UNLOCKING DIVINE ACTION

Unlocking Divine Action

CONTEMPORARY SCIENCE & THOMAS AQUINAS

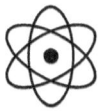

Michael J. Dodds, O.P.

The Catholic University of America Press
Washington, D.C.

Copyright © 2012
The Catholic University of America Press
All rights reserved
The paper used in this publication meets the minimum requirements of
American National Standards for Information Science—Permanence of Paper
for Printed Library Materials, ANSI z39.48-1984.
∞

Library of Congress Cataloging-in-Publication Data
Dodds, Michael J.
Unlocking divine action : contemporary science and Thomas Aquinas /
Michael J. Dodds.
p. cm.
Includes bibliographical references (p.   ) and index.
ISBN 978-0-8132-2961-4 (pbk : alk. paper)   1. Providence and government of God
—Christianity.   2. Causation.   3. Religion and science.   4. Thomas,
Aquinas, Saint, 1225?–1274.   I. Title.
BT135.D63 2012
231.7—dc23   2012003185

To my Dominican Brothers and Sisters

Contents

	Preface	ix
	Abbreviations	xi
	Introduction	1
1.	Causality in Aquinas	11
2.	Causality Locked and Unlocked in Empirical Science	45
3.	Locking Divine Action in Modern Science	105
4.	Unlocking Divine Action through the New Theories of Contemporary Science	119
5.	Unlocking Divine Action through the New Causality of Contemporary Science	160
6.	Divine Action and the Causality of Creatures	205
7.	Providence, Prayer, and Miracles	229
	Conclusion	259
	Glossary	265
	Bibliography	267
	Index of Names	303
	Index of Subjects	309

Preface

This research began over fifteen years ago as I became convinced that an essential element was missing in the theology/science dialogue on divine action: namely, a sufficiently rich understanding of the nature of causality. If God in some way acts in the world, then God is in some sense a cause. But what does it mean to say that God causes something? While many theologians, philosophers, and scientists noticed how shallow the idea of causality had become with the advent of Newtonian science, few were offering a deeper understanding of this concept. At the same time, the dialogue chronicled a burgeoning expansion of the idea of causality in contemporary science itself. Aspects of this blossoming notion of causality were remarkably reminiscent of accounts of causality in the writings of Aristotle and Thomas Aquinas. It seemed the time was ripe to place traditional notions of causality in dialogue with the theories of contemporary science. The project promised new seeds of insight for the theology/science discussion. It is my hope that this research may yield some first fruits of an abundant harvest.

In writing this work, I am grateful to many people. To the Western Dominican Province and Dominican School of Philosophy and Theology for granting me a sabbatical year. To the Dominican communities at Blessed Sacrament Priory, Seattle; Blackfriars, Oxford; and San Esteban, Salamanca, for hospitality during the year, and to my own community and the parish of St. Mary Magdalen in Berkeley (who have to put up with me whether I'm on sabbatical or not). To Richard Schenk, O.P., for fraternal *Gemütlichkeit* and guidance at the *Forschungsinstitut für Philosophie Hannover* and the *Häuslein am Fuchsweg,* where this research began many years ago. To Glenn Ambrose for his work as research assistant in the early stages of the work. To Marilyn Knight for hospitality at the "view from the ridge" in Tiburon, and to Jack Harvey for hospitality at Camano Island. To William Carroll and

Vivian Boland, O.P., for invitations to lecture and participate in seminars at Blackfriars Hall in Oxford. To Ignacio Silva for coffee and conversations on instrumental causality. To my brother, Bill, for collaboration and advice on publishing. To Gabriele Gionti, S.J., Ph.D., for employing his expertise in quantum physics to read the manuscript and save me from many scientific blunders. Any that remain are my own doing. To Marie George for her meticulous review of the manuscript and her most valuable advice on its improvement. To the faculty and students of the Dominican School of Philosophy and Theology and the Graduate Theological Union for insights and questions over many years of teaching. To Bob Russell, for his vision and leadership in founding the Center for Theology and the Natural Sciences whose programs and publications have been a font of inspiration and challenge, and for his friendship and support which have been a source of great encouragement. I also wish to acknowledge my gratitude to Alejandro Garcìa-Rivera, who passed from this life on November 13, 2010, for his insightful review of the manuscript and his warm encouragement. Finally, I am grateful to my family for love and blessings too many to count.

Abbreviations

ABBREVIATIONS FOR THE WORKS OF THOMAS AQUINAS

Comp.	Compendium theologiae
De ente	De ente et essentia
De malo	Quaestiones disputatae de malo
De pot.	Quaestiones disputatae de potentia
De prin. nat.	De principiis naturae
De sp. cr.	Quaestio disputata de spiritualibus creaturis
De ver.	Quaestiones disputatae de veritate
In de an.	In Aristotelis librum De anima commentarium
In de div. nom.	In librum beati Dionysii De divinis nominibus expositio
In meta.	In Metaphysicam Aristotelis commentaria
In peri herm.	Commentarium in Aristotelis libros Peri hermeneias
In phys.	In octo libros Physicorum Aristotelis expositio
Q. de an.	Quaestio disputata de anima
Quodl.	Quaestiones quodlibetales
SCG	Summa contra gentiles
Sent.	Scriptum super libros Sententiarum
ST	Summa theologiae
Super ad col.	Super epistolam ad Colossenses lectura
Super ad hebr.	Super epistolam ad Hebraeos lectura
Super ad rom.	Super epistolam ad Romanos lectura
Super de causis	Super librum De causis expositio

Super de trin.   *Expositio super librum Boethii De Trinitate*
Super ev. matt.   *Super evangelium S. Matthaei lectura*
Super iob   *Expositio super Iob ad litteram*
Super sym. apos.   *Expositio super symbolo apostolorum*

OTHER ABBREVIATIONS

Meta.   Aristotle, *Metaphysics*, ed. Richard McKeon
Phys.   Aristotle, *Physics*, ed. Richard McKeon

UNLOCKING DIVINE ACTION

Introduction

In the beginning, God created the heavens and the earth.

These first words of Genesis tell us two fundamental things about God: God is and God acts. If we believe in a God who acts, we can talk about God only if we speak about action, and to do that we need a language of causality. What we think about causality influences our understanding of how God acts and so also of who God is. Before the advent of modern Newtonian science, theologians found a rich doctrine of causality in the writings of St. Thomas Aquinas who developed the thought of Aristotle. With modern science, our understanding of causality shrank and so did our ability to speak of God's action. We might say the discussion of divine action became locked into that narrower notion of causality.[1] Now, through developments in contemporary science, our understanding of causality is again expanding in a manner remarkably reminiscent of the thought of Aristotle and Aquinas.

The developments in science offer theologians two fundamentally new ways to unlock the discussion of divine action. One incorporates the developments themselves or, more precisely, certain interpretations of the scientific theories surrounding them. This route has been well traveled by many theologians, notably in the works of Ian Barbour and the joint projects of the Center for Theology and the Natural Sciences at the Graduate Theological Union in Berkeley and the Vatican Observatory in Castel Gandolfo,

---

1. "The present-day crisis in the notion of divine action has resulted as much as anything from a shift in the notion of causation. In premechanistic science, science dominated by the influence of Aristotle, a component of divine causal action or teleology was included in every action. Thus Thomas Aquinas insisted that every event involved not only the efficient cause (what we would now speak of as the cause of an occurrence), but also the formal and material causes, or the influence of the matter and the form on the outcome. As a fourth type of causality, Thomas stressed the role of 'final causes', that is, the overall purposes of God, which act as one of the causal forces in every event" (Philip Clayton, *God and Contemporary Science* [Edinburgh: Edinburgh University Press, 1997], 189).

Italy.² The second way employs the expanded understanding of causality implicit in the new interpretations of science rather than the interpretations themselves.³ This road has been less traveled.⁴ In what follows, we will explore both avenues.

Our discussion is based on three fundamental assumptions that are widely shared by participants in the theology/science dialogue. The first is *(mirabile dictu)* that we can actually know something about the world. Albert Einstein points out that "those individuals to whom we owe the great creative achievements of science were all of them imbued with the truly religious conviction that this universe of ours is something perfect and susceptible to the rational striving for knowledge."⁵ That the cosmos is knowable is a central tenet of the philosophy of Aristotle and Aquinas, as James Weisheipl notes: "The fundamental assumption in the Aristotelian conception of nature is that natural phenomena ... are intelligible; there is a

---

2. See Ian Barbour, *Religion in an Age of Science* (San Francisco: HarperSanFrancisco, 1990); Robert John Russell, William R. Stoeger, and George Coyne, eds., *Physics, Philosophy, and Theology: A Common Quest for Understanding* (Vatican City State: Vatican Observatory; Berkeley, Calif.: Center for Theology and the Natural Sciences, 1988); Robert John Russell, Nancey Murphy, and C. J. Isham, eds., *Quantum Cosmology and the Laws of Nature: Scientific Perspectives on Divine Action* (Vatican City State: Vatican Observatory; Berkeley, Calif.: Center for Theology and the Natural Sciences, 1993); Robert John Russell, Nancey Murphy, and Arthur R. Peacocke, eds., *Chaos and Complexity: Scientific Perspectives on Divine Action* (Vatican City State: Vatican Observatory; Berkeley, Calif.: Center for Theology and the Natural Sciences, 1995); Robert John Russell, Willliam R. Stoeger, and Francisco J. Ayala, eds., *Evolutionary and Molecular Biology: Scientific Perspectives on Divine Action* (Vatican City State: Vatican Observatory; Berkeley, Calif.: Center for Theology and the Natural Sciences, 1998), Robert John Russell, Nancey Murphy, Theo Meyering, and Michael Arbib, *Neuroscience and the Person: Scientific Perspectives on Divine Action* (Vatican City State: Vatican Observatory; Berkeley, Calif.: Center for Theology and the Natural Sciences, 1999); Robert John Russell, Philip Clayton, Kirk Wegter-McNelly, and John Polkinghorne, eds., *Quantum Mechanics: Scientific Perspectives on Divine Action* (Vatican City State: Vatican Observatory; Berkeley, Calif.: Center for Theology and the Natural Sciences, 2001); Robert John Russell, Nancey Murphy, and William R. Stoeger, eds., *Scientific Perspectives on Divine Action: Twenty Years of Challenge and Progress* (Vatican City State: Vatican Observatory; Berkeley, Calif.: Center for Theology and the Natural Sciences, 2008). For a comprehensive overview of contemporary approaches to divine action, see Paul Gwynne, *Special Divine Action: Key Issues in the Contemporary Debate (1965–1995)* (Rome: Pontificia Universita Gregoriana, 1996).

3. "The shift in thinking just described creates a completely different context for theological reflection on divine action.... Though perhaps not impossible, it is certainly difficult to recreate the pre-scientific framework—or to develop an alternative one—that allows one, alongside the network of scientific explanations, to speak of another causal system which is equally constitutive of the events in question" (Clayton, *God and Contemporary*, 190).

4. The topic of causality has not, however, been entirely neglected in the theology/science dialogue on divine action. See, for instance, the related articles in the journal, *Philosophy in Science*, published by the Center for Interdisciplinary Studies (Tucson, Arizona), and the relevant articles by William Stoeger, Nancey Murphy, Thomas Tracy, and Robert Russell in the bibliography.

5. Albert Einstein, *Ideas and Opinions*, trans. Sonja Bargmann (New York: Bonanza Books, 1954), 52.

regularity, a determined rationality, about these phenomena which can be grasped. This must be the basic assumption of all science, for without it science itself is impossible."[6]

In the theology/science dialogue, this assumption often goes under the name "critical realism." Ian Barbour first introduced the term into that discussion: "[W]e must recognize the *difficulties in any naive realism* which overlooks the role of man's mind in the creation of theories.... A *critical realism* must acknowledge both the creativity of man's mind, and the existence of patterns in events that are not created by man's mind."[7] Many have adopted the term, notably John Polkinghorne and Arthur Peacocke.[8] There are others, however, who criticize critical realism. Nancey Murphy, for instance, offers "a critique of critical realism as a way of understanding the epistemological status of theology and science and of justifying a dialogue between them." She finds that "critical realism in theology and science ... is based on a confusion" that arises from an uncritical blending of "modern and postmodern perspectives."[9] Andreas Losch agrees that "'critical realism' as such is a rather ambiguous term which needs to be determined by the epistemological consideration of a distinctive philosophical tradition."[10]

Etienne Gilson examines several variations of critical realism and concludes that "the critique of knowledge is essentially incompatible and irreconcilable with metaphysical realism. There is no middle ground. You must

---

6. James A. Weisheipl, "The Concept of Nature," in *Nature and Motion in the Middle Ages*, ed. William E. Carroll (Washington, D.C.: The Catholic University of America Press, 1985), 9.

7. Ian G. Barbour, *Issues in Science and Religion* (Inglewood Cliffs, N.J.: Prentice-Hall, 1966), 172. "My own conclusion is that the *meaning* of truth is correspondence with reality. But because reality is inaccessible to us, the *criteria* of truth must include all four of the criteria mentioned above [agreement with data, coherence, scope, fertility].... Because correspondence is taken as the definition of truth, this is a form of realism, but it is a *critical realism* because a combination of criteria are used. I will be advocating such critical realism throughout this volume" (Barbour, *Religion*, 35). On Barbour's role in introducing the term, see Andreas Losch, "On the Origins of Critical Realism," *Theology and Science* 7 (2009): 85–106.

8. "The view I am defending is called critical realism. 'Realism', because it claims that science actually does tell us about the physical world, even if it does not do so finally and exhaustively. 'Critical', because it recognizes the subtlety and ultimate unspecifiability of the scientific method" (John C. Polkinghorne, *Beyond Science: The Wider Human Context* [New York: Cambridge University Press, 1998], 18). See also John C. Polkinghorne, *Belief in God in an Age of Science* (New Haven, Conn.: Yale University Press, 1998), 101–24; Arthur Peacocke, *Intimations of Reality: Critical Realism in Science and Religion* (South Bend, Ind.: University of Notre Dame Press, 1984).

9. Nancey Murphy, "On The Role of Philosophy in Theology-Science Dialogue," *Theology and Science* 1 (2003): 87; Nancey Murphy, "Scientific Realism and Postmodern Philosophy," *British Journal for the Philosophy of Science* 41 (1990): 291.

10. Losch, "On the Origins," 98.

either begin as a realist with being, in which case you will have a knowledge of being, or begin as a critical idealist with knowledge, in which case you will never come in contact with being.... We can say, therefore, that a realist theory of knowledge and a realist critique of knowledge are both possible and necessary, but neither the one nor the other is equivalent to critical realism, and they should not be called by that name."[11] He favors the term "methodical realism."[12] William Wallace speaks simply of a "realist philosophy of science"; Ernan McMullin uses the term "scientific realism"; Stanley Jaki refers to "moderate realism"; and Peter Kosso argues for "realistic realism."[13] However named, the assumption that the world is knowable is common to both science and common sense, as Nancey Murphy observes: "The commonsense (and correct) idea is that the world and our interaction with it are given; the problem is to find the best way of talking about it as we go along. The realist-antirealist debate has things backwards: participants in the debate assume that we have our descriptions and the problem is whether or not we can know if there is anything out there for those descriptions to describe."[14]

A second assumption is that science and theology, inhabiting the same world and the same human minds, are capable of dialogue.[15] Theology, there-

---

11. Etienne Gilson, *Thomist Realism and the Critique of Knowledge*, trans. Mark A. Wauck (San Francisco: Ignatius Press, 1986), 149, 170.

12. Etienne Gilson, *Methodical Realism*, trans. Philip Trower (Front Royal, Va.: Christendom Press, 1990), 30.

13. William A. Wallace, *Causality and Scientific Explanation* (Ann Arbor: University of Michigan Press, 1972), 2:276, 326. See also William A. Wallace, *The Modeling of Nature: Philosophy of Science and Philosophy of Nature in Synthesis* (Washington, D.C.: The Catholic University of America Press, 1996), 422; Ernan McMullin, "A Case for Scientific Realism," in *Scientific Realism*, ed. Jarrett Leplin (Berkeley and Los Angeles: University of California Press, 1984), 8–40; Paul L. Allen, *Ernan McMullin and Critical Realism in the Science-Theology Dialogue* (Burlington, Vt.: Ashgate, 2006); Stanley L. Jaki, "The Demarcation Line between Science and Religion," *Angelicum* 87 (2010): 81; and Peter Kosso, *Appearance and Reality: An Introduction to the Philosophy of Physics* (New York: Oxford University Press, 1998), 177–86.

14. Murphy, "On the Role of Philosophy," 90.

15. "Yet since for the believer in God the world and history do actually constitute the field of God's activity, evocatively communicated to us, then religious discourse (or faith-language) and scientific discourse, however mutually distinct, really must have something to do with each other; they are both talking about the same reality: our world and our history" (Edward Schillebeeckx, *Jesus: An Experiment in Christology* [New York: Seabury Press, 1979], 628). "In fact science and theology seem to me to have in common that they are both exploring aspects of reality. They are capable of mutual interaction which, though at times it is puzzling, can also be fruitful" (John C. Polkinghorne, *One World: The Interaction of Science and Theology* [Princeton, N.J.: Princeton University Press, 1986], xi). Philosophy is also a necessary partner in this dialogue as William Stoeger observes: "[I]t is worthwhile to complete our disciplinary summary by locating philosophy with respect to the natu-

fore, cannot afford to be ignorant of developments in science. As the Jesuit astrophysicist William Stoeger observes: "Obviously, philosophy and theology must take these new cosmic and human perspectives and possibilities seriously.... To the extent that they do not critically assimilate and confront these truths and perspectives, they will fail to articulate authentically and truthfully who we really are, what the world and the universe really is, and who God really is or is not. For God has expressed the divine nature in the reality we experience around us and experience in ourselves."[16] Owen Thomas argues that "theologians must participate in the discussion of all of the problems in the philosophy of science, including the status and epistemology of scientific theories, terms, and laws (realism, reductionism, etc.), the scope and limits of science, the clarification and justification of the assumptions of science, the interpretation of scientific theories in order to make proposals to further their development, and the interpretation of the theological significance of such theories as relativity, quantum mechanics, and cosmology."[17] Arthur Peacocke observes: "Any affirmations about God's relation to the world, any doctrine of creation, if it is not to become vacuous and sterile, must be about the relation of God to, the creation by God of, the world that the natural sciences describe."[18] Aquinas also thinks that our understanding of the world affects our understanding of God: "The opinion is false of those who asserted that it made no difference to the truth of the faith what anyone holds about creatures, so long as one thinks rightly about God.... For error concerning

---

ral sciences and to theology. Philosophical knowledge, though it does not rely upon divine revelation, is oriented toward the pervasive aspects and the ultimate issues of reality and the possibility of our knowledge of it—and not toward well-defined, easily isolated phenomena, as the natural sciences are. Philosophy often deals with questions which are either presupposed by or neglected by the sciences" (William R. Stoeger, "Reductionism and Emergence: Implications for the Interaction of Theology with the Natural Sciences," in *Evolution and Emergence: Systems, Organisms, Persons*, ed. Nancey Murphy and William R. Stoeger [New York: Oxford University Press, 2007], 232). See also William R. Stoeger, "The Evolving Interaction between Philosophy and the Sciences: Towards a Self-Critical Philosophy," *Philosophy in Science* 1 (1983): 21–43. Christian de Duve notes: "Yet scientists and philosophers must talk to each other. Unless philosophy is merely to be an exercise in pure thought, it must take account of science. And scientists ask metaphysical questions, like everyone else, but they seek answers from the vantage point of their expertise" (Christian de Duve, *Vital Dust: Life as a Cosmic Imperative* [New York: Basic Books, 1998], 291).

16. William R. Stoeger, "Key Developments in Physics Challenging Philosophy and Theology," in *Religion and Science: History, Method and Dialogue*, ed. W. Mark Richardson and Wesley J. Wildman (New York: Routledge, 1996), 194.

17. Owen Thomas, "Metaphysics and Natural Science," *Theology and Science* 7 (2009): 42.

18. Arthur Peacocke, "God's Action in the Real World," *Zygon* 26 (1991): 456. See also Arthur Peacocke, *Science and the Christian Experiment* (London: Oxford University Press, 1971).

creatures ... spills over into false opinion about God, and takes men's minds away from Him, to whom faith seeks to lead them."[19]

Contrary to this second assumption, it is sometimes argued that theology and science cannot speak to each other (whether in agreement or conflict) since they use two different languages. Science uses the language of fact; and theology, of value. The languages cannot conflict since they are fundamentally equivocal and really have nothing to do with each other. Francisco Ayala employs a version of this argument: "Science and religious beliefs need not be in contradiction. If they are properly understood, they *cannot* be in contradiction because science and religion concern different matters. Science concerns the processes that account for the natural world: how the planets move, the composition of matter and the atmosphere, the origin and function of organisms. Religion concerns the meaning and purpose of the world and of human life, the proper relation of people to their Creator and to each other, the moral values that inspire and govern people's lives."[20]

It is evident, however, that theology does sometimes intend to make factual statements about the real world, as in the fundamental scriptural assertion: "Then they crucified him."[21] A number of theologians reject the division of theology and science into absolutely separate realms of discourse. E. T. Oakes asserts: "For too long, in my opinion, there has been a rather facile division of labor between science and theology according to the hoary fact/value distinction. By that I mean that we must reopen for investigation the assumed dichotomy between meaning ('why') and cause ('how') and investigate more closely their potential conflicts and harmonies."[22] John Polkinghorne maintains the how/why distinction, but thinks that conversation is possible: "A simple way of putting the matter would be to say that

---

19. *SCG* II, 3. no. 6. Translations are those of the author except when another published translation is given in the bibliography.

20. Francisco J. Ayala, *Darwin's Gift to Science and Religion* (Washington, D.C.: Joseph Henry Press, 2007), ix. See also Francisco J. Ayala et al., *Science, Evolution, and Creationism* (Washington, D.C.: National Academies Press, 2008), 12. For a refutation of Ayala's arguments, see Joshua M. Moritz, "Rendering unto Science and God: Is NOMA Enough?" *Theology and Science* 7 (2009): 363–78.

21. Mark 15:24. *The New American Bible* (Nashville, Tenn.: Catholic Bible Press, 1987) is used throughout this work, except in translations of passages quoted by Aquinas and in the quotation from Genesis 1: 1, at the heading of this introduction, which is taken from the Revised Standard Version (*The Holy Bible* [New York: Collins, 1973]).

22. E. T. Oakes, "Final Causality," *Theological Studies* 53 (1992): 536. See also Edward Booth, "The Dialogue of Metaphysics and Religion with Natural Science: Continental Examples," *New Blackfriars* 83 (2002): 160–72.

science's concern is with process (how things happen), and theology's concern is with purpose and meaning (why things are happening). Therefore science and theology are not direct rivals.... The true relationship between science and theology is therefore complementary, rather than competitive. Yet this certainly does not imply that the two disciplines have nothing specific to say to each other. A positive dialogue is necessary, not least because the way each subject answers its own questions must bear some fitting relationship to the answers offered by the other, if it is indeed the one world of reality that both are seeking to speak about. There will be no strict logical entailment between the two sets of answers, but there certainly needs to be a significant degree of consonance. How? and Why? are distinct questions, but the forms of their answering must fit compatibly together."[23] Since theology and science make statements about the same world, conversation (and therefore conflict) is possible.[24]

This brings us to a third assumption: although conflict is possible, there can be no fundamental contradiction between truth as discovered by reason and as revealed by God. Aquinas affirms this: "Although the truth of the Christian faith ... surpasses the capacity of reason, nevertheless that truth that the human reason is naturally endowed to know cannot be opposed to the truth of the Christian faith."[25] John Henry Newman echoes Aquinas's conviction: "As to physical science, of course there can be no real collision between it and Catholicism. Nature and grace, reason and revelation come from the same divine Author, whose works cannot contradict each other."[26] The Second Vatican Council expresses the same assurance: "Consequently,

---

23. John C. Polkinghorne, *Theology in the Context of Science* (New Haven, Conn.: Yale University Press, 2009), 97–98.
24. Ian Barbour formulated what have now become four classic ways of relating science and theology: conflict, independence, dialogue, and integration; see his *Religion*, 3–30. John F. Haught describes the alternatives as conflict, contrast, contact, and confirmation in his *Science and Religion: From Conflict to Conversation* (New York: Paulist Press, 1995), 27–46. Robert John Russell provides a detailed diagram of possible "creative mutual interaction" between science and theology; see Robert John Russell, *Cosmology from Alpha to Omega: The Creative Mutual Interaction of Theology and Science* (Minneapolis, Minn.: Fortress Press, 2008), 23; Robert John Russell, "Eschatology and Physical Cosmology: A Preliminary Reflection," in *The Far-Future Universe: Eschatology from a Cosmic Perspective*, ed. George F. R. Ellis (London: Templeton Foundation Press, 2002), 275–79; Robert John Russell, "Bodily Resurrection, Eschatology, and Scientific Cosmology," in *Resurrection: Theological and Scientific Assessments*, ed. Ted Peters, Robert John Russell, and Michael Welker (Grand Rapids, Mich.: Eerdmans, 2002), 12.
25. *SCG* I, 7, no. 1.
26. John Henry Cardinal Newman, *The Idea of a University* (New York: Longmans, Green and Co., 1947), 194.

methodical research in all branches of knowledge, provided it is carried out in a truly scientific manner and does not override moral laws, can never conflict with the faith, because the things of the world and the things of faith derive from the same God."²⁷

The resolution of apparent conflicts, however, is seldom easy, as may be witnessed in "The Galileo Affair" and contemporary arguments between creationists and evolutionists. Aquinas offers a nuanced teaching on the relative certitude of faith and reason.²⁸ He also provides some principles for resolving apparent conflicts. These can be illustrated in his discussion of Genesis 1: 7, on "the waters above the heavens." With Augustine, he maintains that "these words of Scripture have more authority than the most exalted human intellect. Hence, whatever these waters are, and whatever their mode of existence, we cannot for a moment doubt that they are there."²⁹ When it comes to deciding what the waters are, however, he consults the science of his day and rejects any interpretations that are scientifically (or philosophically) impossible. If an interpretation "can be shown to be false by solid reasons, it cannot be held to be the sense of Holy Scripture."³⁰ He

---

27. *The Church in the Modern World* [*Gaudium et spes*], no. 36, in *The Documents of Vatican II*, ed. Austin P. Flannery (New York: Pillar Books, 1975). See also John Paul II, *Fides et Ratio: On the Relationship between Faith and Reason*, Encyclical Letter (Washington, D.C.: United States Catholic Conference, 1988); Peter M. J. Hess and Paul L. Allen, *Catholicism and Science* (Westport, Conn.: Greenwood Press, 2008); Don O'Leary, *Roman Catholicism and Modern Science: A History* (New York: Continuum Press, 2006); and Gennaro Auletta, "Science, Philosophy and Religion Today: Some Reflections," *Theology and Science* 5 (2007): 267–87.

28. Using the term "science" in a broad sense that may apply to any branch of human knowing, Aquinas argues that the science of theology or *sacra doctrina* is "of greater certitude" than other sciences since they "derive their certitude from the natural light of human reason, which can err; whereas this derives its certitude from the light of divine knowledge, which cannot be misled" (*ST* I, 1, 5, co.). Yet, because faith lacks the evidence that science can provide for its conclusions, it is in some ways "less than scientific knowledge" (*De ver.* 14, 2, co.). Science has a "more perfect mode of knowing its object"(*ST* I-II, 67, 3, ad 1). As the "evidence of things not seen" (Heb. 11:1), faith "of its very nature, contains an imperfection on the part of the subject, viz., that the believer sees not what he believes" (*ST* I-II, 67, 3, co.). This means that, although the certitude of faith is always greater in itself than that of science, it is not always so to us: "It may well happen that what is in itself the more certain may seem to us the less certain on account of the weakness of our intelligence.... Hence the fact that some happen to doubt about articles of faith is not due to the uncertain nature of the truths, but to the weakness of human intelligence" (*ST* I, 1, 5, ad 1). See Lawrence Dewan, "Faith and Reason from St. Thomas Aquinas's Perspective," *Science et Esprit* 58, no. 2 (2006): 113–23; Kenneth J. Konyndyk, "Aquinas on Faith and Science," *Faith and Philosophy* 12 (1995): 3–21; John Jenkins, *Knowledge and Faith in Thomas Aquinas* (Cambridge: Cambridge University Press, 1997); and Robert Sokolowski, *The God of Faith and Reason* (Washington, D.C.: The Catholic University of America Press, 1995).

29. *ST* I, 68, 2, ad 2.

30. *ST* I, 68, 3, co. "Since Holy Scripture can be explained in a multiplicity of senses, one should adhere to a particular explanation, only in such measure as to be ready to abandon it, if it be proved

criticizes believers who present errors of reason as truths of faith: "Faith is made ridiculous to the unbeliever when a simple-minded believer asserts as an article of faith that which is demonstrably false."[31] After eliminating false interpretations, he offers some alternatives that fit both the sense of Scripture and the truth of science as known to him.[32] Though we must reject his medieval science, we can still appreciate his principles.[33] These have been sadly neglected since his time, as G. K. Chesterton points out:

> For instance, in the matter of the inspiration of Scripture, he fixed first on the obvious fact, which was forgotten by four furious centuries of sectarian battle, that the meaning of Scripture is very far from self-evident; and that we must often interpret it in the light of other truths. If a literal interpretation is really and flatly contradicted by an obvious fact, why then we can only say that the literal interpretation must be a false interpretation. But the fact must really be an obvious fact. And unfortunately, nineteenth-century scientists were just as ready to jump to the conclusion that any guess about nature was an obvious fact, as were seventeenth-century sectarians to jump to the conclusion that any guess about Scripture was the obvious explanation. Thus, private theories about what the Bible ought to mean, and premature theories about what the world ought to mean, have met in loud and widely advertised controversy, especially in the Victorian time; and this clumsy collision of two very impatient forms of ignorance was known as the quarrel of Science and Religion.[34]

With these assumptions in mind, we will consider the opportunities for unlocking the discussion of divine action that arise through developments of contemporary science. We will first give a brief account of the understanding of causality that preceded modern science in the thought of Aquinas and Aristotle (chapter 1). We will then trace how that understanding was contracted in modern science and is now expanding again in contemporary science (chapter 2). How the diminishment of the idea of causality affected

---

with certainty to be false; lest Holy Scripture be exposed to ridicule by unbelievers and obstacles be placed to their believing" (ST I, 68, 1, co.).

31. *De pot.* 4, 1, co. The Second Vatican Council echoes his criticism: "We cannot but deplore certain attitudes (not unknown among Christians) deriving from a shortsighted view of the rightful autonomy of science; they have occasioned conflict and controversy and have misled many into opposing faith and science" (*The Church in the Modern World*, no. 36).

32. See *ST* I, 68, 3 and 4.

33. His principles have much in common with those proposed by Galileo for resolving such questions. See Galileo Galilei, *Letter to the Grand Duchess Christina*, in *Discoveries and Opinions of Galileo*, trans. Stillman Drake (Garden City, N.Y.: Doubleday, 1957), 173–216. See also William E. Carroll, "Galileo, Science, and the Bible," *Acta Philosophica* 6 (1997): 5–37; and William E. Carroll, *Galileo: Science and Faith* (London: Catholic Truth Society, 2009).

34. G. K. Chesterton, *Saint Thomas Aquinas: The Dumb Ox* (Garden City, N.Y.: Doubleday, 1960), 88.

the discussion of divine action will next be examined (chapter 3). We will then turn to the two opportunities for speaking of divine action that arise through contemporary science. We will look first at how interpretations of current scientific theories themselves may be used in the discussion of divine action (chapter 4). Secondly, we will consider how the broader understanding of causality that arises from those theories may be employed. This will involve a retrieval of certain notions of causality from the thought of Aquinas and Aristotle (chapter 5).[35] We will then look more closely at the relationship between divine and creaturely action, especially with respect to the often neuralgic issues of chance and freedom (chapter 6). Finally we will discuss how the two ways for speaking of divine action that are opened by contemporary science may be applied to the specific theological issues of Providence, prayer, and miracles (chapter 7).

---

35. We might see this as a response to Philip Clayton: "The challenge that philosophers and theologians face is to sketch a new theory of causation. But how is one to reintroduce talk of formal and final causes alongside the efficient causes that are the bread and butter of modern science? The grounds and motivation for the argument must be based on the changes that have occurred as science has moved further and further from the once-regnant ideal of universal reduction to physics. Resources for the new approach can be found, inter alia, in entanglement phenomena in quantum mechanics, mental causes in psychology, information theory and epigenesis in biology, and the structure of emergence that appears again and again as one climbs the ladder of complexity in the natural world" (Philip Clayton, "Natural Law and Divine Action: The Search for an Expanded Theory of Causation," *Zygon* 39 [2004]: 631). "Clearly, it is an urgent task for theologians to provide a clear account of what they mean when they assert that God acts as a causal force within the world. To succeed at this task we need nothing less than a new theory of causation" (Philip Clayton, *Adventures in the Spirit: God, World, Divine Action*, ed. Zachary Simpson [Philadelphia: Fortress Press, 2008], 190).

1

Causality in Aquinas

Today's theoretical physicists look for a "theory of everything" to explain all that is. The earliest Greek philosophers asked a similar question: What is everything, *really*? They decided everything must be composed of four basic elements, earth, air, fire, and water. But which is the most basic, the most fundamental cause of all? Thales (620–550 B.C.) was for water. He thought that, down deep, everything must be water in one form or another. Anaximines (570–500 B.C.) argued for air, while Heraclitus (fl. 500 B.C.) favored fire. Anaximander (610–525 B.C.), rather remarkably, chose "none of the above." He argued that if any particular substance were most fundamental, it would annihilate all the others. Instead, he claimed that "the indeterminate" or "the infinite" must be the most basic component of all things.[1]

These early philosophers were all looking for some basic stuff, some fundamental matter. We might call it the "material cause" of everything. Plato (427–347 B.C.) found it necessary to look beyond material causes. Since material things are constantly changing, they cannot really be known. Even as one starts to know or name one, it changes and becomes something else. He concluded that changeable things must be mere shadows or reflections of unchangeable realities that he called ideas or forms. They are the true objects of knowledge. Changeable things somehow participate or reflect the reality of those unchanging forms. In addition to material causes, therefore, there are formal or exemplar causes.[2]

---

1. See Milton Nahm, ed., *Selections from Early Greek Philosophy* (New York: Appleton-Century-Crofts, 1964), 31–45, 62–77. On the remarkably contemporary overtones of the questions of pre-Socratic philosophy, see Moritz Schlick, *Philosophy of Nature* (New York: Philosophical Library, 1949), 18; and Polkinghorne, *Theology in the Context*, 153–54.
2. See Frederick Copleston, *A History of Philosophy* (Garden City, N.Y.: Doubleday, 1985), 1.163–

Aristotle (384–322 B.C.) further expanded the list of causes. Any explanation of reality requires not only material and formal causes, but also efficient and final ones. Unlike Plato, he did not see formal causes as ideas existing apart from matter, but as intrinsic principles inherent within material substances.[3] Each changeable thing is composed of two intrinsic principles, form and matter. The formal cause explains why the thing exists as a particular kind of thing, and the material cause explains why it can cease to be what it is and become something else. The form of a chair, for instance, is not some esoteric principle existing in a realm of ideas, but the intrinsic structure or arrangement of some matter (such as wood) that makes that particular wood exist as a chair (and not as a table or cabinet). The material cause of the chair (the wood), explains why it can cease to be a chair and become something else (such as tooth picks). The efficient cause is the agent, such as the carpenter who makes the chair. The final cause is the purpose or aim behind the making, perhaps the desire to make money that sets the carpenter to work. It is "that for the sake of which" something is done. Aristotle believed that, with these four causes, he had a complete account of material things and the ways they change.[4]

Thomas Aquinas (1225–1274) agreed that Aristotle's four causes provide an exhaustive account of causality: "Here the Philosopher [Aristotle] reduc-

---

206; and Luc Brisson, "Plato's Natural Philosophy and Metaphysics," in *A Companion to Ancient Philosophy*, ed. Mary Louise Gill and Pierre Pellegrin (Malden, Mass.: Blackwell, 2006), 212–31.

3. In fact, he explicitly rejected the extrinsic formal causality of Plato: "Above all one might discuss the question what on earth the Forms contribute to sensible things, either to those that are eternal or to those that come into being and cease to be. For they cause neither movement nor any change in them.... And to say they are patterns and the other things share in them is to use empty words and poetical metaphors" (*Meta.* I, 9 [991a 8–24]).

4. "[W]e must proceed to consider causes, their character and number.... In one sense, then, (1) that out of which a thing comes to be and which persists, is called 'cause,' e.g., the bronze of the statue, the silver of the bowl, and the genera of which the bronze and the silver are species. In another sense (2) the form or the archetype, i.e., the statement of the essence, and its genera, are called 'causes' (e.g., of the octave, the relation of 2:1, and generally number), and the parts in the definition. Again (3) the primary source of the change or coming to rest: e.g., the man who gave advice is a cause, the father is cause of the child, and generally what makes of what is made and what causes change of what is changed. Again (4) in the sense of end or 'that for the sake of which' a thing is done, e.g., health is the cause of walking about" (*Phys.* II, c. 3, [194b 23–33]). "It is evident, then, even from what we have said before, that all men seem to seek the causes named in the *Physics*, and that we cannot name any beyond these" (*Meta.* I, c. 10 [993a11–16]). Cf.: *Phys.* II, c. 7 (198a 15–34); *In phys.* II, lect. 5 (§177–181). For an overview of the four causes, see Wallace, *Modeling*, 3–18, 70–73, 92–97, 100–106, 158–63; Leo J. Elders, *The Metaphysics of Being of St. Thomas Aquinas in a Historical Perspective* (New York: Brill, 1993), 290–307; Joseph Bobik, *Aquinas on Matter and Form and the Elements* (South Bend, Ind.: University of Notre Dame Press, 1997); and Francis X. Meehan, *Efficient Causality in Aristotle and St. Thomas* (Washington, D.C.: The Catholic University of America Press, 1940), 29–40, 167–98.

es all causes into the four modes of causality we have mentioned, saying that all things which are called causes fall into these four modes."[5] In the category of formal causality, however, he found a place for Plato's exemplars.[6] Unlike Plato, he did not see these as subsistent forms but as ideas in the mind of God: "In the divine wisdom are the types of all things, which types we have called ideas—i.e., exemplar forms existing in the divine mind."[7]

Aquinas associates causality with action. Formal, final, and efficient causality are all types of action.[8] To act means "to make something to be in act."[9] This happens in a number of ways. When a boy makes a snowball, for example, he is the agent or efficient cause that turns the clump of snow into a ball. But the formal cause or structure, what we might call "roundness," also makes the clump of snow to be a ball. For all the boy's squishings and squashings, the clump will not be a ball until it has that shape or form or structure. Final causality is also active in the making of the snowball. If the boy makes it for the fun of throwing it (perhaps at Susie Derkins), that fun (as a good to be attained) is also in some way the cause of the snowball.

The snowball depends in various ways on all four causes in order to come into being and continue to exist. Without the efficient and final causes (the boy who is looking for fun), it would not come to be. Without the material and formal causes (the snow with its particular shape), it would not continue to exist. (If the snow melts or gets squashed, the ball will cease to be.) To Aquinas, such dependency is the hallmark of causality: "Those things are called causes upon which things depend for their existence or

---

5. *In meta.* V, lect. 3, no. 1. "There must be four causes" (*In phys.* II, lect. 10, no. 15 [§240]). "Every cause is either matter, or form or agent or end" (*SCG* III, 10, no. 5). Cf.: *ST* I, 105, 5, co.

6. "A form always has the nature of a cause, for a form is, in a sense, the cause of that which it informs—whether this informing takes place by inherence, as it does in the case of intrinsic forms, or by imitation, as it does in the case of exemplary forms" (*De ver.* 3, 3, co.). Cf.: *In meta.* V, lect. 2, no. 2.

7. *ST* I, 44, 3, co. Cf. *ST* I, 3, 8, ad 2; I, 15, 1. For a detailed account of such causes, see Gregory T. Doolan, *Aquinas on the Divine Ideas as Exemplar Causes* (Washington, D.C.: The Catholic University of America Press, 2008), and Gregory T. Doolan, "The Causality of the Divine Ideas in Relation to Natural Agents in Thomas Aquinas," *International Philosophical Quarterly* 44 (2004): 393–409; Vivian Boland, *Ideas in God according to Saint Thomas Aquinas: Sources and Synthesis* (Leiden: E. J. Brill, 1996); John F. Wippel, *Thomas Aquinas on the Divine Ideas* (Toronto: Pontifical Institute of Mediaeval Studies, 1993); Fran O'Rourke, *Pseudo-Dionysius and the Metaphysics of Aquinas* (Leiden: E. J. Brill, 1997); and James Weisheipl, "Thomas' Evaluation of Plato and Aristotle," *New Scholasticism*, 48 (1974): 100–124.

8. "A thing is said to act [*agere*] in a threefold sense. In one way formally, as when we say that whiteness makes white;... In another sense a thing is said to act effectively, as when a painter makes a wall white. Thirdly, it is said in the sense of the final cause, as the end is said to effect by moving the efficient cause" (*ST* I, 48, 1, ad 4). Cf.: *ST* I, 82, 4, co; 105, 5, co.

9. *ST* I, 115, 1, co.

their coming to be."[10] Causality is an analogous notion that can be employed in a number of ways. The material stuff of the universe is a cause, but so are ideas in the mind of God. The sculptor is the cause of a statue, but so is the statue's form or shape and the purpose or goal that motivates the artist. A cause is always that upon which something depends for its being or becoming, but the modes of dependency vary greatly depending on the kinds of causes involved.[11]

THE FOUR CAUSES

It may be helpful to give a brief description of the four causes since they are often misunderstood.[12] Basically, they explain two things: why something is what it is and why it can cease to be what it is and become something else.

---

10. *In phys*. I, lect. 1, no. 5. "This term 'cause' seems to mean diversity of substance, and dependence of one from another" (*ST* I, 33, 1, ad 1). This note of dependency is characteristic of all four kinds of causes: "An effect must needs depend on its cause. This is part of the very nature of cause and effect; and is evidenced in formal and material causes, seeing that on the removal of any of its material or formal principles, a thing at once ceases to exist, because such principles enter into its essence. The statement applies to efficient causes even as to formal and material causes: since the efficient cause produces a thing by inducing the form or disposing the matter. Hence a thing depends equally on its efficient cause, its matter and its form since through the one it depends on the other. As to final causes the same is to be said of them as of efficient causes: because the end is a cause only for as much as it moves the efficient cause to act, since it comes first not in existence but in the intention. Consequently there is no action where there is no final cause" (*De pot*. 5, 1, co.). See also Lawrence Dewan, "Saint Thomas and the Principle of Causality," in Lawrence Dewan, *Form and Being: Studies in Thomistic Metaphysics* (Washington, D.C.: The Catholic University of America Press, 2006), 61–80.

11. Aristotle explains: "As the word has several senses, it follows that there are several causes of the same thing ... e.g., both the art of the sculptor and the bronze are causes of the statue. These are causes of the statue *qua* statue, not in virtue of anything else that it may be—only not in the same way, the one being the material cause, the other the cause whence the motion comes" (*Phys*. II, 3 [195a 4–8]). Aquinas notes: "Since the term cause is used in many senses, there may be several causes of one thing not accidentally but properly. For the fact that there are many causes of one thing accidentally presents no difficulty, because many things may be accidents of something that is the proper cause of some effect, and all of these can be said to be accidental causes of that effect. But that there are several proper causes of one thing becomes evident from the fact that causes are spoken of in various ways. For the maker of a statue is a proper cause and not an accidental cause of a statue, and so also is the bronze, but not in the same way. For it is impossible that there should be many proper causes of the same thing within the same genus and in the same order, although there can be many causes providing that one is proximate and another remote; or that neither of them is of itself a sufficient cause, but both together. An example would be many men rowing a boat. Now in the case in point these two things are causes of a statue in different ways: the bronze as matter, and the artist as efficient cause" (*In meta*. V, lect. 2, no. 11 [§ 773]).

12. Holmes Rolston III, for example, characterizes matter as a backward-looking principle "wherefrom" and form as a forward-looking principle "whereto." He fails to see that both are present, immanent principles of substances. His characterization of formal cause as belonging to "subjectivity" rather than to the "objective side of reality" is also puzzling since both form and matter are objective principles of being. See his *Science and Religion: A Critical Survey* (New York: Random

Material and Formal Causality

To understand material and formal causality, we must begin with the reality of change in the natural world. Any change always involves two principles: something that stays the same and something new. We do not say that one thing has become another unless some aspect of the first remains in the second. If I merely substitute one pen for another as I am writing, for instance, I do not say the first pen has become the second, since nothing of the first is present in the second. Nor do I generally say my pen is changing as it simply sits on my desk, since there is nothing new about it (no new place, size, weight, color, etc.). Any change requires both continuity and novelty.

Aristotle recognizes two fundamental kinds of change in the natural world. In one, usually called "accidental change," a substance or thing is modified incidentally while remaining the same basic kind of thing (as a log may become part of a cabin, while still remaining a log). In the other, called "substantial change," the substance or thing itself becomes a different kind of thing (as a dog ceases to be a dog when it dies).[13] The principle of continuity in this kind of change cannot be a substance since it is the substance itself that is changing. The substance is precisely what does *not* endure through the change. Nor can the principle of newness be some mere, incidental factor (such as the rearrangement of more basic substances, analo-

---

House, 1987), 34. Mario Bunge manifests a fundamental misunderstanding of the material cause in his discussion of the Scholastic principle that "whatever is in the effect must be first in some way in the cause." He comments: "The scholastic aphorism, entailing as it does the assertion that change is nothing but the unrolling or unfolding of pre-existing potentialities, excludes flatly the emergence of authentic novelty" (Mario Bunge, *Causality and Modern Science* [New York: Dover Publications, 1979], 206). What he describes here is actually Parmenides' position that treats being univocally and so considers it impossible that new being emerge from existent being. Through his discovery of potency as a real aspect of the material world, Aristotle shows that being is analogous and overcomes Parmenides' dilemma, making genuine novelty possible. Such potency is precisely not "preexisting;" it is the mere possibility of existing. See *Phys.* I, 2–3 (185a 20–187a 10). Nancy Murphy sees primary matter as "only a theoretical construct within the system" rather than as a real ontological principle of existing things. See Nancey Murphy, "Divine Action in the Natural Order: Buridan's Ass and Schrödinger's Cat," in *Chaos and Complexity: Scientific Perspectives on Divine Action*, ed. Robert John Russell, Nancey Murphy, and Arthur R. Peacocke (Vatican City State: Vatican Observatory; Berkeley, Calif.: Center for Theology and the Natural Sciences, 1995), 335.

13. "When the change from contrary to contrary is in *quantity*, it is 'growth and diminution'; when it is in *place*, it is 'motion'; when it is in property, i.e., *in quality*, it is 'alteration': but when nothing persists of which the resultant is a property (or an 'accident' in any sense of the term), it is 'coming-to-be,' and the converse change is 'passing-away'" (Aristotle, *On Generation and Corruption*, I, 4 [320a 1–2], in *The Basic Works of Aristotle*, ed. Richard McKeon [New York: Random House, 1941]). On the reality of substantial change, see William Norris Clarke, *The One and the Many: A Contemporary Thomistic Metaphysics* (South Bend, Ind.: University of Notre Dame Press, 2001), 140–41.

gous to the rearrangement of the logs when they become a cabin) since it is not mere, incidental novelty that needs to be explained, but substantial newness—a new substance, a new being. The principle of continuity is not a substance, but the mere "possibility" of being a substance. Nor is the principle of newness a substance. It is not a "thing" or a "what." It is rather "that by which" a thing is the sort of thing that it is.

In Aristotelian philosophy, the principle of possibility is commonly called "primary matter" and the principle of newness is known as "substantial form." To avoid confusion with other meanings of "matter," I will here refer to "primary matter" simply as "possibility-of-being." Each changeable substance is composed of two principles: possibility-of-being (which explains why it can cease to be what it is and become something else) and substantial form (which explains why that "possibility-of-being" is currently actualized as this particular kind of substance). Neither of these principles is a mere idea or abstraction. Each is a real, physical principle—a real aspect of the *physis,* or nature, of a particular material entity.

Primary Matter Broadly speaking, the material cause is the stuff out of which something is made. Marble, for instance, is the material cause of a marble statue. The material cause explains why a thing, presently existing in one way, can cease to be what it is and become something else. The marble in the statue, for instance, has the potency or "potentiality" to become a heap of marble dust. Since it has this potency, the change is possible. Existing as a statue, the marble does not have (lacks) the form of a pile of marble dust. It does, however, have the possibility or potentiality to possess that form. This possibility or potentiality is the mark of the material cause. In this example, the principle of possibility is a particular substance—the marble that acquires the new shape. The marble is a *thing* which, while remaining that thing, is capable of incidental modification in shape, size, and so forth.

On a deeper level, the principle of potentiality explains not just why a particular substance may acquire or lose some incidental feature (such as shape), but why it may cease to be that substance altogether and become something else. When a dog dies, for instance, it ceases to be the one organically unified substance we call "dog" and becomes something else—a carcass. Although we can name the dead dog with the single term "carcass," we realize that it is no longer really one thing, but a collection of independent substances gradually breaking down into still more basic substances or elements. While marble remains marble when a statue is broken or pulverized, the dog does not remain a dog when it becomes a carcass. Here the principle of possibility is not merely the potentiality of a substance to be differently shaped or structured, but the potentiality of one substance to become an entirely different kind of substance. More simply stated, it is the sheer possibility of being a substance at all. This possibility is not itself some *thing*; it is the mere possibility of being a thing. Aristotle called this most basic principle of possibility "primary matter" *(prōtē hulē)*.[14] This sheer "possibility of being something" cannot exist apart from one form or another. It will always exist as some particular thing. As such, it is a real constituent principle of that thing. Considered in itself, however, it is not an existing "thing" but the mere possibility of being. It is, for instance, the possibility present in the dog to exist as something other than a dog.

Primary matter is a notoriously difficult principle to conceptualize, mostly because "there's no there there." Our minds are geared toward knowing what is actual: the existing dog, for example, and the actual principle (substantial form) by which it is a dog. We recognize potentiality only in view of actuality. If we admit the reality of substantial change, we see that there must be a "real" principle of "mere" possibility-of-being (primary matter) that persists through such a change. We cannot directly know that principle, and that principle can never exist by itself. Aristotle is able to give only an evocative description of it: "As the bronze is to the statue, or the wood to the bed, or the matter and the formless before receiving form to any thing which has form, so is the underlying nature to substance, i.e., the 'this' or existent."[15] Aristotle can define primary matter only in terms of the substantial change in which it is recognized: "My definition of matter is just this—the primary substratum of each thing, from which it comes to be without qualification, and which persists in the result."[16]

---

14. *Phys.* II, 1 (193a 29). See also *Meta.* V, 4 (1015a 7–10); VIII, 4 (1044a 23); IX, 7 (1049a 24–27); *Phys.* I, 7 (191a 7–12); I, 9 (192a 31); *In phys.* I, lect. 13, no. 118; I, lect. 15, no. 139. For a complete list of all the places Aristotle uses this phrase, see William Charlton, "Appendix: Did Aristotle Believe in Prime Matter?" in *Aristotle's Physics, Books I–II*, ed. William Charlton (Oxford: Clarendon Press, 1984), 129–45.

15. *Phys.* I, 7 (191a 7–12).

16. *Phys.* I, 9 (192a 31). "By matter I mean that which in itself is neither a particular thing nor of a certain quantity, nor assigned to any of the other categories by which being is determined" (*Meta.* VII, 3 [1029a 20]). "From this argument of Aristotle it is clear that substantial generation and corruption are the source from which we derive our knowledge of prime matter" (*In meta.* VIII, lect. 1 [§1689]). It is important not to confuse Aristotle's idea of primary matter as mere potency with the notion of mat-

Commenting on Aristotle's definition, Aquinas tries to explain why "the ancient philosophers" (the Presocratics) did not discover the principle of substantial form. They thought that one of the "sensible bodies" (such as air or water) must be the most fundamental stuff of the natural world. They did not see that these bodies themselves, since they undergo substantial change, must in turn be composed of the more primary principles of substantial form and primary matter which are "perceptible only indirectly" through an analysis of substantial change.[17]

Substantial Form   It is important to be clear from the outset on the kind of causality that substantial form exercises. Empirical science tends to deal with efficient causes—forces or agents that produce change. Substantial form does not exercise its causality in that way. It acts, not as an efficient cause, but as a formal cause in determining possibility-of-being to exist as one kind of substance or another.[18]

---

ter as the most basic actual "stuff" of the universe. Empirical science is usually concerned with matter as stuff as it investigates the basic building blocks of the universe, such as atoms, electrons, and more fundamental particles. It approaches Aristotle's idea when it speaks of the Big Bang as having the "possibility" of becoming the present universe or of the first organisms as having the "possibility" of evolving into higher forms of life. On this distinction, see Norbert Luyten, "Matter as Potency," in *The Concept of Matter in Greek and Medieval Philosophy*, ed. Ernan McMullin (South Bend, Ind.: University of Notre Dame Press, 1965), 102–13.

17. *In meta.* VII, lect. 2, no. 14 (§1284). The same tendency is evident in some contemporary interpreters of Aristotle who reject primary matter as sheer possibility of being ("the traditional interpretation") and instead affirm some actual substance as the primary substratum of material things: "The traditional interpretation of Aristotle's treatment of this problem is that he posits a prime matter, a bare 'stuff,' lacking all positive determinations, which is the matter of the elements and which makes elemental change possible. This prime matter is nothing but a potentiality which can exist only as actualized in some determinate matter—i.e., in one of the elements—and which is what persists when one contrariety is replaced by another and the identity of an element changes.... And then there is the novel interpretation. According to the new reading: the elements are the most fundamental sort of matter. This alternative theory is the only one open to someone who rejects the traditional notion" (Sheldon M. Cohen, *Aristotle on Nature and Incomplete Substance* [Cambridge: Cambridge University Press, 1996], 55–56). "I have suggested a different picture, though in some ways it resembles the traditional scheme. At the top of the system is God, pure form and actuality, and at the bottom is pure matter. But, contrary to the traditional scheme, the pure matter at the foundation is not an indeterminate potentiality but a set of simple elements—earth, water, air, and fire in the lower cosmos, aether in the higher sphere. Although the elements have definite natures, they are not composites of matter and form. A composite consists of simpler ingredients that can exist as separate bodies or be structured into a higher complex" (Mary Louise Gill, *Aristotle on Substance: The Paradox of Unity* [Princeton, N.J.: Princeton University Press, 1989], 242). See also William Charlton, "Commentary" and "Appendix: Did Aristotle Believe in Prime Matter?" in *Physics Books I & II*, 76–79, 129–245.

18. Some contemporary Aristotelian scholars, however, do interpret formal cause or nature as a kind of efficient cause. On the merits of their arguments, see Thomas Larson, "Natural Motion in Inanimate Bodies," *Thomist* 71 (2007): 555–76.

An example of accidental change may be helpful here. In making the *Pietà*, Michelangelo begins with a block of marble and gradually carves it into the statue. The marble (the material cause) initially has the possibility of becoming a statue and actually becomes the statue when it attains a certain shape (the formal cause). The artist is the efficient cause, while the artist's goal is the final cause. The artist hacks and whittles until the new shape is realized and so causes the statue. For all his chipping and chiseling, however, the marble will not be the statue until it possesses the intended shape. If the shape is never attained, the statue will never come into being. In some way, therefore, it is the shape itself that makes the marble to be a statue. The shape does not do this by pushing, pulling, or exerting any kind of force. It does not act as an efficient cause, but rather as a formal cause. A formal cause exercises its causality by making something to be the kind of thing it is.[19] In this example we are dealing with an accidental, formal cause—a particular shape. The shape is the formal cause that makes the marble to be that statue. The shape is "that by which" the marble is a statue.

In an analogous way in substantial change, substantial form is "that by which" primary matter or possibility-of-being exists as a particular kind of substance. There are, however, important differences between substantial and accidental form. The accidental form merely causes an existing substance to exist "in a certain way" (e.g., "with a certain shape"). The substantial form makes the substance to be a substance, as Aquinas explains: "The substantial form differs from the accidental form in this, that the accidental form does not make a thing to be 'simply' [*simpliciter*], but to be 'such' [*secundum quid*], as heat does not make a thing to be simply, but only to be hot. Therefore by the coming of the accidental form a thing is not said to be made or generated simply, but to be made such, or to be in some particular condition; and in like manner, when an accidental form is removed, a thing is said to be corrupted, not simply, but relatively. Now the substantial form gives being simply; therefore by its coming a thing is said to be generated simply; and by its removal to be corrupted simply."[20]

Although the accidental form makes a whole thing to be what it is, it does not cause the parts of the thing to be what they are. When logs are joined into a cabin, for instance, the accidental form (the structure of the cabin)

19. *Phys.* II, c.7 (198a 15–20). Cf.: *In phys.* II, lect. 10, (§ 240).
20. *ST* I, 76, 4, co.

causes the whole to be a cabin, but it does not cause the parts to be logs. They remain logs as the cabin is built and are simply given a new structure or arrangement. The new structure (accidental form) accounts for the fact that they are now a cabin (and not a table or something else). It accounts for the whole structure of the cabin, but not for the individual logs that compose it. Simply put, it explains why the logs are now a cabin, but it does not explain why they are logs.

The substantial form, however, explains the being of the whole and of the part. For the parts of a substantial whole are the same kind of thing as the whole itself, in virtue of the one substantial form by which the thing is what it is. In a human being, for instance, a hand is not a foot, but each is human in virtue of the one substantial form that makes the whole being to be human (so long as each remains an integral part of a living human being). As Aquinas explains: "Now the substantial form perfects not only the whole, but each part of the whole. For since a whole consists of parts, a form of the whole which does not give existence to each of the parts of the body, is a form consisting in composition and order, such as the form of a house; and such a form is accidental. But the soul is a substantial form; and therefore it must be the form and the act, not only of the whole, but also of each part."[21]

This aspect of formal causality explains how a single whole can be composed of apparently diverse substances. Aquinas thought that the most basic elements were earth, air, fire, and water, and believed that humans are composed of these four elements. But he also thought that earth or water, existing as an integral part of human flesh, did not exist simply as earth or water, but "as human" in virtue of the one human form. To explain the apparent presence of such basic elements in the larger whole, he argued that they are "virtually" present—that is, their *virtus* or power is present. To put his argument into contemporary terms, we might say that the carbon and nitrogen (or electrons and protons) that are part of the integral structure of a human being are distinct from each other, and yet each is human because of the one substantial form that makes the whole human to be human. They are virtually present in the human being since some of their characteristic

---

21. *ST* I, 76, 8, co. "According to St. Thomas an artifact can be said to have a form, but it is a form that belongs to the artifact as a whole and not to each of the parts. The form of a natural thing, on the other hand, is not only the form of the whole but also the form of each of the parts" (John Goyette, "Substantial Form and the Recovery of an Aristotelian Natural Science," *Thomist* 66 [2002]: 524).

activities are evident. As integral parts of the whole human person, however, each exists not simply as carbon or nitrogen, but as human in virtue of the single human substantial form.[22]

In all of its causal action, the substantial form acts as a formal cause, not an efficient cause. It exerts no force and supplies no energy. As a formal cause it simply makes the possibility-of-being to be actually a particular kind of substance, such as hydrogen, carbon, dog, or cat.[23] A dog ovum, for instance, is the kind of substance it is because of its substantial form, but it can become a different substance because of its primary matter or "possibility-of-being." The same is true of the dog sperm: it is what it is because of its substantial form and can become something else because of its possibility-of-being. With the union of sperm and ovum, a new substantial form (the substantial form of dog) is educed from the now properly disposed possibility-of-being present in the egg and sperm, resulting in a new being—the new puppy (or at least the beginning of one).[24] The substantial form is not a ghost or spirit. It does not float in from outer space. It is educed from (brought out of) the potency of the matter when that matter is disposed to exist as the new substance.[25] It is a physical principle of each material substance which makes the substance to be the kind of thing it is—which actualizes or determines possibility-of-being to be a particular kind of substance.[26]

In making the thing to be what it is, the substantial form is the cause

---

22. See Christopher Decaen, "Elemental Virtual Presence in St. Thomas," *Thomist* 64 (2000): 271–300.

23. To avoid dualism, we must be careful to maintain that what the substantial form actualizes or determines is not some existing material thing, but sheer possibility-of-being. In doing so, it accounts (by way of formal causality) for the entire being, structure, and activity of the individual substance.

24. This philosophical account of the generation of a dog in terms of substantial form and primary matter is not meant to compete or conflict with the biological explanation of the event in terms of the chemistry of DNA. It is simply meant to explain why the whole substance that comes into being is one substance—to explain, in other words, why the DNA molecules in the cells of a living dog are not simply the chemical "DNA," but are in fact "dog."

25. "The form ... is educed from the potency of matter by a natural agent" (*De pot.* 3, 4, ad 7). "One may inquire where [substantial] forms ... come from. The answer an Aristotelian philosopher such as Aquinas provides is somewhat surprising; they are not preexistent as forms, nor are they created in any way; instead, they are simply 'educed' from the potency of protomatter" (Wallace, *Modeling*, 60).

26. "The form of the natural body is ... that by which the thing is" (*ST* I, 45, 8, co). "For the form is that through which a thing is the very thing that it is" (*Q. de an.* Q. 9, co.). "It is this characteristic of forms—namely, that they make their subjects what they are—that explains why Aristotle identifies forms with essences" (Jennifer Whiting, "Aristotle on Form and Generation," in *Proceedings of the Boston Area Colloquium in Ancient Philosophy,* ed. John J. Cleary and Daniel C. Sharatin [Lanham, Md.: University Press of America, 1991], 45).

of the particular structure of the thing as well as of its characteristic activities.[27] A substantial form is not itself an existing entity, but a real principle inherent in a substance, making it to be the kind of thing that it is: "The form is called a being, not as that which is, but as that by which something is."[28] It is difficult to say *what* a substantial form is since it is precisely not a *what,* but a *that-by-which.* Some *that-by-whiches* are also *whats. That by which* I eat my ice cream, for instance, is a spoon. But the spoon is also a *what*—an existing implement. A substantial form is a *that-by-which* that is not itself a *what.* It is a principle that makes a *what* (a substance) to be a certain kind of *what* (bird, frog, chicken, etc.).[29]

---

27. "The form of every natural body is the principle of the characteristic movement of that particular kind of body—e.g., the form of fire is cause of fire's movement" (*In de an.* II, lect. 7, no. 323). William Wallace explains this, using the example of the substantial form of sodium: "At once it is a unifying form, conferring a unity on the components; a specifying form, making those components be and react in a way characteristic of sodium; and a stabilizing form, preserving the identity of that element and maintaining the unity of its components under external influences to the extent possible" (William A. Wallace, "A Place for Form in Science: The Modeling of Nature," *Proceedings of the American Catholic Philosophical Association* 69 [1995]: 41).

28. *ST* I, 110, 2, co. Cf.: *SCG* II, 87, no. 3; *In de an.* 2, lect. 1, no. 255. "A natural, generated thing is said 'to be' properly and *per se* inasmuch as it has being *(esse)* and subsists in that being. Form, in contrast, is not said 'to be' since it neither subsists nor has being *per se.* Rather, form is said to exist or to be a being *(ens)* only inasmuch as something exists by it" (Doolan, "Causality," 396). "Aristotle denies in principle that the form may be an autonomous thing.... Its introduction into matter therefore does not mean that two distinct things come into relation with each other, but rather that the matter assumes a different character than it had before" (Johannes Hübner, *Aristoteles über Getrenntheit und Ursächlichkeit: Der Begriff des eidos choriston* [Hamburg: Meiner, 2000], 173–74).

29. Eleonore Stump and Norman Kretzmann define substantial form inaccurately as the "set of characteristics" that a substance manifests: "On Aquinas's view, every thing has a substantial form. The substantial form of any thing is the set of characteristics that place that thing in its species and that are thus essential to it in Aquinas's sense of essential'" (Eleonore Stump and Norman Kretzmann, "Being and Goodness," in *Divine and Human Action: Essays in the Metaphysics of Theism,* ed. Thomas V. Morris [Ithaca, N.Y.: Cornell University Press, 1988], 285). For Aquinas, on the contrary, the substantial form is not the set of characteristics that a substance manifests, but the principle by which a substance is a particular kind of substance, which substance (consequently) manifests certain characteristics. Elsewhere, Stump defines substantial form as the "configurational state" of a thing: "On the basis of this brief consideration of Aquinas's views of forms, including the form that is the soul, it seems not unreasonable to think that by 'form' Aquinas means an essentially configurational state. In general, a substantial form is the configurational state of something that makes it a member of the kind or species to which it belongs" (Eleonore Stump, "Non-Cartesian Substance Dualism and Materialism without Reductionism," *Faith and Philosophy* 12 [1995]: 509). She adds, however, that she has doubts about her definition: "I am not convinced that my phrase 'configurational state' is the only or even the best way of conveying the meaning of the Latin *'forma'*" (ibid., 524n10). I would agree that the definition is less than adequate. The form is not itself a "set of characteristics" or the "configurational state" of a thing. It is rather the principle that make the thing to be what it is, and so causes it to have a certain configurational state and to exhibit a certain set of characteristics. In a later work, Stump's understanding of substantial form seems more in accord with Aquinas: "A substantial form is the form in virtue of which a material composite is a member of the species to which it belongs, and it configures prime matter.... On Aquinas's view,

Substantial form can be recognized as a real and necessary principle of nature. It cannot, however, be pictured or imagined—much less measured, weighed, or otherwise detected empirically.[30] One grasps its reality by taking substantial change seriously as *substantial* change (the generation of a new substance) and not merely as accidental change (the rearrangement or restructuring of other substances). In such a change, there must be a principle that endures (primary matter or possibility-of-being) and a principle of newness that accounts for the new substance in its integrity and wholeness (substantial form).

Formal causality can act both intrinsically and extrinsically. It acts intrinsically as the substantial form, the immanent principle that makes a substance to be the kind of thing that it is. It acts extrinsically as the exemplar cause. For an example of such causality, we can again consider Michelangelo's *Pietà*. Before that statue came to be a finished work, it was already present (somehow) as an idea or image in the mind of the artist. It existed there as an exemplar cause, the model or ideal in accordance with which he shaped the stone. Analogously, Aquinas sees divine ideas as the exemplar causes of all things. With this insight, he moves beyond both Aristotle (who recognized only intrinsic formal causes in nature) and Plato (who envisioned exemplar causes as subsisting ideas).

Aquinas also surpasses his predecessors in his account of the act of existence *(esse)*. Here he is indebted not to Aristotle, but to Avicenna and the Islamic tradition.[31] Aristotle recognized the actuality of substantial form

---

there is just one substantial form for any substance which makes it what it is; the one substantial form of a cat makes the cat a material object, a living thing, an animal, and a cat" (Eleonore Stump, *Aquinas* [New York: Routledge, 2003], 194–95).

30. "It is this natural or substantial form that is apprehended when we grasp the nature of an entity and attempt to define it. Like nature itself, this formal component is not an empirical concept: it is not given immediately in sense experience, though it is derivable from such experience" (William A. Wallace, "Is Finality Included in Aristotle's Definition of Nature?" in *Final Causality in Nature and Human Affairs*, ed. Richard F. Hassing [Washington, D.C.: The Catholic University of America Press, 1997], 56).

31. On the advance of Aquinas and Islamic philosophers over Aristotle, see David Burrell, "Analogy, Creation, and Theological Language," *Proceedings of the American Catholic Philosophical Association* 74 (2000): 35–52; David Burrell, *Freedom and Creation in Three Traditions* (South Bend, Ind.: University of Notre Dame Press, 1993); David Burrell, "Aquinas and Islamic and Jewish Thinkers," in *The Cambridge Companion to Aquinas* (Cambridge: Cambridge University Press, 1999), 60–84; John F. Wippel, "The Latin Avicenna as a Source for Thomas Aquinas's Metaphysics," *Metaphysical Themes in Thomas Aquinas II* (Washington, D.C.: The Catholic University of America Press, 2007), 31–64; John F. Wippel, *Metaphysical Themes in Thomas Aquinas* (Washington, D.C.: The Catholic University of America Press, 1984); John F. Wippel, *The Metaphysical Thought of Thomas Aquinas: From Finite Being to Uncreated Being* (Washington, D.C.: The Catholic University of America Press, 2000).

and the potency of primary matter. Aquinas sees a second level of act and potency—the act of existing *(esse)* and the potency of essence. While substantial form makes the thing to be a particular kind of thing, the act of existing *(esse)* causes the thing to exist rather than not to exist.[32]

The discovery that essence is related to existence *(esse)* as potency to act is an insight belonging properly to Aquinas and found neither in Aristotle nor Avicenna.[33] Every creature possesses an act of existing *(esse)* by which it is. In material things, this results in a twofold composition of act and potency. There is a union of substantial form and primary matter and a conjunction of essence (matter and form considered together as "what it is") and *esse* (the act of existing).[34] Form or essence is a principle of potency with respect to the act of existing, which is "compared even to the form itself as act."[35] *Esse* is the act by which a thing exists. As such, it is "the act of all acts and the perfection of all perfections."[36]

The Question of Dualism   Though substantial form and primary matter are two distinct principles, they do not (when rightly understood) imply any sort of dualism. Aristotle begins with the substantial unity of a being and notices that, because it undergoes substantial change, it must involve two principles, one to account for what it is (substantial form) and another to explain its possibility of becoming something else (primary matter).[37] If either or both of these principles were a complete substance or entity in itself, they could not together form the substantial unity of a single substance, but only the accidental unity of two substances. To conceive of form and matter as complete substances in themselves is to open the door to dualism. René

---

32. *SCG* II, 54; *ST* I, 7, 1.

33. Albert Judy, "Avicenna's *Metaphysics* in the *Summa Contra Gentiles*." *Angelicum* 52 (1975): 210; Joseph de Finance, *Etre et agir dans la philosophie de saint Thomas* (Rome: Presses de l'Université Grégorienne, 1965), 110.

34. *SCG* II, 54, no. 9. In spiritual creatures (angels), there is a single composition of act and potency: the potency of the spiritual form or essence and the act of existing *(esse)*. See *SCG* II, 54, nos. 7–8.

35. *SCG* II, 54, no. 5.

36. *De pot*. Q.7, 2, ad 9. See also William Norris Clarke, "The Limitation of Act by Potency: Aristotelianism or Neoplatonism?" *New Scholasticism* 26 (1952): 167–94.

37. "Aristotle bases his own doctrine on the primacy, in our experience, of the dog, the cat, the human being. It is these unities that are primary beings.... We begin with the doctrine of substantial unity.... We consider that any change involves something one and the same being otherwise now than it was before" (Lawrence Dewan, *St. Thomas and Form as Something Divine in Things* [Milwaukee, Wis.: Marquette University Press, 2007], 27).

Descartes is probably the modern paradigm of such thinking.[38] Unfortunately many thinkers conflate the hylomorphism of Aristotle with the dualism of Descartes, often without explanation or argument.[39] If one maintains, however, that neither substantial form nor primary matter is a complete entity in itself, one can admit a duality of potentiality and actuality in the composition of a substance without sacrificing substantial unity.[40] When Aristotle asks himself what holds substantial form and primary matter together, he answers "nothing." They are principles that are so related to each other that they naturally form a single whole, the complete substance. Their union and their unity as a single substance require no other cause except perhaps the agent that initiated the change and so was responsible for generation of the new substance:

> In the case of all things which have several parts and in which the totality is not, as it were, a mere heap, but the whole is something besides the parts, there is a cause.... What then is it that makes man one; why is he one and not many? ... [I]f, as we say, one element is matter and another is form, and one is potentially and the other actually, the question will no longer be thought a difficulty.... The difficulty disappears, because the one is matter, the other form. What, then, causes this—that which was potentially to be actually—except, in the case of things which are generated, the agent? ... [T]he proximate matter and the form are one and the same thing, the one potentially, and the other actually. Therefore it is like asking what in general is the cause of unity and of a thing's being one; for each thing is a unity, and the potential and the actual are somehow one. Therefore there is no other cause here, unless there is something which caused the movement from potency into actuality.[41]

---

38. Descartes saw the human body as one substance (an "extended thing") and the soul as a completely other substance (a "thinking thing"): "It follows that this mind (soul), by which I am what I am, is entirely distinct from the body ... and that even if the body were not, the soul would not cease to be all that it now is" (René Descartes, *Discourse on Method*, Part 4, in *Discourse on Method and Meditations*, trans. L. Lafleur [New York: Bobbs Merrill, 1977], 25).

39. See, for instance, Philip Clayton: "Considering the mind as an object invites charges of dualism, since (as Descartes argued) an object that is non-physical, immaterial, not composed out of parts, and not located in space and time must be a different kind of thing altogether, which he called *res cogitans*. (The same is also true of that other type of dualism which is implied by the Aristotelian-Thomistic concept of the soul as the form of the body)" (Philip Clayton, *Mind and Emergence: From Quantum to Consciousness* [Oxford: Oxford University Press, 2004], 110; see also 164, 189).

40. "Just as a substantial form does not have through itself an absolute act without that to which it is added, so neither does that to which it is added, namely, matter. Therefore from their union arises that act of existing in which the thing subsists through itself, and from them is produced something that is one through itself" (*De ente* c. 6). Cf.: *De pot.* 3, 8, co.; *In meta.* VIII, lect. 1, (§1689). On how Aristotle's hylomorphism avoids Cartesian dualism, see Stump, "Non-Cartesian"; Sally Haslanger, "Parts, Compounds, and Substantial Unity," in *Unity, Identity, and Explanation in Aristotle's Metaphysics* (Oxford: Clarendon Press, 1994), 129–70; and Laura L. Landen, "Of Forests and Trees, Wholes and Parts," *Proceedings of the American Catholic Philosophical Association* 69 (1995): 81–89.

41. *Meta.* VIII, c.6, (1045a 8–1045b 24). "That is why we can wholly dismiss as unnecessary the

Primary matter and substantial form together constitute a single, unified being, not a duality of beings.[42] Aquinas explains that any substance can have only one substantial form since substantial form is the first actualizer of primary matter, causing a thing to be the kind of substance that it is. Any further actualization of the substance must involve only accidental forms, causing various modifications to the existing substance, such as color, shape, and so on.[43] The unity of the substantial form accounts for the unity of the substance.[44]

A substance, like a dog or a cat, is a single whole, not just a conglomeration of parts.[45] Aristotle argues that, though a substance may be composed

---

question whether the soul and the body are one: it is as meaningless as to ask whether the wax and the shape given to it by the stamp are one, or generally the matter of a thing and that of which it is the matter. Unity has many senses (as many as 'is' has), but the theory most proper and fundamental sense of both is the relation of an actuality to that of which it is the actuality" (Aristotle, *On the Soul*, II, 1 [412b 6–8] in *The Basic Works of Aristotle*, ed. Richard McKeon [New York: Random House, 1941]). Aquinas agrees: "Aristotle proves in the *Metaphysics* there is nothing that makes a unitary thing out of matter and form except the agent which reduces the potentiality to act, for matter and form are related as potentiality and act" (*SCG* II, 71, no. 2). "He [Aristotle] gives the reasons for the error in the above positions. He says that the reason why these thinkers held such views is that they sought for some principle which makes potentiality and actuality one thing, and looked for the differences of these as though it were necessary for them to be brought together by some one mean like things which are actual and diverse. But, as has been stated, both the ultimate matter, which is appropriated to a form, and the form itself are the same; for one of them is as potentiality and the other as actuality. Hence to ask what causes a thing is the same as to ask what causes it to be one, because each thing is one to the extent that it is a being. And potentiality and actuality are also one in a certain respect, for it is the potential that becomes actual; and thus it is not necessary for them to be united by some bond like those things which are completely different. Hence there is no other cause that produces the unity of things which are composed of matter and form except that cause which moves things from potentiality to actuality" (*In meta*. VIII, lect. 5, [§1767]).

42. "Aristotle's concept of natural substance issues in a theory of living things as irreducibly organic unities" (Sarah Waterlow, *Nature, Change, and Agency in Aristotle's Physics: A Philosophical Study* [New York: Oxford University Press, 1988], 1).

43. "The substantial form makes a thing to exist absolutely, and its subject is something purely potential. But the accidental form does not make a thing to exist absolutely but to be such, or so great, or in some particular condition; for its subject is an actual being" (*ST* I, 77, 6, co.).

44. "Nothing is absolutely one except by one form" (*ST* I, 76, 3, co.). Cf.: *De sp. cr.* a. 3, co.

45. "[O]rganic creatures can properly be regarded as ontologically fundamental substances in their own right, rather than arrangements of other, physically more primitive, substances. They are, in other words, *per se* unities. This conclusion does not make it illegitimate to say that they are also combinations of components. In the first place, they have organic parts, both the structured organs and the various homoeomerous stuffs such as flesh that the organs are made of. But these are not self-sufficient substances having each its own inner principle of change which it exhibits in actual change whenever not physically prevented. That would imply that even (if not especially) when separated from the organic context the objects in question would change naturally so as to express autonomous natures. But in fact organs and flesh etc. are never found except in the organic context, and if separated they begin at once to decay. Thus although the organic whole is in a sense a combination of them, it is not a *per accidens* combination of independent substances. Secondly, the organic whole does in a sense consist of the simple bodies, and these are indeed autonomously

in some way of simple elements (he is thinking of flesh as composed of fire and earth), it is not simply a collection of elements, just as a syllable is not simply a collection of letters. The whole is distinctively different from its parts precisely because of its substantial form:

> [N]ow the syllable is not its elements, *ba* is not the same as *b* and *a*, nor is flesh fire and earth (for when these are separated the wholes, i.e., the flesh and the syllable, no longer exist, but the elements of the syllable exist, and so do fire and earth); the syllable, then, is something—not only its elements (the vowel and the consonant) but also something else, and the flesh is not only fire and earth or the hot and the cold, but also something else.... But it would seem that this "other" is something, and not an element, and that it is the *cause* which makes *this* thing flesh and *that* a syllable. And similarly in all other cases.[46]

The added "something" that makes flesh to be flesh rather than just a collection of more basic elements cannot be just another element. It is "not an element but a principle" of the substance and the "primary cause of its being."[47] This is the substantial form that causes primary matter to exist as a substantial whole of a certain kind. Only if the substance ceases to exist will its primary matter come to be actualized by the respective substantial forms of more basic elements. (If the dog dies, for instance, the carcass may break down into "fire and earth" in Aristotle's cosmology or carbon, nitrogen, and so forth in ours.) So long as the substance exists, it remains a single whole in virtue of its one substantial form, not a mere collection of lesser elements.[48]

---

natured substances (at least in the *Physics* they are so treated). But they, unlike the flesh and organs, are not actually present in the organism, i.e., not as the autonomous beings that they actually are when actual. Hence the organism, which is actual, cannot be viewed as a *per accidens* combination of them either. The *per se* unity of the whole is not diminished by its being composed of different things, for the actually present components are not substances, while the substantial components are not as such actually present" (Waterlow, *Nature*, 88–89).

46. *Meta.* VII, 17 (1041b 11–20). A caution from Johannes Hübner is important here: "One ought not in any case put too much weight on these examples by which Aristotle simply wants to show that what accounts for the difference between the whole and the component part is not itself a component part. For the syllable and 'flesh' are not substances and do not have substantial, that is self-explained unity" (Hübner, *Aristoteles*, 178).

47. *Meta.* VII, 17 (1041b 25–31).

48. "A substance cannot consist of substances present in it in complete reality; for things that are thus in complete reality two are never in complete reality one, though if they are potentially two, they can be one (e.g. the double line consists of two halves—potentially; for the complete realization of the halves divides them from one another); therefore if the substance is one, it will not consist of substances present in it and present in this way" (*Meta.* VII, 13 [1039a 3–7]). "The reality of a thing implies that it is separate and numerically distinct from other bodies. If therefore the parts out of which the thing is composed really existed, it would be a divided body, i.e., it would not be a single thing but an aggregate of individual bodies. If something is a part of a whole being, it can therefore exist only in potency; it will only be actual through the breakdown of the whole. Since the parts of a whole exist only

Efficient and Final Causality

In addition to material and formal causality, a complete explanation of change requires efficient and final causes. These are most easily understood through the example of human causality. The efficient cause is the agent. This is broadly conceived. The artist who shapes the marble, for instance, is the efficient cause of the statue, but so is the teacher who advises her.[49] An efficient cause does not act except in view of some end or purpose—the final cause. The artist, for instance, might be making the statue in order to earn money. Final causes can be subordinated to one another. The artist might make the statue *so that* she can make money, *so that* she can buy groceries, *so that* she can feed her family, and so on.[50]

Efficient and final causality are intimately related to formal causality. Each thing exists as a certain type of substance in virtue of its form. It then acts (exhibits efficient causality) in accordance with the kind of thing that it is in order to produce effects that are suitable to its nature (final cause). Sometimes the formal cause, that is, the ground of the creature's being and the source of its efficient activity, is also in some way the final cause or goal of its action. We find this in the activity of generation or reproduction in which formal, efficient, and final causality may coincide:

> We should also realize that three of the causes—form, end, and efficient cause—can coincide. The generation of fire offers a clear example of this. Fire generates fire; therefore fire is an efficient cause, insofar as it generates. Fire is a form, insofar as it makes that which formerly was in potency to be in act. Finally, fire is an end, insofar as it is intended by the agent and insofar as the operation of the agent is terminated in it.... Sometimes the end of the generating process coincides with the two other above-mentioned causes: form and efficient cause. This occurs when generation proceeds from one thing to another thing that is similar in species to the first, as when a man generates a man, or an olive tree an olive tree.... We should realize that the end and the form are numerically identical, inasmuch as the form of the thing generated and the end of the generation are numerically the same.[51]

---

in potency as long as they constitute that whole, one can speak of a subordination under 'something' that endows unity.... The form is this sought-for 'something'" (Hübner, *Aristoteles*, 177). See also Theodore Scaltsas, "Substantial Holism," in *Unity, Identity, and Explanation in Aristotle's Metaphysics*, ed. Theodore Scaltsas, David Charles, and Mary Louise Gill (Oxford: Clarendon Press, 1994), 107–28.

49. "The man who gave advice is a cause" (*Phys.* II, c.3, [194b 30]).

50. Aristotle's example is that, in the practice of medicine, instruments may be used *for* making drugs, which are used *for* purgation, which is done *for* reducing weight, which is *for* attaining health. See *Phys.* II, 3 (194b 33–37); *In phys.* II, lect. 5, no. 6 (§181).

51. *De prin. nat.* c. 4, nos. 27–28. For a detailed analysis, see also Wallace, "Is Finality," 63, 69.

Efficient Causality   Efficient causality may involve just one agent or a number of agents acting together. If two men carry a table, for instance, each is to some extent the cause of its motion (depending on how much weight each bears). Each is responsible for some *part* or percentage of the effect. There are other cases, however, where two agents produce a single effect and yet each is responsible for the whole effect. When a student writes with a pencil, for instance, the words produced on the page are wholly from her and wholly from the pencil. There is no word on the page that she did not write and no mark that the pencil did not make. Such a coincidence of two causes is called "instrumental causality." One efficient cause, the student (called the "principal cause"), employs another efficient cause, the pencil (called the "instrumental cause"), to produce a single effect. In instrumental causality, the effect always exceeds the capacity of the instrumental cause acting alone. It is proper to the pencil, for instance, to make marks, but it cannot write words unless moved by the principal cause. To use Aquinas's example, it is proper to a saw (as an instrumental cause) to divide a piece of wood, but it cannot divide it evenly in accordance with a certain pattern unless moved by a craftsman (as principal cause).[52]

It is also possible for one efficient cause to work through another to produce an effect that does not exceed but is precisely proportionate to the capacity of the other. This is called "secondary causality." Here, the first agent is called the "primary cause," and the second agent the "secondary cause."[53] Ar-

---

52. "A thing is said to work toward the production of an effect instrumentally if it does not do so by means of a form inherent to it but only in so far as it is moved by an agent that acts of itself. It is the nature of an instrument as instrument to move something else when moved itself. The motion by which the instrument is moved by the principal agent is therefore related to the instrument as a complete form is related to an agent acting of itself. It is in this way, for instance, that a saw works upon a bench. Now although the saw has an action which attaches to it in accordance with its own form, that is, to divide, nevertheless it has an effect which does not attach to it except insofar as it is moved by a craftsman, namely, to make a straight cut agreeing with the pattern. Thus an instrument has two operations, one which belongs to it is according to its own form, and another which belongs to it in so far as it is moved by the principal agent and which rises above the ability of its own form" (*De ver.* 27, 4, co.). "An instrument is related to an action more like that by which it is done than like that which does it; for the principal agent acts by means of the instrument" (*De ver.* 27, 4, ad 8). Cf.: *Sent.* III, 18, 1, 1, ad 4; *SCG* III, 147, no. 6; *ST* III, 19, 1, co.; 45, 5, co.; 62, 1, co.; ad 2; Q. 62, 4, co.; 66, 5, ad 1; *Quodl.* X, 4, 1, ad 2.

53. "The terms 'primary' and 'secondary' come into play when we are faced with the situation where one thing is what it is by virtue of the other. So each can be said properly to be a cause, yet what makes one secondary is its intrinsic dependence on the one which is primary. This stipulation clearly distinguishes a secondary cause from an instrument, which is *not* a cause in its own right: it is not the hammer which drives the nails but the carpenter using it" (Burrell, *Freedom and Creation*, 97). See also Etienne Gilson, *The Christian Philosophy of St. Thomas Aquinas*, trans. L. K. Shook (New York:

istotle used this kind of causality in his cosmology to describe how organisms produce offspring only under the influence of the sun as the first cause of generation. Humans produce offspring, for instance, through the generative power that is proper to their nature, but they do this only under the influence of the sun as primary cause. In this activity, they are not mere instrumental causes (producing something beyond their natural capacity), but secondary causes (producing an effect that is entirely in accord with and proportionate to their nature, but one that they can only achieve under the influence of some other cause). This is the meaning of Aristotle's phrase that "man is begotten by man and by the sun as well."[54] Aquinas sees this kind of causality exemplified cosmologically when "lower bodies act through the power of the celestial bodies" and in the realm of voluntary agents when "all lower artisans work in accord with the direction of the top craftsman."[55] In each case, the secondary cause produces an effect proportionate to its own nature, but does this only under the influence of the primary cause. We might find a contemporary example of secondary causality in the activity of an orchestra. All of the musicians are secondary causes, acting under the influence of the conductor as primary cause. Though none of the musicians is producing an effect beyond his or her own skill and training, they could not produce the combined sound of the symphony without the influence of the conductor. The performance may be attributed wholly to the conductor and wholly to the musicians.

Efficient causality may sometimes, but not always, be described as quantitative force. The efficient causality exercised by an artist, for instance, may be described quantitatively in terms of how many pounds of pressure per

---

Random House, 1956), 182–83. Aquinas clearly distinguishes a cause (the secondary cause) that, under the influence of another cause, produces an effect proportionate to its nature, from a cause (the instrumenal cause) that, under the influence of another, produces an effect that exceeds its nature. His terminology, however, is somewhat fluid. Sometimes, for instance, he refers to the instrumental cause as a particular kind of secondary cause. In this sense, every cause that acts under the influence of another is a secondary cause, but the one that produces an effect exceeding its natural capacity is an "instrumental secondary cause [*causa secunda instrumentalis*]" (*ST* I, 45, 5, co.).

54. *Phys.* II, 2 (194b 13). Aquinas explains such celestial genetics: "In the case of animals generated from putrefaction [spontaneous generation], the substantial form is caused by a corporeal agent, namely, the celestial body which is the first agent of alteration; and so all things that produce a change of form in these lower bodies do so by its power. And for this reason the celestial power is enough, without a univocal agent, to produce some imperfect forms. But to produce perfect forms, like the souls of perfect animals, there is also required a univocal agent [of the same species as the offspring] together with the celestial agent. In fact, such animals are not generated except from semen. And that is why Aristotle says that 'man and the sun generate man'" (*SCG* III, 69, no. 24). Cf.: *De pot.* 3, 8, ad 15; *ST* I, 118, 1, ad 3.

55. *SCG* III, 67, no. 5.

square inch she exerts on the clay she is shaping. The activity of the teacher advising her, however, though also a mode of efficient causality, can by no means be described in terms of quantitative force.[56]

For Aristotle, the efficient cause is always in some way a cause of motion or change. It acts on some existing thing to alter it either accidentally (as the sculptor shapes the marble) or substantially (as the cat kills the mouse). Aquinas, building on the traditions of Christian and Islamic thought, sees that an efficient cause may be the source not just of change but also of existence—of being itself. We will have more to say about this in our discussion of divine action.

Final Causality   The final cause, as a good to be attained, is what moves the agent to act. As such, it is the first cause—the foundation of all causal activity.[57] We cannot describe this influence in terms of quantitative force. The final cause acts, but only in the mode of final causality—as the end or good that induces the efficient cause to act. The mode of causality proper to the final cause cannot be reduced to efficient causality, much less to that mode of efficient causality we call "force."

Aristotle believes that final causality is at work not only in human agents, but throughout the natural world.[58] He argues that anyone who denies final causality "entirely does away with nature."[59] Of course, final causality cannot be operative in inanimate substances or even in plants and animals in

---

56. Aristotle uses the example of "the man who gave advice" (*Phys.* II, 3 [194b 30]). Cf.: *In phys.* II, lect. 5, no. 5.

57. "Plainly, however, that cause is the first which we call the final one. For this is the Reason, and the Reason forms the starting-point, alike in the works of art and in the works of nature" (Aristotle, *On the Parts of Animals* I, 1 [639b 14–15], in *The Basic Works of Aristotle*, ed. Richard McKeon [New York: Random House, 1941]). Aquinas agrees: "This species of cause is the most powerful of all the causes, for the final cause is the cause of the other causes.... The end is called the cause of causes" (*In phys.* II, lect. 5, no. 11 [§186]). Cf.: *ST* I, 5, 2, ad 1; *In meta.* V, lect. 2 (§775); *De prin. nat.* c. 4, no. 24. See also Alan Code, "The Priority of Final Causes over Efficient Causes in Aristotle's *Parts of Animals*," in *Aristotelische Biologie: Intentionen, Methoden, Ergebnisse*, ed. Wolfgang Kullmann and Sabine Föllinger (Stuttgart: Franz Steiner, 1997), 127–43.

58. "For those things are natural which, by a continuous movement originated from an internal principle, arrive at some completion: the same completion is not reached from every principle; nor any chance completion, but always the tendency in each is toward the same end, if there is no impediment" (*Phys.* II, 8 [199b16–18]). On the pervasiveness of final causality in Aristotle's view of nature, see Helen S. Lang, *The Order of Nature in Aristotle's Physics: Place and the Elements* (Cambridge: Cambridge University Press, 1998), 274–75; Charlotte Witt, *Substance and Essence in Aristotle: An Interpretation of Metaphysics VII–IX* (Ithaca, N.Y.: Cornell University Press, 1989), 85–86; and Jeffrey Wattles, "Teleology Past and Present," *Zygon* 41 (2006): 449.

59. *Phys.* II, 8 (199b 15–16).

the same way it is in human beings who have proper knowledge of the ends they are seeking. The term "end," as William Wallace points out, has various meanings. It may mean simply the point at which some action ends, as the fall of a stone ends when it hits the ground. It may also indicate the good that is achieved by a particular action. Finally, it may imply the achievement of some conscious goal or aim.[60] Although only humans and higher animals consciously pursue goals or ends, final causality may still be operative throughout nature as a good to be attained.

Aristotle does not posit a deliberative process in nonrational creatures, and he certainly does not see final causality as a kind of preexistent, quasi-efficient cause pulling things toward certain goals.[61] He uses the example of skill or art to show how action for an end need not involve deliberation. We might think of a skilled pianist who does not constantly pause to deliberate what key to strike next. Nature, in an analogous way, may be understood to have a kind of a built-in art and so does not need to deliberate when acting for an end.[62] Aristotle, the biologist, saw this most clearly in living beings that act to produce offspring with forms similar to themselves.[63] But it

---

60. See Wallace, "Is Finality," 60–61.

61. "For Aristotle, final causality ... is not exerted by a future goal or preexisting end-state; rather, the potency proper to form, latent within the individual, simply takes its natural course and comes to fruition under the influence of efficient agents in its environment. Aristotle stresses the dynamic unity of formal and final cause. In order to grasp this, it is first necessary to affirm the unquestionable reality of potency; otherwise it makes no sense. To suggest that 'end-states' of themselves initiate the action whereby they are brought to completion involves the contradiction that something preexists itself and causes its own existence" (Fran O'Rourke, "Aristotle and the Metaphysics of Evolution," *Review of Metaphysics* 58 [2004]: 35).

62. "It is absurd to suppose that purpose is not present because we do not observe the agent [in nature] deliberating. Art does not deliberate. If the ship-building art were in the wood, it would produce the same result *by nature*. If therefore purpose is present in art, it is present also in nature" (*Phys.* II, 8 [199b 26–27]). Cf.: *Phys.* II, 5 (196b 16–18). "The analogy with art, then, assists us to recognize the presence in nature of a cause analogous to that which is intelligence in the operations of man, but we do not know what this cause is. The notion of a teleology without consciousness [*connaissance*] and immanent in nature remains mysterious to us. Aristotle does not think that this should be a reason to deny its existence" (Etienne Gilson, *From Aristotle to Darwin and Back Again: A Journey in Final Causality, Species and Evolution*, trans. John Lyon [South Bend, Ind.: University of Notre Dame Press, 1984], 10). Fran O'Rourke, noting that "the term 'teleology' was coined in 1728 by Christian Wolff," argues that the term "teleonomy" (which was "introduced in 1958 by the American biologist C. S. Pittendrigh, to refer to the finality of nature without any suggestion of outside conscious design") is more apt for describing Aristotle's idea of finality in nature since it does not include the notion of consciousness: "The more limited term 'teleonomy,' therefore, more adequately describes Aristotle's grasp of finality and is helpful since it allows biology to proceed to the limits of its inquiry with a clearly circumscribed model of investigation, free from metaphysical or theological concern" (O'Rourke, "Aristotle and the Metaphysics," 21–22).

63. "This is most obvious in the animals other than man: they make things neither by art nor

is operative also in inanimate nature. The preferred example in Aristotle's cosmology is the stone that naturally falls down in order to attain its "natural place" in the cosmos, the place where it finds rest and which is accordingly "good" for it to be. Robert Spaemann points out how Aquinas puts the philosophical question of finality in nature to a theological use: "If we perceive teleological structures in nature, and teleology necessarily implies consciousness, then nature requires us to speak of God; teleology becomes an argument in the proof for the existence of God. Aristotle rejected the premise with the remark that in nature art works as non-deliberatively as in a perfect artist. Thomas qualifies this thought: indeed art is non-deliberative in things, but how did it get into them?"[64]

THE MODES OF CAUSALITY: NECESSITY, CONTINGENCY, FREEDOM, AND CHANCE

In Aquinas's cosmology, there are several modes of causality. Some things happen necessarily; others, contingently. Necessary causes produce their effects in such a way that they cannot not happen. Contingent causes generate their effects in such a way that they may or may not happen.[65] Among things that occur contingently, some may happen freely and others by chance.

---

after inquiry or deliberation. Wherefore people discuss whether it is by intelligence or by some other faculty that these creatures work, spiders, ants, and the like. By gradual advance in this direction we come to see clearly that in plants too that is produced which is conducive to the end—leaves, e.g., grow to provide shade for the fruit. If then it is both by nature and for an end that the swallow makes its nest and the spider its web, and plants grow leaves for the sake of the fruit and send their roots down (not up) for the sake of nourishment, it is plain that this kind of cause is operative in things which come to be and are by nature. And since 'nature' means two things, the matter and the form, of which the latter is the end, and since all the rest is for the sake of the end, the form must be the cause in the sense of 'that for the sake of which'" (*Phys.* II, 8 [199a 20–34]).

64. Robert Spaemann and Reinhard Löw, *Die Frage Wozu? Geschichte und Wiederentdeckung des teleologischen Denkens* (Munich: Piper, 1985), 85. "It must be pointed out that nature is among the number of causes which act for the sake of something. And this is important with reference to the problem of providence. For things which do not know the end do not tend toward the end unless they are directed by one who does know, as the arrow is directed by the archer. Hence if nature acts for an end it is necessary that it be ordered by someone who is intelligent. This is the work of providence" (*In phys.* II, lect. 12, no. 1 [§250]). "Hence, it is clear that nature is nothing but a certain kind of art, i.e., the divine art, impressed upon things, by which these things are moved to a determinate end. It is as if the shipbuilder were able to give to timbers that by which they would move themselves to take the form of a ship" (*In phys.* II, lect. 14, no. 8 [§268]). Cf.: *De ver.* 5, 2, co.; *ST* I, 2, 3, co.

65. "Again, the contingent differs from the necessary according to the way each of them is found in its cause. The contingent is in its cause in such a way that it can both not-be and be from it; but the necessary can only be from its cause.... Just as from a necessary cause an effect follows with certitude, so it follows from a complete contingent cause if it be not impeded" (*SCG* I, 67, nos. 3–4). Cf. *ST* I, 14, 13, co.

Whether a particular action is necessary or contingent depends on the agent that is acting and the object it acts on. The action is necessary if it proceeds necessarily from the agent and is received necessarily in the object. In Aquinas's cosmology, for instance, the uniform motions of the heavens are necessary actions. The lower heavenly body always and necessarily receives the constant and uniform influence of the higher heavenly body.[66]

An event may be contingent because of the object that is acted upon, even when the agent acts necessarily. When heavenly bodies act on earthly substances, for instance, their effects may be contingent because of some defect in the ability of the earthly substance to receive their influence.[67] Events can also be contingent because of both the agent that is acting and the object that receives its action. When earthly substances act on each other, for instance, contingency may result either from a defect in the agent or in the receiver of the act.[68] The action of making a statue may fail, for instance, either because the sculptor becomes incapable of further work (defect in the agent) or because the marble turns out to be too coarse to hold the fine details the sculptor wants to impart (defect in the receiver of the act). Contingency may also arise when one natural agent interferes with another. Here we might think of the unhappy student who cannot turn in his homework because the dog ate it.[69] A contingent event may also result from the intersection of the activity of two causes: "From the concurrence of two or more causes it is possible for some chance event to occur, and thus an unintended end comes about due to this causal concurrence. For example, the discovery of a debtor, by a man who has gone to market to sell something, happens because the debtor also went to market."[70] William Wallace accordingly describes chance as "an in-

66. "[N]othing comes to be spontaneously in the heavens" (*Phys.* II, 4, [196b 2]). "Since the power of a celestial body is incorruptible and impassible, no effect can escape from the sphere of its causality because of any defect or weakness of its power" (*In meta.* VI, lect. 3 [§1211]).

67. "[T]he germination of a plant is contingent by reason of the proximate contingent cause, although the movement of the sun which is the first cause, is necessary" (*ST* I, 14, 13, ad 1). "[I]t can happen that the power of a celestial body fails to produce its effect because the matter [of the natural being upon which it acts] is not disposed" (*In meta.* VI, lect. 3 [§1211]). Cf.: *ST* I, 19, 3, ad 4.

68. "Many natural causes usually [*frequenter*] produce their effects in the same way, but not always. Sometimes, indeed, though rarely [*ut in paucioribus*], an event occurs in a different way, either due to a defect in the power of an agent, or to the unsuitable condition of the matter, or to an agent with greater strength" (*SCG* III, 99, no. 9). "The philosopher concludes that it is not true that, granted the cause, the effect must be granted; since there are some causes which can fail" (*SCG* III, 94, no. 2). Cf.: *In meta.* VI, lect 2 (§1186); lect. 3 (§1210).

69. "A certain cause, though it may be the direct, proper and sufficient cause of a given effect, may be hindered by the interference of another cause so that the effect does not result" (*SCG* III, 86, no. 12). Cf. *ST* I, 115, 6, co.; *ST* I-II, 75, 1, ad 2.

70. *SCG* III, 74, no. 4. Cf. *In meta.* VI, lect. 3 (§1210).

terference between, or an intersection of, two lines of natural causality not determined, by the nature of either, to interfere with one another."[71]

Not all contingent events may be attributed to chance. Free human actions are contingent, for instance, but are the result of careful deliberation, not of chance. Many events in nature also happen contingently, but are not attributed simply to chance. Whether a daffodil blossoms or not, for instance, is a contingent event dependent on many factors, but its eventual flowering follows from its nature and not just from chance.[72]

To show what distinguishes chance from other events, Aristotle divides events into three groups. The first comprises necessary events that "always happen in the same way." The second consists of events that occur "for the most part." Such events, whether intended by nature or by human free will, are normally realized, but sometimes fail to occur. The "third class" comprises events that cannot "be identified with any of the things that come to pass by necessity and always, or for the most part." These are events that "all say are 'by chance.'"[73] While events in the first group are necessary, those in the second and third are contingent in that they may or may not happen.

To further specify the nature of chance events, Aristotle then divides events in another way: "some events are for the sake of something, others are not." Again, among events that are for the sake of something, some of them come about because of the "deliberate intention" of nature or human free will, but others do not. So it is possible for an event to be the kind of thing that is "done for the sake of something" but not be the result of deliberate intention. Such events "are said to be 'by chance.'"[74]

---

71. William A. Wallace, *Elements of Philosophy: A Compendium for Philosophers and Theologians* (New York: Alba House, 1977), 47.

72. "Aquinas wishes it to be well understood that there is a difference between events that occur by mere chance or fortune and those that occur with some degree of regularity, though not always" (Wallace, *Causality and Scientific*, 1.75). See *SCG* III 75, no. 2.

73. "First then we observe that some things always come to pass in the same way, and others for the most part. It is clearly of neither of these that chance is said to be the cause, nor can the 'effect of chance' be identified with any of the things that come to pass by necessity and always, or for the most part. But as there is a third class of events besides these two—events which all say are 'by chance'—it is plain that there is such a thing as chance and spontaneity" (*Phys.* II, 5 [196b 10–14]). Cf.: *Phys.* II, 4 (195b 30).

74. "But, secondly, some events are for the sake of something, others not. Again, some of the former class are in accordance with deliberate intention, others not, but both are in the class of things which are for the sake of something. Hence it is clear that even among the things which are outside the necessary and the normal, there are some in connexion with which the phrase 'for the sake of something' is applicable. (Events that are for the sake of something include whatever may be done as a result of thought or of nature.) Things of this kind, then, when they come to pass incidentally are said to be 'by chance'" (*Phys.* II, 5 [196b 17–24]).

Necessary events and events that happen "for the most part" always occur for some end determined either by nature or by human free will. Chance events are peculiar. They look like things that happen for an end. Aristotle says that to them, "the phrase 'for the sake of something' is applicable."[75] Behind them, however, there is no determining cause such as nature or human free will.[76] They are the kinds of events that would seem to be the result of intentionality, but occur for some extrinsic reason apart from any direct intention. They are assigned to the "causality" of chance: "Hence it is clear that events which (1) belong to the general class of things that may come to pass for the sake of something, (2) do not come to pass for the sake of what actually results, and (3) have an external cause, may be described by the phrase 'from spontaneity.'"[77]

An example might be useful here. Suppose I want to get in touch with a friend and try phoning him. If I reach him, my purpose explains my action and its result: I got in touch with him because I wanted to. It might happen, though, that before I reach him I go to the supermarket for milk and happen to find him there buying beer. I might say it was a lucky meeting. I've found

---

75. *Phys.* II, 5 (196 b 23). See also Marcelo D. Boeri, "Chance and Teleology in Aristotle's Physics," *International Philosophical Quarterly* 35 (1995): 87–96.

76. "In chance events, everything occurs *as if* an intention (with respect to actions) or a purpose (with respect to nature) were lurking behind some manifest occurrence; and yet, it is this hidden secret that is an illusion.... No one or nothing (neither an agent nor nature) planned what occurred. Yet, an indefinite accidental relation arises *as if it was intended*—the indefinite occurs *as if* it was definite" (Pascal Massie, "The Irony of Chance: On Aristotle's *Physics* B, 4–6," *International Philosophical Quarterly* 43 [2003]: 25).

77. *Phys.* II, 6 (197b 18–20). "When things which come to be simply for the sake of something do not come to be for the sake of that which happens, but for the sake of something extrinsic, then we say that these things come to be by chance" (*In phys.* II, lect. 10 [§233]). "The effect of a natural cause follows from the demand of its form, the effect of a purposive cause from an agent's intention, and whatever goes beyond the demand or the intention is accidental" (Kevin White, "Aquinas on Purpose," *Proceedings of the American Catholic Philosophical Association* 81 [2007]: 136). "The suggestion I have made is that Aristotle is willing to describe chance processes as for the sake of their results provided certain conditions are met. When he says they are for the sake of something without qualification, but not for the sake of what actually results, I suggest he means this: the result was not responsible for (not a cause of) the process that lead to it; nonetheless, the result was valuable for the agent, and was the sort of thing that is typically achieved by goal-directed activity.... The solution I have suggested ... is that Aristotle has a causal and a descriptive sense of 'for the sake of' and that chance processes are for the sake of their results only in the noncausal sense. It is these which 'might have been due to thought or nature,' while *truly* teleological processes *are*. The form of an object of craft, the good perceived as achievable by action, or the nature (form) of a sort of organism are all aspects of the world which Aristotle argues are typically responsible for the processes which produce them. When just these sorts of things are produced and yet are not responsible for the processes which produce them, they are by chance" (James G. Lennox, *Aristotle's Philosophy of Biology: Studies in the Origins of Life Science* [Cambridge: Cambridge University Press, 2001], 256, 258).

him, not because I wanted to, but for some extrinsic reason (my desire to get milk). Contacting my friend is the kind of event that I expect to happen as the end or goal of my deliberate actions. Now, I've suddenly found him through an action (buying milk) that had nothing to do with my plans to contact him. The event seems to be the kind of thing that generally happens as the intended end or goal of some agent, but in fact there was no agent initiating any action with that meeting as its intended end or goal. The event is therefore attributed to the "causality" of chance: I say that I ran into my friend "by chance" or "by luck."[78] Paraphrasing Aristotle, I might say that I met my friend "by chance" since the meeting is (1) the kind of thing that usually results from purposeful intention, but in fact (2) has not happened because of any direct intention, but only through (3) some extraneous intention (getting milk).

I can explain why I went to the store (to get milk) and why my friend went there (for beer). But what is the cause of our encounter? What made our lines of action intersect? The intersection seems to require some proper cause since it is the kind of thing that normally happens as the end or goal of some deliberate action. I am, in a sense, the cause of our encounter since if I had not gone to the store it would not have happened. The same is true of my friend. But neither of us is the proper cause of the meeting, since it occurred only incidentally, apart from our intentions. We are "causes" of the meeting only to the extent that it happens to be joined incidentally to our actions. So, what is the cause of the "coincidence" between our actions and the unintended meeting? The answer is *chance*.[79]

---

78. See *Phys.* II, 5 (196b 34–197a 4). Aristotle and Aquinas distinguish between the term "chance" *(automaton, casus)* which is used of all chance events and "luck" *(tyche, fortuna)* which is used only of those involving rational beings. This distinction, however, is not essential to our present discussion. See *Phys.* II, 6 (197b 22–24); *In phys.* II, lect. 10 (§233).

79. "[Aristotle] says that, since not everything which comes to be has a proper cause, it is therefore evident that in the case of future contingent events the reduction of a future effect to some proper cause goes back to some principle, and that this principle is not reduced to some other proper principle but will be the cause of 'everything that happens by chance,' i.e., an accidental cause, and that there will be no other cause of that accidental cause; just as we have already said that accidental being has no cause and is not generated. For example, the cause of this man being killed by robbers is a proper cause, because he is wounded by robbers; and this also has a proper cause, because he is found by the robbers; but this has only an accidental cause. For if on his way to work this man is wounded by robbers, this is accidental ... and therefore it is not necessary to posit a cause for this. For that which is accidental is not generated, and thus it is not necessary to look for some proper cause which produces it" (*In meta.* VI, lect 3 [§1201]). "[I]t is not simply such or such a cause but *causality as such* that chance and luck put to the question. The accidental factor does not belong to any specific cause but to the relation of the conjoined causes to the outcome. The issue is not to know which cause pro-

Aristotle and Aquinas see chance as a kind of cause, not a proper cause (*causa per se*), but an accidental cause (*causa per accidens*). A *per se* cause produces its effect directly, according to its nature (as a duck directly produces a quack). A *per accidens* cause produces its effect only incidentally (as a duck might incidentally produce an avalanche by its quacking).[80] The *per accidens* cause involves some incidental aspect of either the cause or its effect:

> It must be noted that *per accidens* cause is taken in two ways: in one way on the part of the cause, and in another way on the part of the effect. On the part of the cause, that which is called a *per accidens* cause is joined to the *per se* cause. Thus if the white and the musical are called causes of a house, it is because they are accidentally joined to the builder. On the part of the effect, we sometimes refer to something which is accidentally joined to the effect, as when we say that a builder is the cause of strife because strife arises from the building of a house.... Whatever takes place in the effect outside this intention [of the agent] is *per accidens*.[81]

Chance is understood as a *per accidens* cause in relation to the effect: "In this sense fortune [chance] is said to be a *per accidens* cause when something is accidentally joined to the effect, for example, if the discovery of a treasure is accidentally joined to the digging of a grave."[82] The grave digger is directly

---

duces chance, but whether there could be something indefinite in causality *itself*. Even when essential (and therefore definite) causes are related, accidents (and therefore indefinite) outcomes may occur. Chance is nature operating with indeterminate causality.... Wherever chance happens, an outcome that *in itself* is definite (for instance, to receive payment) is *indefinitely related* to a cause that in itself is *also* definite (for instance, going to the marketplace for the sake of purchasing some goods). The outcome occurred randomly, but the causes could have been indefinitely many. *Conversely*, the cause (going to the market to purchase some goods) is determinate, yet the outcome in relation to this cause is indefinite. In other words, the indefinite does not spring out of some *one* definite cause but from the indefinite coincidence of two definite terms" (Massie, "Irony," 22). Charles De Koninck points out that a given event is not due to chance to the extent that it is determined by a certain constellation of causes, but "to the extent that that constellation itself does not have a determined cause.... The accidental conjunction, as one usually understands it, is not the cause of chance: it is already the effect. That conjunction, so understood, is accidental since it does not have a determined cause" (Charles De Koninck, "Réflexions sur le problème de l'indéterminisme," *Revue Thomiste* 43 [1937]: 242–43, 248).

80. "There are two kinds of causes: *per se* and *per accidens*. The *per se* cause of something is that which is its cause directly through its power, as water is the cause of chill; the *per accidens* cause of something, however, is what causes it indirectly, for instance, by removing the cause of its contrary, as removing fire from a house is the cause of its cooling" (Thomas Aquinas, *Responsio ad magistrum Ioannem de Vercellis de 43 articulis*, in *Opuscula theologica* [Turin and Rome: Marietti, 1955], 1.211–18, article 25).

81. *In phys.* II, lect. 8 (§214).

82. *In phys.* II, lect. 8 (§214). Cf. *De pot.* 3, 6, ad 6; *In meta.* V, lect. 3, no. 13 (§789). "We need to stress here the temporal character of accidental causes: as the Greek expression *kata sumbebēkos* already suggests, a coincidence is a matter of simultaneity, of things that spontaneously 'fall together.' In one and the same instant two things that do not belong by nature to each other nevertheless coincide. Only time holds them together. The cause of death [of the man who, in Aristotle's example, incidentally fell victim to robbers] is something that came to be without going through a *process* of

(*per se*) the cause of the grave. He is only indirectly the cause of the finding of the treasure since that event is joined only incidentally (*per accidens*) to the digging of the grave.

If the grave digger is not the direct cause of the finding of the treasure, what is? The event seems to need a cause since it is among the class of things that would seem to be pursued purposefully. The answer is that there is no direct cause. The event is attributed to the causality of chance. In this sense, chance is a cause, but only an incidental cause. As Aristotle notes: "Things *do*, in a way, occur by chance, for they occur incidentally and chance is an *incidental* cause. But strictly it is not the *cause*—without qualification—of anything."[83]

Note that in this account chance is not merely a name for our ignorance. It is not as if there were "really" some cause of the event lurking in the background that we might discover if only we were smart enough. Chance events really have *no cause*.[84] To illustrate this, we can extend our little supermarket

---

coming into being; it is a cause without a cause. In naming chance as a cause, the inquiry comes to a stop; explanations fail to explain.... The coincidence of simultaneity has no rule and no other unity than the instant of its occurrence. Since there is no knowledge of the indeterminate, a science of the accidental is not even possible. Here, scientific inquiry keeps silent. Aristotle's consideration of chance as a 'cause' is not a 'logical' or 'categorical' mistake; rather it reveals the limit of causality itself. Causality is appropriate in order to account for subsistent entities. By placing chance among the causes, however, we do not merely reduce chance to the all-embracing order of causal explanation, we do not 're-finalize' chance. Rather (and this constitutes a fundamentally aporetic moment for Aristotle), the causal approach to understanding the coming into existence of beings encounters its limit. Chance-events are many and manifest, but chance itself *stands back*. The wonder with chance is that it never appears *as such*, since it is indefinite.... When we talk of chance, nothing determinate comes to the fore; or rather only what is determinate comes to the fore while chance is a cause that remains concealed" (Massie, "Irony," 28).

83. *Phys.* II, 5 (197a 12–14). "Both are then, as I have said, incidental causes—both chance and spontaneity—in the sphere of things which are capable of coming to pass not necessarily, nor normally, and with reference to such of these as might come to pass for the sake of something" (*Phys.* II, 5 [197a 34–35]). "He [Aristotle] says that in a way it is true to say that nothing comes to be by fortune. For all of those things which others say about fortune are in a certain respect true, because they have some meaning [*ratio*]. Since fortune is a *per accidens* cause, it follows that what is by fortune is something *per accidens*. But what is *per accidens* is not simply. Hence it follows that fortune is not the cause of anything simply" (*In phys.* II, lect. 9 [§218]). As an incidental cause, chance cannot be the most fundamental cause in the natural world since it always presupposes other more direct or basic causes: "Spontaneity and chance are causes of effects which, though they might result from intelligence or nature, have in fact been caused by something *incidentally*. Now since nothing which is incidental is prior to what is *per se*, it is clear that no incidental cause can be prior to a cause *per se*: spontaneity and chance are therefore posterior to intelligence and nature" (*Phys.* II, 6 [198a 8–12]). "A *per se* cause is prior to one which is accidental" (*SCG* III, 15, no. 8). Cf. *ST* I 49, 3, co. "But every result of chance presupposes facts which have an individual history, a makeup and intelligibility which are proper to each.... For chance is not a thing but a concurrence; and every concurrence involves things" (Weisheipl, "Concept of Nature," 8).

84. "It is not true that every effect has a direct cause, for something that comes about accidental-

adventure. Suppose a mutual acquaintance has so manipulated my friend and me that we are sure to run into each other at the store. Perhaps he phoned my friend asking to buy him some beer right away and then immediately phoned me to get him some milk. (This argument would, of course, involve the mi-

ly, for instance, that this man who wishes to look for water encounters the robbers, does not have any cause [*non habet aliquam causam*]" (*SCG* III, 94, no. 2). "Therefore we must say ... that everything that is a being 'per se,' has a cause; but what is accidentally, has not a cause [*non habet causam*], because it is not truly a being, since it is not truly one.... Now it is manifest that a cause which hinders the action of a cause so ordered to its effect as to produce it in the majority of cases, clashes sometimes with this cause by accident: and the clashing of these two causes, inasmuch as it is accidental, has no cause [*non habet causam*]. Consequently what results from this clashing of causes is not to be reduced to a further preexisting cause, from which it follows of necessity. For instance, that some terrestrial body take fire in the higher regions of the air and fall to the earth, is caused by some heavenly power; again, that there be on the surface of the earth some combustible matter, is reducible to some heavenly principle. But that the burning body should alight on this matter and set fire to it, is not caused by a heavenly body, but is accidental" (*ST* I, 115, 6, co.). "It has been said that what is accidental is properly speaking neither a being nor a unity. But every action of nature terminates in some one thing. Wherefore it is impossible for that which is accidental to be the proper effect of an active natural principle. No natural cause can therefore have for its proper effect that a man intending to dig a grave finds a treasure" (*ST* I, 116, 1, co.). "An accidental being has no cause [*non habet causam*], least of all a natural cause ... because what occurs accidentally, neither is a being properly speaking, nor is one. For instance, that an earthquake occur when a stone falls, or that a treasure be discovered when a man digs a grave—for these and like occurrences are not one thing, but are simply several things. Whereas the operation of nature has always some one thing for its term, just as it proceeds from some one principle, which is the form of the natural thing" (*ST* II-II, 95, 5, co.). "Things that exist accidentally have no cause [*non habent aliquam causam*]" (*SCG* III, 86, no. 12). "He [Aristotle] says that not everything that takes place has a cause, but only what is *per se* has a cause. What is accidental does not have a cause, for it is not properly being.... Whence *to be musical* has a cause and likewise *to be white*, but *to be musical white* does not have a cause [*non habet causam*]; and the same is the case with all others of this kind" (*In peri herm.* I, lect. 14, no. 11). "To say that an accidental conjunction enters into the causal chain, however, is to say that at some point (the meeting with the murderers) the causal chain breaks down. This chance event has itself no further cause (as Aristotle puts it: 'it does not run back to something else'). And yet, it is this 'lack,' this 'deficiency' that precisely produces chance" (Massie, "Irony," 27). "In Aristotle's opinion, not all that happens has a cause. What is by accident has no cause" (Charles De Koninck, "Thomism and Scientific Indeterminacy," *Proceedings of the American Catholic Philosophical Association* 12 [1936]: 69). Harm Goris points out that in his discussion of chance in his *Commentary on the Metaphysics*, Aquinas "denies altogether" that all that is or happens has a cause: "Not all that is or happens, has a cause. The *ens per accidens* does not have a *causa per se*. The most one can say is that it has a *causa per accidens*: the accidental is either by chance *(casus)* in the case of natural agents, or by luck *(fortuna)* when something happens which was not intended by a voluntary agent" (Harm J. M. J. Goris, *Free Creatures of an Eternal God: Thomas Aquinas on God's Infallible Foreknowlege and Irresistible Will* [Leuven: Peeters, 1996], 283–84). Vincent Edward Smith points out that the intersection of two lines of causality resulting, for example, in a chance meeting does not itself have a cause: "The two orders intersect and we assign the cause of the intersection to chance. This intersection of the two orders is not itself an ordered event, i.e., flowing from a determinate and necessary cause. Rather it is an accidental adjunct to the two lines of causality, in which each follows out its proper order and in neither of which is the meeting essentially included.... As not being ordered by the essential character of any line of natural causality, an event produced by chance has an indeterminate and disconnected causality. The concurrence of the two sequences ... does not have a determined cause" (Vincent Edward Smith, *The General Science of Nature* [Milwaukee, Wis.: Bruce Publishing Company, 1958], 201–2).

nor premise that I have strange friends.) My friend and I might, in ignorance of the manipulation, say our meeting is by chance. We would, however, be wrong. Regardless of our knowledge or ignorance, the meeting would in fact be the result not of chance but of the careful planning of our sneaky acquaintance. And if we ever found out about that planning, we would not say that our encounter has suddenly ceased to be a chance event; we would rather say we were duped and that the meeting never involved chance at all.

Chance is a real feature of the natural world according the Aristotle and Aquinas. Aristotle argues that "it is plain that there is such a thing as chance."[85] Aquinas thinks that "it would be contrary to the character of divine providence if nothing were to be fortuitous and a matter of chance in things."[86] The world is sufficiently complex that there are "innumerable" ways in which an incidental feature may be associated with the effect of some action.[87] The world is therefore rife with chance. Aristotle finds it not only in human affairs but also "in the lower animals and in many inanimate objects."[88] Aquinas discovers it in all earthly things: "These things are said to be under the sun which are generated and corrupted according to the sun's movement. In all such things we find chance: not that everything is casual which occurs in such things; but that in each one there is an element of chance."[89]

THE DYNAMISM OF CAUSALITY AND NATURE IN AQUINAS

Through their understanding of causality, Aquinas and Aristotle present a dynamic vision of the natural world. Substance is not, as in modern philosophy, an "unintelligible chimera" lurking behind perceptible qualities.[90]

---

85. *Phys.* II, 5 (196b 14). "Many things are said both to be and to come to be as a result of chance and spontaneity" (*Phys.* II, 4 [195b 310]).
86. *SCG* III, 74, no. 2.
87. *Phys.* II, 5 (196b 29, 197a 15–18). "The *per se* cause is limited and determinate, whereas the *per accidens* cause is unlimited and indeterminate, because an infinity of things can happen to be united" (*In phys.* II, lect. 8 [§214]).
88. *Phys.* II, 6 (197b 14–15).
89. *ST I*, 103, 5, ad 1.
90. "We have therefore no idea of substance, distinct from that of a collection of particular qualities, nor have we any other meaning when we either talk or reason concerning it.... [T]he particular qualities, which form a substance, are commonly referred to an unknown *something*, in which they are supposed to inhere.... Every quality being a distinct thing from another, may be conceived to exist apart, and may exist apart, not only from every other quality, but from that unintelligible chimera of a substance" (David Hume, *A Treatise of Human Nature*, ed. L. A. Selby-Bigge [Oxford: Clarendon Press, 1960], 16, 222). See also Richard J. Connell, *Substance and Modern Science* (Houston, Tex.: Center for Thomistic Studies, 1988), 17–18; Copleston, *History*, 5.91, 5.269–70.

Substances are actual things, like dogs and ducks.[91] Each substance is what it is and acts as it does because of its nature, which involves both substantial form and primary matter.[92] The form is the dynamic source of a thing's characteristic activity.[93] (So dogs bark and ducks quack in virtue of their substantial forms.) The matter explains why the thing might cease to be what it is and become something else.[94] As one thing becomes another, matter seems to have a natural bent toward higher forms in the interplay of natural things.[95]

Through their particular actions, substances establish mutual relations among themselves. The world is not a collection of isolated substances, but a dynamic harmony of intricate interrelations.[96] If substances had no characteristic actions, the order of nature could not be established: "If actions be taken away from things, the mutual order among things is removed, for, in regard to things that are different in their natures, there can be no gathering together into a unity of order unless by the fact that some of them act

---

91. "Substance, in the truest and primary and most definite sense of the word, is that which is neither predicable of a subject nor present in a subject: for instance, the individual man or horse" (Aristotle, *Categories*, chapter 5 [2a 11–12], in *The Basic Works of Aristotle*, ed. Richard McKeon [New York: Random House, 1941]).

92. Aristotle defines nature as "a source or cause of being moved and of being at rest in that to which it belongs primarily, in virtue of itself and not in virtue of a concomitant attribute" (*Phys.* II, 1, [192b 21–23]). It includes both form and matter, but refers more immediately to form: "This then is one account of 'nature,' namely that it is the immediate material substratum of things which have in themselves a principle of motion or change. Another account is that 'nature' is the shape or form which is specified in the definition of the thing.... The form indeed is 'nature' rather than the matter; for a thing is more properly said to be what it is when it has attained to fulfillment than when it exists potentially" (*Phys.* II, 1 [193a 26–31, 193b 7–8]). On how final cause is also associated with nature, see William A.Wallace, "Aquinas and Newton on the Causality of Nature and of God: The Medieval and Modern Problematic," *Philosophy and the God of Abraham: Essays in Memory of James A. Weisheipl, O.P.*, ed. R. James Long (Toronto: Pontifical Institute of Medieval Studies, 1991), 258–59; and Witt, *Substance and Essence*, 100.

93. "For, since everything acts in so far as it is actual ... and since every being is actual through form, it is necessary for the operation of a thing to follow its form" (*SCG* III, 97, no. 4). Cf.: *Quodl.* VI, 2, 1, co.; *ST* I, 115, 1, co.; *ST* I, 25, 1, co. "Form for Aquinas is not static but dynamic, something that includes the functioning of and the causal interactions among the parts" (Stump, "Non-Cartesian," 509).

94. "A thing is said to be corruptible not merely because God can reduce it to nonexistence by withdrawing his act of preservation; but also because it has some principle of corruption within itself, or some contrariety, or at least the potentiality of matter" (*ST* I, 50, 5, ad 3). See also Goris, *Free Creatures*, 281.

95. "The more posterior and more perfect an act is, the more fundamentally is the inclination of matter directed toward it.... Prime matter is in potency, first of all, to the form of an element. When it is existing under the form of an element it is in potency to the form of a mixed body; that is why the elements are matter for the mixed body. Considered under the form of a mixed body, it is in potency to a vegetative soul, for this sort of soul is the act of a body. In turn, the vegetative soul is in potency to a sensitive soul, and a sensitive one to an intellectual one" (*SCG* III, 22, no. 7).

96. See *SCG* III, 69, no. 26.

and others undergo action. Therefore, it is inappropriate to say that things do not have their own actions."[97] In fact, Aquinas thought that if any alleged part of the world did not really exert some influence and so establish some relation with other parts, it would not be truly part of the cosmos.[98]

The dynamic activities of substances are the reason why science can study them. Since "action follows being,"[99] what things do tells us about what they are. If each were not truly a cause influencing other things in the world and so revealing its own nature, there could be no science: "If created things have no actions productive of effects, it follows that no nature of anything would ever be known through the effect. And thus all the knowledge of natural science is taken away from us, for the demonstrations in it are chiefly derived from the effect."[100]

Empirical science *describes* the spontaneous actions and reactions of things through the laws of nature that it discovers. Those laws, however, do not *prescribe* how things *must* act, since they are themselves merely quantitative descriptions of the ways things *do* act.[101] Ultimately, things act the way they do because of the kinds of things they are. To know why they act as they do, therefore, we must know why they are what they are. For Aristotle and Aquinas, the answer to both questions is *nature*, understood as the substantial form and primary matter of each thing. James Weisheipl explains:

When the great variety of "natural" phenomena has been classified scientifically, their individual characteristics and laws noted, we are still left with the question of their radical source, the ultimate accountability of all such phenomena.... What is the source of any of this activity? It does not make much difference what name is ap-

---

97. *SCG* III, 69, no. 17.
98. "Certain individuals hold that the empyrean heaven has no influence on any bodies since it was not created for the sake of natural effects, but that it might be the dwelling place of the blessed. And so indeed it once seemed to me. But upon more careful consideration, it seems better to say that it influences inferior bodies.... For if the empyrean heaven did not influence inferior bodies, it would not be contained within the unity of the universe" (*Quodl.* VI, Q. 11, co.). Cf.: *SCG* III, 69, no. 17.
99. See *SCG* III, 69, no. 20; *ST* I, 75, 3, co.
100. *SCG* III, 69, no. 18.
101. "[A]lthough the laws of nature do reveal and describe fundamental patterns of behavior and regularities in the real world, we cannot consider them the source of those regularities, much less attribute to them the physical necessity these regularities seem to manifest. Nor can we ascribe to them an existence independent of the reality whose behavior they describe. Instead I claim that they are imperfect abstract descriptions of physical phenomena, not prescriptions dictating or enforcing behavior" (William R. Stoeger, "Contemporary Physics and the Ontological Status of the Laws of Nature," in *Quantum Cosmology and the Laws of Nature: Scientific Perspectives on Divine Action*, ed. Robert John Russell, Nancey Murphy, and C. J. Isham [Vatican City State: Vatican Observatory; Berkeley, Calif.: Center for Theology and the Natural Sciences, 1993], 210).

plied. The important thing is that we must in the last analysis acknowledge a certain internal spontaneity in all things from the smallest to the largest in the universe.... There can be no other "source" for characteristic activities, except internal spontaneity.... All the factors involved in the event must be considered, the circumstances of variation, intensity, prevention, and so forth, but in the last analysis there is the spontaneity "given," as from the body itself. Together with this spontaneity there are also certain receptivities for external influence, receptivities which are compatible with the spontaneous characteristics of each body. To both of these intrinsic sources, the spontaneous and the receptive, Aristotle gives the name nature, which he defines as "the principle of movement and rest in those things to which it belongs properly *(per se)* and not as concomitant attribute *(per accidens).*"[102]

102. Weisheipl, "Concept of Nature," 9–10. "At the outset of scientific investigation it is not necessary that this principle [nature] be comprehended completely, so long as it is seen as a determining internal source of characteristic activity or reactivity. Thus it is that, when we accord a statement law-like status, we treat it as ascribing a property or attribute or process to a subject which we believe has a determinate nature, or generative mechanism, or structure, without feeling bound to state in detail what that mechanism or structure has to be" (William A. Wallace, "Causality, Analogy and the Growth of Scientific Knowledge," in *Il cosmo e la scienza*, Atti del congresso internazionale Tommaso d'Aquino nel suo settimo centenario, no. 9 [Naples: Edizioni Domenicane Italiane, 1975], 38).

Causality Locked and Unlocked in Empirical Science

Empirical science has had an inestimable influence on society, evidenced perhaps most visibly in the technology of contemporary culture. It deeply affects the way we see and think about the world.[1] Of course, broader modes of human thought have also influenced science and the way it interprets its empirical findings.[2] E. A. Burtt traced the metaphysical assumptions of modern science to see their influence on contemporary philosophical conundrums.[3] Thomas Kuhn has famously analyzed how the paradigms that guide scientific research also influence the way scientists see the world.[4] Among other things, science has profoundly influenced our understanding of causality. The meaning and scope of causality was narrowed with

---

1. "[W]ith the Enlightenment reception of science, something radically changed in the Western worldview. It eventually led to a situation in which the theories and methods of science came to shape and guide our thinking and attitudes. Since then, science no longer pertains solely to the material world, but also to the way we think about certain things; it guides our attitude towards reality in general" (Taede Smedes, *Chaos, Complexity, and God: Divine Action and Scientism* [Leuven: Peeters, 2004], 208). "In so far as philosophy involves reflection on the world, philosophic thought will obviously be influenced in some way by the picture of the world that is painted by science and by the concrete achievements of science" (Copleston, *History*, 3.275–76). See also Bryan Appleyard, *Understanding the Present: Science and the Soul of Modern Man* (New York: Doubleday, 1992).

2. "It is, of course, true that many distinctly philosophical assumptions go into the making of science, including its most exact kind which is physics. Such an assumption is that matter is uniform throughout the universe, that the reactions of matter are consistent, that matter cannot come into existence or go out of it at will.... Thoroughly philosophical is the assumption that nature works in the simplest way and therefore the simplicity of a scientific theory should be a vote in its favor" (Stanley L. Jaki, *Means to Message: A Treatise on Truth* [Grand Rapids, Mich.: Eerdmans, 1999], 45).

3. Edwin A. Burtt, *Metaphysical Foundations of Modern Physical Science* (Garden City, N.Y.: Doubleday, 1954).

4. Thomas S. Kuhn, *The Structure of Scientific Revolutions* (Chicago: University of Chicago Press, 1970).

the advent of modern science, but has broadened again in contemporary science. Here we will briefly trace that contraction and expansion.

LOCKING CAUSALITY IN MODERN SCIENCE

One hallmark of science is its method. Procedures devised by Galileo but having roots in Aristotle and Pre-Socratic Greek philosophy have become formalized into the scientific research program known as the hypothetical-deductive method.[5] It involves four steps: observation, hypothesis, deduction/prediction, and verification. Beginning with certain empirical observations, the scientist asks questions about the data and invents a hypothesis to answer them. Once the hypothesis has been formulated, the scientist makes certain deductions or predictions from it. The predictions must then be verified (or falsified). This is usually done by setting up controlled experiments. A verified hypothesis may be considered a valid theory until some new theory is invented which is better able to explain the data.

Though simple enough to state, the method can be quite difficult to implement. Inventing a hypothesis, for instance, requires a good deal of creativity and imagination.[6] Finding a way to test it is also challenging. In some areas of science, such as geology, astronomy, and evolutionary biology, it is simply not possible to duplicate in the laboratory what has occurred historically in nature. When rigorous experiment is not possible, scientists rely on other factors such as the explanatory power of the hypothesis to confirm its validity. Ernst Mayr notes: "Eventually the physicists also realized that they could not always give absolute proof, and the new theory of science no longer demands it. Instead, scientists are satisfied to consider as true either that which appears most probable on the basis of the available evidence, or

---

5. James A. Weisheipl, "The Evolution of Scientific Method," in James A. Weisheipl, *Nature and Motion in the Middle Ages*, ed. William E. Carroll (Washington, D.C.: The Catholic University of America Press, 1985), 239–60; Burtt, *Metaphysical*, 81; Ernst Mayr, *The Growth of Biological Thought: Diversity, Evolution, and Inheritance* (Cambridge, Mass.: Belknap Press of Harvard University Press, 1982), 25; Wallace, *Modeling*, 246–49. On the nature of the hypothetical-deductive method, see also Ernest Hirschlaff Hutten, *The Language of Modern Physics: An Introduction to the Philosophy of Science* (New York: Macmillan, 1956), 222–30; and Barbour, *Religion*, 32–35.

6. "The methods used in empirical science are anything but an automatic application of prefabricated rules. Creativity and interpretation play a central role in scientific progress. In the natural sciences we want to explain the known by the unknown; therefore, we must propose hypothetical explanations that go beyond the available data and we must then test them, creating new experiments and interpreting their results" (Mariano Artigas, *The Mind of the Universe: Understanding Science and Religion* [Philadelphia: Templeton Foundation Press, 2000], 187).

that which is consistent with more, or more compelling, facts than competing hypotheses."[7]

It is also difficult to interpret the meaning of an experimental success or failure. Failure does not always mean that the hypothesis is wrong since extraneous factors may account for it.[8] On the other hand, success does not necessarily imply that the world really behaves just as the model represents it, since some other quite different model may explain the data equally well.[9]

Following Galileo's basic intuition, science continues to express its observations, theories, and conclusions in quantitative or mathematical terms.[10] He once wrote that philosophy (his broad term for scientific knowledge of all kinds) "is written in this grand book, the universe, which stands continually open to our gaze. But the book cannot be understood unless one first learns to comprehend the language and read the letters in which it is composed. It is written in the language of mathematics, and its characters are triangles, circles, and other geometric figures without which it is humanly impossible to understand a single word of it; without these, one wanders about in a dark labyrinth."[11] It is especially this quantitative character of empirical science that will have implications for our understanding of causality.

Science deals with observable phenomena that are mathematically representable and develops hypotheses or predictions that can be empirically tested. It therefore looks for causes that are observable, quantifiable, and

---

7. Mayr, *Growth*, 26.

8. "It seems if one is working from the point of view of getting beauty in one's equations, and if one has really a sound insight, one is on a sure line of progress. If there is not complete agreement between the results of one's work and experiment, one should not allow oneself to be too discouraged, because the discrepancy may well be due to minor features that are not properly taken into account and that will get cleared up with further developments of the theory" (Paul Adrien Maurice Dirac, "The Physicist's Picture of Nature," *Scientific American* 208, no. 5 [1963]: 47).

9. "So, two theories, although they may have deeply different ideas behind them, may be mathematically identical, and then there is no scientific way to distinguish them" (Richard P. Feynman, *The Character of Physical Law* [Cambridge, Mass.: M.I.T. Press, 1987], 168). "Physics provides theories which typically consist of a mathematical formalism and some procedures for applying that formalism to particular concrete situations. But both the formalism and the procedures may admit of alternative ontological interpretations.... It may not be clear which mathematical models represent real physical possibilities, and which do not. And it may not be clear which pairs of mathematical models represent the same physical situation" (Tim Maudlin, "Distilling Metaphysics from Quantum Physics," in *The Oxford Handbook of Metaphysics*, ed. Michael J. Loux and Dean W. Zimmerman [Oxford: Oxford University Press, 2003], 461).

10. "The success of that science, as worked out by Galileo and Newton, rested on the systematic elimination of all considerations other than the quantitative" (Jaki, *Means*, 92).

11. Galileo Galilei, *The Assayer*, in *Discoveries and Opinions of Galileo*, trans. Stillman Drake (Garden City, N.Y.: Doubleday, 1957), 237–38.

capable of empirical investigation. Mario Bunge finds seven basic characteristics of causality in science: "(a) the restriction of causation to *natural* causation (naturalism); (b) the further restriction of all varieties of natural causation to *efficient* causation; (c) the endeavor to reduce efficient causes to *physical* ones (mechanism); (d) the requirement of *testing* causal hypotheses by means of repeated observations and, wherever possible, through reproduction in controllable experiments; (e) an extreme *cautiousness* in the assignment of causes and a ceaseless striving toward the minimization of the number of allegedly ultimate natural causes (parsimony); (f) the focusing on the search for *laws*, whether causal or not; (g) the *mathematical* translation of causal connections."[12]

Studying the world through empirical observation and measurement, modern science had no place in its method for causes that could not be so observed and quantified. Formal and final causes were therefore abandoned since they were "beyond the reach of experiment."[13] According to Francis Bacon (1561–1626): "Matter rather than forms should be the object of our attention, its configurations and changes of configuration, and simple action, and law of action or motion; for forms are figments of the human mind, unless you will call those laws of action forms."[14] Bacon also dismisses final causality: "As Physic and the inquisition of Efficient and Material causes produces Mechanic, so Metaphysic and the inquisition of Forms produces Magic. On the other hand the inquisition of Final Causes is barren, and like a virgin consecrated to God produces nothing."[15] Isaac Newton observes: "The moderns, rejecting

---

12. Bunge, *Causality*, 226.

13. Ibid., 32. "Substantial form could not be measured by mathematics or verified through experiment and was thus rejected by the new physics " (O'Rourke, "Aristotle and the Metaphysics," 22). See also Gilson, *From Aristotle*, 17; Robert M. Augros, "Nature Acts for an End," *Thomist* 66 (2002): 570–71; Goyette, "Substantial Form"; and John W. Keck, "The Natural Motion of Matter in Newtonian and Post-Newtonian Physics," *Thomist* 71 (2007): 529–54.

14. Francis Bacon, *The New Organon*, book 1, no. 51, in *The Works of Francis Bacon*, ed. James Spedding, Robert Leslie Ellis, and Douglas Denon Heath (London: Longman and Co., 1858), 4.58. See also Robert Sokolowski, "Formal and Material Causality in Science," *Proceedings of the American Catholic Philosophical Association* 69 (1995): 59.

15. Francis Bacon, *Of the Dignity and Advancement of Learning*, book 3, chap. 5, in *The Works of Francis Bacon*, ed. James Spedding, Robert Leslie Ellis, and Douglas Denon Heath (London: Longman and Co., 1858), 4.365. "After the critique of the formal cause comes that of the other metaphysical cause, the final one. With great penetration, Bacon goes right to the center of the problem. His main objection is that the contemplative enjoyment of the spectacle of final causes is what averted the attention of the ancient philosophers from the study of material and efficient causes, the only ones the knowledge of which might have some practical usefulness. On this point Bacon was certainly right. Entirely absorbed by the 'harmonies of nature,' lost in the contemplation of their beauty, the Ancients thought they had understood nature, although they had only admired it" (Gilson, *From Aristotle*, 23).

substantial forms and occult qualities, have endeavored to subject the phenomena of nature to the laws of mathematics."[16] Including the idea of formal causality within the new discipline of empirical science would only impede its progress, as Henry Oldenburg once noted to Robert Boyle: "You have driven out that drivel of substantial forms that, as it has hitherto done all the feats the schools have been entertained with, so it has stopped the progress of true philosophy, and made the best of scholars not more knowing as to the nature of particular bodies than the meanest ploughmen."[17] Though science retained the notion of matter, it was not seen as anything so unmeasurable as Aristotle's pure potentiality. Instead, it was thought of as the most basic actuality, the fundamental "stuff" of the universe—the atoms or ultimate particles of which all things are composed.[18] Of Aristotle's four causes, only efficient causality remained since it alone could be expressed mathematically, observed empirically, and controlled experimentally. As Mario Bunge notes:

The Aristotelian teaching of causes lasted in the official Western culture until the Renaissance. When modern science was born, formal and final causes were left aside as standing beyond the reach of experiment; and material causes were taken for granted in connection with all natural happenings—though with a definitely non-Aristotelian meaning, since in the modern world view matter is essentially the subject of change, not "that out of which a thing comes to be and which persists." Hence, of the four Aristotelian causes only the efficient cause was regarded as worthy of scientific research.[19]

---

16. Isaac Newton, *Mathematical Principles of Natural Philosophy*, in *Sir Isaac Newton's Mathematical Principles of Natural Philosophy and His System of the World*, trans. Andrew Motte, revised by Florian Cajori (Berkeley and Los Angeles: University of California Press, 1946), xvii.

17. Henry Oldenburg, "Oldenburg to Boyle, no. 501 (24 March 1665/6)," in *The Correspondence of Henry Oldenburg*, ed. and trans. A. Rupert Hall and Marie Boas Hall (Madison: University of Wisconsin Press, 1966), 3.67. See also Robert Pasnau, "Form, Substance, and Mechanism," *Philosophical Review* 113 (2004): 31.

18. "Likewise potency is jettisoned since it cannot be grasped in a clear and distinct idea" (O'Rourke, "Aristotle and the Metaphysics," 23).

19. Bunge, *Causality*, 32. "Modern physics, by reducing all of nature to the quantifiable and measurable, has effectively eliminated all but one of the four causes" (Keck, "Natural Motion," 530–31). "Aristotle delineated four types of causes: formal, material, efficient and final. Of these, only efficient cause was retained explicitly in the mechanical sciences of Galileo and Newton" (Robert John Russell, "The Meaning of Causality in Contemporary Physics," in *Free Will and Determinism: Papers from an Interdisciplinary Research Conference, 1986*, ed. Viggo Mortensen and Robert Sorensen [Aarhus: Aarhus University Press, 1987], 14). "The Cartesian assimilation of corporeality to pure mathematics, based on Descartes's own distrust of sense experience, has boxed science into, one could say, living a life of extension without any reference to the nature of reality" (Wojciech P. Grygiel, "Quantum Mechanics: A Dialectical Approach to Reality," *Thomist* 65 [2001]: 224). See also Gerald Kreyche, "Some Causes of the Elimination of Causality in Contemporary Science," *Thomist* 29 (1965): 60–78; and Wallace, *Causality and Scientific*, 2.246.

Yet efficient causality was also contracted. It was no longer a broad enough concept to include such things as counselors who advise their leaders.[20] It was understood strictly in terms of the force or energy that moves the atoms of the universe.[21]

As a methodological strategy, there can be no objection to this limiting of the notion of causality. A purely quantitative method cannot embrace such nonquantitative notions as formal causality, purpose, and mere possibility-of-being. As Stanley Jaki points out: "Purpose was not to be found through physics for the simple reason that physics deals only with measurable parameters, that is, quantities."[22]

The very success that science enjoyed by omitting causes that could not be measured eventually led to the conviction that such causes should not only be ignored methodologically but denied metaphysically. The methodological assumptions that science had used for studying the world became ontological assertions about its nature.

The reductionistic method that investigated the world by breaking it down into its smallest parts, became reductionism—the philosophical assertion that the most basic parts of the world are also the most real.[23] Parsimony, the practice of introducing as few causes as possible into a scientific explanation, turned into the ontological conviction that there could be no causes in the real world other than those employed by empirical science. The method of quantitative measurement became materialism, the belief that only the material and measurable is real. The practice of studying the world though efficient causality understood as physical force became mechanism, the tenet that the world is fundamentally mechanical and may be under-

---

20. See *Phys.* II, 3 (193b 30).

21. Burtt, *Metaphysical*, 30, 98–99, 208–9. See also John B. Cobb, "Natural Causality and Divine Action," in *God's Activity in the World: The Contemporary Problem*, ed. Owen C. Thomas (Chico: Scholars Press, 1983), 102.

22. Jaki, *Means*, 92. See also Gilson, *From Aristotle*, 17; Kirk Wegter-McNelly, "Fundamental Physics and Religion," in *The Oxford Handbook of Religion and Science*, ed. Philip Clayton and Zachary Simpson (Oxford: Oxford University Press, 2006), 160; and Artigas, *Mind*, 138.

23. "The whole magnificent movement of modern science is essentially of a piece; the later biological and sociological branches took over their basic postulates from the earlier victorious mechanics, especially the all-important postulate that valid explanations must always be in terms of small, elementary units in regularly changing relations. To this has likewise been added, in all but the rarest cases, the postulate that ultimate causality is to be found in the motion of the physical atoms" (Burtt, *Metaphysical*, 30). On the varieties of reductionism, see Nancey Murphy, "Reductionism: How Did We Fall into It and Can we Emerge from It?" in *Evolution and Emergence: Systems, Organisms, Persons*, ed. Nancey Murphy and William R. Stoeger (New York: Oxford University Press, 2007), 23–24.

stood only through mechanical explanations.[24] The practice of describing the world through mathematically based laws became determinism, the conviction that the laws of science are not merely descriptive but prescriptive and absolutely determinative of all that occurs in the world.[25] The methodological assumption that the laws of science apply uniformly throughout the cosmos became a metaphysical assertion that such laws form a closed causal nexus that cannot be violated. The practice of considering only quantifiable material causes in nature turned into naturalism, the metaphysical conviction that the world, precisely as science studies it, is all that is or can exist.[26]

The net result was not science, but *scientism*.[27] As Gennaro Auletta explains: "The absence of a true philosophy of nature transformed (already in Newton's *Principia*) this methodological reductionism into a metaphysical one, with the consequence that modern science was built on 'faith' in a certain (mechanical) conception of matter and the universe."[28] Scientism has

---

24. "We have seen how the development of astronomy and of mechanics at the time of the Renaissance promoted the growth of a mechanical view of the world. This outlook was reflected in the field of philosophy" (Copleston, *History*, 3.290–91). Etienne Gilson observes: "The pure mechanist in biology is a man whose entire activity has as its end the discovery of the 'how' of the vital operations in plants and animals. Looking for nothing else, he sees nothing else, and since he cannot integrate other things in his research, he denies their existence. This is why he sincerely denies the existence, however evident, of final causality" (Gilson, *From Aristotle*, 11).

25. This is often illustrated with the famous statement of the French mathematician Pierre-Simon de Laplace: "We ought then to regard the present state of the universe as the effect of its anterior state and as the causes of the one which is to follow. Given for one instant an intelligence which could comprehend all the forces by which nature is animated and the respective situation of the beings who compose it—an intelligence sufficiently vast to submit these data to analysis—it would embrace in the same formula the movements of the greatest bodies of the universe and those of the lightest atom; for it, nothing would be uncertain and the future, as the past, would be present to its eyes" (Pierre Simon de Laplace, *Philosophical Essay on Probabilities*, trans. Frederick Wilson Truscott and Frederick Lincoln Emory [New York: John Wiley and Sons, 1902], 4).

26. Francisco Ayala describes this as the difference between a methodological naturalism, the scientific practice of studying the world "by formulating hypotheses, laws, and theories that can be tested, by observation and experiment," and epistemological naturalism, the claim that "science is the only way of knowing" (Francisco J. Ayala, "From Paley to Darwin: Design to Natural Selection," in *Back to Darwin: A Richer Account of Evolution*, ed. John B. Cobb [Grand Rapids, Mich.: Eerdmans, 2008], 50n1). See also Andrew P. Porter, *By the Waters of Naturalism: Theology Perplexed among the Sciences* (Eugene, Ore.: Wipf and Stock, 2001).

27. Scientism is fundamentally the transformation of the methodology of empirical science into a metaphysics, a move from the quantitative investigation of nature to the assumption that being is always quantitative. While the former is a legitimate methodology, the latter is mere ideology: "Whenever one comes across the concept of 'science,' in the singular, being used ... to support sweeping assertions to the effect that here, and here alone, is truth to be obtained, then one is in the presence neither of science, nor of history, but ideology" (Nicholas Lash, "Where Does *The God Delusion* Come From?" *New Blackfriars* 88 [2007]: 517).

28. Auletta, "Science," 273.

far-reaching consequences, as Wolfgang Smith testifies: "I have no doubt that the ongoing de-Christianization of Western society is due in large measure to the imposition of the prevailing scientistic world-view."[29] Huston Smith describes the sweep of scientism: "Itself occupying no more than a single ontological plane, science challenged by implication the notion that other planes exist. As its challenge was not effectively met, it swept the field and gave the modern world its soul."[30]

We can see this shift from methodology to ontology in the thought of René Descartes (1596–1650). Influenced by the mathematics and mechanism of modern science, he found no place for the traditional notions of form and matter in his account of the natural world.[31] He and his contemporaries did not so much refute the notion of substantial form as ignore it.[32] The upshot for causality was that formal, final, and material causality (as pure potentiality) were not simply omitted methodologically but denied ontological existence.[33] The term "causality" was no longer an analogous notion, applicable to a range of causes, but a univocal idea applied to the one unique type of

---

29. Wolfgang Smith, "From Schrödinger's Cat to Thomistic Ontology," *Thomist* 63 (1999): 49.

30. Huston Smith, *Forgotten Truth: The Common Vision of the World's Religions* (San Francisco: HarperSanFrancisco, 1992), 6. See also Avery Dulles, "God and Evolution," *First Things* 176 (2007): 19–24.

31. "René Descartes presents a good example of a philosopher who never was able to comprehend matter and form as ontological co-principles. It was inconceivable for him that there be any such things as substantial principles since their status in being would evade precise mathematical determination. In his view matter must be an extended, actual thing, since 'potency' is only a confused notion. And, if a form is substantial, it must be capable of subsisting by itself and hence must be a thing or complete substance. His insistence on 'clear and distinct ideas' as a starting point effectively blocked for him access to the concepts of protomatter and natural form" (Wallace, *Modeling*, 18). On the influence of the new science on Descartes's philosophy, see Copleston, *History*, 3.289–91.

32. "It is safe to say that substantial forms were never refuted, because the most prominent early modern critics—with the notable exception of Boyle—never took the theory seriously enough to mount a vigorous refutation" (Pasnau, "Form," 46). Writing over two centuries later, Charles Darwin also questioned the reality of form or essence—with the result that the term "species" itself became a rather amorphous concept in his writings. See Charles Darwin, *The Origin of Species* (New York: Modern Library, 1998), 78–79, 644. As Leo Elders points out, Darwin "dissolved the species into an endless variety of individuals without any specific community" (Leo J. Elders, "The Philosophical and Religious Background of Charles Darwin's Theory of Evolution," *Doctor Communis* 37 [1984]: 52).

33. "The essential feature of this mechanical philosophy was the rejection of *physis*, or nature, as an explanatory principle in natural science. With this rejection also went potency and act, substance, formal and final causality, and even the ontological reality of true causality" (Weisheipl, "Evolution," 260). "If philosophy identifies true knowledge with useful knowledge, as modern scientism does, final causality will be by the same stroke eliminated from nature and from science as a useless fiction" (Gilson, *From Aristotle*, 19). See also Dominique Dubarle, "Causalité et finalité chez saint Thomas et au niveau des sciences modernes de la nature," in *Il cosmo e la scienza*, Atti del congresso internazionale Tommaso d'Aquino nel suo settimo centenario, no. 9 (Naples: Edizioni Domenicane Italiane, 1975), 12.

causality to be found in the cosmos: the efficient causality of the energy that moves the atoms.[34]

With David Hume, even this narrow idea of efficient causality was questioned. Since the supposed influence of a cause upon its effect was not directly evident to sense observation, Hume concluded that the connection between cause and effect was not an aspect of the real world, but only a habit of our thinking as we become accustomed to see one thing constantly conjoined to another.[35] Causality became a property not of things but of thought. It was no longer an *ontological* reality in the world outside ourselves, but an *epistemological* property of the way we think about the world. The hallmark of causality was now found in the epistemological category of *predictability* rather than the ontological category of *dependence*.[36]

UNLOCKING CAUSALITY IN CONTEMPORARY SCIENCE

We can link the constriction of causality to the advent of modern science and its expansion to the coming of contemporary science provided we do not make these associations too strictly. In some circles, causality was shrinking even before modern science and in others it remained broad even after its advent. Robert Pasnau points out, for instance, that well before the dawn of modern science some stodgy Scholastics were already shrink-

---

34. "Causality is viewed as an external, efficient relation; Aristotle's comprehensive understanding of *aitia* is abandoned. Reduced in this manner to the dimensions of external extension, the natural world is ... deprived of its inner dynamism and natural tendency. Some of Aristotle's richest insights are lost, namely, intrinsic form and the potency of being. Unless we affirm, however, the presence in natural beings of some element akin to immanent form, it is difficult to understand why they act in the determinate and intelligible ways continually disclosed by science at ever more microcosmic depths. Bereft of form and potency, bodies are deprived of the dynamic structure which orients them by natural tendency" (O'Rourke, "Aristotle and the Metaphysics," 23–24).

35. See David Hume, *An Enquiry Concerning Human Understanding* (Chicago: Open Court, 1930), 75–81. For Immanuel Kant, causality will remain an aspect of thought, not acquired through cumulative experience as in Hume, but known *a priori*. As Frederick Copleston explains: "If I say that every event must have a cause, my judgment expresses *a priori* knowledge: it is not simply the expression of an habitual expectation mechanically produced by the association of ideas. The necessity, Kant insists, is not 'purely subjective'; the dependence of any event or happening or change on a cause is known, and it is known *a priori*" (Copleston, *History*, 6.218).

36. "The reduction of causation to regular association, as propounded by Humeans, amounts to mistaking causation for one of its tests; and such a reduction of an ontological category to a methodological criterion is the consequence of epistemological tenets of empiricism, rather than a result of an unprejudiced analysis of the laws of nature.... A trait of reality (causation) should not be identified with a criterion (predictability) for the empirical test of scientific hypotheses.... Unlike causation, which is an ontological category, predictability is an epistemological category" (Bunge, *Causality*, 47, 327). See also Cobb, "Natural Causality," 111.

ing the scope of causality: "[S]ome of the most significant changes in how form has been understood seem to have occurred not at the hands of modern anti-Aristotelians, but with an earlier generation of scholastics.... The demise of Aristotelian metaphysics might in part be laid at the door of philosophers who were ostensibly Aristotelians."[37] Even in the rise of modern science, some of its practitioners maintained a broad notion of causality. Francis Bacon did not deny the existence of formal and final causality, but simply excluded them from the discipline of empirical science.[38] William Harvey (1578–1657) continued to use final causality in his biology.[39] Newton himself employed thoroughly Thomistic categories of causal explanation in his nonscientific writings and did not hesitate to invoke the influence of the Divine Being in the natural world.[40]

37. Pasnau, "Form," 72.

38. "For Metaphysic, we have assigned unto it the inquiry of Formal and Final Causes.... [T]he invention of Forms is of all other parts of knowledge the worthiest to be sought, if it be possible to be found. As for the possibility, they are ill discoverers that think there is no land when they can see nothing but sea.... But if any man shall keep a continual watchful and severe eye upon action, operation, and the use of knowledge, he may advise and take notice what are the Forms, the disclosures whereof are fruitful and important to the state of man.... In the same manner to inquire the Form of a lion, of an oak, of gold; nay, of water, of air, is a vain pursuit; but to inquire the Forms of sense, of voluntary motion, of vegetation, of colors, of gravity and levity, of density, of tenuity, of heat, of cold, and all other natures and qualities, which like an alphabet are not many, and of which the essences (upheld by matter) of all creatures do consist; to inquire, I say, the *true forms* of these, is that part of Metaphysic which we now define of. Not but that Physic doth make inquiry and take consideration of the same natures: but how? Only as to the Material and Efficient Causes of them, and not as to the Forms" (Francis Bacon, *The Proficience and Advancement of Learning: Divine and Humane*, in *The Works of Francis Bacon*, ed. James Spedding, Robert Leslie Ellis, and Douglas Denon Heath [London: Longman and Co., 1857], 3.355–56). "Bacon adamantly opposed the inclusion of formal and final causes within science.... For Bacon, formal and final causes belonged to metaphysics and not to science. Science, according to Bacon, needed to limit itself to material and efficient causes, thereby freeing science from the sterility that inevitably results when science and metaphysics are conflated" (William A. Dembski, "Signs of Intelligence: A Primer on the Discernment of Intelligent Design," *Touchstone: A Journal of Mere Christianity* 12, no. 4 [1999]: 77).

39. Wallace, *Causality and Scientific*, 2.246. In fact, biologists of the modern period were quite different from physicists in their attitude toward Aristotle, as Marjorie Grene and David Depew point out: "For its part, modern physics, as is well known, began by rejecting not just scholastic Aristotelianism, but the fundamental principles of Aristotle's physics itself.... It is important to recognize, however, that the development of modern biology did *not* follow this pattern. Indeed, biologists who worked after Descartes made increasingly systematic use of the concepts of end and form in their explanations of living things, and the name of Aristotle was often spoken reverently among them. Modern biologists have, in fact, returned again and again to Aristotle as their master" (Marjorie Grene and David Depew, *The Philosophy of Biology: An Episodic History* [Cambridge: Cambridge University Press, 2004], 1–2).

40. "This most beautiful system of the sun, planets, and comets, could only proceed from the counsel and dominion of an intelligent and powerful Being. And if the fixed stars are the centers of other like systems, these, being formed by the like wise counsel, must be all subject to the dominion of One;... and lest the systems of the fixed stars should, by their gravity, fall on each other, he

Today, even with the coming of contemporary science, constricted notions of causality are still current in some circles. Charles De Koninck observes: "Ever since Darwin, the opinion remains prevalent that the notion of purpose in nature is unscientific and unnecessary."[41] Robert Sokolowski thinks that a "reductionist and utilitarian attitude" continues to "pervade our contemporary scientific enterprise and, beyond that, the assumptions of almost all people who have gone to college or in some other way have breathed in the general opinions that circulate in our world."[42] Stanley Jaki sees scientism as the source of this continued contraction of causality: "[I]t is the restriction to the univocal within science and the universal validity assigned by scientism to that restriction which represent the starkest and most timely contrast to the doctrine of the analogy of being, the cornerstone of realist metaphysics."[43] Taede Smedes agrees that scientism remains "a pervasive

---

hath placed those systems at immense distances from one another. This Being governs all things, not as the soul of the world, but as Lord over all.... We know him only by his most wise and excellent contrivances of things, and final causes; we admire him for his perfections; but we reverence and adore him on account of his dominion: for we adore him as his servants; and a god without dominion, providence, and final causes, is nothing else but Fate and Nature. Blind metaphysical necessity, which is certainly the same always and everywhere, could produce no variety of things. All that diversity of natural things which we find suited to different times and places could arise from nothing but the ideas and will of a Being necessarily existing" (Isaac Newton, *Mathematical Principles*, 544–46). "Newton has a fuller discussion of causality and agency, where he invokes such Thomistic concepts as essentially subordinated series of causes, the divine *concursus*, agents that act by contact and those that act only virtually, that is, by their power, and action that comes directly from an agent and action that comes only indirectly *per emanationem et resultantiam*.... Here it may suffice to observe that, at the age of twenty, Newton already had a clear grasp of how God can act in the world through his causality, while still leaving room for nature also being a cause under God's prevenient causality" (Wallace, "Aquinas and Newton," 258). "For Newton, then, gravitation is not to be explained by magnetic-like forces inherent in bodies which 'attract,' but by the direct action of God operating through space" (James A. Weisheipl, "Space and Gravitation," *New Scholasticism* 29 [1955]: 206).

41. Charles De Koninck, *The Hollow Universe* (London: Oxford University Press, 1960), 97. In Jacques Monod's words: "The cornerstone of the scientific method is the postulate that nature is objective. In other words, the systematic denial that 'true' knowledge can be got at by interpreting phenomena in terms of final causes—that is to say, of 'purpose'" (Jacques Monod, *Chance and Necessity: An Essay on the Natural Philosophy of Modern Biology* [New York: Alfred A. Knopf, 1972], 21).

42. Sokolowski, "Formal and Material," 59. Sokolowski also sees sinister implications in Darwin's elimination of purpose or final cause: "The other historical development that has led us to our present situation in regard to form was Darwin's introduction of the theory of the descent of species through natural selection.... What looks like the regularity and the necessity of form is really the outcome of random occurrence joined with environmental opportunity. Note that such a theory of development and life holds up as the highest good not the excellence of the individual in a species, but sheer survival. The lowest common denominator, survival, is the good that rules in evolution, just as the elementary forces expressed in the laws of nature, the lowest common denominator in matter, rule over the whole of nature" (Sokolowski, "Formal and Material," 59).

43. Stanley L. Jaki, *Chesterton: A Seer of Science* (Urbana: University of Illinois Press, 1986), 9–10.

feature of our Western society."[44] Simon Conway Morris points out its prevalence among evolutionary biologists.[45] It is also evident in discussions of the phenomenon of emergence, when materialist assumptions are sometimes presented not just as methodological tools but as ontological truth.[46] John Greene points out a possible reason for the tendency to scientism: "Every great scientific synthesis stimulates efforts to view the whole of reality in its terms.... But the views of reality that originate in this way are not themselves scientific, nor are they subject to scientific verification."[47]

Though the constriction of causality did not immediately end with the advent of contemporary science, its theories and discoveries have nonetheless been the catalyst for broader understandings. We will look at these widening notions of causality in the phenomenon of emergence and then consider the sciences of quantum mechanics, cosmology, and evolution.

Emergence

The theory of emergence asserts that, at many levels in the natural world, new features arise that cannot be explained simply by reference to their parts.[48] To study them, one must begin with the whole (from the top down) rather than the part (from the bottom up). The phenomenon of emergence

---

44. Smedes, *Chaos*, 208. He characterizes the logic of scientism in this way: "What is justifiably or reasonably knowable is what can be established by scientific methods. What is scientifically knowable is what is considered to be 'real.' If this is true, then what is not scientifically knowable, i.e., what cannot be established by scientific methods ... is not real. If only what is physically possible or actual is real, then what falls outside of this category (i.e., the rest of the logical possibilities) is considered not real" (ibid., 183–84).

45. He names Richard Dawkins and E. O. Wilson, among others. See Simon Conway Morris, *Life's Solution: Inevitable Humans in a Lonely Universe* (Cambridge: Cambridge University Press, 2003), 311–30.

46. Philip Clayton, for instance, names "ontological monism" as the first feature of the concept of emergence and defines it, not as a methodological assumption, but as an ontological truth: "Reality is ultimately composed of one basic kind of stuff" (Clayton, *Mind*, 4). He is building on a similar ontological claim by Charbel Nino El-Hani and Antonio Marcos Pereira in what he calls their "classic definition" of emergence (idem, 3–4). They assert: "All that exists in the space-time world are the basic particles recognized by physics and their aggregates" (Charbel Nino El-Hani and Antonio Marcos Pereira, "Higher-Level Descriptions: Why Should We Preserve Them?" in *Downward Causation: Minds, Bodies and Matter*, ed. Peter Bogh Andersen, Claus Emmeche, Niels Ole Finnemann, and Peder Voetmann Christiansen [Aarhus: Aarhus University Press, 2000], 133). A similar tendency to slide from methodological assumptions to metaphysical claims can be found in Clayton's arguments for limiting God's action to the realm of the human mind in his "The Impossible Possibility: Divine Causes in the World of Nature," in *God, Life, and the Cosmos*, ed. Ted Peters, Muzaffar Iqbal and Syed Nomanul Haq (Aldershot, U.K.: Ashgate, 2002), 249–80.

47. John C. Greene, *Darwin and the Modern World View* (Baton Rouge: Louisiana State University Press, 1974), 132.

48. See Clayton, *Mind*, 66–69.

appears in both living and nonliving things. Ernst Mayr affirms emergence in biology, but finds it "equally characteristic of inorganic systems."[49] Jonathan Powers maintains that there are "several features of the present-day theory of elementary particles" which suggest that "at certain levels of complexity, matter exhibits 'emergent properties' and 'emergent laws' which can neither be defined nor explained in terms of the properties and laws at a lower level of complexity."[50] George Ellis points out that "top-down action affects the nature of causality significantly" and can "modify the properties of the constitutive elements at the lower levels." He gives the example of neutrons, which are "unstable with a half-life of eleven minutes when unbound, but stable with a half-life of billions of years when bound into a nucleus. A change of context results in a major difference in local physical behavior." His conclusion is that "complex systems are not just conglomerates of unchanged elementary constituents; rather, by their specific structuring, at all scales they profoundly affect the nature of the constituents out of which they are made."[51] Pier Luigi Luisi avers: "I would like to make the point here that chemistry offers very clear examples of downward causation.... Actually, chemical examples show that emergence must go hand in hand with downward causation—one is the consequence of the other, and the two phenomena take place simultaneously.... Obviously, the emergence of the novel entity water obliges the two components to a relatedness (chemical bonding and the corresponding mixing of the electronic orbitals) that profoundly affects the properties of both hydrogen and oxygen. Obviously, the chemical properties of H and O bound to each other in the water molecules have nothing to do with the physical properties of the free gases."[52]

Emergence is especially evident in living things. Paul Davies notes, for instance, that a cell "commandeers chemical pathways and intermolecular

---

49. "Actually, emergence is equally characteristic of inorganic systems.... Such emergence is quite universal and, as Popper said, 'We live in a universe of emergent novelty'" (Mayr, *Growth*, 63). "Such *emergence* of new properties occurs also through the inanimate world" (Ernst Mayr, *Toward a New Philosophy of Biology: Observations of an Evolutionist* [Cambridge, Mass.: Harvard University Press, 1988], 15).

50. Jonathan Powers, *Philosophy and the New Physics* (New York: Methuen, 1982), 155.

51. George F. R. Ellis, "Physics, Complexity, and the Science-Religion Debate," in *The Oxford Handbook of Religion and Science*, ed. Philip Clayton and Zachary Simpson (Oxford: Oxford University Press, 2006), 753.

52. Pier Luigi Luisi, "Emergence in Chemistry: Chemistry as the Embodiment of Emergence," *Foundations of Chemistry* 4 (2002): 195–96. See also Clayton, *Mind*, 66; Philip Clayton, "The Emergence of Spirit: From Complexity to Anthropology to Theology," *Theology and Science* 4 (2006): 294; and Connell, *Substance*, 81–86.

organization to implement the plan encoded in its genome."[53] Ernst Mayr notes that biological systems act as wholes that cannot be reduced to their constituents.[54] George Ellis observes that in the process of evolution, "top-down action from the environment" may affect the "detailed biological microstructure" of an organism, explaining, for instance, why polar bears have genes for white fur (in their snowy environment) while black bears have genes for black fur (in their dark forest surroundings). There is "no way you could predict or explain this coding on the basis of biochemistry or microphysics alone."[55] Philip Clayton invokes emergence to describe human consciousness: "The subjective states of experiencing joy or being self-conscious have an irreducibly mental component; such phenomena exercise a type of causal influence that includes but is also more than the physical and biological states on which they supervene."[56]

There are many different understandings of the phenomenon of emergence.[57] Basically, we can distinguish "weak emergence" (which recognizes only the "bottom-up" emergence of new features such as the "wetness" of water that is not characteristic of a single water molecule) from "strong emergence" (which admits, in addition, that a new whole may emerge from and then exercise a distinctive causality on its parts).[58]

---

53. Paul Davies, "The Physics of Downward Causation," in *The Re-Emergence of Emergence: The Emergentist Hypothesis from Science to Religion* (New York: Oxford University Press, 2006), 48.

54. "Systems at each hierarchal level have two properties. They act as wholes (as though they were a homogeneous entity), and their characteristics cannot be deduced (even in theory) from the most complete knowledge of the components, taken separately or in other combinations. In other words, when such a system is assembled from its components, new characteristics of the whole emerge that could not have been predicted from a knowledge of the constituents" (Mayr, *Toward a New Philosophy*, 15). See also Clayton, *Mind*, 73–101; John Dupré, "It Is Not Possible to Reduce Biological Explanations to Explanations in Chemistry and/or Physics," in *Contemporary Debates in Philosophy of Biology*, ed. Francisco J. Ayala and Robert Arp (Chichester, U.K.: Wiley-Blackwell, 2010), 32–47; and Arthur Peacocke, "Emergent Realities with Causal Efficacy: Some Philosophical and Theological Applications," in *God's Action in Nature's World: Essays in Honor of Robert John Russell*, ed. Ted Peters and Nathan Hallanger (Aldershot, U.K.: Ashgate, 2006), 191.

55. G. F. R. Ellis, "Physics, Complexity," 753.

56. Clayton, "Natural Law," 626. See also William R. Stoeger, "The Mind-Brain Problem, the Laws of Nature, and Constitutive Relationships," in *Neuroscience and the Person: Scientific Perspectives on Divine Action*, ed. Robert John Russell, Nancey Murphy, Theo Meyering, and Michael Arbib (Vatican City State: Vatican Observatory; Berkeley, Calif.: Center for Theology and the Natural Sciences, 1999), 129–46.

57. For a brief history and critique of various understandings of emergence, see Gregory R. Peterson, "Species of Emergence," *Zygon* 41 (2006): 689–712; Niels Henrik Gregersen, "Emergence and Complexity," in *The Oxford Handbook of Religion and Science*, ed. Philip Clayton and Zachary Simpson (Oxford: Oxford University Press, 2006), 767–73; and Clayton, *Mind*, 1–37.

58. "Emergence ... shows that upward propagation of causes is not the whole story. The state of the whole ... affects the behavior of the particles and the causal interactions that they have. Admit-

Emergence includes the theories of "complexity" and "chaos." As Ian Stewart and Jack Cohen explain, complexity begins with the complex and moves to the simple. It studies how "highly complex interactions taking place in large populations of systems can conspire to create large-scale but simple patterns."[59] It looks at such things as "principles of self-organization and the formation of complex systems" and studies "the interaction between many components of various kinds and the principles that affect their correlation, coupling, and feedback relationships."[60] The enormously complex processes within the growing embryo, for instance, give rise to the mature organism, and the complex interaction of billions of neurons in the brain are understood to produce consciousness.[61]

Chaos theory, in a sense, moves in the opposite direction. It begins with the simple and moves to the complex, studying how "simple rules" may give rise to "complex behavior."[62] It had its origins in studies of weather predictions. Researchers noticed that small fluctuations in otherwise determined atmospheric models could produce widely different results. The phenomenon became known as "the butterfly effect" since conceivably "a butterfly stirring the air today in Peking can transform storm systems next month in New York."[63] Chaos provides a mathematical account of how determined systems, through minor fluctuations, can produce a wide range of random or unpredictable results. It has been applied to many things,

---

tedly, some argue that no actual downward causal forces are involved.... We might speak of these positions as involving at most weak emergence, emergence without downward causation. By contrast, I have argued that the phenomena allow for, and may actually require, the notion of a downwardly propagating causal influence—a view that we might call strong emergence" (Clayton, "Natural Law," 632). "The more robust version, which I have labeled 'strong emergence' and defended in my work, makes two claims. First, new things emerge in natural history, not just new properties of some fundamental things or stuff; and, second, these emergent things exercise their own types of causal power. Such 'downward causation' occurs at many different levels in nature. Strong emergence is a thesis about the nature of natural evolution" (Clayton, "The Emergence of Spirit," 294–95). See also Philip Clayton, "Emergence from Physics to Theology: Towards a Panoramic View," *Zygon* 41 (2006): 677; Clayton, *Mind*, 9. "For most emergentists, it usually is not enough to say that emergent entities exist; it also is important to claim that they are causally efficacious. Thus, emergent entities are said to employ a top-down causality, in contrast to the bottom-up causality of their constituent parts" (Peterson, "Species," 694).

59. See Ian Stewart and Jack Cohen, "Why Are There Simple Rules in a Complicated Universe?" *Futures* 26 (1994): 648–49.

60. Clayton, "Emergence of Spirit," 293–94.

61. Roger Lewin, *Complexity: Life at the Edge of Chaos* (Chicago: University of Chicago Press, 1999), 13–14.

62. See Stewart and Cohen, "Why," 648.

63. James Gleick, *Chaos: Making a New Science* (New York: Penguin Books, 1988), 8. See also Lewin, *Complexity*, 11.

"from the weather, to ecological systems, to the functioning of our hearts."[64]

In chaos theory, "determinism at one level ... generates randomness at the next level, which produces regularity at the next higher level of aggregation."[65] In this way, randomness (chaos) can result from order (determinism) and order can result from randomness.[66] In physics, chaos theory helps to explain how undetermined quantum entities can produce a determined and orderly universe.[67] In biology it shows how myriad chance events can result in highly structured organisms. Chaos theory teaches us that both chance and determinacy play a role in the events of nature. Science does not need to choose between a world of pure chance or of pure determinism. Both are real aspects of the world.[68]

Chaos theory admits both "bottom-up" and "top-down" causation.[69] In bottom-up causation, minor fluctuations may produce holistic results. When magnetic material cools, for instance, the chance alignment of some parts eventually results in the common alignment of the whole magnet. Such causation is operative in many places in nature, from the construction of termite pillars to events in the initial formation of the universe.[70] In top-down causation, wholes may influence their parts or exhibit behaviors that the parts cannot explain. Atoms and molecules, for instance, "have distinctive principles of organization as systems and therefore exhibit properties and activities not found in their components."[71]

---

64. Niels Henrik Gregersen, "Providence in an Indeterministic World," *CTNS Bulletin* 14, no. 1 (1994): 21.

65. David J. Bartholomew, *God of Chance* (London: SCM Press, 1984), 74–75. "The new insight from chaos theory is that even systems that are covered throughout by deterministic descriptions (by way of computer simulations) show a range of indeterministic properties. The reason for this is that the deterministic mathematical formalisms that cover the non-linear dynamics have the in-built function ... of amplifying even the slightest fluctuations. This sensitivity to the initial conditions has an effect like an avalanche. In fact such a non-linear dynamics applies to by far the biggest parts of our medium-scale world, from the weather, to ecological systems, and to the functioning of our hearts. Chaotic behavior is the rule rather than the exception" (Gregersen, "Providence," 21).

66. Bartholomew, *God of Chance*, 78. Although "chance" and "randomness" are sometimes used interchangeably, they can be distinguished since randomness involves statistical order while chance does not. See V. E. Smith, *General*, 204–7.

67. See John C. Polkinghorne, *Science and Creation: The Search for Understanding* (Boston: Shambhala, 1989), 42.

68. See John C. Polkinghorne, *Reason and Reality: The Relation between Science and Theology* (Philadelphia: Trinity Press International, 1991), 39–42; Polkinghorne, *Science and Creation*, 43.

69. See John C. Polkinghorne, *Science and Providence: God's Interaction with the World* (Boston: New Science Library, 1989), 29.

70. Polkinghorne, *Science and Creation*, 37, 45–46.

71. Barbour, *Religion*, 105. "Complex entities possess holistic properties that are unforeseeable and inexplicable in terms of a purely constituent analysis" (Polkinghorne, *Theology in the Context*, 121).

The presence of such emergent properties and behaviors implies that the "bottom-up" method of reductionism is no longer adequate to account for the phenomena that science observes in the world. Philip Clayton sees the rejection of reductionism as an essential aspect of emergence: "The discussion of emergence makes no sense unless one conducts it against the backdrop of reductionism. Emergence theories presuppose that the project of explanatory reduction—explaining all phenomena in the natural world in terms of the objects and laws of physics—is finally impossible."[72] James Gleick argues: "Chaos is anti-reductionist. This new science makes a strong claim about the world; namely, that when it comes to the most interesting questions, questions about order and disorder, decay and creativity, pattern formation and life itself, the whole cannot be explained in terms of the parts. There are fundamental laws about complex systems, but they are new kinds of laws.... They are laws of structure and organization and scale, and they simply vanish when you focus on the individual constituents of a complex system."[73]

Even if the theory of emergence rejects reductionism, it remains ambiguous about the ontological status of the emergent whole. If we say the whole is really "nothing but" its parts, we fall back into reductionism; but if we assert that the whole is "something more," we seem to slide toward dualism or vitalism. If the whole is not merely the sum of the parts but something new, what accounts for the newness? And what sort of newness is it? Is it a distinctively new identity bespeaking an ontological wholeness or oneness,

---

"Another answer given by reductionists is to interpret chemical combination as a simple, mechanical addition of parts. In such a combination no greater comes from the less, since a 'sum is equal to its parts.' This interpretation, however, is not adequate to our present understanding of the molecule which has wave-mechanical unity in which the constituting atoms perdure only in a modified and integrated form. Thus the orbital electrons of the constituting atoms may no longer belong to a single nucleus within the molecule but to several. A new network of relations between the elementary particles within the molecule forms a unitary system, not a mere juxtaposition of previous systems" (Benedict Ashley, "Causality and Evolution," *Thomist* 36 [1972]: 207).

72. Clayton, *Mind*, 2. For a brief history of the debate between reductionists and emergentists, see Murphy, "Reductionism."

73. James Gleick, "Chaos and Beyond," in *Chaos: The New Science*, Nobel Conference 26, ed. John Holte (Saint Peter, Minn.: Gustavus Adolphus College, 1993), 125–26. "Chaos theory ... has already placed complex systems beyond the grip of any mechanistic determinism. The reason is that such systems can reach wildly unpredictable results from very simple initial conditions. While these conditions are in principle mathematically sufficient to project the entire future behavior of the system, they turn out in fact to be unknowable" (Christopher Mooney, *Theology and Scientific Knowledge* [South Bend, Ind.: University of Notre Dame Press, 1996], 101). See also Polkinghorne, *Reason and Reality*, 39; and Barbour, *Nature*, 22.

or is it merely an incidental newness, indicating only an incidental unity, a new pattern or arrangement of ontologically more fundamental parts?

Recognizing the need to ground the being of the whole in accounts of emergence or top-down causality, a number of thinkers have been led back to the philosophical notion of form. To Gregory Peterson, the presence of irreducible, "information-bearing patterns" in theories of emergence is generally reminiscent of Platonic forms, while the specificity of such patterns suggests an Aristotelian understanding of form. He believes that "arguments both for and against Platonic and Aristotelian forms have some relevance here, although this connection has been poorly explored."[74] Philip Clayton uses the notion of form to distinguish his approach to evolution from the reductionist/materialist understanding of Richard Dawkins: "I suggest placing renewed emphasis on the ontological significance of form. In classical philosophy, form meant meaningful structure. For Plato, for example, it meant ideational content (the idea of a thing); for Aristotle, the comprehensible nature or essence of a thing."[75] Terrence Deacon also emphasizes the significance of form as a type of causality that "takes us back to Aristotle."[76] A new appreciation of the causality of the whole makes room for the Aristotelian notion of "form" as a nonreducible principle of causality that allows us to see complex entities in the natural world not as mere conglomerations of parts, but as truly unified "wholes" with their own proper characteristics and activities.[77]

If emergence suggests formal causality, it also evokes the notion of final causality insofar as it implies, as Mariano Artigas says, that "different components collaborate to reach a common goal."[78] The emergence of more complex wholes from basic parts suggests a directionality that is somehow built into the natural world: "It is not difficult to find examples of directionality and cooperativity. If we begin with the most elementary components of the world, we find out that subatomic particles and the four basic interactions behave according to well known specific patterns and collaborate to build up successive levels of organization—atoms, molecules, macromolecules, and the bigger inorganic and organic beings. The entire construction

74. Peterson, "Species," 702–3.
75. Clayton, "The Emergence of Spirit," 12.
76. Terrence Deacon, "Response [to Philip Clayton]," *CTNS Bulletin* 20, no. 4 (Fall, 2000): 27.
77. See E. Herbert Granger, "Aristotle and the Concept of Supervenience," *Southern Journal of Philosophy* 31 (1993): 166.
78. Artigas, *Mind*, 130.

of our world is the result of the deployment of tendencies that collaborate to make up unitary systems. The existence of tendencies means that selective channels of behavior exist. It is easy to perceive that natural entities, on both the biological level and the physicochemical level, display a tendency-like behavior. Moreover, tendencies often favor the cooperation of different elements to form higher levels of organization."[79] Such tendencies suggest the presence of teleology in the natural world.[80] Emergence may indeed invite a retrieval of the four modes of causality of Aquinas and Aristotle.[81]

Quantum Mechanics

Quantum mechanics had its beginnings early in the last century with Max Planck's discovery that radiant energy was emitted and absorbed not continuously but in discrete packets or "quanta." Albert Einstein applied Planck's ideas to light and saw that its behavior must be described sometimes as waves and sometimes as discrete particles or "photons."[82] Werner Heisenberg formulated the "uncertainty principle" that asserts that there is "a certain limit on the accuracy with which position and momentum can be known simultaneously."[83] As William Wallace explains, the principle "specifies the limits within which one can reconcile the concept of a particle localized at a point in space and time with that of a wave field precisely determined in momentum (or energy)" and allows "both notions to be used concurrently within the limits stated in the principle, in probability statements that correctly describe the observed phenomena."[84]

79. Ibid., 129.
80. "The world is full of teleological dimensions. When we search for them, we can easily see that virtually any of the main aspects of our world can be taken as a particular case of teleology. Although this holds especially for living beings, the physicochemical world also exhibits many directional features that acquire a special meaning when seen as necessary conditions for the existence of living beings" (ibid., 129). See also Bartholomew, *God of Chance*, 75; and Peacocke, "God's Action," 468.
81. Mark Graves offers a careful analysis of emergence in terms of Aristotle's four kinds of causality in his *Mind, Brain, and the Elusive Soul: Human Systems of Cognitive Science and Religion* (Aldershot, U.K.: Ashgate, 2008), 118. See also Alwyn Scott, "Nonlinear Science and the Cognitive Hierarchy," in *Evolution and Emergence: Systems, Organisms, Persons*, ed. Nancey Murphy and William R. Stoeger (New York: Oxford University Press, 2007), 180–81.
82. See Rolston, *Science and Religion*, 42; and John C. Polkinghorne, *The Quantum World* (Princeton, N.J.: Princeton University Press, 1984), 5–7.
83. Polkinghorne, *Quantum World*, 46.
84. Wallace, *Causality and Scientific*, 2.191. For general introductions to quantum theory, see John C. Polkinghorne, *Quantum Theory: A Very Short Introduction* (New York: Oxford University Press, 2002); John C. Polkinghorne, *Quantum World* (London: Penguin Books, 1986); and Nick Herbert, *Quantum Reality: Beyond the New Physics* (Garden City, N.Y.: Doubleday, 1987).

Physicists agree on the mathematics of quantum theory, but not on its interpretation.[85] Some, such as Albert Einstein, Max Planck, and David Bohm, think that the theory's indeterminism or uncertainty is the result of human ignorance: quantum events must have natural causes and follow determined laws but the causes have yet to be discovered.[86] Heisenberg, on the contrary, sees indeterminism as an objective feature of nature that he likens to Aristotle's primary matter.[87] An ontological indeterminacy characterizes the material universe at its most fundamental level. If no causes of

85. "We all agree how to do the sums, and our answers fit experiment like a glove, but we cannot all agree on what is going on" (Polkinghorne, *One World*, 47). "[S]cience, by itself, cannot adjudicate between epistemic and ontological interpretations of unpredictability. The fact that there are two interpretations of the probabilistic nature of quantum mechanics, each with exactly the same experimental consequences, in one of which the Heisenberg uncertainty principle is simply a matter of necessary ignorance while in the other it is a matter of irreducible indeterminacy, makes the point clearly enough" (John C. Polkinghorne, "Evolution and Providence: A Response to Thomas Tracy," *Theology and Science* 7 [2009]: 318–19). "Though there is almost universal agreement on the equations and predictions of quantum theory, there have been endless debates over its interpretation" (R. J. Russell, "Meaning of Causality," 23). John Polkinghorne lists four basic lines of interpretation for quantum mechanics; Ian Barbour and Holmes Rolston find three; and Mario Bunge finds three, each with numerous subsets. See Polkinghorne, *One World*, 47–49; Rolston, *Science and Religion*, 48–49; Barbour, *Religion*, 101–4; Mario Bunge, "Survey of the Interpretations of Quantum Mechanics," *American Journal of Physics* 24 (1956): 272–86; Bunge, *Causality*, 14, 328. See also Karl R. Popper, *Quantum Theory and the Schism in Physics* (Totowa, N.J.: Rowman and Littlefield, 1982).

86. "It is sometimes said that only Einstein in his old age supported the idea of a deterministic substratum to quantum mechanics, so it should be mentioned that he was not the only physicist to oppose the Copenhagen interpretation. Among others one may mention Planck, de Broglie, von Laue, Schrödinger, Dirac, Fermi, Feynman, and Bohm—hardly a negligible group" (Peter E. Hodgson, "God's Action in the World: The Relevance of Quantum Mechanics," *Zygon* 35 [2000]: 514). See also Peter E. Hodgson, *Science and Belief in the Nuclear Age* (Naples, Fla.: Sapientia Press, 2005), 188–90. "In the view of Einstein, Schrödinger, L. de Broglie and others, indeterminism results from the conditions under which the experiments are done: indeterminism is not an objective fact but a subjective product" (Elders, *The Metaphysics of Being*, 278). "The principle of indeterminacy is epistemological" (Arthur Stanley Eddington, *The Nature of the Physical World* [New York: Macmillan, 1929], 225). For a thorough account of Einstein's views, see Arthur Fine, *The Shaky Game: Einstein, Realism and the Quantum Theory* (Chicago: University of Chicago Press, 1997). For a contemporary defense of Einstein's realism, see Jerzy Rayski, "A Philosophy of Quantum Mechanics," *Philosophy in Science* 1 (1985): 139–48. For a very readable account of the history of the debate, see Manjit Kumar, *Quantum: Einstein, Bohr, and the Great Debate about the Nature of Reality* (New York: W. W. Norton, 2009).

87. "All the elementary particles are made of the same substance, which we may call energy or universal matter; they are just different forms in which matter can appear. If we compare this situation with the Aristotelian concepts of matter and form, we can say that the matter of Aristotle, which is mere 'potentia,' should be compared to our concept of energy, which gets into 'actuality' by means of the form, when the elementary particle is created" (Werner Heisenberg, *Physics and Philosophy* [New York: Harper and Row, 1958], 160). "Heisenberg was convinced that such indeterminacy arose from the behavior of individual particles and not from the statistical behavior of particle ensembles. Hence he concluded that classical notions including causality and continuity of motion therefore no longer applied to microscopic processes, favoring an Aristotelian ontology of potential being" (R. J. Russell, "The Meaning of Causality," 24–25).

quantum phenomena have been discovered, it is because there simply are no causes.[88]

Such indeterminacy is the hallmark of what has come to be called the "Copenhagen interpretation" of quantum mechanics. As Philip Clayton notes: "Copenhagen theorists came to the startling conclusion that quantum mechanical indeterminacy was not merely a temporary epistemic problem but reflected an inherent indeterminacy of the physical world itself."[89] Far from seeing the world as a chain of determined causes, this interpretation rejects the principle of causality altogether, as Heisenberg famously declared in 1927: "[T]he invalidity of the law of causality is definitively proved by quantum mechanics."[90] John von Neumann came to the same

---

88. "[I]n the usual interpretation of the quantum theory, the precise magnitudes of the irregular fluctuations in the results of individual measurements at the atomic level are not supposed to be determined by any kinds of causes at all, either known or unknown. Instead, it is assumed that in any particular experiment, the *precise* result that will be obtained is *completely arbitrary* in the sense that it has no relationship whatever to anything else that exists in the world or that ever has existed.... Whether this nucleus will decay tomorrow, next week, or in two thousand million years from now is something that the present quantum theory cannot predict. According to the usual interpretation, however, *nothing* determines this time. It is supposed to be completely arbitrary, and not capable of *ever* being related to anything else by means of any kinds of laws at all" (David Bohm, *Causality and Chance in Modern Physics* [Philadelphia: University of Pennsylvania Press, 1971], 87–88). "Thus, the name *uncertainty* principle is somewhat misleading. Uncertainty implies an inexactness in our knowledge of things.... Uncertainty is an epistemological fuzziness, but the inexactness in position and momentum is deeper than that. It is metaphysical. The object cannot *have* an exact position and an exact momentum at the same time. One or the other is indeterminate, not just uncertain to us.... A system that is an even superposition of spin-up and spin-down ... will, when measured, be entirely spin-up or entirely spin-down. Nothing in nature determines which of these two possibilities will be realized. The outcome is, in the nature of things, random" (Kosso, *Appearance*, 133, 159).

89. Clayton, *Mind*, 3. "Those of a realist cast of mind will tend to correlate epistemology closely with ontology, believing that what we know, or what we cannot know, is a reliable guide to what is the case. If this metascientific strategy is followed, unpredictability will be seen as the sign of a degree of causal openness in physical process. In the case of quantum theory, this is indeed the line that has been followed by the majority of physicists, who join with Bohr in interpreting Heisenberg's uncertainty principle as an ontological principle of indeterminism and not merely an epistemological principle of ignorance in the way that Bohm suggests" (John C. Polkinghorne, "Space, Time, and Causality," *Zygon* 41 [2006]: 979). As William Michael Dickson characterizes what he calls the "orthodox" view of quantum physics, "the outcome that we witness as the result of the measurement was not determined to occur by anything prior to the measurement" (William Michael Dickson, *Quantum Chance and Non-locality: Probability and Non-locality in the Interpretations of Quantum Mechanics* [New York: Cambridge University Press, 1998], 14).

90. "Regarding the exact formulation of the law of causality ('If we know the present precisely, we can calculate the future'), it is not the conclusion but the premise that is false. We cannot in principle know the present in all determined parts. For this reason, all perception involves a selection from a plenum of possibilities and a constriction of future possibility. Since the statistical character of quantum theory is now tied so closely to the imprecision of all perception, one might be tempted to the supposition that behind the perceived statistical world a 'real' world lies hidden in

conclusion: "There is at present no reason to speak of causality in nature—because no experiment indicates its presence and ... quantum mechanics contradicts it."[91] Bertrand Russell concurred, but found a more poetical way of putting it: "To me it seems ... that the reason why physics has ceased to look for causes is that, in fact, there are no such things. The law of causality, I believe, like much that passes muster among philosophers, is a relic of a bygone age, surviving, like the monarchy, only because it is erroneously supposed to do no harm."[92]

These different interpretations have their roots in philosophy rather than science. [93] Whether one finds a place for causality or determinism in the quantum world depends on one's philosophical understanding of causality. To illustrate this, we can apply the notions of causality in Aquinas and Hume to quantum theory. Aquinas saw causality as an ontological reality involving the influence of one thing on the being of another. Here, the hallmark of causality is dependency.[94] Hume regarded it as an epistemological principle describing how our knowledge of one thing leads us to think of

---

which the law of causality is valid. But such speculations seem to us—we emphasize it emphatically—unfruitful and senseless. Physics should formally describe only the interrelation of perceptions. One can characterize the true state of affairs much better in this way: Since all experiments are subject to the laws of quantum mechanics and so to [its] equation, the invalidity of the law of causality is definitively proved by quantum mechanics" (Werner Heisenberg, "Über den anschaulichen Inhalt der quantentheoretischen Kinematik und Mechanik," *Zeitschrift für Physik* 43 [1927]: 197).

91. John von Neumann, *Mathematical Foundations of Quantum Mechanics*, trans. Robert T. Beyer (Princeton, N.J.: Princeton University Press, 1955), 328.

92. Bertrand Russell, "On the Notion of Cause," *Proceedings of the Aristotelian Society for the Systematic Study of Philosophy* 13 (1913): 1.

93. "[Max] Born allows the possibility that quantum indeterminism could be underpinned by a more fundamental determinism. Indeed, Born claims that no purely physical argument could ever decide the issue: 'I myself am inclined to give up determinism in the world of atoms. But that is a philosophical question for which physical arguments alone are not decisive'" (Dickson, *Quantum Chance*, 17). "We have also seen that this indeterminism is not forced on the theory directly by empirical results, since deterministic interpretations such as Bohm's can handle the archetypal quantum phenomena" (Maudlin, "Distilling," 481). "Of course, the ontological value of the HUP [Heisenberg Uncertainty Principle] remains deeply linked to the philosophical assumption that what cannot be known has no existence" (Nicholas Saunders, *Divine Action and Modern Science* [New York: Cambridge University Press, 2002], 137). See also William R. Stoeger, "Epistemological and Ontological Issues Arising from Quantum Theory," in *Quantum Mechanics: Scientific Perspectives on Divine Action*, ed. Robert John Russell, Philip Clayton, Kirk Wegter-Mcnelly, and John C. Polkinghorne (Vatican City State: Vatican Observatory; Berkeley, Calif.: Center for Theology and the Natural Sciences, 2001), 81–98; Peter E. Hodgson, *Theology and Modern Physics* (Aldershot, U.K.: Ashgate, 2005), 134–40; Wolfgang Smith, *The Quantum Enigma: Finding the Hidden Key* (Peru, Ill.: Sherwood Sugden, 1995); and William A. Wallace, "Thomism and the Quantum Enigma," *Thomist* 61 (1997): 455–67.

94. "The term cause implies some influence on the being of the thing caused" (*In meta.* V, lect. 1, §751). Cf. *In phys.* I, lect. 1, no. 5; *ST* I, 33, 1, ad 1.

another as we become accustomed to seeing a "constant conjunction" between the two. Here, the mark of causality is prediction.[95]

If we take causation in the Humean sense, no interpretation of quantum theory allows us to assign a cause to a particular quantum event. If causation means the prediction of a second event from knowledge of a first and if the first event cannot be known, the second cannot be predicted and so cannot be caused. Quantum theory always prevents us from knowing the first event since we cannot simultaneously know both the speed and the position of an elementary particle. It therefore eliminates causality, as Mario Bunge points out: "The equation of causality with predictability is, of course, common among the upholders of the positivistic interpretation of the quantum theory. Thus Heisenberg, in a famous paper, held that what prevents modern physics from retaining causality is the physical impossibility of measuring simultaneous, exact values of conjugate variables, such as the position and the momentum of a 'particle'; and this, in turn, prevents us from formulating accurate predictions about the future states of the 'particle.'"[96] Since the prediction of individual quantum events is not possible, no cause in the Humean sense can be postulated for them. The Humean notion of causality also prevents a deterministic interpretation of individual quantum events, as Peter Hodgson points out: "The strict formulation of determinism—that if we know the present we can calculate the future—is inadequate because now we cannot know the present accurately."[97] Statistical determinism, however, is still possible.[98]

---

95. On the influence of Humean causality in science, see Cobb, "Natural Causality," 111; and Bunge, *Causality*, xv.

96. Bunge, *Causality*, 327–28.

97. Hodgson, *Science and Belief*, 180–81. "[I]t is impossible to say that the state of a system can ever be accurately determined by measurement. But since a determination of this kind is a prerequisite for the strict application of the principle of causality, it follows that modern science must renounce the exact truth of this principle and be satisfied with predictions that have probability. Science is thus no longer deterministic in character" (Schlick, *Philosophy*, 69–70). "The fact that the resulting state is unpredictable in advance, that is, that it cannot be explained by a deterministic law, is the basis for the philosophical interpretation that such an event is ontologically indeterministic" (R. J. Russell, *Cosmology*, 167).

98. "The usual presentation of the quantum theory, as advanced by Bohr and Heisenberg, does eliminate causality as regards the results of observation, in the sense that the 'same' physical situation may be followed in an unpredictable way by a large (usually infinite) number of different states. But this restriction on *causality* does not entail a breakdown of *determinism*, since statistical determinacy is definitely retained in that interpretation—not to speak of the obviously nonstatistical laws of quantum mechanics, such as the conservation laws, the selection rules, or the exclusion principle.... The usual interpretation of quantum mechanics does not sweep out causes and effects, but rather the rigid causal nexus among them.... In short, the usual interpretation of the quantum

When we apply Aquinas's idea of causality to quantum physics, some interpretations of quantum theory allow us to say that individual quantum events are caused, but others do not. If we follow the Copenhagen interpretation, where indeterminism is viewed as an objective feature of the physical world, we will not be able to postulate causes for quantum events. The interpretation itself simply rules them out. As John Collins notes: "[T]he most widely accepted interpretation of present theory holds that as far as we can tell, the fate of a single particle is not determined by any prior conditions: there are no causes."[99] We can hardly assign causes while also accepting, as John Polkinghorne says, "the belief of conventional quantum theories that individual quantum events are radically uncaused."[100]

This "belief" that quantum events are uncaused, however, is grounded not in science but in philosophy (however widely it may be accepted in the scientific community and beyond). When science reaches the limits of what it can measure, all it can say scientifically, in accordance with its method, is that it has reached the limits of what it can measure. It may go on to assert that what is unmeasurable is uncaused or unreal only if it assumes that causes must always be measurable or that reality must always be quantifiable. These are philosophical assumptions, however, not findings of empirical science. Physicist Peter Hodgson points this out using the example of radioactive decay: "Radioactive decay is often cited as an example of the statistical nature of reality. We can calculate the probability of decay per unit time but not the actual instant of decay. If this is combined with the belief that quantum mechanics gives a complete account of reality, then we must conclude that radioactive decay provides an example of an uncaused event. If, however, we do not accept this view of quantum mechanics, then we can say that, indeed, each decay has a cause that we do not yet know. There are many possibilities: maybe the decay happens when the motions of the

---

theory actually does not eliminate determinism in the general sense; moreover it retains a certain dose of causality. But it does drastically restrict the Newtonian form of determinism, according to which all physical processes boil down to changes of position determined by both the previous state of motion and externally impressed forces.... It may also be said that Newtonian determinism is sublated in quantum mechanics in its orthodox interpretation, since it is found to obtain on the average" (Bunge, *Causality*, 14–15).

99. John Collins, "Science and the Denial of the Miraculous: Another Look," *Perspectives in Religious Studies* 10 (1983): 130. See also Bohm, *Causality*, 87–88

100. John C. Polkinghorne, "The Quantum World," in *Physics, Philosophy, and Theology: A Common Quest for Understanding*, ed. Robert J. Russell, William R. Stoeger, and George V. Coyne (Vatican City State: Vatican Observatory and and Berkeley, Calif: The Center for Theology and the Natural Sciences, 1988), 339.

constituent nucleons reach a suitable configuration, or perhaps it is due to some external influence. These are possibilities that could provide a subject for future research. Certainly, radioactive decay cannot be proved to be uncaused."[101]

If we follow Einstein rather than the Copenhagen interpretation, we may be able to postulate causes for quantum events. In Einstein's understanding, quantum uncertainty is not an ontological feature of the natural world but a product of our lack of knowledge. Since for Aquinas a cause is simply something that influences the being of another, nothing prevents us from asserting that such causes may be operative in the natural world apart from or beyond our knowledge. In this way, they seem appropriate candidates for the as yet undiscovered causes of quantum events.[102]

Using Einstein's interpretation of quantum indeterminacy and Aquinas's idea of causality, scientists might look for something like David Bohm's "hidden variables" or other as yet undiscovered causes of quantum events.[103] Wojciech Grygiel proposes that "the alternative interpreta-

---

101. Hodgson, "God's Action," 509. "[R]adioactivity involves an apparently statistical process; and, as such, it is often alleged as an example of chance or randomness. Because the behavior of individual radioactive atoms cannot be precisely known, it is often said that this behavior is disordered and chance-like and hence that chance is not merely a real cause but a cause that is quite common in nature.... In radioactivity... our laws are unable to predict which individual atoms will decay or when any one atom will decay, but the behavior of the whole aggregate, which enables us to determine a half-life period for every radioactive element, shows that we are dealing with an order, although it is an order we do not fully understand.... In regard to quantum physics, the fact that our macroscopic world is ordered proves that there is order among atoms and their parts, even if it is an order we do not comprehend. Those who interpret modern physics as evidence that the world is disordered and chance-like reverse the logical direction for approaching nature. To ask whether order exists in nature is one kind of question; what that order is in its most precise detail is another problem which ... occurs after the first kind of question. On this basis, the failure in the second problem to find the exact contours of the order in nature does not necessarily deny our answer to the first question, namely, that there is order in nature to begin with" (V. E. Smith, *General*, 195, 207).

102. See Hodgson, *Science and Belief*, 187–88.

103. "Among the new kinds of laws that one is now permitted to consider if one ceases to assume the absolute and final validity of the indeterminacy principle, a very interesting and suggestive possibility is then that of a sub-quantum mechanical level containing hidden variables.... [W]hen we attack these problems within the framework of the new interpretation of quantum theory, a large number of interesting new possibilities are seen to open up" (Bohm, *Causality*, 101, 124). Although John von Neumann apparently proved in 1932 that hidden variables are impossible, David Bohm succeeded in constructing a coherent hidden variables theory of quantum mechanics in 1952. According to physicist Peter E. Hodgson, there is "no reason to believe that hidden variables are excluded and with them a fully determined theory of quantum mechanics" (Hodgson, *Science and Belief*, 186). The statistical nature of quantum theory itself suggests that such causality is operative: "[W]e know of no clear, positive exceptions to our common sense cause-effect correlation (even quantum phenomena are not *sheerly* disconnected from their past, and if they were there could be

tion of quantum mechanics proposed by David Bohm could help quantum physicists to recognize the four fundamental Aristotelian causes and to demonstrate the validity of their discipline as a Thomistic *scientia media*. Ultimately it may then be possible to harvest the insights of this and other recent physical theories within a coherent philosophical framework."[104] Wolfgang Smith makes the stronger claim that, if we apply Aquinas's idea of causality to quantum physics, we may be able to resolve the "quantum paradox ... quite naturally on strictly traditional philosophic ground." Smith believes that the "quantum facts" can be "readily integrated into a very ancient and venerable ontology: namely, the Thomistic, which traces back to Aristotle.... [T]his reputedly outmoded medieval speculation proves now to be capable of supplying the philosophic keys for which physicists have been groping since the advent of quantum theory."[105]

Some think that the discovery of the true causes or "hidden variables" behind quantum events might result in determinism. Wojciech Grygiel believes it may lead to a "restoration of determinism."[106] Peter Hodgson predicts it may yield "a fully determined theory of quantum mechanics."[107] David Bohm himself, however, envisions it opening into a new and more integrated understanding of the place of chance in the natural world: "The consideration of the alternative interpretation of the quantum mechanics ... serves to show that when one divests the theory of the irrelevant and unfounded hypotheses of the absolute and final validity of the indeterminacy principle, one is led to an important new line of development, which strikes at the roots of the entire mechanist philosophy. For we now see that there is a whole level in which chance fluctuations are an inseparable part of the mode of being of things, so that they must be interwoven into the fabric of the theory of this level in a fundamental way."[108] Whatever the discovery of the causes of quantum events might mean for quantum indeterminacy, incorporating Aquinas's understanding of causality into quantum theory

---

no sense to talk of 'statistical parameters' in quantum physics)" (G. W. Shields, "Davies, Eternity, and the Cosmological Argument," *International Journal for Philosophy of Religion* 21 [1987]: 24).

104. Grygiel, "Quantum Mechanics," 226.

105. W. Smith, "From Schrödinger's Cat," 50. For his full argument, see his *Quantum Enigma*.

106. "The major difference of this view [Bohm] from the Copenhagen approach is the restoration of determinism at the molecular level. This shifts the indeterminism of the Heisenberg principle from the ontological to the epistemic realm, exactly where it had been located in classical mechanics" (Grygiel, "Quantum Mechanics," 231).

107. Hodgson, *Science and Belief*, 186.

108. Bohm, *Chance*, 126.

would not result in a thoroughgoing determinism since, as we have already seen, "chance" (even apart from quantum mechanics) plays an integral role in his understanding of nature.

Cosmology

Though cosmology, as the study of the macrocosm, seems as old as humanity itself, contemporary physical cosmology sprang from Albert Einstein's theory of relativity.[109] To see how it expands the notion of causality, we will look briefly at the theory of relativity, the Big Bang, and the anthropic principle.

Relativity The theory of relativity views space and time not as absolute characteristics of the universe, but as relative to the motion of one's reference system. It replaces the Newtonian notion of gravity as a force of attraction between masses with the idea of a curved time-space in which objects follow natural paths.[110] Such "natural paths" are in some ways reminiscent of the "natural motions" of bodies in Aristotle's cosmology: "The natural motion of the Aristotelian world is similar to the natural motion of the world of Einstein. In both, motion of bodies is spontaneous and natural, and in both it is a consequence of properties of space, which influence the motion of bodies."[111]

The Big Bang The mathematics of Einstein's theory of relativity requires that the universe must eventually expand or contract. Einstein initially attempted to avoid this consequence and ensure the unchanging stability of the universe by introducing a "cosmological constant" into his equations. He later called this "his biggest blunder," as it became evident that the universe was indeed expanding in accordance with his original theory.[112]

The first evidence for the expanding universe was found in 1911, when the observed "red shift" of light coming from spiral nebulae suggested that

---

109. "[C]osmology attained the status of a proper science only in 1915, when the advent of general relativity—the modern theory of gravity—gave the subject a secure mathematical basis" (Bernard Carr, "Cosmology and Religion," in *The Oxford Handbook of Religion and Science*, ed. Philip Clayton and Zachary Simpson [Oxford: Oxford University Press, 2006], 140).

110. See R. J. Russell, "Meaning of Causality," 17–18.

111. Antonio Moreno, "The Law of Inertia and the Principle '*Quidquid movetur ab alio movetur,*'" *Thomist* 38 (1974): 327–28.

112. "Einstein rejected this model [of the expanding universe] at the time because he believed that the universe (i.e., the Milky Way) was static, and he even introduced an extra repulsive term into his equations—the cosmological constant—to allow this possibility. After Hubble's discovery, he described this as his 'biggest blunder'" (Carr, "Cosmology," 142).

they were moving away from the earth. In 1927, the Belgian priest Georges Lemaître suggested that the universe began from the initial "explosion" of a "primal atom." This was confirmed in 1929, when Edwin Hubble noticed that the observable nebulae were all moving away from one another. He concluded that the universe was expanding and that each part was rapidly moving away from all the others like dots on a rapidly inflating balloon. Using his discovery, scientists began to calculate back to the moment when the initial expansion occurred. That moment has become known as the "Singularity," and its expansion as the "Big Bang." It is usually fixed at about 14 billion years ago.[113] Science is unable to describe that first moment precisely since the laws and models of science are not applicable to it.[114]

The Big Bang involves a notion of potentiality reminiscent of Aristotle's material causality. We must say, for instance, that the Singularity had the potentiality to become our present universe, since our universe has indeed evolved from it. As the biologist Christian De Duve observes: "The universe has given life and mind. Consequently, it must have had them, potentially, ever since the Big Bang."[115] Such fundamental potentiality is like Aristotle's idea of primary matter. The Big Bang also provides a caution regarding the limits of science. If the laws of science themselves break down as one approaches the Singularity, those laws must be of limited explanatory power. They cannot themselves be the universal explanation of all things if they point to an initial condition of the universe to which they are not applicable.

The Anthropic Principle   Speculations on the origins of the universe as a place capable of intelligent life gave rise to what has been called the "an-

---

113. Bernard Carr, "Cosmology," 142. More detailed accounts of the Big Bang theory can be found in Barbour, *Religion*, 124–29; George F. R. Ellis, *Before the Beginning: Cosmology Explained* (New York: Boyars/Bowerdean, 1993); and Willem B. Drees, *Beyond the Big Bang: Quantum Cosmologies and God* (LaSalle, Ill.: Open Court, 1990), 211–24.

114. "The Big Bang theory is often extrapolated to 't = 0', the Singularity. However, the theory is reliable only when the underlying theories of both the structure of space and time and the behavior of matter and radiation are known and corroborated by evidence independent of cosmology. In that sense, the Big Bang theory is not a theory about the origin of the Universe, but rather a well-supported theory about the evolution of structures in the Universe from, perhaps, one-billionth of a second up to the present. Theories beyond that limit . . . are more speculative. The boundary might be pushed back. . . . But such developments on the experimental side will not remove this kind of boundary to our knowledge" (Drees, *Beyond*, 224).

115. Christian de Duve, *Life Evolving: Molecules, Mind, and Meaning* (New York: Oxford University Press, 2002), 298. "Moreover, even if the present biological world *is* only one of an already large number of possibilities, the original primeval cloud of fundamental particles at the 'hot big bang' must have had the *potentiality* of being to develop into the complex molecular forms we call modern biological life" (Peacocke, "God's Action," 467).

thropic principle." Using astronomy and high-energy physics, cosmologists tried to reconstruct conceptually the earliest stages of the Big Bang. It became evident that a very delicate balance of forces must have existed in the first moments of the universe. If these had varied even slightly, the universe as we know it would never have formed.[116] Faced with these serendipitous circumstances, the human mind seeks an explanation. Things might have happened differently. Why was it that everything occurred in just the "right" way to make our universe and our own human life possible?

This is not simply a question about efficient causality or one that can by answered by finding the forces involved in the evolution of the universe. Science may know the forces involved, but the more it understands about these forces the more surprising it seems that they should have been so intricately balanced and coordinated. Simon Conway Morris notes that on "a cosmic scale it is now widely appreciated that even trivial differences in the starting conditions would lead to an unrecognizable and uninhabitable universe."[117] Observing that the "laws of science, as we know them at present, contain many fundamental numbers," Stephen Hawking finds it a "remarkable fact" that "the values of these numbers seem to have been very finely adjusted to make possible the development of life."[118] What accounts for their delicate interrelationships? Can this all be attributed to chance or does it suggest something more?

Some have tried to use chance to solve the conundrum by postulating many, possibly limitless, universes and so increasing the "odds" that our universe might occur.[119] Just as the chances of rolling a six go up the more dice one throws, so the chances of getting a universe like ours go up the more uni-

---

116. For a thorough account of the improbable circumstances involved in the development of life in our universe, see Michael J. Denton, *Nature's Destiny: How the Laws of Biology Reveal Purpose in the Universe* (New York: Free Press, 1998); Robin Collins, "Evidence for Fine-Tuning," in *God and Design: The Teleological Argument and Modern Science*, ed. Neil A. Manson (London: Routledge, 2003), 178–99; David J. Bartholomew, *God, Chance and Purpose: Can God Have It both Ways?* (New York: Cambridge University Press, 2008), 82–85; and Leslie, "Anthropic Principle Today," 163–87.

117. Morris, *Life's Solution*, 327.

118. Stephen Hawking, *A Brief History of Time: From the Big Bang to Black Holes* (New York: Bantam Books, 1988), 125.

119. "[It] is not surprising that the apparent peculiarities of our universe (famously in terms of the apparent 'fine tuning' of the physical constants) sharpen the desire to find an 'escape clause' from the ominous sense of a world designed for our habitation and understanding. It is hardly surprising, therefore, if many scientists believe the best course of action is to appeal to multiverses, endlessly generated, with no ultimate beginning and without a conceivable end" (Simon Conway Morris, "What Is Written into Creation?" in *Creation and the God of Abraham*, ed. David Burrell, Carlo Coglioti, Janet Soskice, and William R. Stoeger [New York: Cambridge University Press, 2010], 176).

verses one postulates. Science has a number of ways of allowing for multiple universes. There may be a series of "Big Bang" expansions followed by "Big Crunch" contractions, producing an endless succession of universes.[120] Perhaps there are parallel and wholly unrelated universes, as postulated by certain interpretations of quantum physics. Or, we may find ourselves in one of the many universes comprising the "multiverse" of string theory.[121]

Though scientifically possible and statistically coherent, such approaches seem to violate the scientific principle of "parsimony" or "Ockham's razor." That principle directs us to look for a minimum number of causes and not to multiply beings without necessity. Here we are multiplying not just beings, but universes. As David Bartholomew points out: "It is certainly a possible explanation though it strains the imagination to the limit and requires the use of words in contexts in which their meaning becomes so fluid as to undermine the very reasoning which they are trying to convey. Indeed, it is arguable that it is more difficult to believe in the multiplicity of universes than in the coincidences which they were introduced to explain."[122] Rodney Holder provides a wide-ranging critique of the multiverse, noting that the idea is "violently anti-Ockhamite."[123] William Stoeger, George Ellis, and U. Kirchner offer a careful account of the multiverse in relation to the anthropic principle, noting that the idea "has gained prominence in cosmology, even though there is so far only inadequate theoretical and observa-

---

120. For a sustained argument in favor of the Big Bang/Big Crunch model, see Paul J. Steinhardt and Neil Turok, *Endless Universe: Beyond the Big Bang* (New York: Doubleday, 2007).

121. Leonard Susskind finds four basic routes to multiple universes (the "multiverse") in contemporary science, two from theoretical physics and two from astronomy: "On the theoretical side an outgrowth of inflationary theory called Eternal Inflation is demanding that the world be a megaverse, full of pocket universes that have bubbled out of inflating space, like bubbles in an uncorked bottle of champagne. At the same time String Theory is producing a Landscape of enormous diversity. The best estimates are that 10^{500} distinct kinds of environments are possible." He finds these theories supported by astronomical data on the size of the universe, which is "much bigger than the standard ten or fifteen billion light-years" and by the value of the cosmological constant which is "not quite zero as it was thought to be" (Leonard Susskind, *The Cosmic Landscape: String Theory and the Illusion of Intelligent Design* [New York: Little, Brown and Co., 2005], 21–22). See also Brian Greene, *The Elegant Universe: Superstrings, Hidden Dimensions and the Quest for the Ultimate Theory* (New York: Vintage Books: 1999), 366–70. William Stoeger notes that "there are well supported but still preliminary indications that whatever process or event gave birth to our universe or domain also generated a large number of other universes or domains" (William R. Stoeger, "Are Anthropic Arguments, Involving Multiverses and Beyond, Legitimate?" in *Universe or Multiverse*, ed. Bernard Carr [New York: Cambridge University Press, 2007], 449).

122. Bartholomew, *God of Chance*, 64.

123. Rodney D. Holder, *God, the Multiverse, and Everything: Modern Cosmology and the Argument from Design* (Aldershot, U.K.: Ashgate, 2004), 157.

tional support for its existence.... The relative untestability or unprovability of the multiverse idea in the usual scientific sense is however problematic—the existence of the hypothesized ensemble remains a matter of faith rather than of proof, unless it comes to enjoy long-term fruitfulness and success. Furthermore in the end, the multiverse hypothesis simply represents a regress of causation. Ultimate questions remain: Why this multiverse with these properties rather than others? What endows these with existence and with this particular type of overall order? What are the ultimate boundaries of possibility-what makes something possible, even though it may never be realized?"[124]

Another way to approach such improbable numbers is to begin with the fact that we humans are in fact here asking questions about them. Whatever the conditions of the early universe, they must be such as to allow for this present reality. This approach has been dubbed the "anthropic principle." As formulated by Brandon Carter, it states that "what we can expect to observe must be restricted by the conditions necessary for our presence as observers."[125] David Bartholomew explains that the anthropic principle "requires that, in reasoning about these improbabilities, we should reckon with our own existence without which there could be no speculation at all."[126] In light of this principle, the age of the universe and the forces involved in its formation do not seem entirely arbitrary. Instead, they appear constrained by the conditions necessary for the eventual appearance of humans. They must have values consistent with the eventual formation of a universe where human life could eventually develop.

---

124. William R. Stoeger, G. F. R. Ellis, and U. Kirchner, "Multiverses and Cosmology: Philosophical Issues," (2008), 1–2, 34, available at http://arxiv.org/PS_cache/astro-ph/pdf/0407/0407329v2.pdf (accessed 18 September, 2009). See also William Stoeger, "The Origin of the Universe in Science and Religion," in *Cosmos, Bios, Theos: Scientists Reflect on Science, God and the Origins of the Universe, Life, and Homo Sapiens*, ed. Henry Margenau and Roy Abraham Varghese (LaSalle, Ill.: Open Court, 1992), 267–68.

125. Brandon Carter, "Large Number Coincidences and the Anthropic Principle in Cosmology," in *Confrontation of Cosmological Theories with Observational Data: Symposium no. 63 (Copernicus Symposium II) Held in Cracow, Poland, 10–12 September, 1973*, ed. M. S. Longair (Boston: D. Reidel, 1974), 291. On the anthropic principle, see also John D. Barrow and Frank J. Tipler, *The Anthropic Cosmological Principle* (Oxford: Oxford University Press, 1986); John Leslie, "Observership in Cosmology: The Anthropic Principle," *Mind* 92 (1983): 573–79; Leslie, "Anthropic Principle Today;" Christopher Mooney, "The Anthropic Principle in Cosmology and Theology," *Horizons* 21 (1994): 105–29; and Ernan McMullin, "Anthropic Reasoning in Cosmology," in *Science and Theology: Ruminations on the Cosmos*, ed. Chris Impey and Catherine Petry (Vatican City State: Vatican Observatory, 2003), 79–108.

126. Bartholomew, *God of Chance*, 64.

The anthropic principle comes in both a "weak" and a "strong" form.[127] In its weak form, it does not claim that the universe must necessarily produce human beings, only that its initial conditions are constrained by the fact that it did so.[128] The weak form of the principle may seem almost trivial, as David Bartholomew notes: "In the weak form, it says that what we can expect to observe is constrained by the conditions which are necessary for our existence as observers. That is, if a particular set of physical constants is necessary for intelligent life to appear, then it is not at all surprising that in a universe containing living beings that just these coincidences should be observed. If they were not, there would be no one to observe them!"[129]

In its strong form, the principle asserts that the universe must allow for the development of observers at some point.[130] This assertion is often supported by reference to a divine plan. If the delicate interrelationship of the forces of the universe and the fortunate circumstances of its development demand some explanation beyond chance, it is to be found in God who designed a universe where human life might evolve. David Bartholomew argues that without reference to a divine cause, this version of the anthropic principle would be without support.[131] Rodney Holder concludes: "If the probabilities do indeed fall out in the way they appear to in this book, then

---

127. John Leslie cautions us on this distinction: "People have often imagined that he [Carter] was proposing some deep philosophical division here. Their belief has been that the weak anthropic principle just reminds us that our surroundings must be life-permitting, whereas the strong principle declares dramatically that our universe, or absolutely any real universe, is forced to be life-containing. But although so many have had this belief that it may now no longer be wrong (since custom eventually gives respectability to many an error), Carter has repeatedly made clear that he intended nothing of the kind" (Leslie, "Anthropic Principle Today," 171).

128. "Weak Anthropic Principle (WAP): The observed values of all physical and cosmological quantities are not equally probable but they take on values restricted by the requirement that there exists sites where carbon-based life can evolve and by the requirement that the Universe be old enough for it to have already done so" (Barrow and Tippler, *Anthropic Cosmological*, 16). As Willem Drees explains: "The Weak Anthropic Principle (WAP) states that what we see must be compatible with our existence. We see a Universe with planets because we depend on planets. We see a Universe which has existed for some billions of years because it took billions of years to develop beings which are capable of thinking about the age of the Universe" (Drees, *Beyond*, 79).

129. Bartholomew, *God of Chance*, 64. See also Drees, *Beyond*, 79–83.

130. "Strong Anthropic Principle (SAP): The Universe must have those properties which allow life to develop within it at some stage in its history" (Barrow and Tippler, *Anthropic Cosmological*, 21).

131. "The so-called strong form of the principle is really a quite different principle altogether. It says that the universe must be such as to allow the creation of observers within it at some stage of its evolution. This is essentially the same as saying that the universe exists with ourselves in it because God intended it to be so. In its neutral form it really offers no explanation at all and seems to be without rational basis. The theistic version does, at least, have the merit of claiming other kinds of evidence in its support" (Bartholomew, *God of Chance*, 64).

the chances are that there is in actual fact a Cosmic Designer. This Designer meant us to be here. Perhaps with Aquinas we can dare to say of the Designer, '... and this we call "God."'"[132]

Both versions of the anthropic principle implicitly involve arguments from final causality. They do not begin with material and efficient causality (the conditions of the early universe) and then argue to the production of human beings (the end or final cause). They begin with the final cause and show the efficient and material causes required for its attainment.[133] In the weak form, the fact of human existence is the outcome (final cause) from which the reasoning proceeds to explain the initial conditions of the universe (material and efficient causes). In the strong form, human existence is the purpose toward which the universe is directed by necessity or by design. In both cases, teleology plays a central role.[134]

Evolution

To discuss causality in evolution, we have to know what evolution is. If it involves change of species, we need to understand what a species is and what it means for one species to become another. We also have to be clear on the kinds of causality science invokes to explain how evolution happens. These involve notions of chance, law, reductionism, vitalism, emergence, teleology, and design. All of these are controversial issues. Our goal here is only to see how the concepts and controversies surrounding evolution may contribute to unlocking the idea of causality inherited from modern sci-

---

132. Holder, *God, the Multiverse*, 159, citing *ST* I, 2, 3, co. John Polkinghorne observes that "the unrestrained speculation of such ontological prodigality seems wholly contrary to the scientific spirit. A much more economic metascientific option would be to see the world as a divine creation" (Polkinghorne, *Theology in the Context*, 107). See also Ira M. Schnall, "Anthropic Observation Selection Effects and the Design Argument," *Faith and Philosophy* 26 (2009): 361–77.

133. "The rejection [of the idea of finality] in classical science is only a moment, since the evolution of science in the twentieth century seems ... to be a return to the explanation through finality, which is traditional in the sciences.... The anthropic cosmological principle completes the return of science to unity in explaining it through finality" (Jean-Michel Maldamé, *Le Christ pour l'univers: Pour une collaboration entre science et foi* [Paris: Desclée, 1998], 98). See also Wallace, *Causality and Scientific*, 1.75–79; and Marie I. George, "On the Tenth Anniversary of Barrow and Tipler's Anthropic Cosmological Principle: Thomistic Reflections on Anthropic Principles," *American Catholic Philosophical Quarterly* 72 (1998): 39–58.

134. "Physicists and astrophysicists ... point to many characteristics of our universe, such as its present size, rate of expansion, and the life cycle of stars, that are inexplicable unless we assume that the universe is aimed at making life possible. This kind of reasoning from an end to the means necessary for it has been named the Anthropic Principle" (Augros, "Nature Acts," 544–45). On the teleology of the anthropic principle, see also Drees, *Beyond*, 83; Bartholomew, *God of Chance*, 63; and Denton, *Nature's Destiny*, 12–16.

ence. We will start with Darwin's formulation of his evolutionary theory and then consider the notions of species, chance, purpose, and design.

Charles Darwin (1809–1882) begins *The Origin of Species* with the question of causality. He asks whether a study of the natural world might show that the species of living things are "descended from other species" and not "independently created." He thinks this inquiry must explain "how the innumerable species inhabiting this world have been modified" and demonstrate "the means of modification and coadaptation."[135] In other words, the inquiry must show the cause or causes of evolution. For Darwin, the fundamental cause is "natural selection," which he describes in this way: "As many more individuals of each species are born than can possibly survive; and as, consequently, there is a frequently recurring struggle for existence, it follows that any being, if it vary however slightly in any manner profitable to itself, under the complex and sometimes varying conditions of life, will have a better chance of surviving, and thus be naturally selected. From the strong principle of inheritance, any selected variety will tend to propagate its new and modified form."[136]

Darwin recognizes that the causality of natural selection depends on other causes, but he does not know what those causes are. He uses plant and animal husbandry as an analogy for natural selection. As breeders select certain traits to improve their stock, so "Nature" somehow "selects" advantageous traits.[137] Darwin realizes that neither husbandry nor natural selection could occur unless new traits sometimes appeared that could then be passed on: "[U]nless such [variations] occur, natural selection can do nothing."[138] He does not know by what mechanism new traits are produced and passed on. He believes they cannot result simply from chance: "I have hith-

---

135. Darwin, *Origin*, 20
136. Ibid., 21. "This preservation of favorable individual differences and variations, and the destruction of those which are injurious, I have called Natural Selection, or the Survival of the Fittest" (ibid., 108). See also ibid., 88–89.
137. Ibid., 88. Darwin sometimes personifies natural selection as "a power incessantly ready for action," one that is "immeasurably superior to man's feeble efforts, as the works of Nature are to those of Art" (ibid., 88–89, 112–13). Other times, he admits that natural selection is only "a metaphorical expression," but finds "it is difficult to avoid personifying the word Nature" (ibid., 109). Darwin's definition of "nature" is also notable: "I mean by nature, only the aggregate action and product of many natural laws, and by laws the sequence of events as ascertained by us" (ibid.). This definition, far from presenting nature as a kind of personal "selector," seems to reduce it simply to the events that are actually happening in the world. For nature is called "the product of many natural laws," but those laws themselves are simply "the sequence of events as ascertained by us" (ibid.). On Darwin's understanding of natural selection as a cause and a law of nature, see Armand Maurer, "Darwin, Thomists, and Secondary Causality," *Review of Metaphysics* 57 (2004): 501–3.
138. Darwin, *Origin*, 110.

erto sometimes spoken as if the variations ... were due to chance. This, of course, is a wholly incorrect expression, but it serves to acknowledge plainly our ignorance of the cause of each particular variation."[139] Variations must be the product of some cause, as yet unknown: "There must be some efficient cause for each slight individual difference, as well as for more strongly marked variations which occasionally arise; and if the unknown cause were to act persistently, it is almost certain that all the individuals of the species would be similarly modified."[140]

The cause of new traits and their preservation was later discovered through the genetic studies of the Augustinian monk Gregor Mendel (1822–1884) and the work of James Watson and Francis Crick on the DNA molecule. The melding of Darwin's evolutionary model with modern genetics has become known as "neo-Darwinism" or the "modern synthesis."[141] Spontaneous variations occur through genetic change, and new traits are passed on through genetic inheritance. Contrary to Darwin's instincts, spontaneous changes are now usually attributed to chance, while the preservation of characteristics both through individual inheritance and through the process of natural selection is seen as part of the lawful and stable structure of nature.[142] Still, some fortuitous factors are involved in natural selection. Sudden changes in the environment because of meteors or other external factors may affect the process, and the very presence of organisms that have become adapted to a certain environment may affect that environment, which in turn affects the selection of advantageous traits.[143]

---

139. Ibid., 172. 140. Ibid., 268. Cf. Ibid., 251, 319–20.

141. "This largely expanded theory of evolution has been, since the 1950s, generally referred to as the synthetic theory of evolution, the modern synthesis of evolutionary theory, or the modern theory of evolution. These labels are still used among biologists, although evolutionary biologists most often simply speak of the theory of evolution. The term 'neo-Darwinism' has little currency among evolutionary biologists. . . . In current use, it seems that the term 'neo-Darwinism' and its cognates are mostly confined to the writings of philosophers and theologians" (Ayala, "From Paley," 53). On the historical development of the theory of evolution, see Edward J. Larson, *Evolution: The Remarkable History of a Scientific Theory* (New York: Modern Library, 2006); Francisco Ayala, "The Evolution of Life: An Overview," in *Evolutionary and Molecular Biology: Scientific Perspectives on Divine Action*, ed. Robert John Russell, William R. Stoeger, and Francisco J. Ayala (Vatican City State: Vatican Observatory; Berkeley, Calif.: Center for Theology and the Natural Sciences, 1988), 21–57; Ted Peters and Martinez Hewlett, *Evolution from Creation to New Creation: Conflict, Conversation and Convergence* (Nashville, Tenn.: Abingdon Press, 2004), 35–50; and Martinez Hewlett, "Molecular Biology and Religion," in *The Oxford Handbook of Religion and Science*, ed. Philip Clayton and Zachary Simpson (Oxford: Oxford University Press, 2006), 172–86.

142. See Ayala et al., *Science, Evolution*, 50.

143. "Biological evolution involves chance of the first two types: coincidence and disorder.

Species A key concept in the theory of evolution is the notion of "species." At its inception, the theory was revolutionary in its assertion that the number of species is not permanently fixed in nature, but that new species may arise through natural processes. If species are in a constant state of evolution, however, the very notion of "species" becomes rather fluid. Any particular species is only a momentary product, a sort of snapshot, of the ongoing varietal differences that accumulate gradually and continuously over time. Darwin himself avers that the difference between a "species," a "variety" within a species, and individual "differences" within a variety become rather arbitrary distinctions in the general flux of evolution: "From these remarks it will be seen that I look at the term species as one arbitrarily given, for the sake of convenience, to a set of individuals closely resembling each other, and that it does not essentially differ from the term variety, which is given to less distinct and more fluctuating forms. The term variety, again, in comparison with mere individual differences, is also applied arbitrarily, for convenience sake."[144]

If species are not significantly different from varieties within a species, and if the appearance of new varieties requires no explanation beyond the ordinary processes of nature, then neither does the production of new species: "On the view that species are only strongly marked and permanent varieties, and that each species first existed as a variety, we can see why it is that no line of demarcation can be drawn between species, commonly supposed to have been produced by special acts of creation, and varieties which are acknowledged to have been produced by secondary laws."[145] If Darwin frees himself in this way from looking for a transcendent cause for the origination of species, he also frees himself from the need for intrinsic causes to account for their present differentiation: "In short, we shall have to treat species in the same manner as those naturalists treat genera, who admit that genera are merely artificial combinations made for convenience. This may not be a cheering prospect; but we shall at least be freed from the

---

Indeed, whereas certain phases in the evolution of the Earth favor some forms of life, they harm others. Think of continental drifts, meteoritic impacts, oceanic currents, glaciations, floods, and droughts. And once organisms emerged, they altered the composition of the soil and the atmosphere, which changes in turn induced transformations in organisms—which is why ecologists speak of the biosphere, as well as of active niche (or habitat) construction" (Mario Bunge, *Chasing Reality: Strife over Realism* [Toronto: University of Toronto, 2006], 98).

144. Darwin, *Origin*, 78–79.
145. Ibid., 624–25.

vain search for the undiscovered and undiscoverable essence of the term species."[146]

We might say that Darwin eliminates the need for any special creation of species by eliminating the very notion of species itself. On this view, there are no discrete, naturally occurring kinds of life in the natural world. There is only a minutely graded flux of life. Over time, as intermediary gradations disappear, we may categorize the distinctive types that remain. While such classification is useful for our study, it is really arbitrary and corresponds to nothing real in nature.[147] If there are no naturally occurring kinds of life, there is no need for an intrinsic form or soul to account for each particular type of organism since (really) there are no "particular types." In this way, Aristotle's substantial form, that disappeared from physics with Galileo and Newton, can now quietly vanish from biology as well. With Darwin, the difference of species is only a nominal difference that humans impose on nature as a handy means of classification. It is not an intrinsic aspect of nature itself.

Philosophers and biologists since Darwin have recognized, however, that if species becomes an entirely subjective idea, the very notion of evolution itself as the origin of one species from another becomes incoherent.[148] They have therefore tried to find ways to define species objectively.[149] One effort in this direction may be seen in the proponents of vitalism, who, in

---

146. Ibid., 644.

147. Robert Spaemann and Reinhard Löw accordingly refer to Darwin's "nominalism of species," according to which "the concept of species is only a concept of classification introduced by human beings that matches nothing in nature" (Spaemann and Löw, *Die Frage Wozu?* 215).

148. "Naturalists such as Darwin, however, sometimes call natural species merely artificial devices.... This is equivalent to the denial of their objective reality and would seriously jeopardize the whole concept of evolution since, then, evolution would exist only in our mind" (Antonio Moreno, "Some Philosophical Considerations on Biological Evolution," *Thomist* 37 [1973]: 422–23). "Whatever the correct reading of this story, and of Darwin's role in it, it is certainly the case that since 1859 there has been a rampant 'species problem'—and it has not yet petered out. Indeed, a recent account finds twenty-two species concepts in the literature! Darwin's own position ... was ambiguous: On the one hand, he was equating species and varieties, and so doing away with the species as special or unique; on the other hand, he was rereading the concept of species as one of a lineage rather than a special collection somehow to be classified as permanent. It seems he was both questioning the reality of species and affirming their reality in a more perspicuous sense" (Grene and Depew, *Philosophy*, 292).

149. "It has been one of the most important developments in post-Darwinian biology that the species have made their comeback as classes of living beings based upon objective facts. It is now widely admitted again that nature itself forces us to admit that there are specifically different forms of life which possess characteristics (and the underlying organic organization) which other forms of life do not have" (Elders, "Background," 52). Cf. ibid., 53–55.

the nineteenth and early twentieth centuries, invoked the presence of a "life force" to distinguish living things from nonliving things. As Ernst Mayr has noted, however, this "life force" is now a "dead issue" in biology.[150] Today's biologists reject vitalism, but also reject reductionistic references to chemical or physical structures, finding these an inadequate explanation of living things.[151] They define species dynamically in terms of structures, behaviors, and genetic makeup.[152] They often invoke the notion of emergence in order to maintain the distinctiveness of biological life without falling into vitalism and reductionism.[153] This reference to emergence may provide an opportunity to revisit the Aristotelian notion of formal causality.

Chance   Darwin rejected chance as an adequate explanation for the origin of species. Chance might account for minor variations but not for the

150. "However, by the 1920s or 1930s biologists had almost universally rejected vitalism, primarily for two reasons. First, because it virtually leaves the realm of science by falling back on an unknown and presumably unknowable factor, and second, because it became eventually possible to explain in physico-chemical terms all the phenomena which according to the vitalists 'demanded' a vitalistic explanation. It is fair to say that for biologists vitalism has been a dead issue for more than fifty years" (Mayr, *Growth*, 52).

151. "This rejection of vitalism was made possible by the simultaneous rejection of a crude 'animals are nothing but machines' conceptualization. Like Kant in his later years, most biologists realized that organisms are different from inanimate matter and that the difference had to be explained not by postulating a vital force but by modifying rather drastically the mechanistic theory. Such a theory begins by granting that there is nothing in the processes, functions, and activities of living organisms that is in conflict with or outside of any of the laws of physics and chemistry. All biologists are thorough-going 'materialists' in the sense that they recognize no supernatural or immaterial forces, but only such that are physico-chemical. But they do not accept the naive mechanistic explanation of the seventeenth century and disagree with the statement that animals are 'nothing but' machines. Organismic biologists stress the fact that organisms have many characteristics that are without parallel in the world of inanimate objects. The explanatory equipment of the physical sciences is insufficient to explain complex living systems and, in particular, the interplay between historically acquired information and the responses of these genetic programs to the physical world. The phenomena of life have a much broader scope than the relatively simple phenomena dealt with by physics and chemistry" (Mayr, *Growth*, 52–53). See also Renzo Morchio, "Reductionism in Biology," in *The Problem of Reductionism in Science* (Dordrecht: Kluwer Academic Publishers, 1991), 149–60; and Peterson, "Species," 702.

152. For a review of the nature and importance of species in contemporary biology, see Moreno, "Some Philosophical Considerations," 422–25; and Ayala et al., *Science, Evolution*, 7.

153. "In contrast to the earlier holistic proposals which usually were more or less vitalistic, the newer ones are strictly materialistic. They stress that the units at higher hierarchical levels are more than the sums of their parts and, hence, that a dissection into parts always leaves an unresolved residue—in other words, that explanatory reduction is unsuccessful. More importantly, they stress the autonomous problems and theories of each level and ultimately the autonomy of biology as a whole. The philosophy of science can no longer afford to ignore the organismic concept of biology as being vitalistic and hence belonging to metaphysics. A philosophy of science restricted to that which can be observed in inanimate objects is deplorably incomplete" (Mayr, *Growth*, 66). See also ibid., 73–76; and Clayton, *Mind*, 91.

Causality in Empirical Science • 83

production of new species: "Mere chance, as we may call it, might cause one variety to differ in some character from its parents, and the offspring of this variety again to differ from its parent in the very same character and in a greater degree; but this alone would never account for so habitual and large a degree of difference as that between the species of the same genus."[154]

Jacques Monod assigns a larger role to chance (at least rhetorically) in his account of evolution:

> We call these events [genetic mutations] accidental; we say that they are random occurrences. And since they constitute the *only* possible source of modifications in the genetic text, itself the *sole* repository of the organism's hereditary structures, it necessarily follows that chance *alone* is at the source of every innovation, of all creation in the biosphere. Pure chance, absolutely free but blind, at the very root of the stupendous edifice of evolution: this central concept of modern biology is no longer one among other possible or even conceivable hypotheses. It is today the *sole* conceivable hypothesis, the only one compatible with observed and tested fact. And nothing warrants the supposition—or the hope—that on this score our position is likely ever to be revised.... [M]an knows at last that he is alone in the universe's unfeeling immensity, out of which he emerged only by chance.[155]

Yet Monod recognizes that chance alone does not provide the whole explanation of evolution.[156] Christian de Duve argues that certain "constraints" on chance made the evolution of more complex life forms inevitable.[157] As Francisco Ayala explains, chance may account for the production of new traits, but it is through the determining influence of natural selection that new species are generated: "Chance is, nevertheless, an integral part of the evolutionary process. The mutations that yield the hereditary variations available to natural selection arise at random, independently of whether they are beneficial or harmful to their carriers. But this random process (as well as others that come to play in the great theater of life) is counteracted by natural selection, which preserves what is useful and eliminates the harmful. Without hereditary mutation, evolution could not happen because there would be no variations that could be differentially conveyed from one

---

154. Darwin, *Origin*, 143. See also ibid., 172, 268, 637.
155. Monod, *Chance and Necessity*, 112–13, 180.
156. "Drawn out of the realm of pure chance, the [genetic] accident enters into that of necessity, of the most implacable certainties. For natural selection operates at the macroscopic level, the level of organisms" (ibid., 118).
157. "[T]he natural constraints within which chance operates are such that evolution in the direction of increasing complexity was virtually bound to take place, if given the opportunity. Chance does not exclude inevitability" (de Duve, *Life Evolving*, 297).

to another generation. But without natural selection, the mutation process would yield disorganization and extinction because most mutations are disadvantageous. Mutation and selection have jointly driven the marvelous process that starting from microscopic organisms has yielded orchids, birds, and humans."[158]

Purpose Since Darwin's theory of evolution relies heavily on chance, it is often seen as inimical to the notion of purpose, and so to the idea of final causality.[159] In presenting his theory, however, Darwin himself often uses the language of purpose.[160] Animals and plants, for instance, "which live close round any small piece of ground ... may be said to be striving to the utmost to live there." Similarly, "each species and each variety of grass is annually sowing almost countless seeds; and is thus striving, as it may be said, to the utmost to increase in number."[161] Such striving sets up a struggle for survival that results in the natural selection of traits or structures that are beneficial to the survival of particular organisms. Surviving traits may be described teleologically in that "every detail of structure has been produced for the good of its possessor."[162] In fact "the good of the possessor" is the only purpose for which new traits or structures are produced and preserved. Darwin says that any introduction of other purposes, such as "for the sake of beauty, to delight man or the Creator, ... or for the sake of mere variety" would be "absolutely fatal to my theory."[163] Creatures strive to survive and, if new structures result from that striving, each can have no other

---

158. Francisco J. Ayala, "Intelligent Design: The Original Version," *Theology and Science* 1 (2003): 23–24. See also Ayala, *Darwin's Gift*, 77; Ayala, "From Paley," 74–75; and Ayala et al., *Science, Evolution*, 50.

159. "Darwinians argue that nature does not act for an end, but produces things at random and only those organisms with favorable characteristics survive. So what looks like purpose in natural things is not intended at all but is the result of survival of the fittest. Nineteenth-century biologist Thomas Huxley declared that 'teleology ... received its death blow at Mr. Darwin's hands'" (Augros, "Nature Acts," 538). "Indeed it was the Darwinian theory of evolution, with its combination of chance variation and natural selection, which completed the extrusion of teleology from nature. Having become redundant even in the story of life, purpose retired wholly into subjectivity" (Hans Jonas, *The Phenomenon of Life: Toward a Philosophical Biology* [New York: Harper and Row, 1966], 44).

160. "Darwin uses teleology throughout his works, particularly *The Descent of Man*" (Lyman A. Page, "Teleology in Biology: Who Could Ask for Anything More?" *Zygon* 41 [2006]: 428). "In Darwin's theory purpose is absolutely indispensable to his reasoning.... The survival value is the ultimate purpose in Darwin's theory" (Moreno, "Some Philosophical Considerations," 447). For Darwin's views on purpose, see also Phillip Sloan, "The Question of Natural Purpose," in *Evolution and Creation*, ed. Ernan McMullin (South Bend, Ind.: University of Notre Dame Press, 1985), 121–50.

161. Darwin, *Origin*, 146.   162. Ibid., 251.
163. Ibid., 251–52.

Causality in Empirical Science · 85

purpose than "the good [i.e., the survival] of its possessor."[164] To suggest that such structures are produced for any other purpose would subvert the very process through which natural selection is perfecting and developing the qualities of each organism: "And as natural selection works solely by and for the good of each being, all corporeal and mental endowments will tend to progress towards perfection."[165] Through such language, Darwin allows the notion of purpose or final causality a place in natural science. At the same time, however, he denies that natural selection involves any overarching direction or purpose.[166]

Contemporary scientists generally follow Darwin's lead in denying an overall purpose in evolution. They differ on whether survival itself should be viewed as a biological goal, but commonly use the language of teleology to describe the behavior of individual organisms and the function of their parts.[167]

On the question of an overall purpose in evolution, Francisco Ayala seems to express the scientific consensus: "Natural selection does not tend in any way towards the production of specific kinds of organisms or towards organisms having certain specific properties. The overall process of evolution cannot be said to be teleological in the sense of proceeding towards certain specified goals, preconceived or not."[168] Philip Clayton argues in a similar vein: "Biological evolution does not make use of purpose as an overarching explanatory category; one does not speak of evolution as such as having purposes."[169] Some scientists, however, though not proposing an intentional purpose or goal, do find identifiable patterns or trends in evolution that may be interpreted teleologically.[170]

---

164. Ibid., 251.   165. Ibid., 648.
166. "In my theory there is no absolute tendency to progression, excepting from favorable circumstances!" (Charles Darwin, "Notebook N [1838–1839]," in *Charles Darwin's Notebooks, 1836–1844: Geology, Transmutation of Species, Metaphysical Enquiries,* ed. Paul H. Barrett, Peter J. Gautrey, Sandra Herbert, David Kohn, and Sydney Smith [Ithaca, N.Y.: Cornell University Press, 1987], 576). "[Darwin] viewed an inexorable ascent of life and guaranteed progress as a radical myth" (Maurer, "Darwin," 500). See also Adrian Desmond and James Moore, *Darwin* (New York: Warner Books, 1992), 275.
167. For an overview of approaches to understanding the presence of teleology in evolution, see Jozef Zycinski, *God and Evolution: Fundamental Questions of Christian Evolutionism* (Washington, D.C.: The Catholic University of America Press, 2006), 95–111.
168. Francisco J. Ayala, "Teleological Explanations in Evolutionary Biology," in *Nature's Purposes: Analyses of Function and Design in Biology,* ed. Colin Allen, Marc Bekoff, and George Lauder (Cambridge, Mass.: MIT Press, 1998), 41–42.
169. Clayton, *Mind,* 97.
170. "Though we cannot scientifically or philosophically support the assertion that evolution is

On whether survival should be viewed as a goal, Ernst Mayr argues: "Natural selection is never goal oriented. It is misleading and quite inadmissible to designate such broadly generalized concepts as survival or reproductive success as definitive and specified goals."[171] Paul Erbrich, on the other hand, sees survival itself as a teleological goal in evolution: "Biologists ... often overlook the fact that selection presupposes purposefulness in the living things that are to be selected. The living things must 'want' something. If they want nothing, if they pursue no goals (such as self-preservation or reproduction, for example), then there is no competition, either, no fight for limited resources."[172]

Without naming survival as a specific evolutionary goal, a number of thinkers find a role for teleology in the evolutionary process. Francisco Ayala argues: "The overall process of evolution cannot be said to be teleological in the sense of directed towards the production of specified DNA codes of information, i.e., organisms. But it is my contention that it can be said to be teleological in the sense of being directed towards the production of DNA codes of information which improve the reproductive fitness of a population in the environments where it lives. The process of evolution can also be said to be teleological in that it has the potentiality of producing end-directed DNA codes of information, and has in fact resulted in teleologically oriented structures, patterns of behavior, and self-regulating mecha-

---

intentionally or consciously directed towards a definite, or even general goal, can we assert that it is directed towards a definite goal or range of goals? Can the directionality we have uncovered in evolution be translated into an end-directed or goal-directed formulation of teleology, and not just a minimalist end-resulting one? We have already seen from our account and analysis of the full gamut of scientific evidence that it definitely can" (William R. Stoeger, "The Immanent Directionality of the Evolutionary Process, and Its Relation to Teleology," in *Evolutionary and Molecular Biology: Scientific Perspectives on Divine Action*, ed. Robert John Russell, William R. Stoeger, and Francisco J. Ayala [Vatican City State: Vatican Observatory; Berkeley, Calif.: Center for Theology and the Natural Sciences, 1998], 186). Christian de Duve sees an "arrow of evolution" pointing horizontally to greater "biodiversity, that is, the extraordinary variety of forms evolution has created on given models, be they of a grass, insect, fish, or mammal," and pointing vertically to "an increase in complexity" (de Duve, *Life Evolving*, 182–83). He does not, however, view this arrow as equivalent to purpose: "I exclude ... finalism, or teleology, which assumes goal-directed causes in biological processes" (de Duve, *Vital Dust*, xiv). See also Daniel W. McShea, "Possible Largest-Scale Trends in Organismal Evolution: Eight 'Live Hypotheses,'" *Annual Review of Ecology and Systematics* 29 (1998): 293–318.

171. Ernst Mayr, "Teleological and Teleonomic: A New Analysis," in *Evolution and the Diversity of Life: Selected Essays* (Cambridge, Mass.: Harvard University Press, 1976), 388. See also Mayr, *Growth*, 50.

172. Paul Erbrich, "The Problem of Creation and Evolution," in *Creation and Evolution: A Conference with Pope Benedict XVI in Castel Gandolfo*, ed. Stephan Otto Horn and Sigfried Wiedenhofer (San Francisco: Ignatius Press, 2008), 72. "The principle of natural selection as based on the 'struggle for life,' presupposes the teleological character of needy organisms striving for food, sex etc. Their striving-character is the cause of their involvement in the struggle for life" (F. J. K Soontiëns, "Evolution: Teleology or Chance?" *Journal for General Philosophy of Science* 22 [1991]: 139).

nisms."[173] Robert Pennock contends: "[E]volutionary theory does include a substantive role for teleology; indeed, it is at the core of Darwin's law—namely, in the way in which adaptations are explained by natural selection. But this is a perfectly scientific notion of teleology."[174] Philip Clayton argues that the absence of an overall purpose in evolution "does not prevent the ascription of protopurposiveness to biological agents. We might call it a theory of purposiveness without purpose in the emergence and behavior of organisms.... [T]he parts of an organism (or organ or cell or ecosystem) work together for its survival. Growth, nurturance, and reproduction function so that the chances of the organism's survival, and thus the survival of its genotype, are maximized."[175] He notes the increased use of the language of purpose in biology: "There are numerous reasons for biologists to be cautious about talk of purpose in evolution. Unfortunately, these reasons have sometimes produced a reticence to acknowledge the significance of teleological systems within the biosphere. Recent years have brought renewed study of macroevolutionary patterns, however, and it is now not uncommon to find treatments of organisms and their behaviors as purposive systems. Many biologists now speak of a 'directionality' to evolution, frequently correlating it with the increase in biological complexity."[176]

In reference to the behavior of individual organisms and the functions of their parts, teleological language is regularly employed. Ernst Mayr argues, for instance: "Goal-directed behavior (in the widest sense of this word) is extremely widespread in the organic world; for instance, most activity connected with migration, food-getting, courtship, ontogeny, and all phases of reproduction is characterized by such goal orientation. The occurrence of goal-directed processes is perhaps the most characteristic feature of the world of living organisms."[177] Francisco Ayala agrees that there are many elements of teleology in the biological world: "The presence of organs, processes and patterns of behavior can be explained teleologically by exhibiting their contribution to the reproductive fitness of the organisms

---

173. Ayala, "Teleological Explanations," 42–43. See also Francisco J. Ayala, "Darwin's Devolution: Design without Designer," in *Evolutionary and Molecular Biology: Scientific Perspectives on Divine Action*, ed. Robert John Russell, William R. Stoeger, and Francisco J. Ayala (Vatican City State: Vatican Observatory; Berkeley, Calif.: Center for Theology and the Natural Sciences, 1998), 101–16.

174. Robert T. Pennock, "The Pre-modern Sins of Intelligent Design," in *The Oxford Handbook of Religion and Science*, ed. Philip Clayton and Zachary Simpson (Oxford: Oxford University Press, 2006), 738.

175. Clayton, *Mind*, 97.   176. Clayton, "Emergence of Spirit," 293.

177. Mayr, *Toward A New Philosophy*, 45.

in which they occur."[178] He finds that teleological explanations have advantages over nonteleological ones: "Although a teleological explanation can be reformulated in a nonteleological one, the teleological explanation connotes something more than the equivalent nonteleological one. A teleological explanation implies that the system under consideration is directively organized. For that reason, teleological explanations are appropriate in biology.... Moreover, and most importantly, teleological explanations imply that the end result is the explanatory reason for the existence of the object or process which serves or leads to it. A teleological account of the gills of fish implies that gills came to existence precisely because they serve for respiration."[179] For this reason, he believes that "teleological explanations in biology are not only acceptable but indeed indispensable."[180]

To get away from the notion of consciousness or intentionality that is often associated with the word "teleology," some biologists prefer the term "teleonomy," the apparent purposefulness resulting from the undirected process of evolution.[181] Mariano Artigas argues that, although biologists "use different terminology or propose different classifications of teleological phenomena, there is a general unanimity in recognizing that finalist phenomena exist and play a most important role in the biological world."[182] Michael Ruse sums up the situation: "Purpose in evolution is obviously alive and well and mixing in the best circles!"[183]

Design   Darwin was skeptical about the notion of chance as an ultimate explanation of things, but leery also of any affirmation of design in the uni-

178. Ayala, "Teleological Explanations," 42.
179. Ibid., 44.
180. Ibid., 44. "Biologists need to account for the functional features of organisms, their 'design,' in terms of the goals or purposes they serve, which they do by teleological hypotheses or teleological explanations" (Francisco J. Ayala, "Reduction, Emergence, Naturalism, Dualism, Teleology: A Précis," in *Back to Darwin: A Richer Account of Evolution* (Grand Rapids, Mich.: Eerdmans, 2008), 84). "[T]he use of teleological explanations in biology is not only acceptable but indeed indispensable.... Teleological explanations are not appropriate in the physical sciences, while they are appropriate, and indeed indispensable, in biology which is the scientific study of organisms. Teleological explanations, then, are distinctive of biology among all the natural sciences" (Francisco J. Ayala, "The Autonomy of Biology as a Natural Science," in *Biology, History and Natural Philosophy*, ed. Allen D. Breck and Wolfgang Yourgau [New York: Plenum Press, 1972], 13, 15).
181. On the various shades of meaning of teleology and teleonomy in biology, see Mayr, *Growth*, 48–50. On the origin and history of the term "teleonomy," see Spaemann and Löw, *Die Frage Wozu?* 218; Mayr, "Teleological," 388–93; and O'Rourke, "Aristotle and the Metaphysics," 21–22.
182. Artigas, *Mind*, 128.
183. Michael Ruse, *Darwin and Design: Does Evolution Have a Purpose?* (Cambridge, Mass.: Harvard University Press, 2003), 286.

verse: "I cannot look at the universe as a result of blind chance. Yet I can see no evidence of beneficent design, or indeed any design of any kind, in the detail. As for each variation that has ever occurred having been preordained for a special end, I can no more believe in it than that the spot on which each drop of rain falls has been specially ordained."[184] The question of design still hovers around contemporary discussions of the origin of life and the evolution of species.

Some scientists think that the property of self-organization allows us to account for the production of life without need of a designer. Peter Coveney and Roger Highfield, for instance, maintain that it "does not seem too much of a leap of faith to believe that in an unrelated stew of millions of possible polymer species, a reaction network could self-organize to form an ecosystem of molecules, a kind of metabolism."[185] Christian de Duve comments: "I believe that the pathway followed by the biogenic process up to the ancestral cell was almost entirely preordained by the intrinsic properties of the materials involved, given a certain kind of environment or succession of environmental conditions."[186]

Others are not so sanguine. Simon Conway Morris notes that "the trillion upon trillion tons of interstellar organics" might provide a "universal 'goo'" with the "essential ingredient for getting life started in terms of basic supplies," but he goes on to point out that "the question of just how inanimate became animate has proved stubbornly recalcitrant. It should all be rather simple, especially if you worship at the crowded shrine of self-organization. Yet, somewhere, somehow the right question has not yet been asked, and not for want of trying."[187] Dean Overman believes that "all of the different self-organization theories fail because they do not present a plausible method of generating sufficient information content in the time available."[188]

Even apart from the question of the origin of life, some wonder wheth-

---

184. Charles Darwin, "Letter to J. D. Hooker (12 July 1870)," in *More Letters of Charles Darwin: A Record of His Work in a Series of Hitherto Unpublished Letters*, ed. Francis Darwin and A. C. Seward (New York: D. Appleton and Co., 1903), 1.321.

185. Peter Coveney and Roger Highfield, *Frontiers of Complexity: The Search for Order in a Chaotic World* (New York: Fawcett Columbine, 1995), 209.

186. Christian de Duve, *Blueprint for a Cell: The Nature and Origin of Life* (Burlington, N.C.: Neil Patterson, 1991), 214. He acknowledges chance as a factor, but finds it subject to multiple "constraints" (de Duve, *Vital Dust*, 292–97).

187. Morris, *Life's Solution*, xiv.

188. Dean L. Overman, *A Case against Accident and Self-Organization* (New York: Rowman and Littlefield, 1997), 74.

er natural selection alone can explain the evolution of new species. Errol Harris argues: "The facts do not permit us to hold that the high degree of improbability generated by natural selection could have been the result of mere random shuffling and accidental change."[189] C. F. A. Pantin also thinks "in our present state of knowledge both organism and environment show an abundance of unique necessary properties for life and that Natural Selection alone does not account for these."[190] The question becomes especially acute when one considers the origin of intelligent life. Owen Gingerich points out:

> To postulate that the formation of intelligent life on earth is entirely accidental leaves us with some very puzzling data. The amount of genetic information content in the DNA in every cell of our bodies is so awesome that many distinguished scientists, such as Francis Crick or Fred Hoyle, have expressed their disbelief that it could have arisen by chance in the time available, that is, within the five billion years of the earth's existence. To the outrage of some evolutionists who have adopted the "blind watchmaker" thesis as their philosophical stance, Hoyle has compared the probability of this happening to the likelihood of a 747 aircraft being assembled by a whirlwind in a junkyard. This, they feel, is a brutal attack on their atheology; and so it is if you assume that mechanistic science and the world it describes are one and the same.[191]

Stephen Meyer suggests that design may be needed to account for natural selection: "An experience-based analysis of the causal powers of various explanatory hypotheses suggests purposive or intelligent design as a causally adequate—and perhaps the most causally adequate—explanation for the

---

189. Errol. E. Harris, *The Foundations of Metaphysics in Science* (George Allen and Unwin, 1965), 259.

190. C. F. A. Pantin, "Life and the Conditions of Existence," in *Biology and Personality: Frontier Problems in Science, Philosophy, and Religion*, ed. Ian Thomas Ramsey (Oxford: Blackwell, 1965), 102.

191. Owen Gingerich, *Space, Time, and Beyond: The Place of God in the Cosmos*, Gross Memorial Lecture, 1992 (Valparaiso, Ind.: Valparaiso University Press, 1993), 11. "The perfect timing of this complex configuration of circumstances [involved in the survival of life on earth] is enough to amaze and bewilder many of my friends who look at all this in purely mechanistic terms—the survival of life on earth seems such a close shave as to border on the miraculous" (Owen Gingerich, "Let There Be Light: Modern Cosmogony and Biblical Creation," in *Is God a Creationist? The Religious Case against Creation-Science*, ed. Roland Mushat Frye [New York: Charles Scribner's Sons, 1983], 133). See also Owen Gingerich, "Dare a Scientist Believe in Design?" in *Science and Theology: Ruminations on the Cosmos*, ed. Chris Impey and Catherine Petry (Vatican City State: Vatican Observatory, 2003), 35–55. Fred Hoyle's original and often-quoted remark is as follows: "A junkyard contains all the bits and pieces of a Boeing 747, dismembered and in disarray. A whirlwind happens to blow through the yard. What is the chance that after its passage a fully assembled 747, ready to fly, will be found standing there? So small as to be negligible, even if a tornado were to blow through enough junkyards to fill the whole Universe" (Fred Hoyle, *The Intelligent Universe* [New York: Holt, Rinehart, and Winston, 1984], 19).

origin of the complex specified information required to build the Cambrian animals and the novel forms they represent. For this reason, recent scientific interest in the design hypothesis is unlikely to abate as biologists continue to wrestle with the problem of the origination of biological form and the higher taxa."[192]

Perhaps the best known proposals regarding design in biology come from proponents of intelligent design [ID]. William Dembski argues for ID from instances of "specified complexity" in the natural world.[193] For any event, he thinks there are "three competing modes of explanation. These are regularity, chance, and design. To attribute an event to a regularity is to say that the event will (almost) always happen. To attribute an event to chance is to say that probabilities characterize the occurrence of the event, but are also compatible with some other event happening. To attribute an event to design is to say that it cannot reasonably be referred to either regularity or chance." Events may be divided into three "sets," according to how they happen. Design is thus the "set-theoretic complement of the disjunction law-or-chance." Dembski claims that "these three modes of explanation will be mutually exclusive and exhaustive." This means that if an event cannot be explained by law or chance, it must be attributed to design. He believes that the "principal advantage of characterizing design as the complement of regularity and chance is that it avoids committing itself to a doctrine of intelligent agency."[194]

Michael Behe thinks there are "irreducibly complex" features of biological life that can be explained only by design.[195] He defines an irreducibly complex system as "a single system which is composed of several well-matched, interacting parts that contribute to the basic function, and wherein the removal of any one of the parts causes the system to effectively

---

192. Stephen Meyer, "The Origin of Biological Information and the Higher Taxonomic Categories," *Proceedings of the Biological Society of Washington* 117 (2004): 234.
193. William A. Dembski, "In Defense of Intelligent Design," in *The Oxford Handbook of Religion and Science*, ed. Philip Clayton and Zachary Simpson (Oxford: Oxford University Press, 2006), 717. See also William A. Dembski, *The Design Inference: Eliminating Chance through Small Probabilities* (New York: Cambridge University Press, 1998); William A. Dembski, *Intelligent Design: The Bridge between Science and Theology* (Downers Grove, Ill.: InterVarsity Press, 1999), 127–39; William A. Dembski, *The Design Revolution: Answering the Toughest Questions about Intelligent Design* (Downers Grove, Ill.: InterVarsity Press, 2004), 81–86.
194. Dembski, *Design Inference*, 36.
195. See Michael J. Behe, *The Edge of Evolution: The Search for the Limits of Darwinism* (New York: Free Press, 2007); Michael J. Behe, *Darwin's Black Box: The Biochemical Challenge to Evolution* (New York: Free Press, 1996).

cease functioning."[196] Behe does not deny natural selection or descent from a common ancestor. He simply argues that certain organisms and organic structures exhibit a degree of complexity that requires an intelligent designer. He poses his argument as an answer to Charles Darwin, who once wrote: "If it could be demonstrated that any complex organ existed, which could not possibly have been formed by numerous, successive, slight modifications, my theory would absolutely break down."[197] Behe thinks he has found such an organ in the bacterial flagellum. He explains that the flagellum propels the organism along by spinning at over twenty thousand revolutions per minute. It is composed of some thirty different proteins, all precisely arranged so that if any one of them were removed it would stop spinning. He illustrates the interdependency of its parts with the analogy of a mousetrap. As a mousetrap will not work if any one of its components is removed, so the flagellum will not function if a part is missing. Behe therefore denies that such a structure could be built piece by piece, by chance and natural selection, since it would be useless (would have no survival value) unless it existed as a complete structure. Its production therefore requires an intelligent designer.[198]

Without entering into all the political, scientific, and religious controversies that surround these ID proposals, we might simply note that such thinking certainly does introduce a new mode of causality into the biological world. William Dembski points out that the methodology of science resists such novel causes:

Critics of intelligent design who hold to methodological materialism say that nature operates only by natural causes and is explained scientifically only through natural explanations. But what do they mean by "nature"? Eugenie Scott, director of the evolution watchdog group the National Center for Science Education (NCSE), explains how methodological materialism construes nature: "Most scientists today require that science be carried out according to the rule of *methodological materialism*: to explain the natural world scientifically, scientists must restrict themselves only to

---

196. Behe, *Darwin's Black Box*, 39. William Dembski explains the relation between Behe's terminology and his own: "The connection between Behe's notion of irreducible complexity and my complexity-specification criterion is now straightforward. The irreducibly complex systems Behe considers require numerous components specifically adapted to each other and each necessary for function. On any formal complexity-theoretic analysis, they are complex in the sense required by the complexity-specification criterion" (Dembski, *Intelligent Design: The Bridge*, 149).

197. Darwin, *Origin*, 232. See Michael J. Behe, "Darwin's Breakdown: Irreducible Complexity and Design at the Foundation of Life," *Touchstone: A Journal of Mere Christianity* 12, no. 4 (1999): 40.

198. See Behe, *Edge*, 120–21, 86–87; Behe, *Darwin's Black Box*, 42–43, 69–72.

material causes (to matter, energy, and their interaction).... By continuing to seek natural explanations for how the world works, we have been able to find them. If supernatural explanations are allowed, they will discourage—or at least delay—the discovery of natural explanations, and we will understand less about the universe."[199]

Scott's "methodological materialism" sounds very much like the constricted causality of Newtonian physics where causality was limited to the forces that move the atoms. At the same time, Scott's concern that the invocation of "supernatural explanations" might delay the progress of science is reminiscent of the conviction we have seen in Oldenberg, Boyle, and Locke that any resort to formal and final causes might retard the progress of science. Dembski argues that ID's search for broader (and not necessarily "supernatural") modes of causality will not impede but foster scientific progress:

> Thus, for Scott, nature is "matter, energy, and their interaction." Accordingly, by natural explanations, Scott means explanations that resort only to such material causes. Yet, that is precisely the point at issue: namely, whether nature operates exclusively by such causes. If nature contains a richer set of causes than purely material causes, then intelligent design is a live possibility, and methodological materialism has misread physical reality. Note, also, that to contrast natural explanations with supernatural explanations further obscures this crucial point. "Supernatural explanations" typically denote explanations that involve miracles and cannot be understood scientifically. But explanations that call upon intelligent causes require no miracles and give no evidence of being reducible to Scott's trio of "matter, energy, and their interaction." Indeed, design theorists argue that intelligent causation is perfectly natural provided that nature is understood aright.[200]

Whatever its possible defects, the intelligent design movement is certainly broadening the notion of causation as it invites science to consider this "richer set of causes."[201]

---

199. Dembski, "In Defense," 723. Cf.: Eugenie C. Scott, "'Science and Religion,' 'Christian Scholarship,' and 'Theistic Science': Some Comparisons," *Reports of the National Center for Science Education* 18, no. 2 (1998): 30–32.

200. Dembski, "In Defense," 724.

201. "To be sure, if one is more liberal about what one means by natural causes and includes among natural causes telic processes that are not reducible to chance and necessity (as the ancient Stoics did by endowing nature with immanent teleology), then my claim that natural causes are incomplete dissolves. But that is not how the scientific community by and large understands natural causes" (William A. Dembski, *No Free Lunch: Why Specified Complexity Cannot Be Purchased without Intelligence* [Lanham, Md.: Rowman and Littlefield, 2002], xiv). Without endorsing present ID theories, Del Ratzsch notes: "If there are natural gaps, or if there are design₂ ramifications of our science [i.e., types of design that imply intentionality], then our restricted methods may well not pick those up either. And our science, then, would fall victim to our own philosophical, methodological, and theoretical human prejudices" (Del Ratzsch, "There Is a Place for Intelligent Design

New Modes of Causality in Contemporary Science

The theories of contemporary science have yielded a greater awareness of the limits of science and opened a deeper appreciation of the rich modes of causality that are needed for understanding the natural world. As science pushes toward the first moments of the cosmos, it is faced with a singularity in which the very laws and categories that it uses to discover the nature of the universe seem to break down. As it penetrates the heart of matter in quantum physics, it comes up against the limits of its ability to measure the world precisely.[202] In chaos theory, it finds itself unable to predict the future states of complex systems.[203] John Polkinghorne observes that "science seems to raise questions which transcend its own ability to answer."[204] Contemporary developments in science have led many to see that science cannot provide an exhaustive explanation of reality.[205]

The limitations of science are part and parcel of its very methodology. Sir Arthur Eddington pointed this out long ago with his famous analogy of the ichthyologist who, after carefully studying ocean life using a net that could catch nothing smaller than two inches, solemnly concluded that "no sea creature is less than two inches long."[206] What one finds depends on the

---

in the Philosophy of Biology: Intelligent Design in (Philosophy of) Biology: Some Legitimate Roles," in *Contemporary Debates in Philosophy of Biology*, ed. Francisco J. Ayala and Robert Arp [Chichester, U.K.: Wiley-Blackwell, 2010]: 356).

202. "We do not know what the most basic level of physical reality is, and perhaps we will never know.... So when we try to reduce all scientific explanations to a most basic level of physical reality, we find that level to be elusive, disputed, and hardly even imaginable" (Keith Ward, *The Big Questions in Science and Religion* [West Conshohocken, Pa: Templeton Foundation, 2008], 257).

203. "[F]uture states of complex systems such as weather systems quickly become uncomputable because of their sensitive dependence on initial conditions (a dependence so sensitive that a finite knower could never predict the evolution of the system—a staggering limitation when one notes what percentage of natural systems exhibit chaotic behaviors)" (Clayton, *Mind*, 3).

204. Polkinghorne, *One World*, xii.

205. "I hereby endorse a regularity view of the laws of nature that serves as a reminder that the laws of physics, even when they are deterministic in their mathematical form, do not offer an exhaustive picture of the real-world regularities-and-irregularities, nor are prescriptive in the sense that a specific event must necessarily occur, even where they mostly do" (Niels Henrik Gregersen, "Divine Action, Compatibilism, and Coherence Theory: A Response to Russell, Clayton, and Murphy," *Theology and Science* 4 [2006]: 221–22). "[P]hysics must give up the claim to give a causally complete description of interactions that affect the real physical world... Hence it does not provide an adequate basis for metaphysical speculations about the nature of existence" (George F. R. Ellis, "Science, Complexity, and the Natures of Existence," in *Evolution and Emergence: Systems, Organisms, Persons*, ed. Nancey Murphy and William R. Stoeger [New York: Oxford University Press, 2007], 139). See also Peter Hodgson, "Presuppositions and Limits of Science," in *The Structure and Development of Science*, ed. Gerard Radnitzky and Gunnar Andersson (Boston: D. Reidl, 1979), 133–47.

206. Arthur Eddington, *The Philosophy of Physical Science* (New York: Macmillan, 1939), 16–17.

method one uses in looking. The very rigor of scientific method, as Mariano Artigas notes, accounts for both its effectiveness and its limitations: "The very same reasons that explain the distinctive reliability of empirical science point out its limits. Empirical science, by its very nature, is limited to those aspects of reality that can be studied using experimental control.... The rigor and reliability of empirical science go hand in hand with its limits."[207]

Only if its method is turned into a metaphysics can science claim that nothing lies beyond its powers of explanation. But in that case, science is no longer science but scientism. As science recognizes its limits, it may well question the scientistic assumption that the world may be described only through mechanism, determinism, and reductionism. Gennaro Auletta argues that quantum mechanics spells the end of the "mechanistic paradigm."[208] Keith Ward maintains that a deterministic worldview is not supported by contemporary physics.[209] John Polkinghorne believes that reductionism can no longer accommodate the complexities that science has discovered.[210] John Hedley Brooke notes that critiques of reductionism now arise within science itself.[211]

Seeing its limits, science also recognizes valid areas of inquiry beyond

---

207. Artigas, *Mind*, 8.

208. "Quantum mechanics was the definitive end of the mechanistic paradigm (consisting in determinism, mechanic actions, reductionism, perfect localization, elementary compounds of matter), and received the greatest opposition from those who believed in the mechanical paradigm" (Auletta, "Science," 275). "In effect, the rigid, mechanical determinism of classical physics seems irreconcilable with the revolutionary and, in large part, definitive triumph of quantum mechanics" (Filippo Selvaggi, *Causalità e indeterminismo: La problematica moderna alla luce della filosofia aristotelico-tomista* [Rome: Editrice Università Gregoriana, 1964], 420).

209. "We can confidently say that a closed and deterministic view of nature is neither a presupposition of nor a deduction from the practice and established findings of modern physics. Universal physical determinism was suggested to many by the work of Newton, though he did not subscribe to it himself. Contemporary views tend to be much more agnostic about the universal applicability and all-encompassing range of physical laws" (Ward, *The Big Questions*, 97–98).

210. "At the very least, it is clear that science has not succeeded in establishing the causal closure of the world in terms of its traditionally reductionist approach. The metascientific possibilities open to discussion are much too diverse and complicated for that to be a necessary conclusion" (Polkinghorne, "Space, Time," 980). "Reductionism is thus an expression of pure faith, grounded in the elegance of mathematical descriptions and a belief that all physical behavior is wholly determined by the behavior of matter's smallest constituents. There is little empirical evidence for it and much empirical evidence against it, even though there are features of classical scientific methodology that made the faith seem a desirable and reasonable one" (Ward, *The Big Questions*, 258).

211. "One extrapolation from the new physics deserves special attention.... This is to justify critiques of scientific reductionism in the name of science itself. No longer, it is argued, does one have the license to reduce the behavior of complex systems to the laws governing the behavior of their parts.... On the interpretation of quantum mechanics that regards the atom as a system vibrant with possibilities, reduction to a single description of the state of its components proves to

its borders. As George F. R. Ellis points out: "There are many limits to what science will ever be able to do that will never change—they are boundaries to its competence, because of its nature and its methods of investigation. There are many areas of concern to humans, of which only a subset are within the ambit of science. Outside this ambit are crucially important areas: in particular, ethics, aesthetics, metaphysics, and meaning. They are outside the competence of science because there is no scientific experiment which can determine any of them. Science can help to illuminate some of their aspects, but is fundamentally unable to touch their core. This is not a 'God of the gaps' argument. It is about absolute boundaries to what science can ever do, because of the very nature of science."[212]

In addition to recognizing its limits, contemporary science also seems to be opening itself to new modes of conceiving the causality at work in the natural world.[213] If Newtonian science tended to reduce the idea of causality to the efficient cause conceived univocally as quantifiable force, contemporary science has enormously broadened the notion. A univocal understanding of causality no longer seems adequate to the scientific enterprise. From the indeterminate potentiality that Heisenberg found in quantum mechanics, to formal causality employed in understanding emergence, to the idea of purpose that has become a fundamental tool in biology, contemporary science is reaching out to new modes of causality.

The new kinds of causality that contemporary science is discovering are strikingly reminiscent of the sorts of causality found in the philosophy of Aristotle and Aquinas. Terrence Deacon remarks that his analysis of causal typologies in contemporary science is in many ways "a modern reaffirmation of the original Aristotelian insight about categories of causality."[214] Filippo Selvaggi argues that the "richness of this philosophy of causality and nature, developed through the intuitive genius of Aristotle and Saint Thomas ... recovers all its importance with the developments of modern

---

be elusive" (John Hedley Brooke, *Science and Religion: Some Historical Perspectives* [Cambridge: Cambridge University Press, 1991], 333–34).

212. G. F. R. Ellis, "Physics, Complexity," 760. "We need also to remember that scientific explanations need not be all-embracing, and indeed it would be surprising if they were" (Morris, *Life's Solution*, 327). See also Clayton, *Mind*, 181; and Ayala, "From Paley," 57–58.

213. On the history of the development of this interest, see Wallace, *Causality and Scientific*.

214. Terrence W. D. Deacon, "Emergence: The Hole at the Wheel's Hub," in *The Re-emergence of Emergence: The Emergentist Hypothesis from Science to Religion*, ed. Philip Clayton and Paul Davies (New York: Oxford University Press, 2006), 148. Deacon also notes: "There has been an erosion of this plural understanding of causality since Aristotle that ... may in part contribute to our present intellectual (and indeed spiritual) dilemma" (ibid., 113–14).

science."²¹⁵ Francisco J. Ayala finds it useful to review Aristotle's four causes in explaining the importance of the notion of teleology in biological evolution.²¹⁶ Fran O'Rourke observes: "As the life sciences reveal more and more marvelous instances of determination and directional behavior throughout the world of nature, these provide fresh illustrations of Aristotle's deepest metaphysical intuitions."²¹⁷ John Herman Randall notes: "Today, the concepts of Aristotle's physics, those notions involved in his analysis of process, have been driving those of Newton out of our theory.... [I]t is often explicitly recognized that the ideas of Aristotle's physics are far closer to present-day physical theory than are the ideas of the nineteenth century.... Today it is Aristotle who often seems strikingly modern, and Newton who appears 'of mere historical interest.' ... It is Aristotle who strikes the present-day student as suggestive, enlightening, and sound."²¹⁸

Many developments in contemporary science hearken back to modes of causality neglected by Newtonian science, but prominent in the philosophy of Aristotle and Aquinas. Potentiality, form, and finality are types of causality that are not measurable and so do not come directly under the scientific microscope. What is studied and discovered in science, however, now seems to invite (or possibly to require) their consideration as categories of explanation.²¹⁹ One might say that today's science recognizes that all causes are not the same. Even within the world that science studies, causality must be understood as an analogical rather than a univocal reality. We will consider briefly how material, formal, and final causality, as well as the quasi-causality of chance, have reappeared in contemporary science.

Material Causality   Beyond the deterministic world of Newtonian physics, quantum theory has opened a realm of spontaneity where, at least in one interpretation, a fundamental indeterminism lies at the heart of material reality. Werner Heisenberg noted a resemblance between quantum indeterminacy and Aristotle's primary matter.²²⁰ It is of course questionable

---

215. Selvaggi, *Causalità*, 419. See also Joseph Meurers, "Thomas und die Naturwissenschaft Heute," in *Il cosmo e la scienza*, Atti del congresso internazionale Tommaso d'Aquino nel suo settimo centenario, no. 9 (Naples: Edizioni Domenicane Italiane, 1975), 59.
216. Ayala, "Teleological Explanations," 47–48.
217. O'Rourke, "Aristotle and the Metaphysics," 24.
218. John Herman Randall Jr., *Aristotle* (New York: Columbia University Press, 1960), 167–68.
219. For an extensive study, applying Aristotelian categories of causality to issues in contemporary science, see David S. Oderberg, *Real Essentialism* (New York: Routledge, 2007), 177–260.
220. See Heisenberg, *Physics and Philosophy*, 160.

whether quantum indeterminacy (which is at least statistically determined) can be equated philosophically with the absolute indetermination or pure potentiality of primary matter.[221] However inaccurate Heisenberg may have been in naming this similarity, his reference to Aristotle's primary matter is evidence of an opening of the notion of causality in contemporary science to include more than simply efficient causality, narrowly conceived as the energy that moves the atoms.

The potentiality that Aristotle called "primary matter" is also implicit in Big Bang cosmology. Since the whole cosmos has in fact evolved from the initial Singularity, it must have been *somehow* present in it. Aristotle's idea of primary matter can help us understand that *somehow*. All that now exists was present then, not actually but potentially—as a possibility. Whatever did actually exist in the Singularity had the potentiality for existing as the myriad things that now populate our universe. Aristotle's primary matter, as William Wallace describes it, is consonant with the dynamism of that process: "[M]atter, seen as nature and as a basic constituent of all natural entities, is not the passive and inert principle it has long been pictured to be. It is a powerful and potential principle that lies at the base of the most cataclysmic upheavals taking place on our planet and in the remote depths of space."[222]

The theory of evolution also involves potentiality. Original terrestrial matter must have *somehow* had the possibility of existing in the form of the higher living things we find today since they have in fact arisen and evolved from it. This again harkens back to Aristotle's primary matter.[223] In fact, the causality of primary matter, as Aquinas explains it, suggests the dynamism of the evolutionary process: "[T]he intention of everything existing in potency must be to tend through motion toward actuality. And so, the more posterior and more perfect an act is, the more fundamentally is the inclination of matter directed toward it. Hence, in regard to the last and most perfect act

---

221. Stanley Jaki, for one, is rather underwhelmed by Heisenberg's insight: "The claim made by Heisenberg, that the wave function reveals something of the Aristotelian potency, certainly proved a rank unfamiliarity on Heisenberg's part with what Aristotle said on the transition from potency to act" (Jaki, *Means*, 59).

222. Wallace, "Is Finality," 55.

223. "Beginning ... our study of the causes of evolution in the light of the Aristotelian-Thomistic doctrine of causality, we notice that all forms of life arise from material in the cosmos and that when decaying and dying they are reabsorbed by the material universe. This means that, as far as material causality goes, all these forms of life are contained within the potency of matter" (Elders, "Background," 54–55).

that matter can attain, the inclination of matter whereby it desires form must be inclined as toward the ultimate end of generation. Now, among the acts pertaining to forms, certain gradations are found. Thus, prime matter is in potency, first of all, to the form of an element. When it is existing under the form of an element it is in potency to the form of a mixed body; that is why the elements are matter for the mixed body. Considered under the form of a mixed body, it is in potency to a vegetative soul, for this sort of soul is the act of a body. In turn, the vegetative soul is in potency to a sensitive soul, and a sensitive one to an intellectual one.... [T]he ultimate end of the whole process of generation is the human soul, and matter tends toward it as toward an ultimate form."[224]

Leo Elders explains the relevance of primary matter to the evolution of new species: "It is sometimes argued that lower forms of life have a natural aspiration to reach beyond their own level, in other words, that there is a transgeneric tendency to reach higher forms of being. By 'tendency' is meant not a conscious desire, but a natural drive or urge which influences the direction of activity. We have seen that Darwin himself speaks of a 'tendency to variation.' Also in scholastic philosophy things are said to have a natural desire. St. Thomas mentions such a desire in lower beings to reach higher levels."[225]

Formal Causality   In the phenomenon of emergence, contemporary science recognizes that certain systems exercise a kind of "top-down" causality on their parts. They exhibit a single action that cannot be explained simply by an analysis of their parts. An adequate explanation of their activity must therefore involve more than a simple reduction of the system to its parts.

Since action follows being, a system that exhibits a single unified action must exist as a single unified being. To explain fundamentally why it acts as a single whole, one must first explain why it exists as a single being. Emergence asserts the distinctive reality of the whole, but does not explain what

---

224. *SCG* III, 22, no. 7. "[E]verything in a lower form of existence is inclined to the maximum possible assimilation to the higher form" (*In de an.* II, lect. 7, no. 315). In all of this, primary matter remains, of course, a passive principle: "So, among beings that is most distant from God which is merely potential; namely, prime matter. Hence, its function is solely to undergo, and not to perform, action" (*SCG* III, 69, no. 27). "For matter to seek form is nothing other than matter being ordered to form as potency to act" (*In phys.* I, lect. 15, no. 10, [§138]).

225. Elders, "Background," 56. See also Jacques Maritain, "Toward a Thomist Idea of Evolution," in *Untrammeled Approaches*, The Collected Works of Jacques Maritain, vol. 20 (South Bend, Ind.: University of Notre Dame Press, 1977), 85–131; and Maurer, "Darwin," 511–14.

makes it to be a whole rather than a conglomeration of many things with a mere incidental unity.[226] Accordingly, many scientists and philosophers are now looking for a way to explain how a being may exist as a single unified entity with its own proper characteristics and activities.[227] Alejandro García-Rivera poses the question well and suggests an answer: "What is this depth that characterizes life? ... To ask this is to ask the question of what makes a living creature be that which it is; that is, What is its form? However, to ask this question is to recognize what is known as formal causality.... Formal causality explains the behavior of the whole as a whole. It is the principle by which the many possibilities of molecules and cell parts and cells become this particular living whole."[228] Ernst Mayr calls for "an uncommitted philosophy of biology, which stays equally far away from vitalism and other unscientific ideologies and from a physicalist reductionism that is unable to do justice to specifically biological phenomena and systems."[229] He suggests a possible starting point in Aristotle: "No one prior to Darwin has made a greater contribution to our understanding of the living world than Aristotle.... Aristotle's outstanding characteristic was that he searched for causes. He was not satisfied merely to ask how-questions, but was amazingly modern by asking also why-questions.... He clearly saw that raw matter lacks the capacity to develop the complex form of an organism. Something additional had to be present, for which he used the word *eidos*, a term which he defined entirely differently from Plato. Aristotle's *eidos* is a teleonomic principle which performed in Aristotle's thinking precisely what the genetic program of the modern biologist performs.... Aristotle taught that natural substances act according to their own properties, and that all phenomena of nature are processes or the manifestations of processes. And since all processes have an end, he considered the study of ends as an essential

---

226. For a study of this ontological liability of emergence, see Derek Jeffreys, "The Soul Is Alive and Well: Non-reductive Physicalism and Emergent Mental Properties," *Theology and Science* 2 (2004): 205–25.

227. "[T]he simple fact that organized bodies exist invites still other modern biologists to look in nature for a principle which presides over the organization of living beings. Without such a principle the functioning of such beings can be explained, but not their existence, which, after all, is as much a fact as is their functioning" (Gilson, *From Aristotle*, 30). "An absolutely crucial development in contemporary understandings of the nature of reality regards its non-reducible hierarchical ordering in terms of increasingly complex systems. In some ways this recognition represents a return to the Aristotelian view that the form (organization, functional capacities) of an entity is equally constitutive of reality as is the stuff of which a thing is made" (Murphy, "Buridan's," 338).

228. Alejandro García-Rivera, *The Garden of God: A Theological Cosmology* (Minneapolis, Minn,: Fortress Press, 2009), 88.

229. Mayr, *Growth*, 76.

component of the study of nature."²³⁰ The Aristotelian-Thomistic notion of substantial form may indeed be the answer to Mayr's quest, as William Norris Clarke explains: "If someone claims that there are no essential changes in the material world, but only aggregates of lower elements undergoing merely accidental changes—this is called Reductionism—then one cannot adequately explain that, at least in living things, as even many scientists now admit, there is a new unitary force in the organism as a whole that exercises positive causal influence downwards on its parts, and this new force, not present before in the elements by themselves, must now be present in order to exercise positive causal influence. This 'holistic' principle of unity fulfills precisely the function, under a different name, of St. Thomas's essential or substantial form, which determines the nature of a being."²³¹

Substantial form can provide a metaphysical ground for the unity that science observes in the phenomenon of emergence, while avoiding reductionism on the one hand and vitalism or dualism on the other.²³² A number of scientists and philosophers make reference to the notion of form in their discussion of the phenomenon of emergence—often with explicit reference to Aristotle or Aquinas. Terence Nichols points out that "a rediscovery of holistic cause, similar to the notion of substantial form, is occurring in the natural sciences, the very disciplines responsible for its rejection in the early modern period."²³³ Terrence Deacon emphasizes the significance of form as a type of causality that "takes us back to Aristotle."²³⁴ Noting that it is "commonly held that Aristotle's teaching on substantial or natural form is in no way relevant to the physical or natural sciences as they have developed since the seventeenth century," William Wallace presents arguments to "counter that view and propose that form in general not only plays a critical role in twentieth-century science, but that this role can now be extended

230. Ibid., 87–88. 231. Clarke, *The One*, 141.
232. "My judgment is that the Socratic question, 'what makes one thing one?' rightly leads to the focus on form, and that Aristotle's hylomorphism is, as Gilson said, 'evident,' but, as Aristotle said, is at the summit of theoretical thought, requiring the solving of a most astonishingly difficult problem, that is, how to conceive of unqualified coming to be and ceasing to be in nature" (Dewan, *St. Thomas and Form*, 88n110). See also Michael J. Dodds, "Hylomorphism and Human Wholeness: Perspectives on the Mind-Brain Problem," *Theology and Science* 7 (2009): 141–62.
233. Terence Nichols, "Aquinas' Concept of Substantial Form and Modern Science," *International Philosophical Quarterly* 36 (1996): 303. "Here [on the biological level] information, function, and form are crucial. In this context, it makes sense to speak of the role of information as formal causality" (Ian G. Barbour, "Indeterminacy, Holism, and God's Action," in *God's Action in Nature's World: Essays in Honor of Robert John Russell*, ed. Ted Peters and Nathan Hallanger [Aldershot, U.K.: Ashgate, 2006], 121).
234. Deacon, "Response," 27.

to include even substancing or natural form."[235] Eleonore Stump explains that in Aquinas's philosophy, "the fact that material objects are composites of matter and form means that material objects can have emergent properties of this sort, and these emergent properties may bring with them further emergent properties, such as causal potentialities which belong to the whole but not to its parts."[236]

Final Causality We have seen how the Big Bang theory invites us to consider the intricacies and contingencies involved in the initial formation of the universe and that the anthropic principle suggests an explanation of those intricacies by introducing the presence of human persons into the equations. Somehow the "wherefrom" of the universe, in the interrelation of initial forces, is intricately related to its "whereto" in the eventual emergence of rational life. Consideration of nature's "whereto" opens the way to looking at purpose or final causality as a category of explanation in the natural world.

We can also see this concern for final causality in biology. To some biologists, purpose is evident globally in the universal pursuit of survival that drives natural selection. Others employ it only locally when, for instance, they describe certain organs in terms of their purposes—as gills for breathing.[237] They do not see its inclusion as contrary to the method of empirical science.[238]

Mariano Artigas finds many areas of contemporary science that point to the reality of final causality and invite its study: "We can conclude that, from the point of view of the present scientific worldview, the existence of teleological dimensions in our world—not only in the biological level, but also in

---

235. Wallace, "A Place," 35. "Formal causality—the influence of the form, structure, or function of an object on its activities—is thus probably the most fruitful of these Aristotelian [causal] options" (Philip Clayton, "Conceptual Foundations of Emergence Theory," in *The Re-Emergence of Emergence: The Emergentist Hypothesis from Science to Religion*, ed. Philip Clayton and Paul Davies [New York: Oxford University Press, 2006], 4). "Despite this, the nonreductive physicalist framework has an Aristotelian edge, for it is the shape (the pattern) and the flow of patterns through time (information) that give emergent entities their reality. The pattern is not completely separate from physical reality, as Plato would have it, but is ultimately connected to the physical, as Aristotle seems to imply. These connections suggest that the arguments both for and against Platonic and Aristotelian forms have some relevance here, although this connection has been poorly explored" (Peterson, "Species," 702–3).

236. Stump, "Non-Cartesian," 510. See also Mayr, *Growth*, 66; Fred D. Miller Jr., "Aristotelian Natural Form and Theology—Reconsidered," *Proceedings of the American Catholic Philosophical Association* 69 (1995): 70; Hans-Dieter Mutschler, "Physik und Neothomismus: Das ontologische Grundproblem der modernen Physik," *Theologie und Philosophie* 68 (1993): 50; Landen, "Of Forests," 86–87; Clayton, "Emergence of Spirit," 12; Clayton, "Natural Law," 621, 629.

237. Ayala, "Teleological Explanations," 44.

238. "It is now clear that seemingly goal-directed processes exist in nature which are not in any way in conflict with a strictly physico-chemical explanation" (Mayr, *Growth*, 48).

the physicochemical—is a plain fact. Until now the state of the sciences did not provide sufficient grounds for it; only the scientific progress of the last decades of the twentieth century has made it possible to reach this vantage point."[239] Michael Denton relates these contemporary developments back to Aristotle: "Four centuries after the scientific revolution apparently destroyed irretrievably man's special place in the universe, banished Aristotle, and rendered teleological speculation obsolete, the relentless stream of discovery has turned dramatically in favor of teleology and design."[240]

Chance Heisenberg's claim that quantum events have "no cause" might seem on one level to invalidate the principle of causality. In another way, however, it is reminiscent of Aquinas's teaching that chance events have no cause.[241] For Aquinas, as for contemporary science, chance is not just a name for our ignorance of actual causes, but a real aspect of the natural world.[242] Mario Bunge points out that "certain scientific advances in the nineteenth century, notably the invention of the calculus of accidental errors of observation, and statistical mechanics, suggested that chance is just as real as causation. The emergence of quantum mechanics, genetics, molecular biology, and communication engineering in the twentieth century confirmed the firm place of chance in the world." He notes that causation and chance "are not just in the mind: they are in the world as well. That is, some real processes are causal, others random, and still others have causal as well as stochas-

---

239. Artigas, *Mind*, 130. "Importantly, then, the onset of third-order emergence defines the onset of telos on this planet and, for all we know, in the universe. Creatures have a purpose, and their traits are for that purpose" (Ursula Goodenough and Terrence W. Deacon, "From Biology to Consciousness to Morality," *Zygon* 38 [2003]: 804). Richard Green finds a hint of final causality in quantum mechanics: "There is an air of teleology surrounding these electronic quantum jumps. For again on its orthodox interpretation, quantum mechanics can assign no meaning to the question of how the collapse of a wave packet is brought about. An atom achieves a certain end, as it were, where the supposed means by which it is achieved is not merely unknown, nor even unknowable, but actually non-existent" (Richard Green, *The Thwarting of Laplace's Demon: Arguments against the Mechanistic World-View* [New York: St. Martin's Press, 1995], 23).

240. Denton, *Nature's Destiny*, 389.

241. "One might be tempted to the supposition that behind the perceived statistical world a 'real' world lies hidden in which the law of causality is valid. But such speculations seem to us—we emphasize it emphatically—unfruitful and senseless" (Heisenberg, "Über den anschaulichen," 197–98). "It is not true that every effect has a direct cause, for something that comes about accidentally, for instance, that this man who wishes to look for water encounters the robbers, has no cause" (*SCG* III, 94, no. 2).

242. "A chance event arises when something happens which we could not predict, but this may be because we do not have enough information. Chance is then the other side of the coin to our ignorance; this is sometimes called epistemological chance. Alternatively, chance may be ontological. That is, it is somehow inherent in the nature of things and there is no knowledge we could possibly have which would make any difference" (Bartholomew, *God, Chance and Purpose*, 4).

tic aspects. That is, the fields of causation and chance have a partial overlap. Moreover, causation on one level may emerge from chance on another, and conversely.... Chance is just as real as causation; both are modes of becoming."[243] Robert Russell observes that today's natural science "opens the possibility of interpreting chance as a sign of ontological indeterminism in nature. Scholars in theology and science have made powerful cases that various fields, including cosmology, thermodynamics, chaos theory, the neurosciences, and quantum mechanics, do indeed point to ontological indeterminism. If this is correct, it would mean that the presence of statistics in these fields arises not from our ignorance of the underlying deterministic forces but from the fact that there are, in reality, no sufficient underlying forces or causes that fully determine particular physical processes, events or outcomes."[244]

Emergence has shown that science is not faced with the alternatives of a world of pure chance or sheer determinism. Both have a role to play in nature. Arthur Peacocke explains that "it is chance, operating within a lawlike framework that is the basis of the inherent creativity of the natural order, its ability to generate new forms, patterns and organizations of matter and energy. If all were governed by rigid law, a repetitive and uncreative order would prevail: if chance alone ruled, no forms, patterns or organizations would persist long enough for them to have any identity or real existence and the universe could never be a cosmos and susceptible to rational inquiry. It is the combination of the two which makes possible an ordered universe capable of developing within itself new modes of existence."[245]

The joining of chance with lawful necessity is especially evident in the theory of evolution, where random mutations together with the regular process of natural selection result in the production of new species.[246]

243. Bunge, *Chasing*, 89, 118. "We conclude that modern science, in particular since the advent of quantum physics, takes it for granted that there are chance events out there and that there are things possessing chance propensities. That is, chance (or randomness) is objective, and it is an ontological category" (Martin Mahner and Mario Bunge, *Foundations of Biophilosophy* [Berlin: Springer-Verlag, 1997], 41). On the implications of contemporary scientific theories for the reality of chance, see also Green, *Thwarting*, xi; and Bartholomew, *God of Chance*, 93–94.
244. Robert John Russell, "Quantum Physics and the Theology of Non-Interventionist Objective Divine Action," in *The Oxford Handbook of Religion and Science*, ed. Philip Clayton and Zachary Simpson (Oxford: Oxford University Press, 2006), 580–81.
245. Arthur Peacocke, *Theology for a Scientific Age: Being and Becoming—Natural, Divine and Human* (Minneapolis, Mich.: Fortress Press, 1993), 65.
246. "It now appears that the universe has potentialities that are becoming actualized by the joint operation in time of random, time-dependent processes in a framework of lawlike properties—and that these potentialities include the possibility of biological, and so of human, life" (Peacocke, "God's Action," 468). See also Ayala, *Darwin's Gift*, 77–78; and Polkinghorne, *Science and Creation*, 47–48.

3

Locking Divine Action in Modern Science

Now that we have seen how the idea of causality, locked in by modern science, has been unlocked and expanded in contemporary science, we need to explore how this locking and unlocking has affected our understanding of divine causality. We will find, not surprisingly, that as the notion of causality became limited, so did our ability to speak of God's action. In this chapter, we will look at how divine action became locked with the advent of modern science. In the next two chapters, we will consider how theology might best employ the developments of contemporary science to unlock it.

DIVINE ACTION AND THE CONSTRICTION OF CAUSALITY IN MODERN SCIENCE

As our understanding of causality narrowed with the advent of modern science, so did our capacity to speak of divine action.[1] Contemporary science is now emerging from the narrow causal paradigms of Newtonian science, but much of theology is still trapped in them. As Langdon Gilkey observes: "[C]ontemporary theology does not expect, nor does it speak of, wondrous divine events on the surface of natural and historical life. The causal nexus in space and time which Enlightenment science and philosophy introduced into the Western mind and which was assumed by liberalism is also assumed by modern theologians and scholars; since they participate in the modern world of science both intellectually and existentially,

---

1. "The present-day crisis in the notion of divine action has resulted as much as anything from a shift in the notion of causation" (Clayton, *God and Contemporary,* 189).

they can scarcely do anything else."[2] Keith Ward echoes this idea: "The scientific world-view seems to leave no room for God to act, since everything that happens is determined by scientific laws."[3]

If causality can be thought of only as the efficient causality of physical force, then divine action must be explained univocally in those terms.[4] E. A. Burtt explains the radical reconception of divinity that this entailed at the time of early modern science: "With final causality gone, God as Aristotelianism had conceived him was quite lost; to deny him outright, however, at Galileo's stage of the game, was too radical a step for any important thinker to consider. The only way to keep him in the universe was to invert the Aristotelian metaphysics and regard him as the First Efficient Cause or Creator of the atoms.... God thus ceases to be the Supreme Good in any important sense; he is a huge mechanical inventor, whose power is appealed to merely to account for the first appearance of the atoms, the tendency becoming more and more irresistible as time goes on to lodge all further causality for whatever effects in the atoms themselves."[5]

Kirk Wegter-McNelly explains the consequences of such thinking for discussions of God and human freedom: "Embracing both the determinism and the reductionism of Newtonian science, early modern scientists quickly distanced themselves from modes of explanations that involved purpose, or *telos*. Increasingly they sought explanations couched exclusively in terms of efficient (i.e., mechanical) causes. It was physics' characterization of the world within this new framework of mechanistic reductionism that led to a significant theological crises in Christian thought, for if the state of the natural world was completely determined by the relevant physical laws acting upon the prior configuration of its various parts in each preceding mo-

---

2. Langdon Gilkey, "Cosmology, Ontology and the Travail of Biblical Language," in *God's Activity in the World: The Contemporary Problem*, ed. Owen C. Thomas (Chico: Scholars Press, 1983), 31.

3. Keith Ward, *Divine Action* (London: Collins, 1990), l.

4. "Newtonian science directed attention increasingly to efficient causes, and the fate of the idea of cause has been deeply shaped by that fact. Further, Biblical language about God strongly suggests this kind of agency on his part. Hence Christian theology and modern philosophy alike have dealt chiefly with God's action in terms of efficient causation. In the dominant Newtonian model of natural causality, what is caused is changed, and change is ultimately explicable in terms of local motion. Change in place (or change in speed or direction) is attributable to the impact of other masses" (Cobb, "Natural Causality," 102). "Because of the cultural scientism in Western society, God's action now is limited to physical and mechanistic categories, thereby letting God compete with innerworldly physical and mechanistic causes" (Taede A. Smedes, "Beyond Barbour or Back to Basics? The Future of Science-and-Religion and the Quest for Unity," *Zygon* 43 [2008]: 247).

5. Burtt, *Metaphysical*, 99.

ment, could one still conceive of human beings as thinking and acting in the world with genuine freedom? And, equally important, could one affirm God's ongoing activity in such a world?"[6] We can find his analysis exemplified in remarks of Albert Einstein: "The more man is imbued with the ordered regularity of all events the firmer becomes his conviction that there is no room left by the side of this ordered regularity for causes of a different nature. For him neither the rule of human nor the rule of divine will exists as an independent cause of natural events."[7]

If God's action is conceived univocally as physical force, it cannot but interfere with other physical forces. It must therefore be excluded from the world lest it encroach on other causes and so disrupt the determined patterns of scientific law. There is simply no "room" for it. Gordon Kaufman accordingly ponders how God can possibly intervene in the world without "violently ripping into the fabric of history or arbitrarily upsetting the momentum of its powers."[8] To David Jenkins, a God who would "insert additional causal events from time to time into that universe to produce particular events or trends by that eventuality alone would be a meddling demigod, a moral monster and a contradiction of himself."[9] Arthur Peacocke speaks with less bombast and more poetry, but his conclusion is the same as he admires "the seamless character of the web which has been spun on the loom of time" and criticizes "interventionist assumptions about God's action in the world" that are "inconsistent and incoherent with what the sciences show about the way the world actually goes."[10]

If there is only one brand of causality, God must subscribe to it and so be a univocal cause alongside of creatures. If such a God acts in the world, there must be a point where his causality intersects with that of the creature—the now famous "causal joint." Austin Farrer introduced the term, but, recognizing the transcendence of God's causality, believed that the causal joint must remain a mystery.[11] Theologians who consider God's causality univocal, however, have little patience with such claims to mystery. John Polking-

---

6. Wegter-McNelly, "Fundamental," 160.
7. Albert Einstein, *Out of My Later Years* (New York: Wisdom Library, 1950), 32.
8. Gordon D. Kaufman, *God the Problem* (Cambridge, Mass.: Harvard University Press, 1972), 147.
9. David E. Jenkins, *Anglicanism, Accident, and Providence* (Wilton, Conn.: Morehouse-Barlow, 1987), 21.
10. Arthur Peacocke, *Creation and the World of Science* (Oxford: Clarendon Press, 1979), 60, 134.
11. Austin Farrer, *Faith and Speculation* (Edinburgh: T & T Clark, 1988; original ed., London: A. & C. Black, 1967).

horne, for instance, complains that any "attempt to exhibit the 'causal joint' by which the double agency of divine and creaturely causalities are related to each other is held to be impossible, or even impious."[12] Philip Clayton also seems to be looking for a univocal account of the causal joint: "If one is to offer a full theory of divine agency, one must include some account of where the 'causal joint' is at which God's action directly impacts on the world. To do this requires one in turn to get one's hands dirty with the actual scientific data and theories, including the basic features of relativity theory; quantum mechanics and (more recently) chaos theory."[13] Frank Dilley insists that "defenders of miracles ought to be bringing forth real explanations, in terms of physics for example, of how it is that God acts. There should be a Christian physics and a Christian mathematics . . . in the sense of showing in science itself how it is that God acts, where he is, what means he uses, and so on. One should be attempting to show that in some cases the actual distribution of physical forces is changed in unnatural ways."[14] Georges Rey has similar, univocal expectations and consequent disappointments with theistic claims about divine action in evolution: "[E]ven for those who regard evolution as simply the manner of God's creation, there is (so far as I know) not the slightest interest in investigating, say, radioisotopes, sedimentary layers, and the fossil record to establish precisely how, when, and where God had any role whatsoever in the creation of atoms, compounds, amino acids, DNA, and so forth that are manifestly required for the development of life, consciousness, and intelligent capacities. Despite what they claim, theists in fact treat Him as an idle wheel that does no serious explanatory work."[15] Leonard Susskind has a similar complaint: "If there is a God, she has taken great pains to make herself irrelevant."[16] If God is a univocal cause, there must be a point of intersection between God and other univocal

---

12. John C. Polkinghorne, "Kenotic Creation and Divine Action," in *The Work of Love: Creation as Kenosis*, ed. John C. Polkinghorne (Grand Rapids, Mich.: Eerdmans, 2001), 97. Polkinghorne does sometimes speak eloquently of divine transcendence: "All theological thinking is a precarious balancing act, seeking recourse to the coincidence of opposites in an attempt to use finite human language to discourse about the infinite reality of God" (ibid., 91). At other points, however, he betrays a fundamentally univocal notion of divine action, locating it in the indeterminacy of chaos theory lest it interfere with other worldly causes.

13. Clayton, *God and Contemporary*, 192.

14. Frank B. Dilley, "Does the 'God Who Acts' Really Act?" in *God's Activity in the World: The Contemporary Problem*, ed. Owen C. Thomas (Chico: Scholars Press, 1983), 54.

15. Georges Rey, "Meta-atheism: Religious Avowal as Self-deception," in *Philosophers without Gods: Meditations on Atheism and the Secular Life*, ed. Louise M. Antony (New York: Oxford University Press, 2007), 256.

16. Susskind, *Cosmic Landscape*, 380.

causes, and the logical place to look for it is in the sciences that study those other causes. The causal joint is therefore a "high-stakes debate for those who wish to pursue Christian theology in dialogue with the sciences and our general knowledge of the world."[17]

As a univocal cause, God will necessarily interfere with the causality of creatures if God acts in the world. When two univocal causes are involved in one action, the causality of one must necessarily diminish that of the other. When several sailors carry a lifeboat, for instance, each carries only part of the total weight. The more weight one lifts, the less there is for the others to carry. If the strongest sailor carries all the weight himself, the others are left with nothing to do. Similarly, if we think of God as a cause like any other in the world, God's causality must interfere with that of other agents. An omnipotent God must therefore rob all other agents of their proper causality. Only if God's power is limited can other agents maintain some causal role.

THEOLOGICAL RESPONSES TO THE CONSTRICTION OF CAUSALITY

Theologians have tried several strategies to address the problem of divine action in response to the causal restrictions of modern science. Kirk Wegter-McNelly notes three of these: deism, liberalism, and interventionism. To his list, we might add process theology and various theologies of divine limitation. Here, we will review these five responses.

Wegter-McNelly sees a fundamental assumption of determinism behind the three responses he discusses: "These three views of special divine action developed by Christian thinkers in response to the rise of Newtonian physics—interventionism, deism, and liberalism—differ sharply from one another, yet they brook a common theological constraint. Each accepts the idea that a God who is understood to alter the course of events in the world must be treated on a par with any other object or causal process in the world. Thus, each accepts the claim that in a Newtonian world of strict determinism there is no 'room' in the physical world for God to act in individual events—a viewpoint I call 'theophysical incompatibilism.'"[18] Thomas Tracy sees the same assumption at work in liberal theology.[19] In all of these

---

17. Clayton, *God and Contemporary*, 196. On "univocal cause," see 153n130 and the Glossary.
18. Wegter-McNelly, "Fundamental," 162.
19. "It is a mistake to conclude that modern human beings have adopted, in general, a 'scientific way of knowing' and/or a 'scientific worldview' that rules out talk of divine agency developed within a theological interpretation of the world. The theologians who have made these claims, and

approaches, God's causality is considered univocal with that of creatures. It is necessarily univocal since only one kind of causality is real: mechanistic, efficient causality. The mechanistic causes of science leave no room in the world for a divine mechanistic cause. The introduction of such a cause must therefore constitute a gross interference with the workings of nature.

Interventionism

Interventionism, as Kirk Wegter-McNelly points out, responds to the dilemma of univocal causality by asserting that God does indeed interfere in the world and "simply breaks the laws of nature whenever God wishes to alter the course of the world by acting in a specific event."[20] It is forced to turn God into a kind of divine "lawbreaker," since it accepts the univocal nature of divine action but still wants to assert that God acts in the world.

Deism

To avoid the conundrum of divine interference, the other approaches to divine action try to limit God's power in some way, and so mitigate God's propensity to interfere. Deism teaches that God's action is limited to the moment of creation. God did indeed create the world, but is no longer needed to explain its continued existence and activity. Deism abandons "the notion of special divine action altogether in favor of a God who brings the world into existence and then refrains from any further interaction with it."[21] Nancey Murphy points out that "for modern thinkers, deism has been the most natural view of divine action."[22] Georges DeSchrijver finds this approach particularly prevalent among contemporary cosmologists.[23] It is

---

used them as the basis for far-reaching theological revision, have almost always uncritically presupposed a deterministic picture of the natural world. We can see this in a long line of religious thinkers, from deists in the eighteenth century to Schleiermacher at the founding of liberal Protestant theology in the early nineteenth century to contemporary theologians like Rudolph Bultmann and Gordon Kaufman. For these thinkers, a general metaphysical picture of the world as a closed causal continuum came to be invested with the authority of science by being treated either as a methodological given of scientific inquiry or as a well-established empirical result" (Thomas F. Tracy, "Creation, Providence, and Quantum Chance," in *Quantum Mechanics: Scientific Perspectives on Divine Action*, ed. Robert John Russell, Philip Clayton, Kirk Wegter-Mcnelly, and John C. Polkinghorne [Vatican City State: Vatican Observatory; Berkeley, Calif.: Center for Theology and the Natural Sciences, 2001], 237).

20. Wegter-McNelly, "Fundamental," 161.   21. Ibid., 162.
22. Murphy, "Buridan's," 325.
23. Georges DeSchrijver, "Religion and Cosmology at the End of the 20th Century," *CTNS Bulletin* 14, no. 1 (1994): 12. See also Richard Sturch, *The New Deism: Divine Intervention and the Human Condition* (New York: St. Martin's Press, 1990), 2–3.

exemplified in Stephen Hawking's contention that the laws of science "may have originally been decreed by God, but it appears that he has since left the universe to evolve according to them and does not want to intervene in it."[24]

Liberal Theology

In contrast to deism, liberal theology continues to maintain that God acts in the world, but denies that God acts outside the laws of nature. Friedrich Schleiermacher, often called the father of liberal Protestantism, argues that "as regards the miraculous, the general interests of science, more particularly of natural science, and the interests of religion seem to meet at the same point, i.e., that we should abandon the idea of the absolutely supernatural because no single instance of it can be known by us, and we are nowhere required to recognize it."[25] Rudolf Bultmann considers it inappropriate to view divine action as a cause "which intervenes between the natural, or historical, or psychological course of events."[26] Events in nature are "linked by cause and effect" in a way that leaves "no room for God's working."[27] Divine action is therefore limited to the realm of personal, existential encounter. Talk of God's action in nature must be "demythologized" or translated into the language of personal encounter. To assert that God is the creator, for instance, is not a cosmological statement, but "a personal confession that I understand myself to be a creature which owes its existence to God."[28]

To avoid divine interference with the actions of creatures, Gordon Kaufman envisions God's action in the world as a single, divine "master act." More specific acts of God are accommodated as "subacts" aligned with the master act. So Kaufman affirms a God "whose action is not completely unintelligible to a mind instructed and informed by modern science and

---

24. Hawking, *Brief History*, 122.
25. Friedrich Schleiermacher, *The Christian Faith*, ed. H. R. Mackintosh and J. S. Stewart (Philadelphia: Fortress Press, 1976), 183.
26. Rudolf Bultmann, *Jesus Christ and Mythology* (New York: Charles Scribner's Sons, 1958), 61. "Mythological thought regards the divine activity, whether in nature or in history, as an interference with the course of nature, history, or life of the soul, a tearing of it asunder—a miracle, in fact" (Rudolf Bultmann, "Bultmann Replies to His Critics," in *Kerygma and Myth: A Theological Debate*, ed. Hans Werner Bartsch, trans. Reginald H. Fuller [New York: Harper and Row, 1961], 197).
27. Bultmann, *Jesus Christ*, 65.
28. Ibid., 69. "Bultmann's position is that God's action in the world is hidden in finite causes and is visible only to the eye of faith, while the finite causal nexus itself is completely intelligible to modern science" (Owen C. Thomas, "Summary Analysis," in *God's Activity in the World: The Contemporary Problem*, ed. Owen C. Thomas [Chico: Scholars Press, 1983], 231). "On the liberal account, one might *perceive* God as acting specially in some particular physical event, but this would be merely a matter of one's own subjective perception" (Wegter-McNelly, "Fundamental," 162).

history."[29] This may seem to imply no limitation on divine action, since the master act includes all that happens in the world as ordained to the achievement of some divine goal. On closer investigation, however, the God of the divine master act is found to be incapable of personal intervention. This is not a God who "walks and talks with me."[30] In the end, Kaufman offers a God who presumably works in all events without explaining how God works in any of them.[31]

Maurice Wiles is concerned that any particular action of God would negate the God-given freedom and autonomy of creation. Like Kaufman, he views divine action "in relation to the world as a whole rather than to particular occurrences within it." He argues that "the whole process of the bringing into being of the world, which is still going on, needs to be seen as one action of God."[32] He employs Kauffman's notion of the subacts of creatures under the one master act of God, but denies any causal involvement of God in those subacts.[33] He acknowledges that this minimalist view of divine action verges on deism: "Talk of God's activity is, then, to be understood as a way of speaking about those events within the natural order or within human history in which God's purpose finds clear expression or special opportunity. Such a view is not deistic in the most strongly pejorative sense, in that it allows for a continuing relationship of God to the world as source of existence and giver of purpose to the whole. It is deistic in so far as it re-

---

29. Kaufman, *God*, 147. "The motivation for this detached, single-action view of divine agency appears to be twofold. One is a feeling that modern science leaves us with little choice. The second reason for a detached, single-action account of divine agency is that, if God does nothing in particular, then God cannot be blamed for anything in particular either" (John C. Polkinghorne, "Chaos Theory and Divine Action," in *Religion and Science: History, Method and Dialogue*, ed. W. Mark Richardson and Wesley J. Wildman [New York: Routledge, 1996], 243).

30. Kaufman, *God*, 146-47.

31. "[Kaufman] finally settles for the liberal position that God somehow acts in and through all the events and processes of nature and history to achieve the divine goal but without explaining how this might be understood" (Owen C. Thomas, "Introduction," in *God's Activity in the World*, 10).

32. Maurice Wiles, *God's Action in the World* (London: SCM Press, 1986), 28-29.

33. "A complex action of this kind necessarily contains within itself a number of secondary actions, which together help to make up the one complex act. Gordon Kaufman, to whose treatment of this topic I am much indebted, speaks of the process as a whole as God's 'master-act,' and then goes on to speak of 'subacts performed by God as he works out his purpose.' . . . And in the account that I have given of divine activity I have not followed Kaufman in speaking of God performing any of the subacts which together contribute to God's one act of creating our world" (ibid., 96-97). "It is clear that Wiles denies here any form of causal relation between God's master-act and the particular acts performed by human agents. In this way, however, the claim that the latter can count as 'subacts' of the former, becomes quite vacuous" (Vincent Brümmer, "Farrer, Wiles, and the Causal Joint," *Modern Theology* 8 [1992]: 3).

frains from claiming any effective causation on the part of God in relation to particular occurrences."³⁴

Some liberal theologians believe that the explanations of science have so influenced the contemporary mind that the whole notion of transcendent divine action has become inconceivable. So Langdon Gilkey asserts: "The ordinary experience of contemporary men and women, and so the world they inhabit, possesses for most of us no transcendent dimension; the horizon of that experience seems closed or cramped; the actuality in which we live is composed only of finite, creaturely factors and causes. What is real to most of us, and so alone effective in natural or historical change, are only those natural or human factors."³⁵ Frank Dilley claims that "most moderns, even quite religious ones, *cannot* bring themselves to think in terms of miracles anymore."³⁶

Despite such claims, we would have to agree with Owen Thomas that any assertion that contemporary human consciousness is incapable of admitting God's action in the world is "simply empirically false."³⁷ Although Thomas made his claim in 1983, he still seems to be on safe ground. After presenting the results of a number of recent surveys, Steven Shapin observes: "The triumph of science over religion trumpeted in the late nineteenth century crucially centered on the question of whether or not supernatural spiritual agencies could intervene in the course of nature, that is to say, whether such things as miracles existed. By that criterion, 84 percent of American adults are unmarked by the triumph of science over religion, which supposedly happened over a century ago."³⁸

---

34. Maurice Wiles, *The Remaking of Christian Doctrine* (London: SCM Press, 1974), 38. "The basic difficulty with such views is precisely the fact that they seem to rule out the notion of God's action in nature and history, which is so central a feature of theism. Existentialist theology may speak of an on-going relation of grace and faith experienced in the self-understanding of the believer, but as far as nature and history are concerned, it differs from deism only in refusing to talk about the relation between God and the natural world at all. And Wiles admits explicitly that his position 'is deistic in so far as it refrains from claiming any effective causation on the part of God in relation to particular occurrences'" (Brian Hebblethwaite, *Evil, Suffering, and Religion*, rev. ed. [London: SPCK, 2000], 95).

35. Langdon Gilkey, *Reaping the Whirlwind: A Christian Interpretation of History* (New York: Seabury Press, 1976), 137.

36. Dilley, "Does the 'God Who Acts,'" 54.

37. Thomas, "Introduction," 6.

38. Steven Shapin, *Never Pure: Historical Studies of Science as if It Was Produced by People with Bodies, Situated in Time, Space, Culture, and Society, and Struggling for Credibility and Authority* (Baltimore: Johns Hopkins University Press, 2010), 381. See also John Micklethwait and Adrian Wooldridge, *God Is Back: How the Global Revival of Faith Is Changing the World* (New York: Penguin Books, 2009); and

PROCESS THEOLOGY

Process theology affirms God's action in nature and human history without limiting God to a single master act.[39] It grew out of the process philosophy of Alfred North Whitehead which was formulated, as David Ray Griffin explains, as a reaction against "the supernaturalistic version of theism, with its 'theology of a wholly transcendent God creating out of nothing an accidental universe.'"[40] In contrast, Whitehead proposed that "God is not to be treated as an exception to all metaphysical principles, invoked to save their collapse. He is their chief exemplification."[41]

David Ray Griffin notes that for Whitehead the problem with supernaturalistic theism is that it "conflicts with an assumption essential to 'the full scientific mentality': namely, 'that all things great and small are conceivable as exemplifications of general principles which reign throughout the natural order,' so that 'every detailed occurrence can be correlated with its antecedents in a perfectly definite manner, exemplifying general principles.'"[42] Whitehead was proposing to "theistic religious communities" that they can best "overcome the conflict of their doctrines with scientific assumptions by replacing supernaturalistic with naturalistic theism."[43] Process philosophy therefore comes to birth with an eye to certain assumptions of science. We have seen, however, that such assumptions, insofar as they involve changing the methodology of science into a metaphysics, are really products not of science but of scientism.

Process theology gives a prominent place to divine action. God's influence is an integral aspect of each instance of becoming in a world made up

---

Elaine Howard Ecklund, *Science vs. Religion: What Scientists Really Think* (New York: Oxford University Press, 2010). In addition, a quick Google search for the key words "belief in miracles" and "pew research" will reveal evidence such as the 2007 Pew Forum on Religion & Public Life/U.S. Religious Landscape Survey: "Nearly eight-in-ten American adults (79%) ... agree that miracles still occur today as in ancient times" (available at http://religions.pewforum.org/pdf/report2religious-landscape-study-key-findings.pdf [accessed August 8, 2009]).

39. See David R. Mason's process critique of Kaufman's views in his article, "Can We Speculate on How God Acts?" *Journal of Religion* 57 (1977): 31.

40. David Ray Griffin, "Interpreting Science from the Standpoint of Whiteheadian Process Philosophy," in *The Oxford Handbook of Religion and Science*, ed. Philip Clayton and Zachary Simpson (Oxford: Oxford University Press, 2006), 454. Cf. Alfred North Whitehead, *Process and Reality*, ed. David Ray Griffin and Donald W. Sherburne (New York: Free Press, 1978), 95.

41. Whitehead, *Process and Reality*, 343.

42. Griffin, "Interpreting," 454. Cf. Alfred North Whitehead, *Science and the Modern World* (New York: Free Press, 1967), 5, 12.

43. Griffin, "Interpreting," 455.

entirely of such "becomings." Yet process theology also limits God's action. God acts in each event, but only as a lure, a persuader, who invites the world to progress. God is not an agent of that progress, but only an inspirer of other agents. Each event or actual occasion in the world determines itself and is the agent of its own becoming as it follows or refuses what God proposes.[44]

Whether the process God is really a persuader or a coercer depends on his powers of persuasion. There is a fine line between the kind of persuasion that can ensure the continued advance of creation and a brand of coercion that would overpower the chooser. John Cobb suggests that God may sometimes be a powerful persuader who "may well take the initiative in presenting himself to human occasions with peculiar force and specific efficacy prior to, and quite independently of, their self-preparation or desire for this occurrence."[45] If God's persuasive power is limited, however, to guarantee the contingency and freedom of other agents, God begins to look like just one more univocal cause among others. The process of persuasion then seems a kind of tug-of-war with the outcome—even the eschatological outcome—ever in doubt. Robert Ellis notes: "With greater freedom [among human agents], the chance of God's lure being flaunted deliberately enters, and the outcome is that much more unpredictable."[46] Lewis Ford observes that classical theism "can be serene in the confidence that some day God will wipe out all evil." Process theism, however, "cannot have this traditional assurance about the future.... The forces of evil could conceivably overwhelm God. Against that there is no metaphysical guarantee."[47]

Since the process God is a persuader only, he seems inadequate to the Christian faith and tradition that require a God who acts sovereignly, not one who merely guides and suggests.[48] John Polkinghorne points this out:

---

44. Robert Anthony Ellis explains this process: "God *acts* in every event.... There is an important sense in which nothing would happen at all without God's (basic) action. He gives each occasion its initial aim, which is the best outcome for that occasion given its situation. When that ideal aim is actualized by the occasion, then God's intention is actualized in the world—the consequence is his *act*" (Robert Anthony Ellis, "Can God Act in History? A Whiteheadian Perspective," Ph.D. diss., Oxford University, 1984, 286).

45. John B. Cobb, *A Christian Natural Theology* (Philadelphia: Westminster Press, 1963), 237.

46. R. A. Ellis, "Can God Act," 295.

47. Lewis S. Ford, *The Lure of God: A Biblical Background for Process Theism* (Philadelphia: Fortress Press, 1978), 119–20.

48. "Certainly the impersonal, unconscious, and deficiently actual primordial nature of God affords no soil for a religious bond between man and God. As for the divine consequent nature, it incorporates data from actual entities which have perished and become objectified for it. The conditions for such a prehension do not permit a relationship to spring up between God and the living human

"More significant theologically is the confining of divine interaction to a purely persuasive role. In the end, true initiative lies with the event itself as it 'selects' its own realization ('concrescence'). God's participation is as pleader rather than agent.... Christian theology must seek a more positive account of divine action."[49] Recognizing this shortcoming, some have tried to find a more central place for divine agency in process theology.[50]

Theology of Divine Limitation

To avoid the dilemmas of divine coercion and interference, some theologians propose that God's knowledge and power are limited. Maurice Wiles, for instance, maintains that "God's creation of our world necessarily implies a divine self-limitation in relation to traditional understandings of omnipotence and omniscience."[51] Arthur Peacocke agrees: "God's omniscience and omnipotence must be regarded, in some respects, as 'self-limited.'"[52] Nancey Murphy argues that God limits himself in order "to respect the innate characteristics with which he has endowed his creatures."[53] John Polkinghorne finds that the "act of creation involves a voluntary limitation, not only of divine power in allowing the other to be, but also of divine knowledge in allowing the future to be open."[54] To him, chance also requires divine self-limitation: "God chose a world in which chance has a role to play, thereby ... accepting limitation of his power to control."[55] For Craig A. Boyd and Aaron D. Cobb, "God's choice to actualize a particular cosmic

---

person. It is not even the integral human person who becomes immortal in God; only those selected aspects which can be transmuted into the divine esthetic experience become immortal.... Whitehead does speak very movingly about the loving concern of the divine companion and cosufferer. In systematic terms, however, it is difficult to see how the search for his own esthetic satisfaction makes God good" (James Collins, *God in Modern Philosophy* [Chicago: Henry Regnery, 1959], 322).

49. Polkinghorne, "Chaos Theory," 245.
50. See Sharon Dowd, "Is Whitehead's God the 'God Who Acts'?" *Perspectives in Religious Studies* 9 (1982): 157–70.
51. Wiles, *God's Action*, 80.
52. Peacocke, *Theology for a Scientific*, 155.
53. Murphy, "Buridan's," 355. Cf. ibid., 339–40, 342–43, 345, 348–51, 356. See also Dennis Bielfeldt, "Nancey Murphy's Nonreductive Physicalism," *Zygon* 34 (1999): 625.
54. Polkinghorne, "Chaos Theory," 250. "The balance between the room for maneuver which God has reserved and that which God has given away is, of course, a delicate issue. It is also an issue familiar to theology, for it is the problem of grace and free will, written cosmically large" (Polkinghorne, "The Laws of Nature and the Laws of Physics," in *Quantum Cosmology and the Laws of Nature: Scientific Perspectives on Divine Action*, ed. Robert John Russell, Nancey Murphy, and C. J. Isham [Vatican City State: Vatican Observatory; Berkeley, Calif.: Center for Theology and the Natural Sciences, 1993], 446).
55. Polkinghorne, *Science and Creation*, 63.

order limits the range of possible states of affairs over which God acts and this constitutes a form of divine self-limitation."[56] To Denis Edwards, divine love implies divine limitation: "If divine love involves divine respect for and patience with created processes as well as human freedom, this means that God is not *absolutely* unlimited in freedom and power to achieve the divine purposes. There may be circumstances, and very many of them, when God embraces limits in God's love and respect for finite creatures. God's nature, as lovingly respectful of both human freedom and the finite limits and autonomy of natural processes, may involve limitations on divine action in particular circumstances."[57]

Brian Hebblethwaite thinks that human freedom implies divine limitation: "Creation is an act of God's omnipotence, but in order to relate himself to the creatures he has made, he must limit himself in a manner appropriate to the nature of what he has made, in the case we are considering, free finite persons.... God's omniscience, like his omnipotence, is self-limited by the nature of what he has made. In each case the limitation is logical, given the actual nature of God's creation. He cannot determine the future precisely without destroying his creatures' freedom. He cannot know the future precisely, if his creatures are indeed free."[58] Langdon Gilkey agrees that in giving freedom to creatures, God must limit himself: "The problems of theodicy, of human freedom, and of the goodness of the future ... can be resolved only by rethinking ontologically the way the God of the present acts in relation to human freedom and to the possibilities of the future, i.e., by an explicitly ontological doctrine of the self-limitation in every present of the divine power in relation to the freedom of the creature."[59] Thomas Tracy argues that God limits himself and yet (somehow) remains omnipotent: "In establishing this relation to creatures, God commits himself to a pattern of interaction that qualifies the scope and direction of his activity. He creates a field of other agents whose integrity he respects and so whose independent actions condition his choices. This amounts to a purposeful limitation of the scope of his own activity, but it does not nullify his omnipotence: he

---

56. Craig A. Boyd, and Aaron D. Cobb, "The Causality Distinction, Kenosis, and a Middle Way: Aquinas and Polkinghorne on Divine Action," *Theology and Science* 7 (2009): 392.

57. Denis Edwards, *How God Acts: Creation, Redemption and Special Divine Action* (Minneapolis, Minn.: Fortress Press, 2010), 51–52. "By creating in love, God freely accepts limitations" (ibid., 50).

58. Brian L. Hebblethwaite, "Some Reflections on Predestination, Providence, and Divine Foreknowledge," *Religious Studies* 15 (1979): 440–41.

59. Gilkey, *Reaping*, 235. Cf. ibid., 249, 279, 281.

remains an all-powerful and radically self-creative agent capable of freely regulating his own pattern of life at every moment of his existence. Intentional self-restraint does not represent a renunciation of omnipotence, but rather a renunciation of certain uses of power, and this is entirely in keeping with God's unlimited self-creativity."[60]

We must view God's action as limited if we believe that it would otherwise disturb or interfere with the proper causality of creatures and the nexus of scientific laws. And we will think that God's action must involve such a disturbance so long as we understand God as a univocal cause. But we will have no other way to understand divine action so long as we think of causality itself as a univocal notion. But why should we continue to view causality so narrowly? Contemporary science suggests a much wider notion of causality which opens broader avenues for speaking of divine action.

---

60. Thomas F. Tracy, *God, Action, and Embodiment* (Grand Rapids, Mich.: Eerdmans, 1984), 143–44.

Unlocking Divine Action through the New Theories of Contemporary Science

The developments of contemporary science suggest novel and sometimes strange ways of viewing the natural world. These provide theologians with two fundamentally new options for speaking about divine action. One is to use the developments themselves (or certain interpretations of the theories associated with them). The other is to employ not the interpretations but the expanded notion of causality that they imply. We will explore both options—the first in this chapter and the second in the next.

FEATURES OF SCIENCE THAT UNLOCK DIVINE ACTION

In the first option, theologians use the new openness in nature that appears in certain interpretations of contemporary science to model divine action in ways that were not possible in the worldview of modern science. Thomas Tracy describes this: "Our interest is in mapping possibilities for conceiving of divine action, and if we reject universal determinism, then a new possibility arises.... In an indeterministic world of the right sort, it would be possible for God to act through the structures of nature, yet leave those structures entirely undisturbed. God's action would realize one of the alternative possibilities generated within, but left open by, the causal history of the world. This would alter the direction of the world's development so that events evolve differently from how they would have had God not so acted; but it would do so without displacing natural causes. The result is a non-interventionist and non-miraculous particular divine action."[1]

William Stoeger sees similar possibilities: "How we describe God's relationship with and action in the world must be tempered and partially determined by what we are discovering in the contemporary sciences. There is the familiar negative criterion of avoiding 'the God of the gaps.' But there is a positive resource here as well. The scope, the interconnectedness, and the intricacy of the laws of nature on so many levels—together with the radically evolutionary character of reality—express very strongly, though always imperfectly, some of the principal modes of divine action, and point tantalizingly to other, more profound, and pervasive modes which lie just beyond the horizons of our understanding and our inquisitive gaze."[2] Keith Ward also sees open spaces for divine action, but suggests it be confined to the spaces provided: "Far from excluding the possibility of further divine actions, such a universe invites the possibility of particular divine acts at those points of contingent process, unknown in detail to us, which are allowed and defined by the structure of the world. It follows that it would be wrong either to think of God as excluded wholly from particular action within the world; or to think of him as doing absolutely anything he wants at any particular moment in the world's history."[3]

This approach avoids the interventionist claim that divine action requires a violation of the laws of nature in order to make a space for itself in the world. Instead, it employs the natural openings envisioned by contemporary science. These are not contrary to but part of the scientific account of nature. We will explore how theologians use these openings to discuss divine action, arranging our discussion under the general headings of emergence, indeterminism, and design.

Emergence

The notion of emergence is utilized in several areas of science. We have seen it in connection with the behavior of atomic particles in physics and the action of organisms in biology. In each instance a new whole emerges from its parts and remains in some way distinct from them. The behavior of the whole is not entirely determined by its parts. It rather exercises a distinctive top-down causality on them. When emergence is applied to divine action,

---

1. Thomas F. Tracy, "Theologies of Divine Action," in *The Oxford Handbook of Religion and Science*, ed. Philip Clayton and Zachary Simpson (Oxford: Oxford University Press, 2006), 601.
2. Stoeger, "Key Developments," 199.
3. Ward, *Divine Action*, 36–37.

the causal influence of an emergent whole on its parts is viewed as analogous to the causal influence of God on the natural world. As the emergent phenomenon does not violate the laws of nature in exercising its causality, so divine action does not interfere with the established patterns of nature.[4]

This general analogy is applied to divine action in various ways. One application requires a major refashioning of the traditional notion of God in order to fit the analogy. Steven Dale Crain points out that in the notion of emergence, "a downwardly-acting causal power is embodied in the system out of whose micro-structure the power emerges" and is "ontologically dependent on (i.e., is sustained by) the very micro-structure upon which it acts. Indeed, it is through this very dependence that the emergent power gains access to lower ontological levels in order to effect change there."[5] If God is to affect the world in an analogous way, God must be an emergent phenomenon of the world. Philip Clayton calls this "radically emergent theism" and finds it exemplified in the Gifford Lectures of Samuel Alexander. In this approach, "the divine itself becomes yet another emergent property in natural history—and indeed, presumably, the final one."[6]

Other theologians propose that the top-down causality of emergence may be applied to divine action without turning God into an emergent property of the world. David Bartholomew suggests that God acts by "some form of 'pressure' on physical processes designed to steer them in desired directions." The "pressure" he has in mind is analogous to what happens when we put our thoughts into action. As we are certain that we do this, although we do not know how, so we can be sure that God acts in the world without knowing how: "An idea in our mind is converted into a tangible change in the world through the agency of our bodies and those of others. If a full explanation of how this happens is lacking, we cannot expect to comprehend how God might achieve his purpose."[7]

---

4. "Since emergence primarily takes place in the merging of coupled systems, theology may escape the unfortunate alternatives of an interventionist God who acts by breaking natural laws 'from the outside,' and a God who only sustains the laws of nature uniformly over time. Since there are no pre-ordained laws to break in coupled systems, God's providential interaction with the evolving world can no longer be said to 'break laws' in an interventionist manner" (Niels Henrik Gregersen, "Complexity: What Is at Stake for Religious Reflection," in *The Significance of Complexity: Approaching a Complex World through Science, Theology and the Humanities*, ed. Kees van Kooten Niekerk and Hans Buhl [Aldershot, U.K.: Ashgate, 2004], 153).

5. Steven Dale Crain, "Divine Action in a World of Chaos," *Faith and Philosophy* 14 (1997): 55.

6. Clayton, "Emergence of Spirit," 300. Cf. Samuel Alexander, *Space, Time, and Deity*, the Gifford Lectures for 1916–1918, 2 vols. (London: Macmillan, 1920).

7. Bartholomew, *God of Chance*, 161.

Arthur Peacocke sees God acting though top-down causality on the world as a whole. He is particularly concerned to avoid any violation of the causal nexus of science: "In a world that is a closed causal nexus, increasingly explicated by the sciences, how might God be conceived of as influencing particular events, or patterns of events, in the world without interrupting the regularities observed at the various levels studied by the sciences?" His answer employs an "analogy with the operation of whole-part influence in natural systems." In this way, "God could affect holistically the state of the world (the whole in this context) at all levels." This might occur "without abrogating any of the laws (regularities) which apply to the levels of the world's constituents." Such divine action is "distinguished from God's universal creative action" in that "particular intentions of God for particular patterns of events to occur are thereby effected; *inter alia,* patterns could be intended by God in response to human actions or prayers."[8] He gives a poetic description of this intimate involvement of God in the world: "So might the creator be imagined to unfold the potentialities of the universe, which he himself has given it, selecting and shaping by his redemption and providential action those that are to come to fruition—an Improviser of unsurpassed ingenuity."[9]

Peacocke, like David Bartholomew, uses the mind-body relationship to describe God's causality in the world. He thinks, however, that the analogy will not work if we have a dualistic understanding of that relationship. If the mind is spirit and the body is matter, it is difficult to see how one affects the other. The "causal joint" between thought and physical action becomes obscure. Peacocke therefore uses a "mind-body identitist view," in which the mind is seen as an emergent property of brain states. It is not something distinct from the brain, but a phenomenon that arises from and consists in the vital interaction of brain cells. Using "top-down" causation, Peacocke argues that "states of the brain-as-a-whole ... could be causally effective at the level of neurones, and so of action."[10] Dualism is overcome since mind and brain

---

8. Arthur Peacocke, "Emergence, Mind, and Divine Action: The Hierarchy of the Sciences in Relation to the Human Mind-Brain-Body," in *The Re-emergence of Emergence: The Emergentist Hypothesis from Science to Religion,* ed. Philip Clayton and Paul Davies (New York: Oxford University Press, 2006), 274–76. "If God interacts with the 'world' at this supervenient level of totality, then he could be causatively effective in a 'top-down' manner without abrogating the laws and regularities (and the unpredictabilities we have noted) that operate at the myriad sub-levels of existence that constitute that 'world'" (Peacocke, *Theology for a Scientific,* 159).

9. Peacocke, "God's Action," 469.

10. Peacocke, *Theology for a Scientific,* 160.

are the same reality. States of the brain-as-a-whole (mind) can affect individual cells and vice versa. The causal joint between the whole (mind) and the part (neurones) is conceived in terms of a "transfer of information rather than of energy." Analogously, "the continuing action of God with the world-as-a-whole might best be envisaged ... as analogous to an input of information rather than of energy."[11] Keith Ward agrees with Peacocke's top-down analysis of divine action.[12] William Norris Clarke concurs that divine action may be modeled as a nonenergetic input of information occurring in a way that is invisible to empirical science.[13] Philip Clayton also thinks that God may act by information input and finds it appropriate in this context to introduce the notions of formal and final causality: "In fact, wherever form or structure influences biological process—and such influences are pervasive in the biosphere—one can speak of informational causation.... According to the analog, God could guide the process of emergence through the introduction of new information (formal causality) and by holding out an ideal or image that could influence development without altering the mechanisms and structures that constrain evolution from the bottom up (final causality)."[14]

Peacocke's mind-body analogy seems to imply that God must be an emergent property of the world just as the mind is an emergent property of the brain. He tries to avoid this consequence by employing the notion of panentheism, which he defines as "the belief that the Being of God includes and penetrates the whole universe, so that every part of it exists in him, but that his being is more than and is not exhausted by, the universe."[15] God's being does not emerge from the universe, but rather includes it. God is then

---

11. Ibid., 161.
12. "One does not have to think of this as a matter of there being a set of deterministic laws of physics or biology, which God interferes with occasionally to push things in the right direction. I prefer to use the idea, canvassed by Arthur Peacocke, of 'top-down' or 'whole-part causation' whereby, roughly speaking, the nature of a complex whole influences the nature of its parts. For a theist, the ultimate complex whole consists of the universe and God. God is the ultimate reality, constantly holding the universe in being and determining its general nature" (Keith Ward, *God, Chance and Necessity* [Rockport, Mass.: Oneworld, 1996], 79).
13. "God is constantly working creatively with the ongoing unfolding of the world's own built-in active potentialities, stepping up his creative collaboration at certain key thresholds to inject new information-sets—not necessarily new physical energy—into the process to enable new qualitatively higher ontological centers with new properties to appear on the scene. Such creative intervention, or perhaps better, creative collaboration of God, acting on a totally spiritual level, would entirely escape all empirical observation, quantitative measurement, or scientific detection in any way" (Clarke, *The One*, 256).
14. Clayton, "Natural Law," 630, 633.
15. Peacocke, "God's Action," 463.

in some way identical with the universe, and yet is also something more. To the extent that God's being is identified with the universe, it becomes difficult to distinguish God's action from the activity of natural agents. It seems that their activity is simply named as divine action if it is expressive of God's "particular intentions."[16] Peacocke says, for instance, that the "processes revealed by the sciences are in themselves God acting as creator, and God is not to be found as some kind of additional influence or factor added on to the processes of the world God is creating."[17] The action of creatures is identified not just with God's action but with his being: "[T]he natural, causal, creative nexus of events *is* itself God's creative action. It is this that the attribution of *immanence* to God in his world must now be taken to convey. God is not some kind of diffuse 'spiritual' gas permeating everything (like the discarded ether of the nineteenth century), but all-that-is in its actual processes *is* God, manifested in his mode as continuous Creator."[18] God is not an emergent property of the world since God is the world (and something more).

John Polkinghorne employs chaos theory to find "room for divine maneuver."[19] He argues that "it is natural to consider" the "infinitesimal differences" that give rise to widely different outcomes in chaos theory as "akin to information input," and that such "informational causality will have a holistic or 'top-down' character to it." Given this context, it seems "entirely conceivable that God also interacts with the creation through the input of active information into its open physical process."[20] As in Peacocke's account, the input of such information need not involve any change in the energy of the system: "I do not believe that God is contained within the mind/matter confines of the world, but it is entirely conceivable that he might interact with it ... in the form of information input.... God is not pictured as an interfering agent among other agencies. (That would correspond to energy input.) Instead, form is given to the possibility that he influences his creation in a nonenergetic way."[21] God's action will "always be hidden. It

16. Peacocke, "Emergence, Mind," 275.
17. Peacocke, "Articulating God's Presence in and to the World Unveiled by the Sciences," in *In Whom We Live and Move and Have Our Being: Panentheistic Reflections on God's Presence in a Scientific World*, ed. Philip Clayton and Arthur Peacocke (Grand Rapids, Mich.: Eerdmans, 2004), 144.
18. Peacocke, "God's Action," 452.
19. Polkinghorne, *Science and Providence*, 31.
20. Polkinghorne, "Chaos Theory," 247-49.
21. Polkinghorne, *Reason and Reality*, 45. See also Peacocke, "Space, Time," 280; Crain, "Divine Action," 45-46.

will be contained within the cloudy unpredictabilities of what is going on. It may be discernible by faith, but it will not be exhibitable by experiment.... It will be part of the complex nexus of occurrence from which it cannot be disentangled in some simplistic way that seeks to assert that God did this but nature did that. All forms of agency intertwine in the inter-relating complexity and sensitivity of a chaotic world."[22]

A number of authors have pointed out, however, that the equations that guide chaos theory are themselves deterministic.[23] They represent not an openness in nature, but in our understanding of nature since we cannot track all the infinitesimal influences on major causal outcomes. Nancey Murphy therefore sees chaos theory as providing "epistemological" rather than "ontological" room for divine action—space in our understanding as distinct from space in the natural world.[24] Polkinghorne recognizes these distinctions, but thinks in this case it is reasonable to equate epistemology and ontology: "Unpredictability is an epistemological property, and it is a matter for philosophical debate and decision to conclude what ontological properties are to be associated with it. Those of a realist cast of mind will tend to correlate epistemology closely with ontology, believing that what we know, or what we cannot know, is a reliable guide to what is the case. If this metascientific strategy is followed, unpredictability will be seen as the sign of a degree of causal openness in physical process."[25] Polkinghorne maintains that in a "critical realist re-interpretation of what is going on, these epistemological uncertainties become an ontological openness, permitting us to suppose that a new causal principle may play a role in bringing about future developments.... Thus a realist reinterpretation of the epistemological unpredictabilities of chaotic systems leads to the hypothesis of an ontological openness within which new causal principles may be held to be operating which determine the pattern of future behavior and which are of an holistic character."[26] He opines that

22. Polkinghorne, "Chaos Theory," 247–49.
23. See Clayton, *God and Contemporary,* 195–96.
24. "The real value of chaos theory for an account of divine action is that it gives God a great deal of 'room' in which to effect specific outcomes without destroying our ability to believe in the natural causal order. The room God needs is not space to work within a causally determined order—ontological room—but rather room to work within our perceptions of natural order—epistemological room" (Murphy, "Buridan's," 38).
25. Polkinghorne, "Space, Time," 979. See also John C. Polkinghorne, "Chaos and Cosmos: A Theological Approach," in *Chaos: The New Science,* Nobel Conference 26 (Saint Peter, Minn,: Gustavus Adolphus College, 1993), 105–17.
26. Polkinghorne, *Belief in God,* 62–63. "The original [chaos] theory had a deterministic ontology (expressed by its Newtonian equations) but this resulted in an unpredictable epistemology.

"many take with undue seriousness the deterministic Newtonian equations from which the exquisitely sensitive solutions of chaos theory were first derived," and maintains that they should rather be seen as "approximations to a more subtle and more supple reality." He concludes that there is "no valid obligation to adhere to the notion of deterministic chaos" and that, instead, "it is possible to be more bold in metaphysical speculation concerning the openness of such systems."[27] Although Polkinghorne presents these arguments as a brand of realism, proceeding from "a realist cast of mind,"[28] it should be noted that such a facile identity of "what we know" with "what is the case" generally goes under the title of idealism rather than realism.[29]

Indeterminism

Indeterminism has been a watchword for the Copenhagen interpretation of quantum mechanics, which views uncertainty or indeterminism not as the result of our limited ability to know and measure, but as an ontological feature of the world itself.[30] This overthrows the deterministic worldview of Newtonian physics by asserting an objective openness or indeterminacy in nature. A number of theologians have made the indeterminacy of this interpretation of quantum mechanics a key factor in their discussion of divine action.[31]

Instead of adopting the conventional strategy of saying that this shows that simple determinism underlies even apparently complex random behavior, I prefer the realist strategy of seeking the closest alignment of ontology and epistemology (theory and behavior) by modifying the theoretical basis along the lines proposed. This strategy then has the additional advantage of accommodating the notion of top-down causality in a natural way" (ibid., 65).

27. Polkinghorne, "Space, Time," 979. Robert Russell allows that, although "chaos theory is indisputably a deterministic theory," Polkinghorne's notion of "holistic chaos" may allow him to "turn to chaos theory and suggest that reality is ontologically open" (R. J. Russell, *Cosmology*, 130–31).

28. Polkinghorne, "Space, Time," 979.

29. Here, Arthur Fine's admonition regarding realist interpretations of quantum physics seems apt: "[N]ot even realism requires that the order of reality be isomorphic to the order of thought. That is rationalist dogma, quite independent of realism" (Fine, *Shaky Game*, 201).

30. "For the most widely accepted interpretation of the equations of quantum probabilities holds that the limitations on our knowledge of quantum states are intrinsic to the world itself. It is not that better theories or measuring apparatus will someday allow us to specify the location and momentum of a subatomic particle with exact precision. Rather, there are good physical reasons to think that precise knowledge of this sort will never be possible (the Heisenberg uncertainty principle), in part because the amount of energy necessary for producing this measurement would change or eliminate the very state we were seeking to measure. More controversial but still widely shared is the so-called Copenhagen interpretation of quantum mechanics, which argues for an actual *ontological indeterminacy*: nature itself is indeterminate at the quantum level" (Clayton, *God and Contemporary*, 193–94).

31. "According to one view God's action is located at the heart of matter where physicists have

As early as 1956, E. L. Mascall suggested that whether or not a Geiger counter registers at a given moment "may be due solely to the primary causality of God."[32] William Pollard sees God as determining all the indeterminacies of quantum physics: "The enigma of history resides in the fact that every event is at one and the same time the result of the operation of universal natural laws and the object of the exercise of the divine will.... As history unfolds, the world moves forward in accordance with the inner requirements of its structure and the universal laws to which it is subjected. This structure is, however, so constituted and the laws under which it operates so framed as to open innumerable alternatives.... Because of this it is possible either to assert that all events without exception are subject to the universal laws of nature and to sift out of the profusion of events those which make manifest the universal scope of this assertion, or to assert with equal validity that all events without exception are responsive to the will of Almighty God and to sift out of the profusion of events those which make manifest His universal sovereignty."[33]

Ian Barbour also sees quantum indeterminacy as a possible locus for divine action: "Quantum events have necessary but not sufficient physical causes. If they are not completely determined by the relationships described by the laws of physics, their final determination might be made directly by God. What appears to be chance ... may be the very point at which God acts.... God does not have to intervene as a physical force pushing electrons around but instead actualizes one of the many potentialities already present—determining, for example, the instant at which a particular radioactive atom decays."[34]

Naming quantum indeterminacy as a locus for divine action, Owen Gingerich suggests that "the intersection between the world of physics and biology and the world of theology could well lie in that hazy netherland of quantum uncertainty."[35] Philip Clayton believes that quantum mechanics

---

revealed a fundamental uncertainty principle. This is the point beyond which causal chains of events can be traced no further. What appears to us, in our ignorance, as chance is, in reality, the guiding hand of God" (Bartholomew, *God of Chance*, 123).

32. E. L. Mascall, *Christian Theology and Natural Science: Some Questions on Their Relations* (New York: Ronald Press, 1956), 201.

33. William G. Pollard, *Chance and Providence: God's Action in a World Governed by Scientific Laws* (London: Faber and Faber, 1958), 114.

34. Barbour, *Nature*, 27.

35. Gingerich, *Space, Time*, 20.

offers "an area in which sense could be made of divine intervention *without* doing damage to the integrity of science *or* making oneself vulnerable to the embarrassment of further scientific progress." In this way, it "offers theology resources found in no other area of the physical sciences."[36]

Thomas Tracy, while careful not to limit God's involvement in the world to quantum indeterminacy, does see it as one possible avenue of divine action: "[T]heists who affirm God's freedom as Creator have no basis for denying that God *could* act this way should God choose to do so."[37] Nancey Murphy argues more strongly that since nature, in the Copenhagen interpretation of quantum mechanics, provides necessary, but not sufficient, causes for quantum events, God must be the cause of all such events: "My proposal is that God's governance at the quantum level consists in activating or actualizing one or another of the quantum entity's innate powers at particular instants, and that these events are not possible without God's action. This is the manner and extent of God's government at this level of reality."[38] She sees this approach as a compromise between the Aristotelian and Newtonian accounts of nature: "Notice also that this view splits the difference between Newton's view of the utter passivity of matter and Aristotle's view of substances as possessing their own inherent powers to act. On this view, created entities have inherent powers, yet they are radically incomplete: they require God's cooperation in order to be actualized."[39] By positing this cooperation between divine and creaturely causality, Murphy believes that she avoids the occasionalism which would otherwise result if God alone determined every quantum event and those events in turn determined all phenomena at the macrolevel.[40]

Murphy contends that God's action at the quantum level may sometimes

---

36. Clayton, *God and Contemporary*, 194, 214. At the same time, he does not see this as the *only* way God might act in the world: "It remains metaphysically possible, of course, that a God who created the universe could bring about any effect within that universe that God might choose to accomplish" (Clayton, "Natural Law," 628).

37. T. F. Tracy, "Theologies," 609. See also Thomas F. Tracy, "Particular Providence and the God of the Gaps," *CTNS Bulletin* 15, no. 1 [1995]: 13–14); Thomas F. Tracy, "Evolution, Divine Action, and the Problem of Evil," in *Evolutionary and Molecular Biology: Scientific Perspectives on Divine Action*, ed. Robert John Russell, William R. Stoeger, and Francisco J. Ayala [Vatican City State: Vatican Observatory; Berkeley, Calif.: Center for Theology and the Natural Sciences, 1998], 517).

38. Murphy, "Buridan's," 342. Like Thomas Tracy, however, Murphy does not limit God's activity to the quantum level only: "In addition to creation and sustenance, God has two modes of action within the created order: one at the quantum level (or whatever turns out to be the most basic level of reality) and the other through human intelligence and action" (ibid., 339).

39. Ibid., 344.

40. "To say that each sub-atomic event is solely an act of God would be a version of occasionalism" (ibid., 340). See also T. F. Tracy, "Theologies," 607.

result in unusual events (miracles), depending on what quantum alternatives God has decided to actualize: "I have just been arguing that by tampering with initial conditions at the quantum level, God can bring about extraordinary events; events out of keeping with the general regularities we observe."[41] God limits himself in the production of such events, however, lest what we experience in the world appear too arbitrary: "I am proposing that the uniformity of nature is a divine artifact. God could produce a macroscopic world that behaved in much less regular ways by manipulating quantum events. However, there are two kinds of limits by which God abides. The first is respecting the inherent characteristics of created entities at both the quantum and higher levels—respecting their 'natural rights.' However, within the degrees of freedom still remaining many more strange things could happen than what we observe.... So we must assume that God restricts extraordinary actions even further in order to maintain our ability to believe in an orderly and dependable natural environment."[42]

Perhaps the most dedicated proponent of divine action through quantum indeterminacy is Robert John Russell.[43] He argues that "we can view God as acting in particular quantum events to produce, indirectly, a specific event at the macroscopic level, one which we call an event of special providence.... [Q]uantum mechanics allows us to think of special divine action without God overriding or intervening in the structures of nature."[44] Like Thomas Tracy, he sees quantum indeterminacy not as the exclusive theater of divine action but as "one location or domain where that action may have an effect on the course of nature."[45]

Quantum indeterminacy provides a context for what Russell calls "quantum mechanics non-interventionist objective divine action," to which he gives the acronym "QM-NIODA."[46] God's action at the quantum level is "noninterventionist" since it does not interfere with or violate any of the established laws of nature. It "brings about events which go beyond those described by the laws of nature without contravening or disproving them." It is

---

41. Murphy, "Buridan's," 347.
42. Ibid., 348.
43. "[T]he physicist-theologian Robert J. Russell ... has been a leading advocate of the view that God could intervene supernaturally within the scope of quantum indeterminacy" (Clayton, *God and Contemporary*, 194).
44. Robert John Russell, "Does the 'God Who Acts' Really Act in Nature?" in *Science and Theology: The New Consonance*, ed. Ted Peters (Boulder, Colo.: Westview Press, 1998), 89, 94.
45. Ibid., 92.
46. R. J. Russell, "Quantum Physics," 585–86.

"objective" since it does not merely involve the way that humans subjectively perceive or interpret events in the natural world. Rather, "what God does in bringing about special events is more than what God does in bringing about ordinary events."[47]

Using the Copenhagen interpretation of quantum mechanics, Russell can argue—almost by definition—that when God acts at the quantum level, God does not act as a natural cause since, according to that interpretation, there simply are no natural agents involved at that level: "QM-NIODA does *not* reduce God to a natural cause, because, according to the philosophical interpretation of quantum mechanics deployed here, there are no efficient natural causes for a specific quantum event. If God acts together with nature to produce the event in which a radioactive nucleus decays, God is not acting as a natural, efficient cause."[48]

Russell wisely refrains from attempting to describe "how" God acts in nature.[49] He does say, however, that the outcome of God's activity may be attributed to both God and nature: "God acts as continuous creator together with nature, which supplies the material and formal causes, to bring about quantum events."[50] He does not explain, however, in what way nature provides material and formal causes. As to efficient causality, he clearly attributes the effect entirely to God: "But I am claiming that God acts together with nature to determine which quantum outcome becomes actual; God can know which potential state will become actual, since *God alone causes it to become actual!* In essence, quantum indeterminism is the result of it being God, not nature, which determines the outcome."[51]

In his earlier writings, Russell maintained that some quantum events

---

47. Ibid., 583.

48. Ibid., 587. "If quantum physics signals ontological indeterminacy, we can conceive of God as acting in specific events in nature without violating the laws of nature. According to these laws, nature provides a set of necessary causes, but this set is not sufficient to bring about the actual event. If that is true, if science claims that there is no complete set of natural causes for a quantum event, then we can argue that the addition of divine causality brings these events to completion without violating these laws or without being equivalent to a natural or secondary cause" (Robert John Russell, "Religion and the Theories of Science: A Response to Barbour," *Zygon* 31 [1996]: 38).

49. "I also want to reiterate that I am not proposing an explanation of *how* God acts in nature (i.e., the 'causal joint' problem or the relation between primary and secondary causality); in addition this is, at most, a proposal about one of many domains in nature where the effects of God's acts arise. Hence, for all that has been said here, my proposal is fundamentally circumscribed and moderated by the profoundly apophatic nature of theological language" (R. J. Russell, "Quantum Physics," 592).

50. Ibid., 586. "In short, quantum events occur in part because of God's special providence, in part because of natural causality" (R. J. Russell, "Religion and the Theories," 38).

51. R. J. Russell, "Quantum Physics," 587.

come about entirely through the spontaneity of nature as described by quantum mechanics and that others are caused by God.[52] Later, however, he combines the positions of Murphy and Tracy, saying that God acts in all quantum events, but more intentionally in some: "Actually, we can combine Murphy's pervasiveness of divine causality with Tracy's concern for the event to be objectively special because of the nature of quantum statistics: God acts in all events. (God's action is never 'more' or 'less', but always equally causative.) Still on certain occasions, God will choose to actualize one state in particular, and not the other, because that state, and not the other, promotes life, thus conveying God's intentionality in this particular event."[53]

NIODA explains how certain effects are brought about in the world through God's action at the level of quantum indeterminacy. Such action may be called providential: "It involves *objective* special providence, for it involves a difference in what actually happens; it is objective special *providence*, since it truly conveys God's intentions through events that nurture life and wellbeing in the world; and it is *special* providence, because it is that event that we use to refer to God's providence against the assumed backdrop of the general situation itself: a wonderful outcome, a healing, a renewal of hope. Most importantly, it is *non-interventionist* objective special providence, because it is an act of objective special providence that God achieves without violating or suspending the ongoing processes of nature and the laws that describe them. So in short, God causes all the processes of the ordinary world (general providence), but a few of them genuinely convey special meaning because the choices God makes in causing *them*, and not the other options available to God, bring them about."[54]

---

52. "An alternative would be to say that most quantum events occur by chance, but God influences some of them without violating the statistical laws of quantum physics. This view has been defended by Robert Russell, George Ellis, and Thomas Tracy, and it is consistent with the scientific evidence" (Barbour, Nature, 28).

53. R. J. Russell, "Quantum Physics," 592. To accommodate human freedom, Russell also suggests that "God acts in all quantum events in the universe until the evolution of organisms capable of even primitive levels of consciousness. God then increasingly refrains from determining the neurophysiological outcomes we associate with conscious choices, leaving room for top-down, mind-brain causality in conscious and self-conscious creatures. This would be one version of the standard 'solution' to the problem of free will: namely, God's voluntary or metaphysically necessary self-limitation, but seen now as a temporal development of the limitations, from minimum to maximum" (ibid., 592–93). See also Robert John Russell, "Special Providence and Genetic Mutation: A New Defense of Theistic Evolution," in *Evolutionary and Molecular Biology: Scientific Perspectives on Divine Action*, ed. Robert John Russell, Wllliam R. Stoeger, and Francisco J. Ayala (Vatican City State: Vatican Observatory; Berkeley, Calif.: Center for Theology and the Natural Sciences, 1998), 215.

54. R. J. Russell, "Quantum Physics," 592.

One significant example of such divine action is evolution: "It turns out there is a tremendously important case in which this kind of understanding of noninterventionist objective special providence is of critical importance, and it is precisely where the critics of Christianity have been the most vocal: neo-Darwinian evolution!"[55] Russell explains God's involvement in the evolutionary process: "If God acts at the level of the DNA molecule, contributing to genetic variation, then the combined effect of molecular biology/genetics and natural selection on phenotypically expressed genotype can amplify the effects of divine action to the level of organisms, species, and ecosystems, thus influencing the course of evolution. Diametrically contrary to Monod, evolution is precisely what is needed for divine action, hidden in the undergrowth of quantum chance, to realize the divine intentions for the world."[56]

Noninterventionist divine acts may be providential, but they are not miracles: "*NIODA is not meant to address 'miracles.'* Objectively special divine acts support and fulfill the meaning of God's general acts that provide for the regularities of nature even as they go beyond their meaning in surprising and novel ways. Still, they are not 'miracles' in the Humean sense: they are not interventions by God which suspend the ordinary regularities of nature or violate the laws of nature that we construct to describe these regularities. Nor are they what theologians for millennia have meant by miracles, namely the nature miracles, the healing miracles, and the central threefold miracle of the Incarnation, Resurrection, and Ascension of Christ—events which involve the transformation of nature as a whole and with it the transformation of the laws of nature."[57]

This leaves us with the question of what sorts of events "nature miracles" and "healing miracles" are, if they are neither instances of NIODA nor

---

55. R. J. Russell, "Does the 'God Who Acts,'" 90–91.
56. R. J. Russell, "Religion and the Theories," 38. See also R. J. Russell, "Quantum Physics," 590. "The lynchpin in Russell's argument was his contention that quantum chance enters necessarily into an explanation of why DNA point-mutations occur. He acknowledged that a host of classic (that is, non-quantum) factors might also play a significant role in evolutionary change, but he argued convincingly that quantum genetic mutation, the source of variation upon which classical factors operate, is ultimately traceable to events that occur at the quantum level (for example, the making and breaking of hydrogen bonds)" (Kirk Wegter-McNelly, "Atoms May Be Small, but They're Everywhere: Robert Russell's Theological Engagement with the Quantum Revolution," in *God's Action in Nature's World: Essays in Honour of Robert John Russell*, ed. Ted Peters and Nathan Hallanger [Aldershot, U.K.: Ashgate: 2006], 99).
57. R. J. Russell, "Quantum Physics," 585. "I want to note here that NIODA is *not* meant to include miraculous divine action" (R. J. Russell, *Cosmology*, 121).

of "the transformation of nature as a whole" (as Russell understands the Incarnation, Resurrection, and Ascension). It is a significant question, since these are precisely the miracles that Bultmann and others found troublesome as violations of the causal nexus of science. Elsewhere, Russell seems to indicate that such miracles are instances of interventionist divine action (a possibility he had never denied): "I agree with Gregersen that God's action, except in such cases as miracles (e.g., some of the key events of the Exodus, the healings in the New Testament, and certainly the Incarnation and Resurrection of Jesus), should best be described as non-interventionist."[58] In a later work, Russell more clearly states his understanding of the relation between miracles and NIODA:

> Note that the liberal and conservative positions can still be articulated in an indeterministic world: Liberals can still assume that all talk about divine acts is merely religious language about ordinary events while conservatives can still insist that God objectively acts by miraculously intervening in the indeterministic processes of nature, but now there is a third alternative as well—NIODA: special acts of God that are objective but not miraculous. This remarkable distinction made possible between miracles and NIODA in an indeterministic world offers theologians for the first time the opportunity to distinguish between objective divine providence in light of science (see, for example, my version of theistic evolution . . .) and those events in scripture and the life of faith which do require the language of miracle, such as the nature miracles and healing miracles in the New Testament. Note: When discussing the resurrection of Jesus, I usually refer to it as "more than a miracle" since his resurrection seems to involve the transformation of nature as a whole rather than an intervention into the processes of nature which leaves them otherwise untouched (as, for example, in the miraculous resurrection of Lazarus).[59]

It seems clear that Russell does not consider NIODA to be the only possible mode of divine action. NIODA is better characterized as a thought experiment, an exploration into one possible mode of divine action.[60] As such it seems an appropriate endeavor for a theology seeking to make divine action intelligible and acceptable to a contemporary scientific audi-

---

58. Robert John Russell, "An Appreciative Response to Niels Henrik Gregersen's JKR Research Conference Lecture," *Theology and Science* 4 (2006): 129.
59. R. J. Russell, *Cosmology*, 128–29
60. "In seeking to explore these possibilities, different people focused initially on different loci of intrinsic unpredictability, some looking to quantum indeterminacy and others to chaotic uncertainty. None of these attempted models should be taken with undue detailed seriousness. They are what a physicist would call 'thought experiments,' attempts to explore and try out ideas in a simplified way, rather than purporting to be complete solutions to the problem of divine action" (Polkinghorne, *Theology in the Context*, 114–15).

ence.[61] Russell suggests as much: "I think we should welcome the specificity of this approach and follow it as far as it can take us. By illuminating the concrete implications of a noninterventionist approach to objective special divine action in light of a particular interpretation of quantum physics, the strengths as well as the limitations of the approach are revealed, which in turn should lead to further insight and new areas of research."[62]

Design

The notion of design appears on the cosmic level in certain discussions of the Big Bang and the anthropic principle. Some religious thinkers, notably Pope Pius XII, have suggested an identification or at least a consonance between the Big Bang and the moment of creation: "In fact, it would seem that present-day science, with one sweeping step back across millions of centuries, has succeeded in bearing witness to that primordial '*Fiat lux*' uttered at the moment when, along with matter, there burst forth from nothing a sea of light and radiation, while the particles of chemical elements split and formed into millions of galaxies."[63] William Dembski also argues that "the big Bang epistemically supports the Christian doctrine of Creation."[64]

Other theologians utilize the anthropic principle to argue for divine de-

---

61. "The Church learned early in its history to express the Christian message in the concepts and languages of different peoples and tried to clarify it in the light of the wisdom of their philosophers: it was an attempt to adapt the Gospel to the understanding of all people and the requirements of the learned, insofar as this could be done.... With the help of the Holy Spirit, it is the task of the whole people of God, particularly of its pastors and theologians, to listen to and distinguish the many voices of our times and to interpret them in the light of the divine Word, in order that the revealed truth may be more deeply penetrated, better understood, and more suitably presented" (*The Church in the Modern World*, no. 44).

62. R. J. Russell, "Divine Action and Quantum Mechanics: A Fresh Assessment," in *Quantum Mechanics: Scientific Perspectives on Divine Action*, ed. Robert John Russell, Philip Clayton, Kirk Wegter-Mcnelly, and John C. Polkinghorne (Vatican City State: Vatican Observatory; Berkeley, Calif.: Center for Theology and the Natural Sciences, 2001), 304. "I believe, in sum, that every approach must be based on a 'what if' approach such as this: an approach which takes a given interpretation of physical theory seriously and resolutely, and yet which recognizes the real possibility that such an interpretation may one day be undermined by advances in physics and philosophy" (R. J. Russell, *Cosmology*, 164).

63. Pope Pius XII, "Modern Science and the Existence of God," *The Catholic Mind* 50 [1952]: 190. The pope immediately goes on to qualify his statement: "It is quite true that the facts established up to the present time are not an absolute proof of creation in time, as are proofs drawn from metaphysics and Revelation in what concerns simple creation, or those founded on Revelation if there be question of creation in time. The pertinent facts of the natural sciences, to which we have referred, are awaiting still further research and confirmation, and the theories founded on them are in need of further development and proof before they can provide a sure foundation for arguments which, of themselves, are outside the proper sphere of the natural sciences" (ibid.).

64. Dembski, *Intelligent Design*, 205.

sign in the origination of the universe.[65] John Polkinghorne, for instance, suggests a divine alternative to the "many worlds" account of the fine-tuning of the universe: "A possible explanation of equal intellectual respectability—and to my mind greater economy and elegance—would be that this one world is the way it is because it is the creation of the will of a Creator who purposes that it should be so."[66]

In the area of biological evolution, Michael Behe and William Dembski argue that certain systems in nature are of such complexity that they cannot be the result of chance or natural selection, but only of design. Although the obvious choice for the designer is God, they do not name God as the only possible designer.[67] Their reticence may stem from their desire to incorporate ID into empirical science rather than consign it to philosophy or theology.[68] Comparing his arguments to those of William Paley (1743–1804), the famous proponent of design arguments for the existence of God, Behe notes:

The most important difference is that my argument is limited to design itself; I strongly emphasize that it is not an argument for the existence of a benevolent God, as Paley's was. I hasten to add that I myself do believe in a benevolent God, and I

---

65. For a review of the theological implications of the anthropic principle, see George Francis Rayner Ellis, "The Theology of the Anthropic Principle," in *Quantum Cosmology and the Laws of Nature: Scientific Perspectives on Divine Action*, ed. Robert John Russell, Nancey Murphy, and C. J. Isham (Vatican City State: Vatican Observatory; Berkeley, Calif.: Center for Theology and the Natural Sciences, 1993), 367–405; and William Lane Craig, "Design and the Anthropic Fine-Tuning of the Universe," in *God and Design: The Teleological Argument and Modern Science*, ed. Neil A. Manson (London: Routledge, 2003), 155–77.

66. Polkinghorne, *One World*, 80. Robert Spitzer also argues that the highly improbable set of initial conditions in the Big Bang implies an "underlying supernatural plan" (Robert J. Spitzer, "Indications of Creation in Contemporary Big Bang Cosmology," *Philosophy in Science* 10 [2003]: 92).

67. "As a result, intelligent design presupposes neither a creator nor miracles. Intelligent design is theologically minimalist. It detects intelligence without speculating about the nature of the intelligence" (Dembski, *Intelligent Design*, 107). "Whereas the creator underlying scientific creationism conforms to a strict, literalist interpretation of the Bible, the designer underlying intelligent design need not even be a deity" (Dembski, *Design Revolution*, 44).

68. "Another important point to emphasize right at the beginning is that mine is indeed a scientific argument, not a philosophical or theological argument.... By calling the argument scientific I mean first that it does not rest on any tenet of any particular creed, nor is it a deductive argument from first principles. Rather, it depends critically on physical evidence found in nature. Second, because it depends on physical evidence it can potentially be falsified by other physical evidence. Thus it is tentative, only claiming that it currently seems to be the best explanation given the information we have available to us right now" (Behe, "Modern Intelligent," 278). "Intelligent design is a strictly scientific theory devoid of religious commitments" (Dembski, *Design Revolution*, 44). Of course, those who argue that ID is not science but pseudoscience are legion. Its merits as a philosophical or theological argument are also disputed: "Statements rejecting intelligent design as science have been issued by more than a hundred scientific organizations, and by dozens of religious denominations" (Peter M. J. Hess, "Creation, Design and Evolution: Can Science Discover or Eliminate God?" *University of St. Thomas Journal of Law and Public Policy* 4, no. 1 [2010]: 107).

recognize that philosophy and theology may be able to extend the argument. But a scientific argument for design in biology does not reach that far. Thus, while I argue for design, the question of the identity of the designer is left open. Possible candidates for the role of designer include: the God of Christianity; an angel—fallen or not; Plato's demiurge; some mystical new-age force; space aliens from Alpha Centauri; time travelers; or some utterly unknown intelligent being. Of course, some of these possibilities may seem more plausible than others based on information from fields other than science. Nonetheless, as regards the identity of the designer, modern ID theory happily echoes Isaac Newton's phrase, *hypothesis non fingo*.[69]

On whether ID's designer is the Christian God, Michael Ruse notes: "Dembski does not want to assert this absolutely . . . but he certainly gives the green light to one who, having accepted an intelligent designer, would understand or interpret this in the light of the Christian faith."[70]

CRITIQUE OF THIS APPROACH TO DIVINE ACTION

By employing interpretations of the theories of contemporary science to speak of divine action, theologians have certainly opened a fruitful path for the theology/science dialogue. To use Robert Russell's metaphor, they demonstrate that the "bridge" between theology and science is already complete and capable of supporting a mutually beneficial exchange of ideas.[71] For all its fruitfulness, however, the approach is not unproblematic. One inherent liability is that if a particular scientific interpretation changes or is superseded, the theology that incorporates it will be invalidated.[72] Some

---

69. Behe, " Modern Intelligent," 277. Behe goes on to point out that quite a "lesser god" might be sufficient for his purposes: "The fact that modern ID theory is a minimalist argument for design itself, not an argument for the existence of God, relieves it of much of the baggage that weighed down Paley's argument. First of all, it is immune to the argument from evil. It matters not a whit to the scientific case whether the designer is good or bad, interested in us or uninterested. It only matters whether an explanation of design appears to be consistent with the biological examples I point to. Second, questions about whether the designer is omnipotent, or even especially competent, do not arise in my case, as they did in Paley's. Perhaps the designer isn't omnipotent or very competent. More to the point, perhaps the designer was not interested in every detail of biology, as Paley thought, so that, while some features were indeed designed, others were left to the vagaries of nature. Thus the modern argument for design need only show that intelligent agency appears to be a good explanation for some biological features" (ibid., 277–78).

70. Michael Ruse, "Modern Biologists and the Argument from Design," in *God and Design: The Teleological Argument and Modern Science*, ed. Neil A. Manson (London: Routledge, 2003), 311.

71. See Robert John Russell, "Completing the Bridge: The New CTNS Logo," *Theology and Science* 6 (2008): 9–11.

72. Consider, for instance, Stephen Dale Crain's critique of John Polkinghorne's account of divine action: "Any discovery or theoretical development that suggested that chaotic systems, or even quantum systems, are not indeterministic would at very least count against his model. This seems

such risk, however, may be inevitable if theology is not to ignore science entirely.[73] A more trenchant difficulty is evident in the starting point of this approach to divine action. Almost all who pursue it begin from a fundamental desire to describe divine action in a way that does not interfere with the laws of science. The desire to avoid such interference of course presupposes that such interference is possible—that the creator might act in such a way as to interfere with the very world he has created. Such causal interference is possible, however, only between univocal causes. It seems then that lurking somewhere behind this mode of discussing divine action there must be a univocal understanding of divine causality.[74]

To some thinkers finding a noninterfering mode of divine action is imperative since only such divine action would be compatible with our contemporary understanding of the natural world.[75] God can act in the world only if God acts without interference. To other thinkers finding a noninterfering approach to divine action is one option among many for naming how God acts in the world.[76] The approach is valuable, not as the only way to understand divine action, but as one possibly fruitful way. In either case, the locus for God's action is established by employing interpretations of scientific theories that posit an objective indeterminism in nature. Any theol-

---

to me an unhealthy, even unacceptable, relationship between science and theology, for in this case a scientific discovery could cast doubt on whether in principle God can act in the world" (Crain, "Divine Action," 57).

73. As Steven Dale Crain notes: "This raises a question of profound importance for the dialogue between theology and science: to what extent should theological proposals depend on current scientific theories? On one extreme, any such dependence is rejected. In this case, developments in science cannot possibly pose risks to theology. This option seems both unwise in principle (theology must address the world as best we understand it) and impossible to carry out in practice (our understanding of the natural world, even on a most basic level, as well as our metaphysical speculations, are inextricably entangled with modern science). The opposite extreme I wish to reject here is pinning the intelligibility and intellectual respectability of a religious belief—in this case, the belief that God acts in the world—on a particular development in contemporary science, something I believe Polkinghorne has done. He does so by making the first, and perhaps the second of the following two claims: (1) if God is to act in the world, macroscopic indeterministic physical systems of some sort must exist (weaker claim); and (2) if God acts in the world, God does so specifically through 'chaotic' systems, which must therefore be indeterministic (stronger claim). If Polkinghorne in fact is only making the weaker claim, his position puts theology far less at risk than if he is asserting both claims" (ibid.).

74. On the meaning of the term "univocal cause," as I am using it here, see the glossary and my remarks in this chapter under "Locking Divine Action into Univocal Causality."

75. See, for example, Peacocke, "Emergence, Mind," 274–76; Peacocke, *Creation*, 60, 134; Peacocke, *Theology for a Scientific*, 159.

76. See, for example, T. F. Tracy, "Theologies," 601, 609; T. F. Tracy, "Particular Providence," 13–14; T. F. Tracy, "Evolution, Divine Action," 517.

ogy that employs this strategy is open to criticism regarding the particular scientific interpretation it employs, the sort of "room" it provides for God's action, and its implicit understanding of the deity who acts in that room. We can review such criticisms under the headings of emergence, indeterminism, and design.

Emergence

We have seen how Arthur Peacocke and John Polkinghorne use the top-down causality of emergence in certain interpretations of complexity or chaos theory as a locus for divine action. God acts by providing an input of information that does not involve an input of energy. One problem for both Peacocke and Polkinghorne, therefore, is whether information input without energy input is possible. Peacocke himself is aware of this issue: "How can God exert his influence on, make an input of information into, the world-as-a-whole without an input of matter/energy? This seems to me to be the ultimate level of the 'causal joint' conundrum, for it involves the very nature of the divine being in relation to that of matter/energy and seems to be the right place in which to locate the problem."[77] Denis Bielfeldt asks "how there can be a real flow of information without the transmission of energy?"[78] After wrestling with "Polkinghorne's notion that God's action does not add energy to a physical system," Wesley Wildman concludes: "I am not sure that zero-energy action makes sense."[79] Willem B. Drees asserts that there "seems to be no basis in physics for the claim that there is transfer of information without transfer of energy."[80]

---

77. Peacocke, *Theology for a Scientific*, 164. See also Peacocke, "God's Interaction with the World: The Implications of Deterministic 'Chaos' and of Interconnected and Interdependent Complexity," in *Chaos and Complexity: Scientific Perspectives on Divine Action*, ed. Robert John Russell, Nancey Murphy, and Arthur R. Peacocke (Vatican City State: Vatican Observatory; Berkeley, Calif.: Center for Theology and the Natural Sciences, 1995), 282, 286–87.

78. Bielfeldt, "Can Western Monotheism Avoid Substance Dualism?" 167. "I have claimed in this section that the noninterventionist account of divine agency must make sense of information transfer without energy transfer or must countenance downward causation. At this point I do not see how either strategy is likely to succeed. We do not have a theory for how information can be propagated in the absence of energy. We do not have empirical evidence for the existence of real irreducible causal power at the higher level that is not finally determined by events and processes at lower levels" (ibid., 173).

79. Wesley Wildman, "Further Reflections on 'The Divine Action Project,'" *Theology and Science* 3 (2005): 72.

80. Willem B. Drees, "Gaps for God?" in *Chaos and Complexity: Scientific Perspectives on Divine Action*, ed. Robert John Russell, Nancey Murphy, and Arthur R. Peacocke (Vatican City State: Vatican Observatory; Berkeley, Calif.: Center for Theology and the Natural Sciences, 1995), 223.

Another liability for Polkinghorne is that his notion of divine action is tied to a particular interpretation of chaos theory that is not widely shared. Chaos theory arises from deterministic equations such as those found in Newtonian science. It does not posit an objective openness or indeterminism in nature, but only in our ability to know the complexities of nature. Polkinghorne, however, argues that the uncertainty of our knowledge points to an indeterminism in nature since epistemology reflects ontology. Although Nicholas Saunders defends his position, many theologians remain skeptical.[81] Wesley Wildman and Robert John Russell point out that "chaos in nature gives no evidence of any metaphysical openness in nature."[82] Kirk Wegter-McNelly agrees that "strictly speaking, chaos theory resides within the deterministic framework of Newtonian physics."[83] Thomas Tracy finds that "Polkinghorne advances an appealing metaphysical conjecture about the open structures of nature 'beneath' the simplifications and idealizations of scientific theory. But it is not clear that chaos theory supports or invites this general metaphysical view. On the contrary, to the degree that we affirm a cautious realism about chaos theory, ... the conclusion would seem to be that the systems in nature described by this theory are in fact deterministic."[84] If chaos theory is ontologically deterministic, it cannot provide the ontological openness for divine action that Polkinghorne is seeking. Denis Bielfeldt therefore thinks that "prospects are bleak for finding a place for divine activity within the processes of a chaotic system."[85]

David Bartholomew points out that even if chaos theory is given an ontologically indeterministic interpretation, God's "room to maneuver" remains rather sparse. "[T]he idea that a large degree of freedom of action is consistent with conforming to a probability law is false." God would have to act sparingly to avoid detection: "[P]rovided that the proportion of occasions on which God chooses to act decisively is negligibly small, it will be impossible to detect his action by scientific means."[86] In the end, Bar-

---

81. See Saunders, *Divine Action*, 173–206.

82. Wesley Wildman and Robert John Russell, "Chaos: A Mathematical Introduction," in *Chaos and Complexity: Scientific Perspectives on Divine Action*, ed. Robert John Russell, Nancey Murphy, and Arthur Peacocke (Vatican City State: Vatican Observatory; Berkeley, Calif.: Center for Theology and the Natural Sciences, 1995), 82.

83. Wegter-McNelly, "Fundamental," 167. Taede Smedes notes that Peacocke also objects to Polkinghorne's theory: "Arthur Peacocke disagrees with Polkinghorne's use of chaos theory, arguing that a full-blown deterministic ontology underlies chaotic behavior" (Smedes, *Chaos*, 173).

84. T. F. Tracy, "Theologies," 606.   85. Bielfeldt, "Can Western," 164.

86. Bartholomew, *God of Chance*, 130.

tholomew finds this account of divine action unsatisfactory: "Some theologians have seen chaos theory as a lifeline offering a means for God to exercise control without disturbing the orderliness of nature. To me this claim seems premature and unconvincing."[87] In a sense, chaos theory opens more pitfalls than possibilities for divine action since God must now avoid interfering both with nature's laws (the causal nexus) and with its randomness.

Indeterminism

The uncertainty principle of the Copenhagen interpretation of quantum mechanics postulates an objective or ontological indeterminism in nature rather than the merely epistemological uncertainty of chaos theory.[88] To that extent, it seems to provide a secure ground for divine action. Its very reliance on that interpretation, however, is open to criticism.

Peter Hodgson points out that the interpretation is based on the philosophy of positivism that is now "largely discredited."[89] Stanley Jaki sees the interpretation itself as the product of an error in logic: "I have already on numerous occasions rendered that fallacy as equivalent to the inference: an interaction that cannot be measured exactly, cannot take place exactly. The fallacy consists in taking the same word 'exactly' in two different senses. The first sense is clearly operational as it refers to the operation whereby an interaction is measured with numerical exactitude, with no margin of numerical error whatever. The other sense is ontological, for the phrase 'to take place' means to happen, to occur, to exist."[90] If Jaki's argument is correct, the Copenhagen interpretation rests on a fundamental error and is hardly a firm foundation for a theology of divine action.

Even if the Copenhagen interpretation is logically valid, however, it remains only one among many possible interpretations of quantum mechanics. Michael Ruse questions the wisdom of tying theology so closely to a par-

---

87. Bartholomew, *God, Chance and Purpose*, 56.
88. "Quantum physics may accept actual or ontological indeterminacy at the subatomic level if, as many believe, there is no single state of affairs or hidden variable 'underneath' the quantum probability functions. By contrast, chaos theory seems to presuppose that the initial conditions are actually one way rather than another. If this is true, the indeterminacy will lie only in the degree of our knowledge of these conditions; the inference from epistemic limit to ontological limit will be blocked" (Clayton, *God and Contemporary*, 195).
89. Hodgson, *Theology and Modern*, 134, 167.
90. Jaki, *Means*, 102. See also Stanley L. Jaki, *Miracles and Physics* (Front Royal, Va.: Christendom Press, 1989), 52–54; Stanley L. Jaki, "Chance or Reality: Interaction in Nature versus Measurement in Physics," in *Chance or Reality and Other Essays* (Lanham, Md.: University Press of America, 1986), 6–7.

ticular scientific theory: "[T]he crux of my discomfort ... is with the general strategy of trying to make science do your theology! I do not want my religious beliefs ... to be a function of the science.... I still think that he [Russell] is willing to entangle science and religion/theology to a degree I want to avoid."[91] Mark Worthing is also cautious. After reviewing some of the liabilities of quantum divine action, he remarks: "Such problems warn of the danger of binding our concept of God and divine providence too closely to any particular theory, whether it be that of classical or quantum physics. Both theories are a rich source of models, metaphors, and paradigms that theology is free to use in its confession of the providential presence of God in the context of modern, scientific worldviews. Yet any attempt to go beyond this would seem an abuse of both science and theology."[92] Niels Henrik Gregersen, on the other hand, is encouraged by the "traction" that the idea of quantum divine action provides between science and theology, even to the extent that "the thesis of a Non-Interventionist Objective Divine Action (NIODA) is crafted as a theological view which is scientifically falsifiable."[93]

Some interpretations of quantum mechanics allow for no ontological indeterminism and so provide no openness for divine action.[94] They assume that there may be or must be natural causes for quantum phenomena

---

91. Michael Ruse, "An Evolutionist Thinks about Religion," *Theology and Science* 6 (2008): 169.

92. Mark William Worthing, *God, Creation, and Contemporary Physics* (Minneapolis, Minn.: Fortress Press, 1995), 134.

93. Niels Henrik Gregersen, "The Complexification of Nature: Supplementing the Neo-Darwinian Paradigm?" *Theology and Science* 4 (2006): 20, 24. See also Philip Clayton, "Toward a Theory of Divine Action That Has Traction," in *Scientific Perspectives on Divine Action: Twenty Years of Challenge and Progress*, ed. Robert John Russell, Nancey Murphy, and William R. Stoeger (Vatican City State: Vatican Observatory; Berkeley, Calif.: Center for Theology and the Natural Sciences, 2008), 85–110.

94. "The crux of the problem ... is that there are several competing interpretations of quantum theory.... These interpretations are all consistent with the scientific evidence, so there is no means by which we can know how things 'really are.' And if we do not know that, it is hard to see how a single theological account can cover all possibilities.... It is not even known whether the reality which quantum theory describes is, in fact, probabilistic; some accounts are deterministic and thus offer no foothold for theistic involvement. Among those on the deterministic side, Einstein was very reluctant to accept that chance is a real element of the world at this level. Others, such as David Bohm, have also sought to find deterministic explanations of the formalism. These often seem rather contrived but, if they are correct, there would be no place for God's action under the guise of chance" (Bartholomew, *God, Chance and Purpose*, 141–42). "It has to be said that religious apologists have not been as circumspect as they might have been in drawing lessons from the new physics. The mathematical formalism of quantum mechanics is open to different philosophical interpretations, making it rash to extrapolate from one alone. The old trap of the god-of-the-gaps has had its victims among those who tried to correlate God's activity with the actualization of one, rather than another, set of physical possibilities inherent in particular states of the subatomic world" (Brooke, *Science and Religion*, 331–32). See also John Hedley Brooke, "Einstein, God, and Time," *Zygon* 41 (2006): 951–52; and Hodgson, *Theology and Modern*, 170; Hodgson, "God's Action," 514.

and criticize the Copenhagen interpretation for arbitrarily cutting off the natural impulse of science to discover those causes.[95] To those still searching for natural causes for quantum events, the introduction of a divine cause must surely seem like a god of the gaps: "I believe that progress in experimental testing and understanding of these theories is such that attempts on the part of theologians to appropriate these theoretical frameworks to provide an avenue for divine action run the risk of the fate of earlier God-of-the-gaps arguments."[96]

Proponents of quantum divine action readily admit that they are relying on a particular interpretation of quantum mechanics and that their approach to divine action might be invalidated if that interpretation were disproved.[97] They seem ready to do so for two reasons. First, they do not think

---

95. "The metaphysical belief in causality seems thus more fertile in its various manifestations than any indeterminist metaphysics of the kind advocated by Heisenberg. Indeed we can see that Heisenberg's comments have had a crippling effect on research. Connections which are not far to seek may easily be overlooked if it is continually repeated that the search for such connections is 'meaningless'" (Karl R. Popper, *The Logic of Scientific Discovery* [London: Hutchinson, 1959], 248). "[I]t has happened many times in the history of science that what seemed impossible at one time became a familiar achievement. Bohr's Copenhagen interpretation would prevent us from even trying to find a new theory, while that of Einstein leaves the door open to future advances" (Hodgson, "God's Action," 508). "Saying that no further advance is possible and that certain questions must not be asked prevents all further progress.... The overwhelming majority of physicists, particularly those who struggle daily in the laboratory, instinctively reject these debilitating beliefs and continue to believe, in the words of Einstein, that 'something deeply hidden had to be behind things'" (Hodgson, *Science and Belief*, 200, 202). "The only constant [in Einstein's writings on quantum theory] is his conception of quantum theory as providing an incomplete description of individual systems. The concept of an incomplete description was meant to be hortatory: that is, to call on us to search for a more complete and better theory" (Fine, *Shaky Game*, 190).

96. Robert J. Brecha, "Schrödinger's Cat and Divine Action: Some Comments on the Use of Quantum Uncertainty to Allow for God's Action in the World," *Zygon* 37 (2002): 921. Michael Langford also sees quantum divine action as merely a "sophisticated version of the 'God of the gaps' approach" (Langford, *Providence* [London: SCM Press, 1981], 79). See also Bartholomew, *God of Chance*, 126.

97. "NIODA [noninterventionist objective divine action based on quantum mechanics] is not undermined by the fact that scientific theories can be given multiple and mutually contradictory interpretations.... I agree that multiple interpretability is a real problem for NIODA, but this is not particularly surprising or unavoidable, since multiple interpretability is a real problem for any theology seeking to engage with scientific theories. In short, every scientific theory is multiply interpretable!... In my view, the best response is to take a 'what if' stance to this problem: be rigorously clear in acknowledging the multiple interpretability of a given theory, in choosing one particular interpretation, and in stressing that this approach to NIODA is hypothetical and tentative. With this stated up front, one can proceed to be as clear as possible about what this interpretation would tell us about the world *if it were true, which it might in fact be*" (R. J. Russell, "Quantum Physics," 584–85). Thomas Tracy echoes this awareness: "[I]n casting our theological lot with a particular interpretation, we take the risk that new developments in physics or in the philosophy of physics will significantly undercut our theological constructions. It is important to acknowledge this possibility in framing our discussion of these matters, and this suggests two caveats. First, the particular interpretive approach we favor should not be presented as 'the' conclusion to be drawn from quantum

they are introducing God to explain some "gap" in the Copenhagen interpretation of quantum mechanics; they are merely exploiting the indeterminism that the theory itself affirms. Though not introducing a "God of the gaps" in the traditional sense of that term, they are very much employing a "God of the gaps" in a new sense insofar as they affirm a God who has created a world with "intrinsic, naturally occurring gaps" in which God may act without disturbing the lawful patterns of nature.[98]

The second reason why proponents of quantum divine action are willing to cast in their lot with the fortunes of the Copenhagen interpretation may be their appreciation of theological method. If theology is "faith seeking understanding," theologians must look for some model or tool that is better known to illumine the necessarily obscure divine mystery that reason cannot penetrate. One of the hazards (or joys) of theology is that a new model may always come along that better illumines the mystery for a particular Christian audience. In this way, Aquinas found Aristotle more useful than Plato in his theology, and St. Patrick presumably found a simple shamrock better for his theological purposes than the intricate trinitarian theology of St. Augustine. For the same reasons, it is theologically justifiable to employ the Copenhagen interpretation as a model for divine action for certain audiences, even though that interpretation may later be discredited. Aquinas, at least, is quite clear that every theological model, itself ever inadequate to the mystery it seeks to illumine, faces the same danger of being overthrown or discarded when a better model is found.[99]

Even if the Copenhagen interpretation is accepted, however, there are still a number of objections to using quantum indeterminacy as a locus for divine action. Otto Hermann Pesch argues that if God is made the hidden cause of quantum events, God becomes just another "part" of the world, one more univocal cause alongside others.[100] Thomas Tracy argues that if

---

mechanics. Second, proposals about the theological relevance of quantum theory should be regarded as tentative and provisional hypotheses reflecting the current uncertainty of the relevant science and the extraordinary difficulty of interpreting it" (T. F. Tracy, "Creation, Providence," 254).

98. "Instead, a successful approach to NIODA must claim that the processes of nature are created by God *ex nihilo* with intrinsic, naturally occurring gaps" (R. J. Russell, "Quantum Physics," 584).

99. See *ST* I, 32, 1, ad 2.

100. "To think of God as a hidden secret in the indeterminateness of natural processes is to think of him as a factor in the world and so as a part of the world" (Otto Hermann Pesch, "Theologische Überlegungen zur 'Vorsehung Gottes' im Blick auf gegenwärtige natur- und humanwissenschwaftliche Erkenntnisse," in *Christlicher Glaube in Moderner Gesellschaft*, ed. Franz Böckle et al. [Freiburg: Herder, 1982], 4.92).

God is made the cause of all quantum events, God's influence will result in a "thoroughgoing determinism."[101] David Bartholomew thinks "it is very doubtful whether there are any quantum events which God could influence whose outcomes might significantly determine what happens at the macro level."[102] John Polkinghorne and Philip Clayton share this concern.[103]

Another problem regarding quantum divine action arises not insofar as its proponents do embrace the Copenhagen interpretation of quantum mechanics, but insofar as they do not. Since the Copenhagen interpretation denies the presence of natural causes for quantum events, proponents of quantum divine action are able to introduce a divine cause for them. This divine cause, almost by definition, cannot interfere with natural causes at the quantum level since, according to the Copenhagen interpretation, there simply are no such natural causes.[104]

The argument appears seamless. If we look more closely, however, we

---

101. T. F. Tracy, "Evolution, Divine Action," 517–18.

102. Bartholomew, *God, Chance and Purpose*, 154–55.

103. "There are a number of difficulties about this proposal in relation to human and divine agency. One relates to the amplification effect. Exactly how the quantum world interlocks with the everyday world is still a question of unresolved dispute.... There is a particular difficulty in using quantum indeterminacy to describe divine action. Conventional quantum theory contains much continuity and determinism in addition to its well-known discontinuities and indeterminacies.... Occasions of measurement only occur from time to time and a God who acted through being their determinator would also only be acting from time to time. Such an episodic account of providential agency does not seem altogether satisfactory theologically" (John C. Polkinghorne, "The Metaphysics of Divine Action," in *Chaos and Complexity: Scientific Perspectives on Divine Action*, ed. Robert John Russell, Nancey Murphy, and Arthur R. Peacocke [Vatican City State: Vatican Observatory; Berkeley, Calif.: Center for Theology and the Natural Sciences, 1995], 152–53). "I am uneasy about it [quantum divine action] as the principal account of God's action in the world. There is an air of contrivance about the whole idea" (Polkinghorne, *One World*, 71–72). See also Polkinghorne, *Reason and Reality*, 40–41. Philip Clayton notes that "on the scientific side, there is as yet no clear understanding of how, if at all, chaotic systems could amplify individual divine actions on the quantum level such that they made a perceptible difference in the physical world" (Clayton, *God and Contemporary*, 221). See also ibid., 203–204, 222; Clayton, *Mind*, 187. In Nicholas Saunders's opinion, "all the existing claims for quantum SDA [special divine action] in relation to current understandings of quantum theory fail" (Saunders, *Divine Action*, 170). See also Timothy Sansbury, "The False Promise of Quantum Mechanics," *Zygon* 42 (2007): 111–21. For a critique of Saunders's arguments, see Wesley J. Wildman, "The Divine Action Project, 1988–2003," in *Scientific Perspectives on Divine Action: Twenty Years of Challenge and Progress*, ed. Robert John Russell, Nancey Murphy, and William R. Stoeger (Vatican City State: Vatican Observatory; Berkeley, Calif.: Center for Theology and the Natural Sciences, 2008), 161–65. See also Russell's response to his critics in R. J. Russell, *Cosmology*, 174–77.

104. "NIODA does *not* reduce God to a natural cause because, according to the philosophical interpretation of the candidate theory of science [the Copenhagen interpretation of quantum physics], there are no efficient natural causes for the specific events in question" (R. J. Russell, "Quantum Physics," 585). "[F]or each event in question, there is no natural efficient cause for science to discover, given that the scientific theory in question is interpreted philosophically as pointing to ontological indeterminism" (R. J. Russell, *Cosmology*, 128).

Unlocking through New Theories of Science • 145

may find that proponents of quantum divine action are able to introduce God as the cause of quantum events only by abandoning the Copenhagen interpretation and adopting a sort of hybrid interpretation that includes elements of both the Copenhagen interpretation and that of its opponents. Scientists solidly situated in the Copenhagen interpretation believe that *no* causes are needed for quantum events. Scientists who oppose the Copenhagen interpretation believe that *natural* causes are needed and should be sought through the usual methods of empirical science. The first group would be puzzled by the postulation of a divine cause for quantum events, since no cause is needed.[105] The second group would wonder at the introduction of a divine cause for quantum events since what is needed is a natural cause.

Only by a selective use of the tenets of both groups can a conceptual framework be forged in which a divine cause for quantum events may seen as possible (Russell) or necessary (Murphy). This is just what the proponents of quantum divine action seem to do. They borrow from the Copenhagen interpretation the tenet that there are no natural causes of quantum events while simultaneously ignoring its conviction that such events require no causes. They then adopt the tenet of the opponents of the Copenhagen interpretation that some causes are needed for quantum events while ignoring their conviction that these causes must be natural and discoverable by empirical science. Proponents of quantum divine action are then in a position to affirm a divine cause for quantum events (since, as the opponents of the Copenhagen interpretation maintain, *some* cause is needed), and to assert that this divine cause cannot interfere with any natural causes (since, as the proponents of the Copenhagen interpretation maintain, there simply are no natural causes at the quantum level with which such a divine cause could possibly interfere).

We can clearly see this selective use and disuse of the Copenhagen interpretation in Nancey Murphy's theology of divine action. She reduces the possible causes of quantum events to four:

Now, the peculiarity of entities at the quantum level is that while specific particles have their distinguishing characteristics and specific possibilities for acting, it is not possible to predict *exactly when* they will do whatever they do. This allows us to

---

105. "Quantum mechanics as currently formulated certainly requires no metaphysical supplementation, and to give it any seems to threaten its very integrity" (Bielfeldt, "Can Western," 163). "[I]f the indeterminacy is part of nature *per se*, then it must be the randomness of that event—its own randomness as it were, not God-guided apparent randomness" (R. A. Ellis, "Can God Act," 88). See also P. Davies, "The Physics," 48.

raise another question: Is the *when*: (1) completely random and undetermined; is it (2) internally determined by the entity itself; is it (3) externally determined by the entity's relations to something else in the physical system; or, finally (4) is it determined by God?

She eliminates the second and third possibilities, using assumptions taken from the Copenhagen interpretation, according to which quantum indeterminacy is not due to our ignorance (epistemological interpretations of quantum indeterminacy) or to determinate causes existing in nature (hidden variables), whether these be internally determined or externally determined. She is then left with two possibilities:

> Insofar as epistemological interpretations of quantum theory and the quest for hidden variables are rejected, we are left with the conclusion that there is no "sufficient reason" either internal or external to the entities at this level to determine their behavior. While these issues are still open, many physicists have rejected both epistemological interpretations and at least local hidden variables. By process of elimination, this leaves options 1 and 4: complete randomness or divine determination.

She then invokes a philosophical argument using "Buridan's ass," the tragic medieval donkey who starved to death when placed immediately between two equally delicious bales of hay since it lacked a "sufficient reason" to choose one over the other. If this parable shows that some cause or sufficient reason is always needed for every event, then quantum events also require a cause, and so option 1 is not viable: "The fact that the inventor of Buridan's ass believed the donkey would starve illustrates the philosophical assumption that all events must have a sufficient reason."[106]

Murphy employs one tenet of the Copenhagen interpretation (that there are no natural causes of quantum events) but ignores another (that such events require no causes). She then uses one intuition of the opponents of the Copenhagen interpretation (that quantum events require some cause) but ignores another (that this must be a natural cause). By her selective use of both the proponents and opponents of the Copenhagen interpretation, Murphy is able to carve out a space for God as the determiner of quantum events: "I shall argue that the better option is divine determination."[107] Since some cause of

---

106. Murphy, "Buridan's," 341. Robert Russell agrees with Murphy that a sufficient reason is needed for quantum events: "Tracy explores the option that God acts in some but not all quantum events. This option seems to violate the principle of sufficient reason, since some quantum events would occur without sufficient prior conditions, constraints or causes" (R. J. Russell, "Special Providence," 215).

107. Murphy, "Buridan's," 341–42.

quantum events is needed (as the opponents of the Copenhagen interpretation maintain) and since no natural causes of quantum events exist (as the proponents of the Copenhagen interpretation insist), a divine cause may be introduced that cannot interfere with the (nonexistent) natural causes.

Her argument may be self-consistent, but it agrees neither with the Copenhagen interpretation nor with that of its opponents. This seems to defeat the very reason for introducing quantum divine action in the first place, since it seems to have been formulated as a theology that would be acceptable (at least in principle) to scientists, especially those who subscribe to the Copenhagen interpretation of quantum physics.[108] Murphy's argument, however, contradicts both the Copenhagen interpretation (that says that no causes are needed) and the views of its opponents (who say that a natural cause is needed).

In addition to questioning Murphy's use (or disuse) of the Copenhagen interpretation, one might also question the univocal nature of the God she introduces as the determiner of quantum events. The opponents of the Copenhagen interpretation are looking for natural causes of quantum events, such as David Bohm's "hidden variables."[109] Murphy seems to be proposing God as a univocal cause—at least this seems to be implied in her facetious (though telling) assertion: "To put it crudely, God is the hidden variable."[110]

In summary, it seems possible to postulate an "ontological gap" in nature using quantum theory only if one borrows both from those who support the Copenhagen interpretation and from those who oppose it. To scientists who subscribe to the Copenhagen interpretation, there is no "gap" into which one might insert a cause of quantum events since they simply have no cause. To opponents of the Copenhagen interpretation, there is no "gap" in nature, only a gap in our knowledge of the natural causes at work in nature. The supposed "ontological gap" then appears as a mirage that becomes visible only if one borrows in highly selective ways from both the proponents and opponents of the Copenhagen interpretation.

---

108. "Murphy has sought to show that both top-down influence and bottom-up causality via quantum-level phenomena are thinkable, and she has speculated that chaos effects might help make quantum effects felt far and wide.... If the question is, 'Is it possible?' I think Murphy has made her case. But if one asks, 'Is it plausible?' many scientists, confronted with Buridan's-ass-like quantum particles and God as the hidden variable, may well have a different response" (Clayton, *God and Contemporary*, 219).

109. See Polkinghorne, *Quantum World*, 56.

110. Murphy, "Buridan's," 342.

Design

The notion of design, as it appears in discussions of the Big Bang, the anthropic principle, and the theory of evolution, has provided theologians with another opportunity to employ the theories of contemporary science to speak of divine action. Some theologians have associated the Big Bang itself with the divine act of creation.[111] Others caution, however, that science cannot establish the Big Bang as an absolute beginning.[112] William Stoeger points out that the Big Bang and the doctrine of creation deal with quite different things: "The origins with which science can deal are always what we might call 'relative origins,' which are indeed very important, absolutely crucial, for us to understand. But they are not absolute, or ultimate, origins."[113]

Invoking the anthropic principle, some theologians point to God as the designer who fine-tunes the intricate forces involved in the first instants of the universe to produce a world capable of human life. David Bartholomew observes, however, that this will be a deistic God if its role is limited to such initial fine-tuning: "Evidence of purpose can ... be found in the rather special combinations of circumstances when things began. This is sufficient to retain a place for theism if only of a very limited kind. At best it amounts to a new style deism in which the universe is set going at the beginning of time along an indeterminate path and according to no clear plan."[114] Aside from

---

111. See, e.g., Pope Pius XII, "Modern Science," 190; Dembski, *Intelligent Design*, 205; and Drees, *Beyond*, 17–40.

112. "Since the Big Bang theory does not in fact exclude the possibility of an antecedent stage of matter, it can be noted that the theory appears to provide merely indirect support for the doctrine of *creatio ex nihilo* which as such can only be known by faith" (International Theological Commission [ITC], *Communion and Stewardship: Human Persons Created in the Image of God*, no. 67, [Vatican City State, 2004], available at http://www.vatican.va/roman_curia/congregations/cfaith/cti_documents/rc_con_cfaith_doc_20040723_communion-stewardship_en.html [accessed December 27, 2008]). See also Drees, *Beyond*, 41–75.

113. Stoeger, "The Origin of the Universe," 263. See also William R. Stoeger, "The Big Bang, Quantum Cosmology, and creatio ex nihilo," in *Creation and the God of Abraham*, ed. David Burrell, Carlo Coglioti, Janet Soskice, and William R. Stoeger (New York: Cambridge University Press, 2010), 152–75; Ernan McMullin, "How Should Cosmology Relate to Theology?" in *The Sciences and Theology in the Twentieth Century*, ed. Arthur Peacocke (South Bend, Ind.: University of Notre Dame Press, 1981), 30; William E. Carroll, "Thomas Aquinas, Creation, and Big Bang Cosmology," in *Science and Theology: Ruminations on the Cosmos*, ed. Chris Impey and Catherine Petry (Vatican City State: Vatican Observatory, 2003), 1–18; Robert John Russell, "The Doctrine of Creation Out of Nothing in Relation to Big Bang and Quantum Cosmologies," in *The Human Search for Truth: Philosophy, Science, Theology: The Outlook for the Third Millennium, International Conference on Science and Faith, The Vatican, 23–25 May 2000* (Philadelphia: Saint Joseph's University Press, 2002), 108–29.

114. Bartholomew, *God of Chance*, 31–32.

the liability of deism, there is also the danger that this designer God might become another god of the gaps if a natural explanation for fine-tuning is discovered: "SAP [strong anthropic principle] explanations are also vulnerable to the future development of scientific theories.... The argument assumes that the anthropic coincidences are here to stay. However, some of these features, which apparently point to design, or perhaps even all of them, might find more traditional scientific explanations in future theories."[115] William Norris Clarke concludes that the "fine tuner" God sounds too much like the god of the gaps who has been "progressively put out of a job" as science advances.[116] Christopher Mooney contends that the anthropic principle offers an inadequate foundation for arguing to a designer God: "It is philosophically deficient because it relies to a great extent on a large gap in present scientific knowledge. If it is to be based only on the current scientific inability to explain the tightly knit character of the cosmos, then it suffers from all the weaknesses of a kind of philosophical 'god of the gaps' remedy. And it must await in the history of science the development of more adequate theories that may or may not incorporate an anthropic principle."[117]

In the area of biological evolution, the notion of design looms large among those who argue for Intelligent Design [ID]. Scientists who make such arguments generally refrain from naming the needed designer. William Dembski argues that "intelligent design is under no obligation to speculate about the nature, moral character or purposes of any designing intelligence it happens to infer." That responsibility lies elsewhere: "Here rather is a task for the theologian—to connect the intelligence inferred by the design theorist with the God of Scripture."[118] Theologians who follow his advice, however, will be attaching their theology to a rather tenuous and often criticized scientific

---

115. Drees, *Beyond*, 84, 86. See also Patrick Frank, "On the Assumption of Design," *Theology and Science* 2 (2004): 122; Simon Conway Morris, "The Paradoxes of Evolution: Inevitable Humans in a Lonely Universe?" in *God and Design: The Teleological Argument and Modern Science*, ed. Neil A. Manson (London: Routledge, 2003), 333; and Stoeger, "Contemporary Physics," 233.

116. Clarke, "Is a Natural Theology Still Possible Today?" in *Physics, Philosophy, and Theology: A Common Quest for Understanding*, ed. Robert J. Russell, William R. Stoeger, and George V. Coyne (Vatican City State: Vatican Observatory; Berkeley, Calif.: Center for Theology and the Natural Sciences, 1988), 104–5.

117. Mooney, "The Anthropic Principle," 124. William Stoeger also cautions that "in going beyond the sciences, we must avoid putting God in the 'scientific gaps.' Perhaps our final theory is not really final! We should ensure that the divine agent is always a primary or ultimate cause—not one that could conceivably be filled by some unknown secondary or created cause" (Stoeger, "Are Anthropic Arguments," 456).

118. Dembski, *Intelligent Design*, 107.

theory. Just as quantum divine action is subject to the fortunes of the Copenhagen interpretation of quantum physics, so a theology based on ID will have to share its lot.

Some critics of ID find its arguments circular or meaningless.[119] Others contend that it is superfluous or at least premature to invoke an intelligent designer for features of the natural world that may be, or have been, explained through natural processes.[120] Darwin himself proposed an argument that might be viewed (anachronistically) as a rebuttal to Behe's mousetrap: "We can no longer argue that, for instance, the beautiful hinge of a bivalve shell must have been made by an intelligent being, like the hinge of a door by man. There seems to be no more design in the variability of organic beings and in the action of natural selection, than in the course which the wind blows."[121] Darwin saw that a particular structure might have been used for different purposes in successive generations: "Now according to our theory during the infinite number of changes, we might expect that an organ used for a purpose [by an ancestor] might be used for a different one by his descendant."[122] So simpler structures might have had different uses before evolving into more complex ones. Kenneth Miller illustrates this

---

119. "Intelligent Design has been proposed as a credible scientific alternative to the theory of evolution as an explanation of life on earth. Its justification depends on an extension of Fisherian significance testing developed by William Dembski. It is shown, in this chapter, that there is a fatal flaw in the logic of his method, which involves a circularity. In order to construct a test to detect design and 'eliminate' chance, one has to know how to recognize design in the first place. Dembski's calculation of the probability required to implement the method is also shown to be erroneous" (Bartholomew, *God, Chance and Purpose*, 97). "Behe's conclusion to the existence of an intelligent designer, however, is a *non sequitur*. The problem with Behe's proposal is not just that it asks us to imagine a designer of this or that organ or biochemical cascade, but of complex biological systems in general. We know how the design of an artifact relates to the plan of the designer because we understand how the design gets translated into concrete systems. In other words, we can comprehend the mechanism of the making. When we transfer this way of thinking to the design of biological systems in nature, unfortunately, the mechanism falls away and we are left with a purported identity of argument that is essentially meaningless" (T. Michael McNulty, "Evolution and Complexity," *American Catholic Philosophical Quarterly* 73 [1999]: 445).

120. "The crucial point is that, given the research procedures which the scientific community is using, we cannot say *a priori* that the remaining gaps in the evolutionary theory cannot be filled by purely scientific explanations of the future. Therefore, we cannot say that the details of evolution *demand* an external designer" (Langford, *Providence*, 93). "[Behe's argument for irreducible complexity] ignores the possibility of an evolutionary process that might, with the help of natural selection, have led to increasing complexity by way of intermediary stages each of which fulfilled a useful function" (de Duve, *Life Evolving*, 52).

121. Charles Darwin, *The Autobiography of Charles Darwin*, ed. Nora Barlow (New York: Norton, 1958), 87.

122. Charles Darwin, *The Foundations of the Origin of Species. Two Essays Written in 1842 and 1844*, ed. Francis Darwin (Cambridge: Cambridge University Press, 1909), 41.

process, refuting Behe's mousetrap with a funky tie clip: "What I have right here is a mousetrap from which I've removed two of the five parts. I still have the base plate, the spring, and the hammer. Now you can't catch any mice with this, so it's not a very good mousetrap. But it turns out that, despite the missing parts, it makes a perfectly good, if somewhat inelegant, tie clip.... And when we look at the favorite examples for irreducible complexity, and the bacterial flagellum is a perfect example, we find the molecular equivalent of my tie clip, which is we see parts of the machine missing—two, three, four, maybe even 20 parts, but still fulfilling a perfectly good purpose that could be favored by evolution. And that's why the irreducible complexity argument falls apart."[123]

If natural causes may eventually explain complex structures, to propose a divine cause is to introduce a god of the gaps. Simon Conway Morris observes: "That alone [the fact that the bacterial flagellum seems to be a convergent product in various species of bacteria] would be sufficient reason to make us very doubtful that god of gaps arguments being applied to the flagellum motor are in any way worth pursuing. And I wouldn't do it even if I believed in intelligent design, and emphatically I do not—simply because once that gap is closed, then credibility is lost."[124]

Theologians may also question whether it is wise to identify ID's intelligent designer with the God of Christian tradition. The refusal of ID propo-

---

123. Kenneth R. Miller, interviewed in "Judgment Day: Intelligent Design on Trial," PBS *NOVA* program, broadcast November 13, 2007, transcript available at http://www.pbs.org/wgbh/nova/transcripts/3416_id_08.html (accessed July 5, 2009). See also Kenneth R. Miller, "Answering the Biochemical Argument from Design," in *God and Design: The Teleological Argument and Modern Science*, ed. Neil A. Manson (London: Routledge, 2003), 292–307; Jeffrey Schloss, "Neo-Darwinism: Scientific Account and Theological Attributions," in *Back to Darwin: A Richer Account of Evolution*, ed. John B. Cobb (Grand Rapids, Mich.: Eerdmans, 2008), 115; Kenneth R. Miller, *Finding Darwin's God: A Scientist's Search for Common Ground between God and Evolution* (New York: Cliff Street Books, 1999), 148; Francisco J. Ayala, *Darwin and Intelligent Design* (Minneapolis, Minn,: Fortress Press, 2006), 77–84.

124. Simon Conway Morris, Gifford Lectures, 2007, number 6: "Towards an Eschatology of Evolution," mp3 recording available at http://www.hss.ed.ac.uk/giffordexemp/2000/details/Professor SimonConwayMorris.html (accessed April 29, 2009). "When we look for a cause of genetic information we are led to consider that reading and writing coded information appear to require an intelligent cause, or at least a cause that is analogous to intelligence. This has led design theorists to propose God as the author of the message written in the DNA. While I do not wish to exclude or belittle the role of God in the design and function of living organisms, I think that the account of the design theorists is dangerous, and ultimately incoherent, because it removes the role of secondary causes from the world, turning living organisms into puppets or, to use a more contemporary analogy, robots. In explaining the cause or principle responsible for inscribing and interpreting the message encoded in DNA, I think we would do better to look for a more proximate cause rather than turn immediately to God" (Goyette, "Substantial Form," 527).

nents to identify the designer impairs their argument.[125] At the same time, their willingness to suggest any sort of designer (space aliens, etc.) may well imply that the intelligence they have in mind is something less than the Christian God.[126] To the extent that ID advocates insist that their arguments are not intended as a way to God, theologians may be wise simply to take them at their word.[127] If ID proponents suggest that their arguments may be used theologically, it is up to theologians to determine whether the arguments are equal to the task.[128] In making that determination, they would do well to consider Chris Doran's conclusions on Dembski's arguments: "Finally, his endeavor to connect the designer behind ID with the God of Jesus Christ is cursory at best and upon further examination causes sizeable

125. "I suggest that appeals to intelligent causality are only legitimate in everyday life and in science when they are accompanied by a reasonable explanation for the existence and nature of the intelligent cause. Not surprisingly, therefore, Darwinists are demanding that ID theorists provide an account of the designer behind the intelligent design. Without it, I contend that the ID proposal remains incomplete because its central thesis of irreducible complexity remains unintelligible" (Nicanor Pier Giorgio Austriaco, "The Intelligibility of Intelligent Design," *Angelicum* 86 [2009]: 104). "Dembski's contention that questions about the designer's identity are philosophical and/or theological in nature and thus play no role in defining ID science not only effectively ignores the fact that one must presuppose something about the identity of the designer in order to attempt ID science, but also that his ID program is already practically presupposing that the designer looks and acts in a particular manner" (Chris Doran, "Implicit Presuppositions Made Explicit: A Critical Appraisal of the Theology of Intelligent Design as Found in the Work of William Dembski," Ph.D. diss., Graduate Theological Union, Berkeley, Calif. [2007], 181).

126. "Possible candidates for the role of designer include: the God of Christianity; an angel—fallen or not; Plato's demiurge; some mystical new-age force; space aliens from Alpha Centauri; time travelers; or some utterly unknown intelligent being" (Behe, "Modern Intelligent," 277). "To be sure, the designer is compatible with the creator-God of the world's major monotheistic religions.... But the designer is also compatible with the watchmaker-God of the deists, the Demiurge of Plato's *Timaeus*, and the divine reason (i.e., *logos spermatikos*) of the ancient Stoics" (Dembski, *Design Revolution*, 44). "The intelligent design community ... understands the 'intelligent' in 'intelligent design' simply to refer to intelligent agency (irrespective of skill or mastery) and thus separates intelligent design from optimality of design" (William A. Dembski, "Introduction: What Intelligent Design Is Not," in *Signs of Intelligence: Understanding Intelligent Design*, ed. William A. Dembski and James M. Kushiner (Grand Rapids, Mich.: Brazos Press, 2001), 7.

127. "ID theory is a minimalist argument for design itself, not an argument for the existence of God" (Behe, "Modern Intelligent," 277). See also Dembski, *Design Revolution*, 44.

128. "I have written that if you look at molecular machines, such as the cilium, the flagellum, and others, they look like they were designed—purposely designed by an intelligent agent.... In my view there is every reason, based on hard empirical observation, to conclude with Joseph Cardinal Ratzinger that 'the great projects of the living creation are not the products of chance and error.... [They] point to a creating Reason and show us a creating Intelligence, and they do so more luminously and radiantly today than ever before'" (Michael J. Behe, "Evidence for Design at the Foundation of Life," in *Science and Evidence for Design in the Universe: Papers Presented at a Conference Sponsored by the Wethersfield Institute, New York City, September 25, 1999* [San Francisco, Calif.: Ignatius Press, 2000], 127–28). Cf. Joseph Ratzinger, *In the Beginning: A Catholic Understanding of the Story of Creation and the Fall* (Grand Rapids, Mich.: Eerdmans, 1986), 54–56.

damage to the traditional theology that he seeks to affirm. Divine transcendence, compassion, holiness, along with the affirmation of creation's goodness, are seriously damaged if we accept his inference that the designer is God."[129]

LOCKING DIVINE ACTION INTO UNIVOCAL CAUSALITY

One overarching criticism applies to all approaches to divine action that directly employ interpretations of the theories of contemporary science. Despite their occasional protestations to the contrary, they all tend to treat God as a univocal cause alongside of natural causes.[130] This becomes evident if we consider their implicit understanding of the relation between God and the laws of nature.

They start with two basic convictions: that Christian faith requires an affirmation of God's action in the world and that the integrity of science demands or at least prefers that such action not break the laws of nature or interfere with the natural causes upon which those laws are based. The theme of not violating the laws of nature looms large, for instance, in Ian Barbour's

---

129. Chris Doran, "Implicit Presuppositions," 181. See also Chris Doran, "Intelligent Design: It's Just Too Good to Be True," *Theology and Science* 8 (2010): 223–37.

130. I am using the term "univocal cause" in a broad sense here to designate simply a cause that belongs to same order as another cause with which it may cooperate to produce a given effect. When two such causes act together, the causality of one inevitably interferes with the causality of the other in such a way that the more one contributes to the effect, the less the other is able to do so. Two men, for instance, belong to the same order of being. When they work together to produce some effect, they act as univocal causes, and the more one contributes to the effect, the less the other is able to do so. When two men carry a table, for instance, the more weight one lifts, the less there is for the other to lift. A "univocal cause" is distinguished from a "transcendent cause." The transcendent cause belongs to a different order from the cause with which it acts to produce some effect. The single effect that the two causes produce is not divided among them, but belongs wholly to both. A human being, for instance, transcends the nonintelligent being of a piece of chalk. If they act together to produce writing on a chalkboard, the causality of one does not interfere with the causality of the other, and the effect belongs wholly to both. Every mark on the chalkboard is produced both by the human being and by the chalk. As Aquinas explains: "One action does not proceed from two agents of the same order. But nothing hinders the same action from proceeding from a primary and a secondary agent" (*ST* I, 105, 5, ad 2). My use of the term "univocal cause" should not be confused with the distinction Aquinas sometimes makes between a "univocal cause" and an "equivocal" or "nonunivocal cause," in which the term "univocal cause" means a cause belonging to the same species as its effect (as when a dog begets a dog) and the term "equivocal" or "nonunivocal cause" designates a cause that transcends the individual members of the species since it is the cause of species itself (i.e., of the substantial form as such). See *ST* I, 4, 2, co. When I assert that some in the theology/science dialogue are thinking of God as a "univocal cause," I do not mean that they see God as belonging to the same species as some creature, only that they view God and creatures as being so alike that it is possible for their causalities to interfere with one another. See the glossary entry "univocal cause."

summary of recent accounts of divine action: "Several recent authors have said that their accounts of divine action do not involve violations of the laws of nature or divine intervention in gaps in the scientific account.... Instead they have tried to show how new scientific concepts either permit divine action or suggest analogies for it.... In all these cases God is seen as working subtly in cooperation with the structures of nature rather than by intervening discontinuously."[131]

Kirk Wegter-McNelly notes the same concern: "[R]ecent developments in physics have allowed for new, but still theologically incompatibilist, approaches to the problem of special divine action, now commonly referred to as 'non-interventionist' strategies.... In these different types of physical processes, so the non-interventionist argument goes, God can be understood to act objectively in the world without needing to violate its laws."[132] Niels Henrik Gregersen reports: "Between 1993 and 2001 the Vatican Observatory and the Center for Theology and the Natural Sciences produced an impressive series of volumes devoted to one pivotal issue: How can a scientifically informed Christian believer conceive of God's objective interaction with the world of nature *within* the constraints and opportunities offered by the natural sciences?"[133] Commenting on the same series, Nancey Murphy notes: "Many of the participants' focus was on the question of where is there 'room' for special divine action in nature."[134] Alvin Plantinga avers: "It would be fair to say, I think, that the main problem for the [Divine Action] Project is to find an account of divine action in the world—action beyond creation and conservation—that doesn't involve God's intervening in the world."[135] Taede Smedes sees this concern especially in the theology of John Polkinghorne: "It is particularly Polkinghorne who emphasizes the incom-

---

131. Barbour, *Nature*, 104–5.
132. Wegter-McNelly, "Fundamental," 162–63.
133. Niels Henrik Gregersen, "Special Divine Action and the Quilt of Laws: Why the Distinction between Special and General Divine Action Cannot be Maintained," in *Scientific Perspectives on Divine Action: Twenty Years of Challenge and Progress*, ed. Robert John Russell, Nancey Murphy, and William R. Stoeger (Vatican City State: Vatican Observatory; Berkeley, Calif.: Center for Theology and the Natural Sciences, 2008), 179.
134. Nancey Murphy, "Science and the Problem of Evil: Suffering as a By-product of a Finely Tuned Cosmos," in *Physics and Cosmology: Scientific Perspectives on the Problem of Natural Evil*, ed. Nancey Murphy, Robert John Russell, and William Stoeger (Vatican City State: Vatican Observatory; Berkeley, Calif.: Center for Theology and the Natural Sciences, 2007), 141. "The real value of chaos theory for an account of divine action is that it gives God a great deal of 'room' in which to effect specific outcomes without destroying our ability to believe in the natural causal order" (Murphy, "Buridan's," 38).
135. Alvin Plantinga, "What Is 'Intervention'?" *Theology and Science* 6 (2008): 383.

patibilist position of divine action and a deterministic natural order. In his view, the universe must be open for God to be able to act in it. If the universe is closed and deterministic, God's action is physically impossible. God's action, in this view, competes with the laws of nature; competes, that is, with natural causality, as if God's action were on the same ontological level as the workings of the natural order."[136]

Implicit in the concern that God's action *not* violate the laws of nature is the conviction that God *could* violate those laws—that the action of the Creator might somehow contradict the very creation which exists from moment by moment only through his sustaining influence. One cause can contradict another, however, only if they are of the same sort—only if they are univocal. If two causes are of different orders—if one transcends the other—their respective causalities cannot be understood univocally but only analogously. This requires the establishment of a new conceptual framework to describe their relationship. Any perceived clash or interference between them will then be taken to mean not that they are actually in conflict, but only that one's concept of their relation is inadequate—that one has slipped back into a univocal understanding of them. It will indicate a problem, not with the two causalities, but with one's conceptualization of them.

The fact that the possible violation of the proper causality of creatures is a central concern of those who approach divine action by employing interpretations of the theories of science shows that these thinkers are implicitly assuming that the divine cause is univocal with the causality of creatures. Even when they explicitly acknowledge divine transcendence, their arguments betray the fact that they are still thinking of God as a univocal cause. Philip Clayton, for instance, avers that "by definition, God cannot be just a cause alongside others in the natural world" and that "an infinite divine being" cannot belong to "the finite causal order in the way that persons do." Still, he is concerned to point out that his model of divine action "allows for divine causal constraints on the aspirations of persons in a way that does not abrogate the functioning of natural law. No physical laws are broken if there is an exchange of information between a divine source and conscious human agents."[137] Arthur Peacocke gives an eloquent affirmation God's transcendence: "We must be clear from the outset that in saying that God is, and that God is Creator, we do not affirm that he/she is any ordinary 'cause'

---

136. Smedes, *Chaos*, 198.
137. Clayton, "Natural Law," 630.

in the physical nexus of the universe itself—otherwise God would be neither explanation nor possible meaning.... This fundamental 'otherness' of God in his own inscrutable, unsurpassable and ultimately incomprehensible Being is essential to what we mean by God. Referred to by the predicate *transcendent,* this is an inexpugnable element of the Judeo-Christian (and Islamic) experience of God."[138] Yet, he also argues: "Our current perception of the world as a closed nexus of events renders the idea of God 'intervening' in the world to rupture its God-given regularities as incoherent."[139] Taede Smedes says of the theology of Arthur Peacocke and John Polkinghorne: "They deal with divine action as if it were an explanatory theory or a hypothesis, similar to scientific theories and hypotheses. Moreover, though they are aware of the peculiar character of God-language, they still talk about God in competition-terms, as if God's action is similar to creaturely, causal and/or intentional action, including the limitations inherent to the creaturely condition."[140]

Robert Russell also affirms God's transcendence: "God's causality is radically different from any of the kinds of causality we know about, just as God's nature as necessary being is ontologically different from ours as contingent beings."[141] Yet he seems to be speaking from a univocal notion of divine causality when he suggests that, with the advent of conscious life, God "increasingly refrains from determining the neurophysiological outcomes we associate with conscious choices, leaving room for top-down, mind-brain causality in conscious and self-conscious creatures."[142] Only univocal causes need to "leave room" lest they interfere with one another. The same conceptual framework is evident in his remark that "quantum events occur in part because of God's special providence, in part because of natural causality."[143] Only among univocal causes is an action partly from one cause and partly from the other. The effect of a transcendent primary cause and a secondary cause is wholly from both. Again, Russell remarks that we must "avoid an ontological gaps argument when these gaps are viewed as disruptions of nature by God's intervention" and instead affirm "that the process-

---

138. Peacocke, "God's Action," 460–61.
139. Arthur Peacocke, "Problems in Contemporary Christian Theology," *Theology and Science* 2 (2004): 2–3.
140. Smedes, *Chaos,* 207. Cf. ibid., 182, 254–55.
141. R. J. Russell, "Quantum Physics," 582.
142. Ibid., 592–93.
143. R. J. Russell, "Religion and the Theories," 38.

es of nature are created by God *ex nihilo* with intrinsic, naturally occurring gaps."[144] The gaps seem to be necessary in any case lest God (as a univocal cause) interfere with the causality of creatures. Russell simply seems to prefer that the gaps be built into the natural world from the beginning and not introduced ad hoc, in violation of the established order of nature, on occasions when God acts.

Theologians who consider God's causality to be univocal with that of creatures and who also want to affirm that God acts in the world without displacing or disturbing the proper causality of creatures, must find some locus in creation where God can act without interference. In the philosophy that grew out of Newtonian science, there was no such locus. The nexus of created causes was conceived as deterministic and inviolable. Divine action was simply impossible. Certain interpretations of contemporary science have provided such a locus by introducing an objective indeterminacy into the world, an ontological break or gap in the causal nexus. Theologians have been able to exploit that indeterminacy as a place where God may act in the world without interfering with created causes. Divine action is therefore possible, but, as Keith Ward points out, only if the web of creaturely causes remains sufficiently slack to accommodate it: "Divine action is, thus, not occasional interference in the laws of nature. It is continuous with natural processes, present throughout the whole cosmos and entirely compatible with our mathematical descriptions of physical behavior—which, accordingly, must be rather looser and more flexible than some Newtonian physicists thought."[145]

Such an indeterministic niche for divine action is needed only if God and creatures are conceived as univocal causes that might otherwise interfere with each other. The very search for indeterministic pockets in the natural world suitable for divine action therefore bespeaks a univocal understanding of divine causality. Any true affirmation of divine transcendence would render such a search unnecessary or at least suspect, as Steven Dale Crain observes: "I believe that the claim that God transcends the world as its creator renders highly suspect attempts like Polkinghorne's to argue that God must exploit a built-in physical feature of the world in order to act in the world."[146]

---

144. R. J. Russell, "Quantum Physics," 584.   145. Ward, *The Big Questions*, 260.
146. Crain, "Divine Action," 58.

When divine action is conceived univocally with the action of creatures, divine being tends to be viewed univocally as well. A univocal God, however, is quite different from the God of Christian tradition.[147] In place of the sovereign Creator, there is a God who must limit himself lest he interfere with creation. Instead of the God who manifests himself in the whirlwind, there is a lurking, rather sneaky God who must function furtively lest his action be discovered.[148] In place of the God who is intimately involved in the life of his people, there is (at least in some accounts) a God who acts only on the universe as a whole and seems indistinguishable from the deistic God.[149] Instead of the God who formed the heavens with a word, there is a sort of divine statistician who must carefully calculate whether his action is sufficiently subtle to remain undetected by empirical science.[150]

If univocal thinking about divine causality leads to such unhappy images, why should we continue to think univocally, especially when contemporary science itself is suggesting broad, new ways of conceiving causality? These take us far beyond the Newtonian notion of the force that moves the atoms. Perhaps what theology should take from contemporary science is not that there are pockets of indeterminacy in nature (according to certain interpretations of some scientific theories) that can be exploited theologically

---

147. "The category mistake is thus a confusion between natural causality and divine action: divine action is supposed to work on the same level as natural causality. In other words, divine action is considered to be limited by the same factors as is human action, thereby blurring the distinction between the order of creation and its inherent limits, and the transcendent order of its Creator. This confusion results in a conceptual 'devaluation' of God, i.e. a reduction of the Creator to its creation" (Smedes, *Chaos*, 198).

148. "However, this strategy is not without its problems, over and above that of wondering whether acting somewhat furtively under cover of randomness is a God-like thing to do" (Bartholomew, *God, Chance and Purpose*, 130). Cf. ibid., 154. Noting that William Dembski "asserts that the designer might deceptively mask its own intelligent causation as a chance or necessary phenomenon," Chris Doran asks how Dembski expects Christians "to infer that a potentially deceptive designer is actually the holy and just God whom we affirm created the universe" (Doran, "Implicit Presuppositions," 171).

149. "Still, in the final analysis Peacocke has to admit that his view, like those of Kaufman and Wiles, ... allows for God's action only 'on the world-as-a-whole'" (Clayton, *God and Contemporary*, 225).

150. "Thus, provided that the proportion of occasions on which God chooses to act decisively is negligibly small, it will be impossible to detect his action by scientific means. We thus have a way of allowing room for God to work in the world without violating his own laws" (Bartholomew, *God of Chance*, 130). "God must be sure to make experiments in which scientists gather quantum statistics come out right. This is definitely an awkward constraint in the sense that human beings can more or less force God to act in a particular way, constraining divine freedom. Yet in practice it is not so severe, particularly if God only acts in some but not all events, because providentially relevant events are unlikely to include anything about which scientists can gather quantum statistics" (Wildman, "Divine Action Project," 161).

as places where God (conceived as a univocal cause) might act without disturbing other natural causes, but that there is now a broader understanding of causality itself to be employed in discussions of divine action.

By embracing that wider concept of causality we may break free of the narrow Newtonian notions that have so long hampered the discussion of divine action.[151] Instead, we might retrieve certain earlier ideas of causality, such as the formal and final causes of Aristotle and Aquinas, to which science itself now seems to be pointing.[152] If broader understandings of causality are now felt to be needed in science, how much more are they needed in those realms of thought which reach far beyond the limits of science, even to the First Cause of all things.

151. "The far-reaching consequences of this common willingness to accept a 'no-inherent-room-for-God' constraint coming from Newtonian physics cannot be overemphasized. Prior to the rise of Newtonian physics, Christian thinkers simply did not perceive the logical difficulty of asserting simultaneously that God acts at specific times and places and that the world retains its own causal efficacy and integrity. However, the supposed compatibility of these two ideas dissolved in the face of Newtonian determinism, which left in its wake human and divine agency as newly felt problems" (Wegter-McNelly, "Fundamental," 162).

152. "Aristotle, it may be recalled, had conceived of four different types of questions, only one of which was the why-question, and each of these he thought could be answered in causal terms. The varieties of causal explanation he proposed, and which we have seen time and again appearing in different guises throughout this historical account, in our estimation are able to provide more powerful instruments for the acquisition of truth than has been acknowledged in the recent past.... I have therefore urged an expansion of causal thinking far beyond the narrow domain of Humean causation, to include what contemporary thinkers have spoken of as 'powers,' 'inner determiners,' and other real 'explanatory factors' that can account for the phenomena being studied by today's scientists" (Wallace, *Causality and Scientific*, 2.240, 326).

5

Unlocking Divine Action through the New Causality of Contemporary Science

We have seen that contemporary science suggests understandings of causality beyond the constricted notions of Newtonian science. At the same time, we have noticed how our ability to speak of divine action is linked to our understanding of causality—shrinking or expanding as our notion of causality grows narrower or broader. We have also discovered that the new and broader understandings of causality in contemporary science are reminiscent of aspects of causality as understood in the philosophy of Aristotle and Thomas Aquinas. Our present task will be to exploit those new (and old) understandings of causality to speak of divine action. Here we address the interests of a number of those involved in the science/theology dialogue as expressed in a question posed by Kirk Wegter-McNelly: "Might it be possible to recover a view of divine activity as the source and guarantor of the integrity of natural processes and creaturely freedom—as one finds it, say, in pre-modern thinkers such as Aquinas, Luther, and Calvin—without giving up the task of serious religious engagement with the natural sciences?"[1]

THE BEING AND ACTION OF GOD

Aquinas begins his discussion of God in the *Summa Theologiae* by noting that certain events in the world point beyond themselves to a transcendent

---

1. Wegter-McNelly, "Fundamental," 163. In his discussion of divine action, Philip Clayton is also eager to "marshal the diverse evidence and arguments that point beyond classical notions of physical causality. Taken together, they now encourage us to accept (as the medieval Islamic philosophers also urged) that the genus 'cause' includes types of influences other than mechanistic ones"

cause. He traces the various kinds of causality they entail (formal, efficient, and final) and shows that they have their origin in God. His arguments here are his famous "five ways" of showing the existence of God.[2] Having established God's existence, Aquinas can then use the five ways to discuss God's nature and attributes. This involves saying certain things about God, but also (and mostly) "unsaying" things, since we more properly know what God is *not* than what God *is*.[3] Once Aquinas has established God's existence and nature by tracing the modes of God's action or causality in the world, he then reverses his steps and, starting with God's being, considers the modes of God's action.[4]

Following Aquinas, we will first consider God's being and then God's action in creating and sustaining the world. Our discussion will involve four related topics: God's transcendence and immanence, the "causal joint" between God and creation, the relationship between God and creatures, and the nature of the language we use to speak of God and God's action. After briefly exploring these issues, we will be ready to tackle the topic of divine action itself in view of the new (and old) modes of causality revealed in contemporary science.

God is unlike all other things.[5] In God, essence and existence are the same; in every creature, they are distinct: "God alone is Being by virtue of

---

(Clayton, "Impossible Possibility," 255). Nancey Murphy concurs: "It is my contention that the problem of divine action is, at base, a metaphysical problem—one that cannot be solved by anything less radical than a revision of our understanding of natural causation" (Murphy, "Buridan's," 326).

2. See *ST* I, 2, 3, co. On the importance of creation as a way to God, see also *SCG* II, 2, nos. 1–5; II, 3, no. 6; and II, 4, no. 1.

3. "Because we cannot know what God is, but rather what He is not, we have no means for considering how God is, but rather how He is not" (*ST* I, 3, prologue). "The most important thing we can know about the first cause is that it surpasses all our knowledge and power of expression. For that one knows God most perfectly who holds that whatever one can think or say about Him is less than what God is" (*Super de causis* 6 [Guagliardo, 46]). Cf.: *ST* I, 3, 4, ad 2; *Super de trin.* 6, 3, co. We are, as Anton Pegis says, to "reach him by unsaying progressively all the things in the universe that the human mind can know and know also that they are not God" (Anton C. Pegis, *St. Thomas and Philosophy* [Milwaukee, Wis.: Marquette University Press, 1964], 72). Niels Henrik Gregersen seems to intuit the same divine mystery: "This reality, God, is even more foreign to our conceptuality than the most unexplained features in the world. Thus, the religious answer to why-questions does not find a solution to a riddle, but rather proposes a language in which we can adequately express and communicate with the puzzles of reality, every morning anew" (Gregersen, "Providence," 19–20).

4. See: *ST* I, 44–119, especially QQ. 103–5 on divine action. See also Alfred Freddoso, "God's General Concurrence with Secondary Causes: Pitfalls and Prospects," *American Catholic Philosophical Quarterly* 68 (1994): 132.

5. "Although it may be admitted that creatures are in some way like God, it must no wise be admitted that God is like creatures.... A creature can be spoken of as in some way like God; but not that God is like a creature" (*ST* I, 4, 3, ad 4).

his own essence, since his essence is his existence; whereas every creature has being by participation, so that its essence is not its existence."[6] Every creature *has* or possesses an existence that is distinct from its nature or essence. (The existence of the duck, for instance, is distinct from its nature. It does not inherently possess the property of existence, as every duck hunter knows.) God, however, "is his own existence."[7] As subsistent existence (*ipsum esse subsistens*), God is the source of existence in all things not only at the moment of creation but at each instant of their continued existence.[8] There is no question, therefore, of *whether* God acts in the world: if God did not act, the world would simply not exist.[9]

The action of God in sustaining the world is, in a sense, simply a continuation of the original act of creation.[10] Yet it is also different from creation, since creation implies "beginning or newness."[11] To name the differ-

6. *ST* I, 104, 1, co. "That thing, whose existence differs from its essence, must have its existence caused by another. But this cannot be true of God; because we call God the first efficient cause. Therefore it is impossible that in God His existence should differ from His essence" (*ST* I, 3, 4, co.). See also Lawrence Dewan, "St. Thomas and the Distinction between Form and Esse in Caused Things," *Gregorianum* 80 (1999): 353–70.

7. *ST* I, 3, 4, co.

8. "God is the essentially self-subsisting Being [*ipsum esse per se subsistens*].... All beings apart from God are not their own being, but are beings by participation. Therefore it must be that all things ... are caused by one First Being, who possesses being most perfectly" (*ST* I, 44, 1, co.). Cf.: *Sent.* I, 37, 1, 1, co.; *De ver.* 5, 8, ad 9; *SCG* III, 65, no. 3; *ST* I, 3, 4, co.; I, 4, 2, co.

9. "A thing is said to preserve another *per se* and directly when what is preserved depends on the preserver in such a way that it cannot exist without it. In this manner all creatures need to be preserved by God. For the being of every creature depends on God, so that not for a moment could it subsist but would fall into nothingness were it not kept in being by the operation of the divine power" (*ST* I, 104, 1, co.). Cf. *In meta.* VI, lect. 3 (§1209). "One indisputable characteristic of the God of Abraham, Isaac and Jacob, the Father of the Lord Jesus Christ, is that he is the creator of all things in heaven and earth.... If one is exploring the idea of divine action, this is where one must begin, for creation is the first act of God in relation to all other things, without which no further acts would be possible" (Ward, *Divine Action*, 4). See also Tracy, "Creation, Providence," 239).

10. "The preservation of things by God is a continuation of that action whereby he gives existence, which action is without either motion or time" (*ST* I, 104, 1, ad 4). "The basic division between 'producing,' 'ordering' and 'preserving and guiding' may perhaps suggest a temporal succession of different acts on the part of God, but that is definitely not what Thomas intends. It concerns three conceptually different aspects of the one single act of creation, coinciding with the single divine essence, which is pure act and, as such, the sufficient cause with respect to any possible being. The logical division in the human manner of conceiving God's act of creation should not be projected onto God himself. The different aspects in which God's work of creation is discursively articulated all relate to the one and undivided *actus purus* of the divine essence" (Rudi A. Te Velde, *Aquinas on God: The "Divine Science" of the Summa theologiae* [Aldershot, Hants, U.K.: Ashgate, 2006], 125). See also Hans Jorissen, "Schöpfung und Heil: Theologiegeschichtliche Perspektiven zum Vorsehungsglauben nach Thomas von Aquin," in *Vorsehung und Handeln Gottes*, ed. Theodor Schneider und Lothar Ullrich (Leipzig: St. Benno Verlag, 1988), 102.

11. "Nor is it necessary that as long as the creature is it should be created; because creation imports a relation of the creature to the Creator, with a certain newness or beginning" (*ST* I, 45, 3, ad 3).

ence, Aquinas distinguishes between creating and ruling or governing: "We should keep in mind that the action of the first cause is twofold: one inasmuch as it establishes things, which is called creation; another inasmuch as it rules things already established."[12] God's rule or care for creatures is generally called providence. But within the notion of providence one may distinguish God's plan of creation, which is called providence in a more specific sense, and the execution of that plan, which is called government.[13] Creation belongs to God alone, but creatures also share in the work of government.[14]

If we recognize that God's way of being is different from that of creatures, we can assert that his way of acting will also be different, since action follows being.[15] Since God's being is one, his action cannot be distinct from his being but must be one with it.[16] His action is therefore utterly different from that of creatures, since the action of no creature is the same as its being.[17]

---

12. *Super de causis*, 24 (Guagliardo, 137). Cf. *In de div nom.* 24 (Saffrey, p. 122, lines 13–17).

13. "Two things pertain to the care of providence—namely the reason of order, which is called providence and disposition; and the execution of order, which is termed government" (*ST* I, 22, 1, ad 2). "The plan or order of providence and governance is to lead all things to their proper end" (*ST* I, 103, 1, co.). Cf. *ST* I, 22, aa. 1–3; *Sent* I, 39, 2, 1, co.; *SCG* III, 65, nos. 1–2.

14. "Creation is the proper act of God alone" (*ST* I 45, 5, co.). "Two things belong to providence—namely, the plan of the order of things towards their end; and the execution of this order, which is called government. As regards the first of these, God has immediate providence over everything, because He has in His intellect the types of everything, even the smallest; and whatsoever causes He assigns to certain effects, He gives them the power to produce those effects. Whence it must be that He has beforehand the type of those effects in His mind. As to the second, there are certain intermediaries of God's providence; for He governs things inferior by superior, not on account of any defect in His power, but by reason of the abundance of His goodness; so that the dignity of causality is imparted even to creatures" (*ST* I, 22, 3, co.). Cf. *ST* I, 104, 1, co.; *SCG* III, 77, no. 2.

15. "Aquinas' distinction between divine causation and creaturely causation is similar to the distinction he draws between divine being and creaturely being.... Aquinas distinguishes the being of the Creator from the being of the creature not in terms of necessary being versus contingent being but more radically in terms of being versus non-being.... Likewise, divine causation differs from creaturely causation as being differs from non-being. Without God's causation, there is no creaturely causation at all. The former constitutes the latter, whether the created cause causes contingently or necessarily" (Goris, *Free Creatures*, 299–300).

16. "Then, too, just as active power is something acting, so is its essence something being. But, as we have seen, God's power is his essence. Therefore, his action is his being. But his being is his substance. Therefore, God's action is his substance.... Furthermore, an action that is not the substance of the agent is in the agent as an accident in its subject; and that is why action is reckoned as one of the nine categories of accident. But nothing can exist in God in the manner of an accident. Therefore, God's action is not other than his substance and his power" (*SCG* II, 9, nos. 4–5). "In God there exists only one real operation, that is, his essence" (*ST* I, 30, 2, ad 3).

17. "The act of the [natural] agent, by which it makes something like itself is something coming forth from the agent into the patient, which cannot be the case with God since his act is his substance" (*In de div. nom.* IX, lect. 2 [§232–59]). "It is clear that God is not a univocal agent" (*ST* I, 25, 2, ad 2).

(The quacking of the duck, for instance, is not the same as the existence of the duck—it is not a case of "I quack therefore I am.")

Recognizing this difference, we should be cautious about trying to say *how* God acts. Aquinas calls God "the cause hidden from every human being."[18] Though we do not know how God acts, we can see that his action cannot be in competition with that of creatures since it is the very source of their existence and action. As Brian Shanley notes: "When conceived primarily in terms of the creative causation of *esse*, the divine motion is not an exterior manipulation of created agents determining them to act one way or another. For just as creation is not a change, so too the divine motion is not the effecting of a change in something with independent existence; divine efficient causation is only a motion in an analogous sense. The primary mode of divine causation is creative and constitutive, not controlling and compelling. God is not rival or auxiliary to created causes, but rather the One who makes all causes be causes."[19]

Divine Transcendence and Immanence

As the cause of being, God both transcends all of creation and is immanently present in it. These two characteristics are not opposed—as if the more transcendent God were the less immanent he could be. As the source

---

18. *SCG* III, 101, no. 1. "One must indeed acknowledge that one cannot conceive how God acts if one is obliged to consider all such acting as partaking in the paradigmatic bestowing of *esse* which is creation" (Burrell, *Freedom and Creation*, 70). "There is a very good reason for an apophatic stance in relation to God's creative act. God's creative act *is* God. Whatever we see, whatever science studies, is not God. We have no direct access to God's creative act, only to its effects: the universe of creatures we find around us, with the relationships between them and the laws that govern them. We never find any particular point of intersection (the "causal joint") between God and creatures, because we have no empirical access to God. In a sense, of course, every creature in the universe is the point of intersection, but what we have empirical access to is simply the creature. So a theology of divine action not only should not spell out how God acts, but should insist that this is something we cannot know" (Edwards, *How God Acts*, 63).

19. Brian Shanley, "Divine Causation and Human Freedom in Aquinas," *American Catholic Philosophical Quarterly* 72 (1998): 105. "God's action must actually be such as to work omnipotently on, in, or though creaturely agencies without either forcing them or competing with them. But as soon as we try to conceive it in action, we degrade it to the creaturely level and place it in the field of interacting causalities. The result can only be (if we take it literally) monstrosity and confusion" (Farrer, *Faith and Speculation*, 62). "To call God the Creator of the world is not just to note that he got the world started. It is also to note that he sustains it in being. If that is so, however, God can hardly be an agent acting on us so as to interfere with us" (Brian Davies, "God and Evil: A Dialogue," *New Blackfriars* 85 [2004]: 283). "God will never be said to 'intervene,' since creating cannot be represented as another vector added to the configuration of forces in the universe" (Burrell, *Freedom and Creation*, 70). See also idem, "Creator/Creatures Relation: 'The Distinction' vs. 'Onto-theology,'" *Faith and Philosophy* 25 (2008): 184; Te Velde, *Aquinas on God*, 141; and Smedes, *Chaos*, 180–82.

of creaturely existence, God must transcend the creaturely mode of being. Creatures have existence by participation, and their being is distinct from their essence. God is subsistent being itself. Yet, precisely as the source of creaturely existence, God must also be immanently present in creation. For nothing is more intimate to any being than its own existence, and God is present to each creature as the source of its being. Aquinas can therefore affirm that "God is in all things, and innermostly."[20] In addition to this global presence, God has a special mode of intimacy in human beings through grace and a unique presence in the God-Man through the union of his divine and human natures in the person of the Logos.[21]

As God's presence in each thing is most intimate, so is his action: "Because in all things God himself is properly the cause of universal being which is innermost in all things, it follows that in all things God works intimately."[22] As William Hill explains: "[T]he very transcendence of God—on which grounds, our awareness of him is more an unknowing than a knowing, but a positive gain for us in that we know him to be unknowable—is itself the ground of the divine immanence in everything that partakes of being. The total otherness of God explains that he is not present and operative in any one place but simultaneously in all places giving them their very powers of location; he is not present to any one order of being but to everything whatsoever that participates in being."[23]

God's presence in the world does not imply that God is identical with the world (pantheism). Nor does it mean that God is a part of the world or that the world is a part of God (panentheism). God is not "present in things in the sense of being combined with them as one of their parts," but rather "in

---

20. *ST* I, 8, 1, co. Cf. *ST* I, 8, 3, co.; *De ver.* 5, 9, ad 10; *De pot.* 3, 7, co. On divine transcendence and immanence, see also Schillebeeckx, *Jesus*, 627–28; and Kathryn Tanner, *God and Creation in Christian Theology: Tyranny or Empowerment?* (New York: Basil Blackwell, 1988), 45–48.

21. Of the mode of presence by grace, Aquinas says: "Above and beyond this common mode [of divine presence], however, there is one special mode belonging to the rational nature wherein God is said to be present as the object known is in the knower, and the beloved in the lover. And since the rational creature by its operation of knowledge and love attains to God himself, according to this special mode God is said not only to exist in the rational creature, but also to dwell therein as in his own temple" (*ST* I, 43, 3, co.). Cf.: *ST* I-II, Q. 110. On the hypostatic union, Aquinas says: "There is, however, another special mode of God's existence in man by union" (*ST* I, 8, 3, ad 4). Cf. *ST* III, QQ. 2–6.

22. *ST* I, 105, 5, co. Cf.: *De pot.* 3, 7, co.

23. William J. Hill, "The Implicate World: God's Oneness with Mankind as a Mediated Immediacy," in *Beyond Mechanism: The Universe in Recent Physics and Catholic Thought*, ed. David L. Schindler (Lanham, Md.: University Press of America, 1986), 88. See also John H. Wright, *A Theology of Christian Prayer* (New York: Pueblo, 1979), 47.

the fashion of an agent cause."²⁴ God is not one part of a greater whole.²⁵ Yet it can be truly said that God is in the world and the world is in God.²⁶

The notion of panentheism perhaps deserves a brief remark here in view of its pervasiveness in the science/theology dialogue on divine action. Many participants embrace it favorably, but some are critical.²⁷ Panentheism has been defined as "the belief that the Being of God includes and penetrates the whole universe, so that every part of it exists in him, but ... that his being is more than, and is not exhausted by, the universe."²⁸ It is often presented as an alternative to deism (transcendence to the exclusion immanence) or pantheism (immanence to the exclusion of transcendence), and is frequently contrasted with "traditional theism."²⁹

---

24. *SCG* III, 68, no. 11.

25. "It is not possible for God to enter into the composition of anything ... because no part of a compound can be absolutely primal among beings" (*ST* I, 3, 8, co.).

26. "Although corporeal things are said to be in another as in that which contains them, nevertheless, spiritual things contain those things in which they are; as the soul contains the body. Hence also God is in things containing them; nevertheless, by a certain similitude to corporeal things, it is said that all things are in God; inasmuch as they are contained by him" (*ST* I, 8, 1, ad 2). "Something is said to be in another in several ways: in one way really, in another way according to the relation of action and passion. Now, according to the first way, all things must be said to be in the first cause in one way, because that by which all things are in the first cause is one and the same thing, namely, divine power, for effects are virtually in their cause. But according to this mode the first cause is in things in diverse ways because the first cause is in the things caused inasmuch as it imprints its likeness on them, while diverse things receive the likeness of the first cause in diverse ways. But in the second way, the opposite is the case. For the first cause acts upon all things according to one mode and so ... it is in all things according to one disposition. But all things do not receive the action of the first cause in the same way" (*Super de causis*, 24 [Guagliardo, 135–36]).

27. See Michael W. Brierley, "The Potential of Panentheism for Dialogue between Science and Religion," in *The Oxford Handbook of Religion and Science*, ed. Philip Clayton and Zachary Simpson (Oxford: Oxford University Press, 2006), 635–51; Owen C. Thomas, "Problems in Panentheism," in *The Oxford Handbook of Religion and Science*, ed. Philip Clayton and Zachary Simpson (Oxford: Oxford University Press, 2006), 662; Polkinghorne, *One World*, 73; Polkinghorne, *Science and Creation*, 53; and Polkinghorne, *Theology in the Context*, 159n6.

28. *The Oxford Dictionary of the Christian Church*, 3rd ed. rev., ed. Frank Leslie Cross and Elizabeth A. Livingstone (Oxford: Oxford University Press, 2005), 1221–22. William Hill defines panentheism as "a doctrine which constitutes divinity as neither identical with the world (pantheism) nor as autonomous from it (classical theism), but as in a state of dependence upon it" (William J. Hill, "Does Divine Love Entail Suffering in God?" in *God and Temporality*, ed. Bowman L. Clarke and Eugene T. Long, 55–71 [New York: Paragon House, 1984]). Panentheism, however, comes in many forms: "There may be as many panentheisms as there are ways of qualifying the world's being 'in God'" (Niels Henrik Gregersen, "Three Varieties of Panentheism," in *In Whom We Live and Move and Have Our Being: Panentheistic Reflections on God's Presence in a Scientific World*, ed. Philip Clayton and Arthur Peacocke [Grand Rapids, Mich.: Eerdmans, 2004], 19).

29. The term "theism" denotes "a philosophical system which accepts a transcendent and personal God who not only created but also preserves and governs the world, the contingency of which does not exclude miracles and the exercise of human freedom" (*The Oxford Dictionary of the Christian Church*, 1608). In addition, theism may include the tenet that God is "all-knowing, all-powerful,

Despite its efforts to tread a middle course, however, panentheism seems to collapse inevitably into pantheism. Its assertion that God's being is "more than and not exhausted by the universe" betrays this pantheistic orientation. For the assertion makes sense only if God's being and the being of the universe are taken univocally. As we can add apples and oranges only by finding a common univocal category, such as "fruit," so we can add God's being to that of the universe (and so conclude that the former is "more than" and "not exhausted by" the latter) only if we think of "being" as a common, univocal category that embraces both. To think of God's being and the being of the world univocally, however, is pantheistic since such a univocal understanding implies that both are essentially the same. As the water in my cup is essentially the same as the water in the pitcher (even if there happens to be more of it in the pitcher than in the cup), so the being of the world is essentially the same as the being of God (even if there happens to be more of it in God than there is in the world).

When Aquinas affirms that "God is in things," and "all things are in God," he does not mean that things are part of God, that God is part of things, or both God and things together are part of some greater totality of univocal being.[30] Rather, God is immanently present in things precisely insofar as he is the transcendent (and so wholly other) source of their being. This entails a most radical sort of immanence, which can be characteristic only of an utterly transcendent Creator: "God is in all things, not indeed as part of their essence, nor as an accident; but as an agent is present to that upon which

---

and all-good" (Brian Davies, *An Introduction to the Philosophy of Religion* [Oxford: Oxford University Press, 1993], 32). John W. Cooper points out the difference between panentheism and traditional theism: "Panentheism affirms that although God and the world are ontologically distinct and God transcends the world, the world is 'in' God ontologically. In contrast, classical theism posits an unqualified distinction between God and the world: although intimately related, God and creatures are always and entirely other than one another" (John W. Cooper, *Panentheism: The Other God of the Philosophers: From Plato to the Present* [Grand Rapids, Mich.: Baker Books, 2006], 18). Theism goes under a variety of names such as "traditional theism," "classical theism," "philosophical theism," "unitarian theism," and "supernaturalistic theism." The term has many shades of meaning, not all of which are compatible with traditional Christian faith. See Ingolf U. Dalferth, "The Historical Roots of Theism," in *Traditional Theism and Its Modern Alternatives*, ed. Svend Andersen (Aarhus: Aarhus University Press, 1994), 15–43; Philip Clayton, "Panentheism in Metaphysical and Scientific Perspective," in *In Whom We Live and Move and Have Our Being: Panentheistic Reflections on God's Presence in a Scientific World*, ed. Philip Clayton and Arthur Peacocke (Grand Rapids, Mich.: Eerdmans, 2004), 73–74; and Clayton, *Adventures*, 118–32.

30. *ST* I, 8, 1, ad 2. As Herbert McCabe puts it, "God is not what is left over when you remove creatures" (Herbert McCabe, *God and Evil in the Theology of St. Thomas Aquinas*, ed. Brian Davies [New York: Continuum, 2010], 129).

it works.... Now since God is very being by his own essence, created being must be his proper effect.... Now God causes this effect in things not only when they first begin to be, but as long as they are preserved in being.... Therefore as long as a thing has being, God must be present to it, according to its mode of being. But being is innermost in each thing and most fundamentally inherent in all things since it is formal in respect to everything found in a thing.... Hence it must be that God is in all things and innermostly."[31]

The "Causal Joint"

By affirming God's intimate action in each thing, we can also address the issue of the "causal joint."[32] Since God's action is one with his being and essence, there is, on his part, no intervening "joint" or "relation" between him and the creature in which he acts. In this, God is unlike creatures who do require a certain disposition in their actions. Aquinas explains that in creaturely actions there is "some disposition through which an agent is adapted or rendered proportionate to a patient, or a recipient. And because [an agent] acts thus in different things it must have different dispositions by which it is adapted to diverse things. In this way a certain multitude occurs in a thing of this sort, that is, one that acts in different ways upon different things according to its different dispositions, which are outside its nature, or essence, which is one. Thus, such a thing, that is, one that acts according to different dispositions, is mixed with the things upon which it acts according to a certain adaptation to them."[33] The action of a creature is distinct from its being and adapted in some way to the thing acted upon. A surgeon, for instance, produces one kind of action when using a scalpel in a delicate operation and another when wielding an axe to split logs for his fireplace.

---

31. *ST* I, 8, 1, co. Cf. *ST* I, 3, 8, co.; *SCG* III, 68, no. 11. Citing some of these passages, Niels Gregersen correctly points out that, although "proponents of panentheism often claim it better articulates the immanence of God than classical theism," such "immanence of God in creatures is indeed asserted" in the "classical theism" of Aquinas. He also correctly identifies a key difference between Aquinas and panentheism: "The real difference, according to Thomas, is that the nature and activities of the creatures do not have a real feedback effect on God.... The world is utterly dependent on God for its existence, while the world cannot really affect the being or mind of God" (Gregersen, "Three Varieties," 24). What Gregersen fails to see is that this utter dependence on God as the source of its being, is not only the reason why the world cannot contribute to the being and knowledge of God but also the ground for God's surpassing immanence in the world. A God that could in any way be actualized by the world could not be as immanent in the world as the God of Aquinas.

32. See the discussion of "the causal joint" in the section "Divine Action and the Constriction of Causality in Modern Science" in chapter three.

33. *Super de causis*, 20 (Guagliardo, 123). Cf. *Sent.* I, 8, 4, 3, ad 3.

God's action is quite different from this. His action is one with his being, and no disposition or "connecting link" stands between God and his action in creatures: "The first cause acts through its being.... Hence it does not act through any additional relation or disposition through which it would be adapted to and mixed with things. And such a 'relation' is called here a 'connecting link' or mediating thing [*continuator vel res media*] because through such a disposition or relation an agent is adapted to a recipient, and [such a relation] is in a certain sense a mediating thing between the essence of the agent and the patient itself."[34] To posit such a relation or "joint" would be to reduce God to the level of other causes which do act only "through such a disposition or relation" and so cannot be as intimately present to one another as God is to each of them.[35] As David Burrell explains: "Divine action must effect its results immediately, yet not in such a way as to replace the created agents at work. The only possible candidate for such a cause is the cause of being itself, and even more precisely, the cause of each thing's existing. For only existing individuals can act, so that the One who empowers each thing to exist thereby empowers it to act.... Thus we are reminded once again that any account of divine causal activity must tailor itself to the paradigm of creation, which requires an activity without any attendant process; one which may be asserted but never tracked. And if the assertion of a free creation is already a faith-assertion, providence will be so as well. So the mode or manner of divine activity will ever escape us, yet we will be able to speak of it consistently, provided we keep referring any divine action to the constituting and originating activity of creation."[36]

The Relation between God and Creatures

As the source of being in creatures, God is beyond the whole order of creaturely reality. This means that the relationship between God and creatures must be quite different from that of one creature to another. The difference implies not that God is more distant from creatures than they are from one another, but infinitely closer.[37]

Aquinas finds two ways in which creatures that belong to the same or-

---

34. *Super de causis*, 20 (Guagliardo, 123–24).   35. *Super de causis*, 20 (Guagliardo, 124).
36. Burrell, *Freedom and Creation*, 122–23.
37. On the nature of the relationship between God and creation in Thomas Aquinas, see Michael J. Dodds, "Ultimacy and Intimacy: Aquinas on the Relation between God and the World," in *Ordo Sapientiae et Amoris: Hommage au Professeur Jean-Pierre Torrell, O.P.*, ed. Carlos-Josaphat Pinto de Oliveira (Fribourg, Switzerland: Editions Universitaires, 1993), 211–27.

der may be related to each other. Such relations may be based either on the property of quantity or on the action of one agent upon another. In the first way, a material thing may, for example, have the relation of being larger or smaller than another. In the second way, creaturely action may ground a relationship, as the act of generating a child may establish the relation of parenthood.[38] All such creaturely relations involve a note of mutual dependency. The existence of the relationship in one term depends in some way on the other term. One thing cannot have the property of being "larger" except with respect to something that is "smaller," and vice versa. One cannot have the relationship of parenthood except with respect to a child that one has generated. Aquinas considers all such relationships to be real. They are not just in our mind, but are actual aspects of the world.[39] They are found in creatures that belong to the same order and so may have mutual dependencies.

Since God is the source of creatures, God neither depends on creatures nor belongs to the same order of being. It would therefore be inappropriate to attribute to God the real relations of mutual dependency that are characteristic of creatures. Since creatures really depend on God and are ordered to God as parts of his creation, they are really related to God. Since God does not depend on creatures and is not part of the order of creation, God has no corresponding relation to creatures: "As the creature proceeds from God in diversity of nature, God is outside the order of the whole creation, nor does any relation to the creature arise from His nature; for He does not produce the creature by necessity of His nature, but by His intellect and will."[40]

Here we find Aquinas's often misunderstood teaching on the relationship between God and creation: "Since therefore God is outside the whole order of creation, and all creatures are ordered to Him, and not conversely, it is manifest that creatures are really related to God himself; whereas in God there is no real relation to creatures, but a relation only in idea, inasmuch as creatures are referred to Him."[41] The statement can readily be

---

38. "Now there are other relations which are realities as regards both extremes, as when for instance a habitude exists between two things according to some reality that belongs to both; as is clear of all relations, consequent upon quantity; as great and small, double and half, and the like; for quantity exists in both extremes: and the same applies to relations consequent upon action and passion, as motive power and the movable thing, father and son, and the like" (*ST* I, 13, 7, co.). Cf. *De pot* 7, 9, co.

39. "Some have said that relation is not a reality, but only an idea. But this is plainly seen to be false from the very fact that things themselves have a mutual natural order and habitude" (*ST* I, 13, 7, co.).

40. *ST* I, 28, 1, ad 3.

41. *ST* I, 13, 7, co. "Therefore there is no real relation in God to the creature; whereas in crea-

taken to imply that God is uncaring or that his love is unreal. William Lane Craig accordingly calls this teaching an "absurdity," and David Tracy argues that it jeopardizes Christianity's "most fundamental religious affirmation."[42] Properly understood, however, the statement is an affirmation of God's transcendence and intimate involvement in creation.

Creaturely relations may be based on quantity or action. God's relation to creation cannot arise from the property of quantity since God is not a material being. It arises rather from God's action. But God's action is fundamentally different from that of creatures. While a creature's action is an incidental aspect of its being, God's action is one with God's being.[43] When one creature acts on another, it is incidentally present to the other. When God acts on or in a creature, God is substantially present.[44] Since God's

---

tures there is a real relation to God; because creatures are contained under the divine order, and their very nature entails dependence on God" (*ST* I, 28, 1, ad 3).

42. William Lane Craig, *God, Time, and Eternity* (Dordrecht, The Netherlands: Kluwer, 2001), 61, 78; and D. Tracy, *Blessed Rage for Order*, 177.

43. "God does not act through a mediating action which is understood as proceeding from God and terminating in the creature. But his action is his substance, and whatever is in it is altogether outside the genus of created being through which the creature is referred to God" (*De pot.* 7, 9, ad 4). "God does not work by an intermediary action to be regarded as issuing from God and terminating in the creature: but his action is his substance and is wholly outside the genus of created being whereby the creature is related to him. Nor again does any good accrue to the creator from the production of the creature: wherefore his action is supremely liberal. . . . It is also evident that he is not moved to act and that without any change in himself he makes all changeable things. It follows then that there is no real relation in him to creatures, although creatures are really related to him, as effects to their cause" (*De pot* 7, 10, co.).

44. "The natural mover or agent moves and acts by an intermediary movement or action that is between the mover and the thing moved, between the agent and the patient: wherefore in this intermediary, at least agent and patient, mover and thing moved must come together. Wherefore the agent as such is not outside the genus of the patient as such: and consequently each has a real relation to the other, especially seeing that this intermediary action is a perfection proper to the agent so that the term of that action is a perfection of the agent. This does not apply to God" (*De pot.* 7, 10, ad 1). "There are two kinds of contact; corporeal contact, when two bodies touch each other; and virtual contact, as the cause of sadness is said to touch the one made sad. According to the first kind of contact, God, as being incorporeal, neither touches, nor is touched; but according to virtual contact He touches creatures by moving them; but He is not touched, because the natural power of no creature can reach up to Him. Thus did Dionysius understand the words, 'There is no contact with God'; that is, so that God Himself be touched" (*ST* I, 105, 2, ad 1). "Human persons then, unlike divine persons, change in every new relation. The relations they establish are through changes in their natures, through and in which they relate to others. Thus human persons are never related to one another as they are in themselves, but always by some changeable mediating action of their nature. This is easily seen in human love. A person grows in love and tries to express it, but he soon realizes that no expression of his love captures and makes real the totality of his love. This is because the person cannot relate himself as he is, with all his love, to the other person, but must use mediating and changeable actions" (Thomas G. Weinandy, *Does God Change? The Word's Becoming in the Incarnation* [Still River, Mass.: St. Bede's Publications, 1984], 184).

most fundamental action is to give being, and since being is most intimate to the creature, God's action makes God's very substance most intimately present to the creature.

A real relation of mutual dependence may arise from the incidental action of one creature on another. Such a relation, however, is simply too tangential to express the intimacy of divine presence that arises through God's substantial action in the creature. Real relations of mutual dependence arise between creatures that are never more than "beside" one another. They cannot capture the closeness of divine presence that arises from the action of God who is never simply beside but most deeply within the creature. To predicate such a relation of God would be to reduce God to the level of one creature existing beside another. In effect, the notion of "real relation" is simply too remote to express the intimacy of God's presence.

This does not mean, however, that there is no relation between God and creation or that the relation is merely imaginary. A relation always has two terms, and in each of them the relation may be real or logical (of idea only). This yields three possibilities.[45] If it is of idea only in both terms, then the relation is purely conceptual; it exists only in the mind and not in the thing. The relationship of identity is of this sort. A thing that is actually one is mentally taken to be two and so found to be "identical" with itself. The relationship exists only in one's head. In another way, the relation may be real in each term. These are the relations of mutual dependency we have seen between creatures that belong to the same order and are somehow "beside" each other. The third possibility is that the relation may be real in one term and of idea only in the other. Here the relationship is not merely imaginary; nor does it imply the mutual dependency of beings that are merely alongside each other.[46] This is often called a "mixed relation."[47] It is the kind of relation that Aquinas predicates between God and creatures. It is the sort

---

45. See *ST* I, 13, 7, co.; *Sent.* I, 30, 1, 3, ad 3.
46. "Some things are relative to each other on an equal basis, as master and servant, father and son, great and small; and he [Aristotle] says that these are relative as contraries; and they are relative of themselves because each of these things taken in its quiddity is said to be relative to something else. But other things are not relative on an equal basis, but one of them is said to be relative, not because it itself is referred to something else, but because something else is referred to it, as happens, for example, in the case of knowledge and the knowable object. For what is knowable is called such relatively, not because it is referred to knowledge, but because knowledge is referred to it" (*In meta.* X, lect. 8, nos. 13–14 [§2087–88]).
47. See A. Krempel, *La doctrine de la relation chez saint Thomas* (Paris: Librairie Philosophique J. Vrin, 1952), 458.

of rapport that attains between beings that belong to different orders of being. Its reality in the creature is the result of God's creative act in calling the creature into existence.[48] Aquinas can therefore affirm that *there is* a relation between the creator and the creature, precisely the mixed relation that pertains to beings that belong to different orders: "If by proportion is meant a definite excess, then there is no proportion in God to the creature. But if proportion stands for relation alone, then there is relation between the creator and the creature: in the latter really, but not in the former."[49]

This teaching preserves at once the reality of the relatedness of God and creatures, the transcendence and immanence of God, and the dependence of the creature.[50] Despite the rather awkward and easily misunderstood terminology, therefore, the teaching seeks to maintain that God is infinitely more intimately involved with each creature than would be possible in the kind of real relation of mutual dependency that is found between creatures.[51]

God's involvement in the world is confirmed in Aquinas's Trinitarian theology. The relationships of knowing and loving that are most intimate to the Trinitarian life of Father, Son, and Holy Spirit, are not without import to the world that God creates in wisdom and love. The name "Word" or "Logos" that is reserved most especially to the Son proceeding from the Father

---

48. See *ST* I, 45, 3.
49. *De pot.* 7, 10, ad 9.
50. "To predicate real relations of God to us . . . would be to deprive him of his divinity, to make him intrinsically dependent upon us" (Krempel, 460).
51. "The Creator, because of his transcendence as Creator, is 'more' and 'more intensely' *in* the world than creatures themselves are capable of being since he is more immanent in individual created things, and so more immanent in the universe, than creatures themselves" (Raphael Schulte, "Wie ist Gottes Wirken in Welt und Geschichte theologisch zu verstehen?" in *Vorsehung und Handeln Gottes*, ed. Theodor Schneider und Lothar Ullrich [Leipzig: St. Benno Verlag, 1988], 141). "Creation, as the coming to be of some share of the divine actuality in the effect, does not necessitate any change or alteration in the divine being itself. Such alteration characterizes, not causality as such, but only finite causality wherein the cause undergoes a transition from being able to cause to actually exercising such causality, a transition alien to a cause that is already and always the fullness of act. In short, God is operative at the heart of all creaturely activity but without being acted upon by creatures in return in such wise as to gain something previously lacking to him. This is the basis of Aquinas' generally misunderstood teaching that the creature is really related to God, whereas God's relation to the creature is a relation of reason only. This is only intended to preclude any relation accruing to God accidentally as an increment (or diminution) of his being which would then have to be conceived as lacking something of the perfection of being to begin with. It is not meant to imply that God does not actually create, know, love, redeem the world, and the like. The resulting relationship is not a mere extrinsic denomination on the part of human knowers. It is designated a relation of reason to convey that the fundament for it is something intrinsically intelligible within God, namely an actual exercise of causality on God's part vis a vis the creature" (Hill, "The Implicate World," 87).

bears a relation to creation: "Word implies relation to creatures. For God by knowing Himself, knows every creature.... Because God by one act understands Himself and all things, His one only Word is expressive not only of the Father, but of all creatures."[52] Likewise the love of the Holy Spirit, uniting the Father and the Son most intimately, expresses a relation to creatures: "The Father loves not only the Son, but also Himself and us, by the Holy Spirit.... Hence, as the Father speaks Himself and every creature by His begotten Word, inasmuch as the Word begotten adequately represents the Father and every creature; so He loves Himself and every creature by the Holy Spirit, inasmuch as the Holy Spirit proceeds as the love of the primal goodness whereby the Father loves Himself and every creature. Thus it is evident that relation to the creature is implied both in the Word and in the proceeding Love, as it were in a secondary way, inasmuch as the divine truth and goodness are a principle of understanding and loving all creatures."[53]

The Language of Divine Action

Starting with God's transcendent being gives us a perspective on what should be said and left unsaid regarding divine action. Aquinas thinks that we can speak of anything to the extent that we know it. Following Aristotle, he also believes that our knowledge of things begins with the senses. Our language and knowledge, then, are geared toward creatures which we know first through our senses and then through our intellect.

Given this epistemological context, our verbal and conceptual abilities should be utterly defeated if we try to speak of God, since God is utterly beyond the being of creatures.[54] The defeat is overcome, however, by the fact that God is the creator, the source of the creatures that we are able to know and speak about.[55] Since effects in some way (however remote and attenu-

---

52. *ST* I, 34, 3, co. Cf.: 34, 3, ad 2.
53. *ST* I, 37, 2, ad 3. See also Gilles Emery, *Trinity in Aquinas* (Ypsilanti, Mich.: Sapientia Press, 2002); Gilles Emery, "The Personal Mode of Trinitarian Action in Saint Thomas Aquinas," *Thomist* 69 (2005): 31–77; and Gilles Emery, *The Trinitarian Theology of Saint Thomas Aquinas* (New York: Oxford University Press, 2007).
54. "The first cause is above being *(ens)* insofar as it is infinite 'to-be' *(ipsum esse infinitum)*. 'Being,' however, is called that which finitely participates 'to be,' and it is this which is proportioned to our intellect, whose object is some 'that which is.' ... Hence our intellect can grasp only that which has a quiddity participating 'to be.' But the quiddity of God is 'to be' itself. Thus it is above intellect" *(Super de causis,* 6 [Guagliardo, 51–52]).
55. "God is not an existent thing in the way that these [creaturely] things are existents since the nature of being is in him eminently. As he is not entirely without being, however, he is also not entirely beyond knowledge as if he could not be known at all. Still, he is not known in the same way as

ated) resemble their cause, creatures are in some way like God.⁵⁶ So, the language that we normally use of creatures can, in some way (however remote and attenuated) also be used of God.⁵⁷

From Pseudo-Dionysius, Aquinas learns three ways to talk about God. First, creaturely attributes may somehow be attributed to God since God is the cause of creatures. Second, such attributes must also be denied of God insofar as creatures fall short of God's perfection. Third, names describing creaturely perfection may be said of God in a supereminent way since God utterly exceeds the perfection of creatures. These are the three ways of causation, negation, and eminence.⁵⁸ Using them, we can say, for instance, that "God is good," as the source of the goodness of creatures (the way of causation), only if we immediately deny that the limited goodness of creatures should be attributed to God (the way of negation), and affirm that the notion

---

other existing things that can be comprehended by the created intellect" (*Sent*. I, 3, 1, 1, ad 1). "The very fact that God the Wholly Other is Creator means that he is also the Ultimate-Intimate One, the One Wholly near at hand. All this implies that in one way or another God's transcendent, creative activity will come to expression in our world; otherwise there would be no ground, no occasion even, for justifying our talk of God's acting in our history—not even in an evocative and analogous way" (Schillebeeckx, *Jesus*, 627). "If God must remain outside of any genus, he is properly unknowable. Such an assertion would seem to end in pure agnosticism. Yet Aquinas refuses to settle for that and goes on to drive a wedge: then God must be improperly knowable, namely by analogy. So far this says no more than the term ana-logos itself suggests: improperly knowledge yet still knowledge. The implication is, of course, that God is at all costs knowable; or rather, Aquinas implies that something must be able to be said about him" (David B. Burrell, *Analogy and Philosophical Language* [New Haven, Conn.: Yale University Press, 1973], 126).

56. "If there is an agent not contained in any genus, its effect will still more distantly reproduce the form of the agent; not, that is, so as to participate in the likeness of the agent's form according to the same specific or generic formality, but only according to some sort of analogy; as existence is common to all. In this way all created things, insofar as they are beings, are like God as the first and universal principle of all being" (*ST* I, 4, 3, co.). Cf. *ST* I, 4, 3, ad 3; I, 44, 3, ad 1; *Sent*. I, 8, 1, 2, co. See also John F. Wippel, "Thomas Aquinas on Our Knowledge of God and the Axiom That Every Agent Produces Something Like Itself," *Proceedings of the American Catholic Philosophical Association* 74 (2000): 81–101.

57. "In this way some things are said of God and creatures analogically, and not in a purely equivocal nor in a purely univocal sense. For we can name God only from creatures. Thus whatever is said of God and creatures, is said according to the relation of a creature to God as its principle and cause, wherein all perfections of things pre-exist excellently. Now this mode of community of idea is a mean between pure equivocation and simple univocation. For in analogies the idea is not, as it is in univocals, one and the same, yet it is not totally diverse as in equivocals; but a term which is thus used in a multiple sense signifies various proportions to some one thing" (*ST* I, 13, 5, co.). Perhaps Aquinas here answers the need identified by Langdon Gilkey: "What we desperately need is a theological ontology that will put intelligible and credible meanings into our analogical categories of divine deeds and of divine self-manifestation through events" (Gilkey, "Cosmology," 40).

58. Aquinas regularly employs these three ways. See, for example, *Sent*. I, 2, 1, 3, co.; d. 3, 1, 1, *div. text*; a. 3, co.; d. 22, 1, 2, obj. 2; d. 35, 1, 1, co.; *ST* I, 12, 12, co.; Q.13, 1, co.; a.8, ad 2; a.10, ad 5; Q.84, 7, ad 3; II-II, 27, 4, co.; *De pot*. Q. 9, 7, obj. 2; co.; *De malo* Q.16, 8, ad 3; *In de div. nom*. I, lect. 3 (§83, 85, 102, 104); VII, lect. 4 (§729, 731); *Super de trin*. Q. 1, 2, co.; Q. 6, 2, co.; a. 3, co.; *Super ad rom*. I, lect. 6 (§115).

of goodness—to the extent that it implies no imperfection in itself—may be said of God preeminently (the way of eminence).

Taken together, these three ways generate an analogous way of speaking about God that maintains the tension between what we may affirm and what we must deny. In using this language, we never overcome our limited, creaturely way of understanding the words and concepts that we employ. John Henry Cardinal Newman reflects on this dilemma:

> We can only speak of Him, whom we reason about but have not seen, in the terms of our experience. When we reflect on Him and put into words our thoughts about Him, we are forced to transfer to a new meaning ready made words, which primarily belong to objects of time and place. We are aware, while we do so, that they are inadequate, but we have the alternative of doing so, or doing nothing at all. We can only remedy their insufficiency by confessing it. We can do no more than put ourselves on the guard as to our own proceeding, and protest against it, while we do adhere to it. We can only set right one error of expression by another. By this method of antagonism we steady our minds, not so as to reach their object, but to point them in the right direction; as in an algebraical process we might add and subtract in series, approximating little by little, by saying and unsaying, to a positive result.[59]

To use Aquinas's phrase, we never escape our creaturely "mode of signifying" when we speak of God. If we say "God is good," for instance, it is always a creaturely kind of goodness we have in mind, since that is the only sort of goodness we know. Our intention, however, is to use the word to point beyond our creaturely limitations to a divine goodness (the "thing signified" by the word, to again use Aquinas's terminology).[60] We can therefore speak truly about God, and know that we are speaking truly, even though we do not comprehend the truth that we are saying in any positive way.[61]

This is our situation when we say anything of God, including our talk of divine action. It is easy to see that it would be a mistake to speak of God's action as if it were univocal or had the same meaning as creaturely action. It would also be untrue to think that divine action is equivocal or had absolutely no relation to creaturely action and so could not be spoken of at all. Our philosophical and theological language about divine action involves the

---

59. John Henry Newman, "On Certainty, Intuition and the Conceivable, 1861–1863," in *The Theological Papers of John Henry Newman on Faith and Certainty*, ed. J. Derek Holmes (Oxford: Clarendon Press, 1976), 102.

60. *ST* I, 13, 6, co.

61. On the nature of analogous language in Aquinas, see Gregory Rocca, *Speaking the Incomprehensible God: Thomas Aquinas on the Interplay of Positive and Negative Theology* (Washington, D.C.: The Catholic University of America Press, 2004); Ralph McInerny, *Aquinas and Analogy* (Washington, D.C.: The Catholic University of America Press, 1996); and Burrell, *Analogy and Philosophical Language*.

inevitable tension of analogy. Even within the tension of that usage, however, we recognize that we may speak truly of God's activity.[62] Such tension, however, is not easy to maintain, as Brian Hebblethwaite and Edward Henderson point out: "Talk about God's action will always require, therefore, the use of analogies drawn from relations among finite agents, and there will always be the danger of applying analogies without the right qualifications or of identifying the relation of God and creature with some relation of creatures to each other."[63]

When we speak philosophically of God's action, we begin with our human knowledge of this world. Based on that knowledge we can reason to the existence and influence of a being that transcends this world and then speak of the action of that being using our human language analogously. When we speak theologically, we begin with God's revelation. We are convinced by faith of the truth, revealed in Scripture and Christian tradition, that God acts both in God's own Trinitarian life and in creation.[64] We then set out to find a model to help us understand that truth. This is the exercise of faith seeking understanding. We grope for some sort of action or activity in the creaturely sphere to use as a model or analog to help us to penetrate—however inadequately—the mystery of God's action. The models we find may be more or less adequate, and one model may eventually replace another. The theological truth of divine action remains the same, however, no matter what model we use and however limited and inadequate it may be.

Aquinas uses the model of immanent action to describe the Trinitarian life of Father, Son, and Holy Spirit, and that of transient action to speak of God's action in the world.[65] Immanent motion includes the activities of

62. "Analogy is very useful when we try to speak about God. On the one hand, God's action on nature should be seen as completely different from natural causality. God cannot simply be a first cause as the mere beginning of a series of causes. God's causality, as the source of all being and becoming and activity, cannot be represented by using the categories that we apply to created causes. We should admit an essential difference between God and creatures, for otherwise we would not really be speaking about God. On the other hand, divine and natural causality must have something in common, insofar as in both cases we are dealing with causes that produce effects. In this context, analogy means that we apply the concept of cause both to God and to creatures, partly in the same way and partly in a different way" (Artigas, *Mind*, 145).

63. Brian Hebblethwaite and Edward Henderson, "Introduction," in *Divine Action: Studies Inspired by the Philosophical Theology of Austin Farrer* (Edinburgh: T & T Clark, 1990), 7. See also Thomas F. Tracy, "Divine Action, Created Causes, and Human Freedom," in *The God Who Acts: Philosophical and Theological Explorations*, ed. Thomas F. Tracy (University Park: Pennsylvania State University Press, 1994), 82.

64. For Aquinas, the starting point for theology is faith. See *ST* I, 1, 1–10.

65. "There are two sorts of operation, as Aristotle teaches in *Metaphysics*: one that remains in the agent and is a perfection of it, as the acts of sensing, understanding, and willing; another that

knowing and willing—acts that are immanent since they remain in the agent who performs them. This model allows Aquinas to explore the rich biblical and traditional themes of Trinitarian theology in terms of the immanent processions of knowledge and love. Transient motion includes such mundane activities as heating and sawing—acts that in some way pass from a doer (such as a carpenter) to a receiver (such as wood). This is used as an analogy for the way that divine actuality is communicated to creatures.[66]

Aquinas saw this use of modeling in the method of theology as similar to the employment of models in the method of the astronomy of his day. As theologians look for models to try to understand the truths of faith (such as divine action), so astronomers look for models to understand the facts of nature (such as the motion of the heavens). As the truths of faith remain the same whatever model one might use for them, so astronomical facts remain constant, whatever model one might use to represent them. Aquinas knew that Aristotle modeled the cosmos as concentric spheres and that Ptolemy did so in a much more complex geometry of circular orbits. He speculated that science might find other, still more adequate, models in the future. As a better model is always possible in astronomy, so, by implication, a more adequate model is always possible in theology:

> Reason is employed in another way, not as furnishing a sufficient proof of a principle, but as confirming an already established principle, by showing the congruity of its results, as in astronomy the theory of eccentrics and epicycles is considered as established, because thereby the sensible appearances of the heavenly movements can be explained; not, however, as if this proof were sufficient, forasmuch as some other theory might explain them.... In the second way, reasons avail to prove the Trinity; as, when assumed to be true, such reasons confirm it. We must not, however, think that the trinity of persons is adequately proved by such reasons [*rationes*].[67]

To put Aquinas's observations in contemporary language, we might say that the data of astronomical observations remains the same whether it is

---

passes over into an external thing, and is a perfection of the thing made as a result of that operation, the acts of heating, cutting, and building, for example. Now both kinds of operation belong to God: the former, in that he understands, wills, rejoices, and loves; the latter, in that he brings things into being, preserves them, and governs them" (*SCG* II, 1, nos. 2–3 [§853–854]). Cf. *De pot*. Q.10, 1, co.; SCG II, 10, no. 2; *ST* II, 3, 2, ad 3; 57, 4, co.

66. See *ST* I, 27; *SCG* II, 1, no. 3. For a brief overview of immanent and transient motion as models for divine action in Aquinas, see Michael J. Dodds, *The Unchanging God of Love: Thomas Aquinas and Contemporary Theology on Divine Immutability* (Washington, D.C.: The Catholic University of America Press, 2008), 161–203.

67. *ST* I, 32, 1, ad 2.

described or explained by the cosmological model of Aristotle, Ptolemy, Copernicus, Galileo, Newton, Kepler, or Einstein. Similarly, divine action remains the same reality whether it is described through the model of quantum mechanics, chaos theory, emergence—or the notions of final, formal, and efficient causality. It is simply a question of what model is more adequate for speaking of divine action and less likely to distort divine action and cause us to conceptualize it as something it is not—such as an action univocal with the activity of creatures. If the models for divine action that directly employ interpretations of contemporary theories of science tend to involve us in univocal thinking, we may have reason to look beyond them to other models that use, instead, the new understanding of causality that stands behind the theories of contemporary science.

THE MODES OF DIVINE ACTION

Contemporary developments in science have opened new ways of thinking about causality beyond the constricted views of classical Newtonian physics. These are reminiscent of the understanding of causality in Aristotle and Thomas Aquinas. The indeterminism that the Copenhagen interpretation of quantum mechanics finds in nature evokes Aristotle's idea of primary matter as mere possibility of being (at least in Heisenberg's account). It steers us away from the deterministic Newtonian universe and invites a new consideration of Aristotle's notion of chance or spontaneity. The "top-down" causality of the theory of emergence that is now widely employed in physics, chemistry, and biology encourages a retrieval of Aristotle's formal causality. The "anthropic principle" in cosmology and teleological language in biology suggest a new consideration of Aristotle's final causality. The scientific understanding of efficient causality has moved far beyond Newton's "force that moves the atoms," and invites a reconsideration of the nuances of efficient causality developed by Aristotle and Aquinas.

Such broad notions of causality dropped out of theology's discussion of divine action with the advent of modern science and the worldview that tacitly or explicitly accompanied it. The discussion and exploration of such modes of causality in contemporary science now invite theology to explore them once again in its discussion of divine action.[68] We will do this through

---

68. See Michael J. Dodds, "Science, Causality, and Divine Action: Classical Principles for Contemporary Challenges," *CTNS Bulletin* 21, no. 1 (2001): 3–12; and Michael J. Dodds, "Unlocking Divine Causality: Aquinas, Contemporary Science, and Divine Action," *Angelicum* 86 (2009): 67–86.

Aristotle's philosophy as developed by Thomas Aquinas. This philosophical tradition already enjoys a close acquaintance with contemporary science.[69]

In this chapter, we will consider God's action in relation to final, formal, and efficient causality.[70] In the next chapter, we will then consider the relation of the action of God to that of creatures, especially with regard to chance and human freedom. The division of this discussion is useful conceptually, but should not be taken to imply that God sometimes acts simply as a final cause and other times as a formal or efficient cause. In all that God does, God is at once the final, formal exemplar and efficient cause of all things.[71] John Cobb underlines the need for this discussion: "Either some sense must be made of divine final and efficient causation or belief in God in the Western sense must be abandoned."[72]

Final Causality

Contemporary science has rediscovered the importance of final causality. In biology, it has become an increasingly respected and necessary category of explanation. The anthropic principle treats human life as a final cause to explain the fine tuning among the fundamental constants of physics.

Aquinas follows Aristotle in giving primacy to final causality as "the cause of the causality of all the causes."[73] Since God is the first cause of all

---

69. See Ralph McInerny's review of the rich interaction between Thomism and science in his article "Thomism," in *A Companion to Philosophy of Religion*, ed. Philip Quinn and Charles Taliaferro (Cambridge: Blackwell, 1997), 162. See also Goris, *Free Creatures*, 289.

70. Material causality is missing from this list since, as might be imagined, Aquinas finds it inappropriate to attribute this to God: "Although there are four causes in created things, the characteristics of all the causes are not found in God. The characteristic of the material cause does not belong to God either with respect to something that is in him or with respect to that which is in creatures because matter is imperfect and in potency" (*Sent* I, 34, 1, 2, co.). Yet, matter is also from God: "Since God is the efficient, the exemplar, and the final cause of all things, and since primary matter is from Him, it follows that the first principle of all things is one in reality" (*ST* I, 44, 4, ad 4). As part of creation, matter is also in some way like God: "Although matter as regards its potentiality recedes from likeness to God, yet, even in so far as it has being in this wise, it retains a certain likeness to the divine being" (*ST* I, 14, 11, ad 3).

71. "God not only gives things their form, but he also preserves them in existence, and applies them to act, and is moreover the end of every action" (*ST* I, 105, 5, ad 3). "In the three aspects of the act of creation it is not difficult to recognize a reference to Aristotle's analysis of the manifold senses of cause. The aspect of production is unmistakably associated with the efficient cause (*causa efficiens*); the distinction refers to the extrinsic formal cause (*causa exemplaris*), and the couple preservation/government is related to the final cause (*causa finalis*). The material cause does not play a distinct role in the causality of creation. The matter of things is not presupposed by the threefold active causality of creation, but rather posited by its universal action. In contrast to natural causation the divine cause of creation does not presuppose a material substrate: God creates the world *ex nihilo*, including its matter" (Te Velde, *Aquinas on God*, 125–26).

72. Cobb, "Natural Causality," 106.   73. *De prin. nat.* c. 4, no. 24.

things and final causality is the first of all causes, God must be the final cause of creation as a whole and of every creature.[74] The influence of God's final causality is present in the least act of every creature. Each one acts in accordance with its nature. In doing this, it is consciously or unconsciously seeking some good, namely, the fulfillment of its nature. Its nature, however, bears some likeness to God since God is the creator of all things, and each thing in some way resembles its creator. The fulfillment of its nature, therefore, also bears some likeness to God, since that fulfillment is proportionate to its nature, and its nature is like God. In seeking its fulfillment as a good proportionate to its nature, therefore, it is also seeking God or divine goodness since the fulfillment of its nature bears a likeness to God.[75] In its every act, therefore, the creature is in some way seeking the goodness of God as its final cause.[76]

This mode of divine influence as the final cause of all things is much more profound than the simple causality of "the force that moves the atoms" in Newtonian science. It involves no force at all—no pushing or pulling. Those are aspects of efficient causality, not final causality. This divine influence that pervades all creation and is present in every creaturely act is nothing less than the very goodness of God, the final cause of all things.[77] Aquinas's argument here might be viewed as a metaphysical account of the "groaning of all creation" for fulfillment in God (Romans 8:22).

74. "The characteristic of final cause is in God with respect to creatures, whose goodness we say is the end of all creatures" (*Sent.* I, 34. 1. 2. co.). Cf. *ST* I, 103, 2, co.; I, 105, 2, ad 2.

75. "To be good belongs preeminently to God. For a thing is good according to its desirableness. Now everything seeks after its own perfection; and the perfection and form of an effect consist in a certain likeness to the agent, since every agent makes its like; and hence the agent itself is desirable and has the nature of good. For the very thing which is desirable in it is the participation of its likeness. Therefore, since God is the first effective cause of all things, it is manifest that the aspect of good and of desirableness belong to Him; and hence Dionysius attributes good to God as to the first efficient cause, saying that, God is called good 'as by Whom all things subsist'" (*ST* I, 6, 1, co.).

76. "All things, by desiring their own perfection, desire God Himself, inasmuch as the perfections of all things are so many similitudes of the divine being.... And so of those things which desire God, some know Him as He is Himself, and this is proper to the rational creature; others know some participation of His goodness, and this belongs also to sensible knowledge; others have a natural desire without knowledge, as being directed to their ends by a higher intelligence" (*ST* I, 6, 1, ad 2). "All things desire God as their end, when they desire some good thing, whether this desire be intellectual or sensible, or natural, i.e., without knowledge; because nothing is good and desirable except forasmuch as it participates in the likeness to God" (*ST* I, 44, 4, ad 3).

77. "God acts in everything that acts.... First as an end. For since every operation is for the sake of some good, real or apparent; and nothing is good either really or apparently, except in as far as it participates in a likeness to the Supreme Good, which is God; it follows that God Himself is the cause of every operation as its end" (*ST* I, 105, 5, co.). Cf. *ST* I-II, 109, 6, co.; *In de div. nom.* IX, lect. 3, lines 54–82.

As the final cause of all things, God does not act to attain some good for himself. His action is therefore unlike that of creatures who are always in some way seeking their own fulfillment: "Some things are both agent and patient at the same time: these are imperfect agents, and to these it belongs to intend, even while acting, the acquisition of something. But it does not belong to the First Agent, Who is agent only, to act for the acquisition of some end; He intends only to communicate His perfection, which is His goodness; while every creature intends to acquire its own perfection, which is the likeness of the divine perfection and goodness. Therefore the divine goodness is the end of all things."[78]

In these arguments, Aquinas's understanding of God is quite different from that of Aristotle. Aristotle also sees God as a final cause, the "unmoved mover" who moves the cosmos as the object of desire. His unmoved mover, however, does not itself create or love the universe it moves. The God of Aquinas, in contrast, is the final cause of all things precisely because he is first the creator, whose love has brought all things into being and who shares his goodness with each creature: "Every love of God is followed at some time by a good caused in the creature, but not co-eternal with the eternal love. And according to the difference of this good, the love of God for the creature is looked at differently. For one [love] is common, whereby he loves 'all things that are' (Wisdom 11:25), and thereby gives things their natural being. But the second [love] is a special love, whereby he draws the rational creature above the condition of its nature to a participation of the divine good. And according to this love, he is said to love someone simply, since it is by this love that God simply wishes the eternal good, which is himself, for the creature."[79]

---

78. *ST* I, 44, 4, co. Cf. *ST* I, 25, 2, co.

79. *ST* I-II, 110, 1, co. Cf. *Sent*. III, 32, 1, 2, co. Etienne Gilson maintains that Aquinas differs fundamentally from Aristotle in seeing God as an efficient cause rather than only a final cause: "It [the immovable mover of Aristotle] moves only by the love it excites—which it excites, observe, but does not breathe in.... The God of St. Thomas and Dante is a God who loves, the god of Aristotle is a god who does not refuse to be loved; the love that moves the heavens and the stars in Aristotle is the love of the heavens and the stars for god, but the love that moves them in St. Thomas and Dante is the love of God for the world; between these two motive causes there is all the difference between an efficient cause on the one hand and a final cause on the other" (Etienne Gilson, *The Spirit of Medieval Philosophy* [New York: Charles Scribner's Sons, 1940], 75). Mark Johnson argues, however, that Aquinas himself maintained that Aristotle's unmoved mover was not only the final cause but also the efficient cause of creation. Whether Aquinas was correct in this claim remains disputed: "For the entirety of his career St. Thomas claimed that Aristotle's God was the one upon whom the *esse omnium* depended, and on this matter he never changed his mind. Whether St. Thomas was right in attributing a doctrine of creation to Aristotle is a fair question, but *that* he did so seems to me

Aquinas's vision of God is also distinct from that of process theology. The process God is in some way seeking its own fulfillment—the increase of value in its consequent nature: "The completion of God's nature into a fullness of physical feeling is derived from the objectification of the world in God."[80] The God of Aquinas does not act for his own enhancement or fulfillment. He simply desires to share his infinite goodness as the end in which creatures find their fulfillment. In this, his love is better characterized as *agape* than as *eros*.[81]

Formal Causality

With the idea of emergence and the causality of the whole, contemporary science seems to have retrieved something of Aristotle's intuition that the whole is ineffably more than just a collection of parts. The recognition of a whole with a distinctive causality of its own beyond the sum of its parts, however, inevitably raises the philosophical question of what constitutes the being of the whole. What makes the whole to be a distinctive entity and not just a hodgepodge of parts? If the answer is simply "the structure of the parts," then the whole ceases to be a distinct entity and, in a sense, collapses back into its parts which are then seen as the ultimate explanation of the apparent identity of the whole. In that case, reductionism has the final word. But if the whole is truly a distinctive being with a characteristic causality that manifests its distinctness, then some causal principle is required beyond merely the structure of its parts.

To the extent that we recognize the distinctive identity of the whole, we will see the unique characteristics of the parts themselves as a product of the causality of the whole and no longer view the whole as an effect or epiphenomenon of the structure of the parts. This difference in perspective can be made clear by a simple question: Is a tiger a tiger because it has stripes, or does it have stripes because it is a tiger? (Note that this question is not about how we recognize or *know* that it is a tiger, but about what makes it to *be* a tiger.) Those who see the whole as an effect or epiphenomenon of the parts will answer that it is a tiger because it has stripes. The whole is a product of the parts. Those who begin with the whole and see it as the source of

---

beyond dispute" (Mark Johnson, "Did St. Thomas Attribute a Doctrine of Creation to Aristotle?" *New Scholasticism* 63 [1989]: 154–55).

80. Whitehead, *Process*, 345.

81. See William J. Hill, "Two Gods of Love: Aquinas and Whitehead," *Listening* 14 (1979): 249–65; Dodds, *Unchanging*, 208–13.

the structure of the parts will say that it has stripes because it is a tiger. The whole will take precedence over the parts. If priority is given to the whole over the part, it must also be given to that principle that accounts for the distinctive identity of the whole.

To identify that principle, we may need to move beyond empirical science as such and engage a philosophy of nature that can field broader questions about the natural world.[82] Like empirical science itself, such a philosophy will be critical about introducing superfluous principles (such as the "vital force" of the vitalists). It may find it necessary, however, to incorporate principles that lie beyond the scope of empirical science (such as primary matter and substantial form) in order to address questions that arise from science but may be broader than science. As John Goyette notes with respect to biological science: "The growth of a living organism, the dramatic corruption of the body after death, and the unity that prevails over the almost startling turnover among the parts of the body all point to the notion of substantial form, a form that is not a result of the coming together of the parts of the body, but their cause."[83] Rightly understood, such principles will not lead to vitalism or dualism. Instead, they will be seen as complementary to the work of science, explaining the phenomenon of the whole that is now recognized in physics, chemistry, biology, and cognitive science.

It is not our task here to pursue such a philosophy of nature. We will suggest only that the causality of form, now broached in empirical science, may also be helpful to theologians in their discussion of divine action. If there is reason to retrieve the notion of substantial form as an immanent principle in natural things to explain the existence and causality of whole entities as distinct from their parts, there is surely justification for theologians to use the idea of formal causality in their discussion of divine action. We might begin with the notion of form as an extrinsic exemplar cause.

Aquinas retrieves the Platonic notion of exemplar causality discarded by Aristotle. Unlike Plato, Aquinas sees exemplar causes not as subsisting entities, but as ideas in the mind of God. The ideas or types (exemplar causes) of all created things are in the divine mind.[84] As the idea in the mind of an artist is the source of the art she produces, so the divine ideas are the

---

82. See Wallace, *Modeling*; Auletta, "Science," 267–87.
83. Goyette, "Substantial Form," 533.
84. See *ST* I, 6, 4, co.; 15, 3, co. "In order to understand that God can be the cause of all creatures in their proper distinctiveness, one must assume in God the specific idea *(ratio speciei)* of each creature, which is the exemplar according to which God creates" (Te Velde, *Aquinas on God*, 126–27).

source of creatures.[85] God's exemplar causality is therefore tied to his efficient causality as creator: "God is the first exemplar cause of all things. In proof whereof we must consider that if for the production of anything an exemplar is necessary, it is in order that the effect may receive a determinate form.... Now it is manifest that things made by nature receive determinate forms. This determination of forms must be reduced to the divine wisdom as its first principle, for divine wisdom devised the order of the universe, which order consists in the variety of things. And therefore we must say that in the divine wisdom are the types of all things, which types we have called ideas—i.e., exemplar forms existing in the divine mind. And these ideas, though multiplied by their relations to things, in reality are not apart from the divine essence, according as the likeness to that essence can be shared diversely by different things. In this manner, therefore God himself is the first exemplar of all things."[86]

As products of God's exemplar causality, creatures are in some way like God and are said to "participate" or possess "in part" the actuality that God possesses infinitely.[87] They also tend toward God as their exemplar.[88] God's exemplar causality is therefore manifest in every action of the creature: "Since any moved thing, inasmuch as it is moved, tends to the divine likeness so that it may be perfected in itself, and since a thing is perfect in so far as it is actualized, the intention of everything existing in potency must be to tend through motion toward actuality."[89] Niels Henrik Gregersen invokes this notion of exemplar causality in his account of evolution: "God is the Divine Pattern that is the wellspring of any concrete pattern-formation in evolution, and hence is the underlying source of novelty during evolution. God is the *forma formarum*, 'the Form of forms' as the Scholastics said."[90]

God's exemplar causality is also related to the substantial forms of exist-

---

85. "The knowledge of God is to all creatures what the knowledge of the artificer is to things made by his art" (*ST* I, 14, 8, co.).

86. *ST* I, 44, 3, co.

87. "Therefore if there is an agent not contained in any 'genus,' its effect will still more distantly reproduce the form of the agent, not, that is, so as to participate in the likeness of the agent's form according to the same specific or generic formality, but only according to some sort of analogy; as existence is common to all. In this way all created things, so far as they are beings, are like God as the first and universal principle of all being" (*ST* I, 4, 3, co.). "Form is something divine and very good and desirable. It is divine because every form is a certain participation in the likeness of the divine being, which is pure act" (*In phys.* I, lect. 15, [§135]). Cf. *SCG* III, 19, no. 4; *ST* I, 3, 4, co.; 6, 4, co.

88. "Now, the function of a perfect image is to represent its prototype by likeness to it; this is why an image is made. Therefore, all things exist in order to attain to the divine likeness, as to their ultimate end" (*SCG* III, 19, no. 4). See also Te Velde, *Aquinas on God*, 141.

89. *SCG* III, 22, no. 7.   90. Gregersen, "Complexification," 26.

ing substances: "The form which is a part of the thing is a likeness of the first agent, flowing from him. Thus, all forms are traced back to the first agent as to the exemplar principle."[91] We will have more to say about God as the cause of substantial forms in our discussion of efficient causality.

Efficient Causality

The notion of efficient causality never disappeared from empirical science. It was reduced in Newtonian science to the force that moves the atoms, and further diminished by David Hume to a mere habit of mind as we notice a constant conjunction between certain events. As such, it was no longer an ontological principle, something that might influence the being of another thing, but only an epistemological principle that might enable us to predict natural events. When such predictions became impossible because of the indeterminism of quantum mechanics, Heisenberg famously declared that the principle of causality had been "definitively disproved."[92] Efficient causality has, however, outlived Heisenberg's declaration and is an integral aspect of contemporary science.[93]

Efficient causality appears more often in discussions of divine action than any other mode of causality. God is seen as an agent who does something in the world. How God manages to do this without interfering with creaturely causes is often viewed as the fundamental problem. Two solutions are generally proposed. Either intrusive divine causality is eliminated by some form of divine self-limitation or it is consigned to a realm of indeterminism in the natural world where, since no natural causes are present, there can be no interference. Both of these solutions, however, presuppose a univocal understanding of divine causality. Absent such an understanding, the problem itself does not arise.

We might wonder what divine causality would look like if God were viewed as a truly transcendent cause. God would no longer appear as an agent whose action might blunder into the domain of created causes, but as a cause whose influence is essential to every instance of creaturely activity. God's action would not distort the proper causality of creatures, but would be its very source.[94]

91. *Sent.* II, 1, 1, 1, ad 5. Cf. *De ver.* 2, 1, ad 6. See also Dewan, *St. Thomas and Form*, 74n62.
92. Heisenberg, "Über den anschaulichen," 197.
93. See Bunge, *Causality*; Bunge, *Chasing*; Wallace, *Causality and Scientific*; and Wallace, *Modeling*.
94. "Thomas' metaphysical understanding of creation in terms of participation enables him to embrace the typically Aristotelian affirmation of the world of nature with its own ontological den-

To establish a framework for understanding the relation between God's causality and that of creatures, we will examine the notions of secondary and instrumental causality. These ideas are not strangers to the theology/science dialogue on divine action.[95] They are quite useful since they allow for both natural and transcendent explanations of worldly events. On the natural level, one can describe what happens in the world entirely in terms of causes that are open to the investigation of empirical science. Descriptions on this level do not require the introduction of causes that exceed the methodology of science—provided one refrains from asking questions that go beyond that method. One can, for instance, ask questions such as "What in the world makes that happen?" One must refrain, however, from such questions as "What is it that makes the world happen?"[96]

Should one want to entertain broader questions, one would have to shift to the transcendent level of explanation. When one moves to that level, however, the first level can remain entirely intact. The cause operating on the transcendent level will be found to act in and through causes on the natural

---

sity and causal efficacy. The whole of nature, with its rich and abundant diversity of forms of being, constitutes a creation: that is to say, a work that allows itself to be understood as the expression of God's ordering wisdom and of the finality of his goodness" (Te Velde, *Aquinas on God*, 142).

95. Denis Edwards explains: "Why, then, opt for the approach to divine action in which the Creator is thought of as acting through secondary causes? Fundamentally, I embrace this approach because it represents a foundational metaphysical understanding of the God-world relationship, which is at the heart of the Christian tradition and which I find intellectually coherent and religiously meaningful. At the center is the idea that the Creator is present to all creatures, closer to them than they are to themselves, conferring existence and the capacity to act on every entity and every process. God does this always and everywhere in our universe. And at the heart of this approach is the idea that God gives creatures independence and integrity, including the capacity to act as real causes. In this view, God consistently respects the proper autonomy of creation" (Edwards, *How God Acts*, 62). For other applications of secondary causality in the theology/science dialogue, see T. F. Tracy, "Divine Action, Created Causes," 77–102; and William R. Stoeger, "Describing God's Action in the World in Light of Scientific Knowledge of Reality," in *Chaos and Complexity: Scientific Perspectives on Divine Action*, ed. Robert John Russell, Nancey Murphy, and Arthur R. Peacock (Vatican City State: Vatican Observatory; Berkeley, Calif.: Center for Theology and the Natural Sciences, 1995), 239–61.

96. "The active and passive powers. of a natural thing suffice for action in their own order: yet the divine power is required for the reason given above [regarding God's action in natural causes]" (*De pot.* III, 7, ad 1). "In particular, from the sciences we still are unable to answer the questions, why there is something rather than nothing, why there is order rather than disorder, and why there is openness to novelty—to new and more complex entities—rather than just sterile uniformity. That is, why are there 'laws of nature' in the first place? And why these 'laws of nature' and not some others? In fact, not even philosophy can adequately answer these questions" (Stoeger, "Describing," 243). "Natural science as such does not ask why there is a universe nor why and in what ways it is intelligible, but simply limits itself to its own intelligible content of mass and energy in space/time ordered ideally through mathematics, and of other internal reciprocal connections" (John H. Wright, "Theology, Philosophy and Natural Science," *Theological Studies* 52 [1991]: 660).

level without changing the quality of their causality or its consequent empirical description. By moving to the transcendent level, one simply allows for a more complete account of the natural world by addressing philosophical or perhaps theological questions that exceed the method of empirical science.

On the transcendent level, one may speak of God as the "First Cause" whose action pervades the world in and through natural causes, which may now be viewed as "secondary" or "instrumental" causes acting under the influence of the First Cause.[97] The notions of secondary and instrumental causality are therefore "science-friendly" since they do not in any way threaten or interfere with the integrity and ability of science to pursue any of the questions that fall within its method.[98]

Both the scientist and the philosopher or theologian, however, must abide by the rules of this discussion. Science may not make claims about causes belonging to the transcendent level of explanation based on studies that fall within its competence. The scientist may not, for instance, claim that empirical science demonstrates that God does not exist. Richard Dawkins is therefore not playing by the rules when he insists that "God's existence or non-existence is a scientific fact about the universe" and that "the presence or absence of a creative super-intelligence is unequivocally a scientific question."[99] Nor may the scientist argue that a successful explanation of certain events through the laws of science excludes the influence of a transcendent cause or shows that such a cause is superfluous to the production of those events.

Aquinas entertains such an argument in one of the objections to his demonstration of the existence of God. The objection is not so much that there is "no room" for God to act (as modern Newtonian science would have

---

97. "This primary divine, existence-endowing causality is always operative, holding things in existence, charging them with realization. It is essential to conceive primary causality very differently from the causes—secondary causes—we discuss and deal with each day. The primary cause is not just another one of these—it completely transcends them and provides their ultimate basis in reality. There are no gaps in the secondary causal chain, but the whole chain demands a primary cause to support and sustain it. Without the primary cause there is no explanation for its existence or for its efficacy" (Stoeger, "Describing," 247).

98. Charles De Koninck points out that this autonomy of science and philosophy is important for both disciplines: "This sapiential function [of philosophy], however, would be devoid of meaning, if the subordinate sciences did not enjoy perfect autonomy in their own field. In fact, experimental science can be useful to the philosopher only in so far as it has established itself in its own right" (De Koninck, "Thomism," 76).

99. Richard Dawkins, *The God Delusion* (New York: Houghton Mifflin, 2006), 50, 58–59. See also Lash, "Where Does," 507–21. For a sustained refutation of Dawkins's arguments, see Alister McGrath, *Dawkins' God: Genes, Memes, and the Meaning of Life* (Oxford, U.K.: Blackwell, 2005).

it), but that there is simply nothing for God to do in the natural world, and so no need for him to bother to exist: "It is superfluous to suppose that what can be accounted for by a few principles has been produced by many. But it seems that everything we see in the world can be accounted for by other principles, supposing God did not exist. For all natural things can be reduced to one principle which is nature; and all voluntary things can be reduced to one principle which is human reason, or will. Therefore there is no need to suppose God's existence."[100] He answers that there is no need to introduce yet another secondary cause, but there is a need for a primary cause: "Since nature works for a determinate end under the direction of a higher agent, whatever is done by nature must needs be traced back to God, as to its first cause. So also whatever is done voluntarily must also be traced back to some higher cause other than human reason or will, since these can change or fail; for all things that are changeable and capable of defect must be traced back to an immovable and self-necessary first principle."[101] The search for natural causes is reasonable, but not if it denies the influence of the primary cause: "Since God wills effects to proceed from definite causes, for the preservation of order in the universe, it is not unreasonable to seek for causes secondary to the divine will. It would, however, be unreasonable to do so, if such were considered as primary, and not as dependent on the will of God."[102]

In discussing secondary causes, theologians and philosophers must also "play fair." They may not attempt to explain a natural event by invoking a transcendent cause to the exclusion of natural causes. Aquinas admonishes:

When we ask the reason *why*, in regard to a natural effect, we can give a reason based on a proximate cause; provided, of course, that we trace back all things to the divine will as a first cause. Thus, if the question is asked: "Why is wood heated in the presence of fire?" it is answered, "Because heating is the natural action of fire"; and this is so "because heat is the proper accident." But this is the result of its proper form, and so on, until we come to the divine will. Hence, if a person answers someone who asks why wood is heated: "Because God willed it," he is answering appropriately, provided he intends to take the question back to a first cause, but not appropriately, if he means to exclude all other causes.[103]

Invoking divine causality immediately, to the exclusion of secondary causes, inevitably leads to the "god of the gaps." When God is invoked as a tran-

---

100. *ST* I, 2, 3, obj. 2.
102. *ST* I, 19, 5, ad 2.
101. *ST* I, 2, 3, ad 2.
103. *SCG* III, 97, no. 17.

scendent cause to explain some "gap" in the scientific account of nature (to account for something that science has not yet explained through natural causes), God is inevitably found to be in retreat as the "gap" is closed by new scientific theories and explanations.

As long as both partners play fair, secondary causality can be a very helpful notion in the science/theology discussion of divine action.

Primary and Secondary Causality   Every creature has a characteristic activity in virtue of its substantial form.[104] So ducks quack, dogs bark, and people think, because of the substantial form that each has—the form that makes each to be the kind of thing it is and so to exhibit the sort of activity it does. Aquinas sees such action as a manifestation of God's power and goodness, since God not only causes each thing to exist but also endows each with its own proper causality.[105]

There is a difference, however, between exercising one's own proper causality and being the absolutely first cause of one's action. Aquinas demonstrates in the "five ways" that the activities of creatures, though the product of their own proper causality, point beyond themselves to a transcendent first cause of all actuality. The influence of that cause is present not only in calling creation forth from nothing and sustaining it in being, but also in every actualization of potency—in every instance of causation in the created world, right down to the production of every human thought.[106]

---

104. "Now every form bestowed on created things by God has power for a determined act, which it can bring about in proportion to its own proper endowment" (*ST* I-II, 109, 1, co.).

105. "Nor is it superfluous, even if God can by himself produce all natural effects, for them to be produced by certain other causes. For this is not a result of the inadequacy of divine power, but of the immensity of his goodness, whereby he has willed to communicate his likeness to things, not only so that they might exist, but also that they might be causes for other things. Indeed, all creatures generally attain the divine likeness in these two ways.... By this in fact the beauty of order in created things is evident" (*SCG* III, 70, no. 7). Cf. *ST* I, 103, 6, co.; 105, 5, ad 1; *SCG* III, 21, no. 2; 69, no. 14; *Sent.* I, 45, 3, ad 4. See also Gilson, *Christian Philosophy*, 176.

106. "We always need God's help for every thought, inasmuch as he moves the understanding to act" (*ST* I, 109, 1, ad 3). "Every operation should be attributed to God, as to a first and principal agent" (*SCG* III, 67, no. 4). Cf. *ST* I-II, 109, 1, co.; *Sent.* I, 37, 3, 3, ad 3. "No cause makes its effect be in act except insofar as it acts by the power of God, which alone has being as its proper effect. In this way, then, God may be called the cause of each action of a created agent" (Te Velde, *Participation and Substantiality in Thomas Aquinas* [New York: Brill, 1995], 171). Cf. ibid., 160–61. "It is true, [Aquinas] says, that God must be operative in every creaturely cause. So the actions of creatures are, in a sense, always God's action" (Brian Davies, *The Thought of Thomas Aquinas* [Oxford: Clarendon Press, 1992], 163). See also Goris, *Free Creatures*, 299; and Alfred Freddoso, "God's General Concurrence with Secondary Causes: Why Conservation Is Not Enough," *Philosophical Perspectives* 5 (1991): 553–85.

Each thing acts to the extent that it is itself actual, but it is never the ultimate source of its own actuality. Therefore every actualization of potentiality, every instance of causality—however much it may be an exercise of the proper causality of some creature—necessarily requires and involves the influence or action of the ultimate source of all actuality, who is God.[107]

In this context, Aquinas calls creatures "secondary causes;" and God the "primary cause."[108] A secondary cause exercises its own proper causality, but does so only under the influence of the primary cause. As Rudi Te Velde notes, the fact that "the second cause is really the cause of its effect is due to the first cause."[109] Since God is the creator, who has gifted each creature with its own proper causality according to its nature, his influence does not interfere with the proper causality of the creature, but is rather its source.[110]

The notion of primary and secondary causes will make sense only if we remember that these causes do not belong to the same order.[111] They are not univocal causes: God's causality infinitely transcends that of creatures.[112]

---

107. "Where there are several agents in order, the second always acts in virtue of the first; for the first agent moves the second to act. And thus all agents act in virtue of God himself; and therefore He is the cause of action in every agent" (ST I, 105, 5, co.). Cf. SCG III, 67, no. 5; De pot. 3, 7, co. See also Mascall, *Christian Theology*, 200; and Doolan, "Causality," 405.

108. See, for example, ST I, 19, 6, ad 3; 19, 8, co.; 22, 3, ad 2; 23, 5, co.

109. Te Velde, *Participation*, 167. "God can be understood to be the cause of any other thing's action, as he actualizes the power of a thing to perform its own action. The point is not that the instrumental cause, by the power of the higher cause, is brought to perform an action which is foreign to it; it is brought to perform its own action" (ibid., 172).

110. "We do not take away their proper actions from created things, though we attribute all the effects of created things to God, as an agent working in all things" (SCG III, 69, no. 28). Cf. ST I, 105, 5, co.; I-II, 10, 4, ad 2. "In the thought of Thomas Aquinas, a competitive model of the relationship between divine and creaturely causality is excluded from the beginning. Rather, God does his all (what he alone is able to do) and the creature does its all (that to which it is empowered by God's creative power), so that God and creature—each in its own way—wholly produce the same effect: '*totius ab utroque*' (SCG III, 70)" (Jorissen, "Schöpfung," 102). "God is not in the midst of secondary causes as a helper or a rival. He does not enter into mutual employment with them. Rather, he founds their causality through the fact that he founds their existence" (Finance, *Être et agir*, 239). See also Mascall, *Christian Theology*, 199; and Gilson, *Christian Philosophy*, 182–83.

111. "One action does not proceed from two agents of the same order. But nothing hinders the same action from proceeding from a primary and a secondary agent" (ST I, 105, 5, ad 2).

112. See ST I, 4, 3, co. "God and creature are not two causes collaborating on the same level to produce a joint effect. God causes on the transcendental level and He thereby constitutes the creatures' causation on the categorical level" (Goris, *Free Creatures*, 301). "God and creatures are, so to speak, on different levels of being, and different planes of causality—something that God's transcendence implies. God does not give on the same plane of being and activity as creatures, as one among other givers, and therefore God is not in potential competition (or co-operation) with them.... Unlike this co-operation among creatures, relations with God are utterly non-competitive because God, from beyond this plane of created reality, brings about the *whole* plane of creaturely being and activity in its goodness. The creature's receiving from God does not then require its passivity in the world:

When two univocal causes interact, their effect always belongs partly to one and partly to the other. When two men carry a table, for instance, the weight is divided between them, and if one lifts more, the other must support less. Their cooperation is always a zero-sum game: the more one does, the less the other can do. When a primary and secondary cause act together, however, the effect belongs entirely to both. The influence of the primary cause does not diminish the action of the secondary cause, but enables it.

When God acts as primary cause in a creature, the effect is not divided between them, but belongs wholly to both: "It is apparent that the same effect is not attributed to a natural cause and to divine power in such a way that it is partly done by God and partly by the natural agent; rather, it is wholly done by both, according to a different way, just as the same effect is wholly attributed to the instrument and also wholly to the principal agent."[113] In this way, God acts in all things. The effect is attributed to both God and the creature, but most especially to God, since God is the source of the very causality of the creature.[114] This teaching will raise some issues (and perhaps some eyebrows) if we remember that sometimes the effect of creaturely action is not good but evil, even the evil of sin. We will discuss those issues in

---

God's activity as the giver of ourselves need not come at the expense of our own activity. Instead, the creature receives from God its very activity as a good" (Kathryn Tanner, *Jesus, Humanity, and the Trinity: A Brief Systematic Theology* [Minneapolis, Minn,: Fortress Press, 2001], 3–4).

113. *SCG* III, 70, no. 8. "There is no distinction between what is from a secondary cause and a first cause" (*ST* I, 23, 5, co.). Cf. *SCG* III, 70, no. 5. See also Jorissen, "Schöpfung," 102; and Schulte, "Wie ist Gottes," 124–25.

114. "The influence of the first cause is more intense than that of the second cause" (*ST* I, 21, 4, co.). Cf. *SCG* III, 67, no. 5; *ST* I, 36, 3, ad 4; *De ver.* 5, 9, ad 10; *De pot.* 3, 7, co. "What Thomas rejects is that the second causes are an instrument of the first cause in such a way that they stand between God's action and the lower creatures. God's infinite power works immediately and most intimately in all things. The relation of God and his creatures is not mediated by anything which differs from God. Yet God is said to produce the natural effects *mediante naturae*; this means that God does not want to produce the effects of nature without nature, by way of a miracle, but that he causes nature to operate and to make its own effect by mediating the natural power of each thing with the being (*esse*) of that effect. This relation of mediation is formulated by Aquinas with great precision. Both causes, God and nature, operate immediately with regard to the effect, though not independently from one another, but according to a certain order in which the first has priority over the other. Now from the point of view of the active subject (*agens suppositum*), the natural cause is immediately related to its effect. It is the fire which causes the burning of the wood, not God acting secretly in the fire. God does not take over the operation of nature by placing himself between the natural cause and its effect. This would be a wrongly conceived mediation. But God is immediate to the effect in a different way, even more immediate than the natural agent itself. For seen from the point of view of the power by which the agent operates, one must say that the power of the higher cause is more immediate to the effect than the power of the lower cause. It is, after all, by the power of the higher cause, which enters more deeply in the effect, that the power of the lower cause is connected with (*coniungitur*) its effect" (Te Velde, *Participation*, 175). See also Gregory T. Doolan, " Causality," 407.

our treatment of providence in chapter seven. First, however, we must look at some other aspects of the relation between divine and creaturely causality.

Principal and Instrumental Causality   Sometimes a creature, even while exercising its own proper causality, achieves something beyond its natural capacity. Chalk, for instance, by its own nature, may be able to leave marks when it is drawn across a surface. If it leaves intelligible marks in the form of letters and words, however, this effect must be due not just to the chalk but to some intelligent agent employing the chalk as an instrument. The chalk is an "instrumental cause," and the one who uses it is a "principal cause."

The hallmark of instrumental causality is that the instrument, while acting in accordance with its own nature and proper causality, achieves something beyond its nature through the influence of the principal cause.[115] As in the case of primary and secondary causality, the effect is attributed wholly to each agent. The marks on the board, for instance, are not partly from the chalk and partly from the teacher who uses it, but wholly from both.[116] Again as in primary and secondary causality, the two agents cannot be simply univocal. The causality of the principal cause must in some way belong to a different order from that of the instrumental cause. The teacher, for instance, as an intelligent agent, belongs to a different order of causality than the chalk, and so the effect can belong wholly to both agents. If the effect were the product of two univocal causes, it would be divided between them. If the marks were made with two pieces of chalk, for instance, some would be due to one, and some to the other.

Given God's utter transcendence, he may act as a principal cause enabling the creature, as an instrument, to produce an effect beyond its natural capacity. In fact, this is what happens in every creaturely action. For every action or exercise of efficient causality involves a bestowal of being, whether substantially or accidentally. But God alone is the source of being

---

115. "[T]he secondary instrumental cause does not participate the action of the superior cause, except inasmuch as by something proper to itself it acts dispositively to the effect of the principal agent. If therefore it effects nothing, according to what is proper to itself, it is used to no purpose; nor would there be any need of certain instruments for certain actions. Thus we see that a saw, in cutting wood, which it does by the property of its own form, produces the form of a bench, which is the proper effect of the principal agent" (*ST* I, 45, 5, co.). "A thing is said to work toward the production of an effect instrumentally if it does not do so by means of a form inherent to it but only in so far as it is moved by an agent that acts of itself" (*De ver.* 27, 4, co.).

116. "The same effect is wholly attributed to the instrument and also wholly to the principal agent" (*SCG* III, 70, no. 8). Cf. *ST* III, 19, 1, co.

since only God is subsistent being itself *(ipsum esse subsistens)*. God must therefore be involved as principal cause in every creaturely action: "Every operating agent is a cause of being in some way, either of substantial or of accidental being. Now, nothing is a cause of being unless by virtue of its acting through the power of God. Therefore, every operating agent acts through God's power."[117] In this way, they participate in God's causal activity.[118]

Creatures cannot serve as instruments in the initial act of creation, when God brings the world into being from nothing: "The proper effect of God creating is what is presupposed to all other effects, and that is absolute being. Hence nothing else can act dispositively and instrumentally to this effect, since creation is not from anything presupposed, which can be disposed by the action of some instrumental agent. So therefore it is impossible for any creature to create, either by its own power or instrumentally, that is, ministerially."[119]

Creatures do, however, act as instrumental causes of the new being that

---

117. *SCG* III, 67, no. 1. Cf.: *SCG* II, 21, no. 4; no 10; III, 66, nos. 1–3; no. 5; *De pot.* 1, 3, co.; 3, 7, co. "Just as the instrument in the order of created causes carries out its instrumental action (the action which belongs to it as instrument) by the power of the mover that flows through it, and not by its own power, so also the second cause effects *esse* (the action which belongs to it as second cause) by the power and operation of the First Cause that is acting in it, and not by its own proper power. The analogy is between the second cause *qua* second cause (that is, as giving *esse*) and the instrument *qua* instrument (that is, as carrying out the instrumental action). The instrument can perform its instrumental action only under the influence of the principal cause, and the second cause can give *esse* only under the influence of the First Cause" (James S. Albertson, "Instrumental Causality in St. Thomas," *New Scholasticism* 38 [1954]: 432). "In contrast to any form of occasionalism, Aquinas does not believe that the universal scope and absolute primacy of divine causation require that God do all the causing, but rather only that God do all the creating. Aquinas safeguards God's causal primacy by reserving the production of *esse* to God alone as its proper cause. Apart from creation, it is not necessary that God do all the causing but rather only that God cause all the causing" (Shanley, "Divine Causation," 102). "Although the creature exercises efficient causality, divine action is nonetheless present most intimately in each effect since it is what gives the act of existing *(esse)*.... Divine action . . . is presupposed in the action of every secondary cause" (Jean-Marie Vernier, *Théologie et métaphysique de la création chez saint Thomas d'Aquin* [Paris: Pierre Téqui, 1995], 247). "[A]s the source of being (the 'primary cause') God is immediately engaged in the most intimate way possible with each creature throughout its history and in all of its interactions with other creatures. There can be no distinction drawn between events in which God acts and those in which God does not; God acts in every event" (Thomas F. Tracy, "Evolutionary Theologies and Divine Action," *Theology and Science* 6 [2008]: 109).

118. "Thomas also mentions the immanence by participation of the power of the higher cause in the instrumental cause. In a certain sense the instrument may be called the cause of the effect which is proper to the principal cause, not by its own power, but inasmuch as it participates in the power of the principal cause. So the instrument is not only 'applied' to its own activity but even raised to a level of an effect that exceeds its own power, just as we cut with a pair of scissors a well-shaped figure out of a piece of paper" (Te Velde, *Participation*, 172–73).

119. *ST* I, 45, 5, co.

is generated through substantial or accidental change.[120] To illustrate this, we can use the example of dogs producing puppies. In this action, the parent dogs exercise their own proper causality and produce an effect (the puppy) that is proportionate to their nature. The puppy comes into being through the causal influence of its parents. Once it exists, however, it does so through its own act of existence *(esse)*. This act cannot be caused simply by its parents. They can produce an effect proportionate to their nature, but their nature does not include existence. Their existence is distinct from their nature, and so they depend on God, moment by moment, for their continued existence. By the nature proper to them, they can produce the nature of a dog, but they cannot produce existence, since this exceeds their nature and is not part of their nature.

Though the parent dogs cannot as such produce existence, they can function as instrumental causes in its production. They produce a puppy that not only has the nature of a dog (through the proper causality of its parents) but also exists (through the instrumental causality of its parents and the principal causality of God). As intelligible marks on a chalkboard are the effect of the principal causality of the teacher and the instrumental causality of the chalk, so the puppy, as regards its existence, is the effect of the principal causality of God and the instrumental causality of its parents. Just as the teacher does not deprive the chalk of its own proper causality in acting through it to write on the board, so God does not deprive the parent dogs (or any other creature) of their own proper causality in acting through them in the generation of new being in substantial and accidental change.[121]

Using the same example, we can discover another way in which creatures regularly act as instrumental causes under God's primary causality.

---

120. "[F]or Thomas, whenever a new substance is efficiently caused by a natural or created agent, that agent's causation applies both to the act of being itself *(esse)* of the new substance and to a particular determination of *esse* as realized in that substance. Causation of the particular determination (this or that kind of form) is owing to the created efficient cause insofar as it operates by its own inherent power as a principal cause. Causation of the act of being itself *(esse)* is assigned to it as an instrumental cause acting with the power of God and to God himself as the principal cause of the same. From this it follows that one should not maintain that Thomas denies that created causes can efficiently cause the act of existing or the act of being, at least in the process of bringing new substances into being" (John F. Wippel, "Thomas Aquinas on Creatures as Causes of *Esse*," *International Philosophical Quarterly* 40 [2000]: 213). See also Doolan, "Causality," 398–402.

121. "The operation of nature is also the operation of the divine power, just as the operation of an instrument is effected by the power of the principal agent. Nor does this prevent nature and God from operating to the same effect, on account of the order between God and nature" (*De pot.* 3, 7, ad 3).

The puppy that the parent dogs produce has the same nature that they have, since it has the same kind of substantial form. Through their agency, the form of dog has been educed from the potency of some matter that did not exist as a dog before.[122] In causing the new dog, they are also in some way the causes of the substantial form by which it is a dog. They cannot, however, be the cause of the substantial form of "dog," as such, since each of them is also a dog in virtue of that form. If they were the cause of the form as such, they would be the cause of themselves.[123] They are not the cause of the form as such, but of the eduction or coming-to-be of that form in the matter that comes to be disposed for that form through their action.[124] As such, they are truly the causes of the puppy, since the new form would not have been produced apart from their agency.[125] With respect to the substantial form of the

---

122. "The form ... is educed from the potency of matter by a natural agent" (*De pot.* 3, 4, ad 7). See also Wallace, *Modeling*, 60.

123. "Now it is clear that of two things in the same species one cannot directly cause the other's form as such, since it would then be the cause of its own form, which is essentially the same as the form of the other; but it can be the cause of this form for as much as it is in matter—in other words, it may be the cause that *this matter* receives *this form*. And this is to be the cause of *becoming*, as when man begets man, and fire causes fire. Thus whenever a natural effect is such that it has an aptitude to receive from its active cause an impression specifically the same as in that active cause, then the *becoming* of the effect, but not its *being*, depends on the agent" (*ST* I, 104, 1, co.). Cf. *SCG* II, 21, no. 8; III, 65, no. 4; *ST* I, 13, 5, ad 1; *De pot.* 5, 1, co.

124. "Thomas explains that as regards two things in the same species, one cannot be a *per se* cause of form in the other, i.e., the cause of its form as such; if it were, it would be the cause of its own form since it shares the same nature as its effect. Thus, e.g., an individual man cannot be the cause of human nature absolutely, for he would then be the cause of himself. Rather, a univocal cause can only be the cause of the form of another individual in the same species inasmuch as that form exists in matter—i.e., only inasmuch as such an agent causes this matter to acquire this form. Thus, while one man cannot be the cause of human nature absolutely, he can be the cause of human nature inasmuch as it exists in this man. And it is this mode of causality that Thomas terms generation, according to which an agent's action presupposes determinate matter.... Because the operations of natural agents proceed from a form that is determined by designated matter, such agents are only particular ones. It is for this reason that they cannot be the cause of a nature absolutely but, rather, only inasmuch as that nature exists in this individual. Consequently, Thomas concludes that although such agents are the cause of the coming-to-be *(causa fiendi)* of a thing, they are not the cause of its being *(causa essendi)*" (Doolan, "Causality," 398–99). "[T]hough a craftsman may make a chair, he does not thereby make 'what a chair is.' And in the same way, nature may produce this or that living being, without being in the least responsible for 'what it is to be alive,' nor for 'what it is to be this kind of living being'" (De Koninck, *Hollow Universe*, 93).

125. "Consequently, it is not correct to say that the form is made in matter, rather should we say that it is educed from the potentiality of matter. And from this principle that the composite and not the form is made the Philosopher proves that forms result from natural agents. Because since the thing made must needs be like its maker, and that which is made is the composite, it follows that the maker must be composite and not a self-subsistent form, as Plato maintained: so that as the thing made is composite, and that by which it is made is a form in matter made actual, so the generator is composite and not a mere form, while the form is that whereby it generates, a form to wit existing in that particular matter such as that flesh, those bones and so forth" (*De pot.* 3, 8, co.). Cf. *ST* I, 65,

puppy, however, they are instruments of God, who is the principal cause of all substantial forms: "Whatever is caused as regards some particular nature cannot be the first cause of that nature, but only a second and instrumental cause; for example, since the human nature of Socrates has a cause, he cannot be the first cause of human nature; if so, since his human nature is caused by someone, it would follow that he was the cause of himself, since he is what he is by virtue of human nature. Thus, a univocal generator must have the status of an instrumental agent in respect to that which is the primary cause of the whole species."[126]

Aquinas teaches that God is the source of substantial form as well as the source of being.[127] As God's continuous action is needed to hold things in being, so his action is also required for the continued existence of substantial forms and of the particular species or natural types that exist in virtue of those forms.[128] God produces substantial forms through the causality of

---

4, co.; *De pot.* 5, 1, ad 5. "This, of course, does not eliminate efficient causality in creatures. Though it may be the case that no creature is able to effect a form as such and that no creature can operate in any way without an influx from the first cause, it is not reasonable, St. Thomas holds, to take the extreme position of certain of the Arabians that no created power ever exerts any influence whatsoever.... Moreover, if the operation be one of generation by a univocal agent, the agent can be only as an instrumental cause with respect to that which is the first cause of the whole species" (Rosemary Lauer, "The Notion of Efficient Cause in the *Secunda Via*," *Thomist* 38 [1974]: 761).

126. (*SCG* II, 21, no. 5). Cf.: *De pot.* 3, 7, co. Aquinas regularly uses the example of human generation in this context. In his philosophy and theology, however, there is a fundamental difference between the production of the human substantial form and that of any other substantial form. Other forms are educed from the potency of matter under God's primary causality and the secondary causality of creatures. Because of the spiritual aspect of the human person, however, the human substantial form cannot be simply educed from the potency of matter. Rather, when matter is properly disposed to the human form, under the influence of divine and secondary causes, the human form is then directly created by God to actualize that matter, generating a human person: "Since every active power of nature is compared to God as an instrument to the primary and principal agent, nothing prevents the action of nature, in that self-same generated subject which is man from terminating in a part of man, and not in the whole, the production of which is due to the action of God. The human body, therefore, is formed at the same time both by the power of God, as principal and first agent, and by the power of the semen, as secondary agent; but it is God's action that produces the human soul, which the seminal power cannot produce, but to which it disposes" (*SCG* II, 89, no. 14). Cf. *ST* I, 118, 2, ad 3. On the compatibility of this understanding of the human substantial form with the general account of hylomorphic philosophy, see Dodds, "Hylomorphism."

127. "Therefore He [God] is the cause of action not only by giving the form which is the principle of action, as the generator is said to be the cause of movement in things heavy and light; but also as preserving the forms and powers of things.... And since the form of a thing is within the thing, and all the more, as it approaches nearer to the First and Universal Cause; and because in all things God Himself is properly the cause of universal being which is innermost in all things; it follows that in all things God works intimately" (*ST* I, 105, 5, co.). See also Dewan, *St. Thomas and Form*, 39; 87n108).

128. "Now this cause [of the human species itself or any other species of natural things] is God, either mediately or immediately. For we have shown that he is the first cause of all things. So he

creatures as secondary and instrumental causes.[129] The use of secondary causes does not bespeak any divine limitation, but (if anything) a divine exuberance in willing to share "the abundance of his goodness" with creatures.[130] As Gilles Emery points out: "[T]he creation is not a 'restriction' of God who would limit himself or give place to the creature through effacing himself *(kenosis)*, but rather it is the gift of a participation in God by a free decision of divine superabundance."[131]

In considering the relation of substantial forms to God as their source we are brought back again to the idea of exemplar causality. All forms are ultimately derived from God as the first exemplar cause.[132] There may, however, be intermediary exemplar causes just as there are intermediary efficient causes among the myriad ways that creatures share in divine causality: "Just as the divine power, the first agent, does not exclude the action of a natural power, so neither does the first exemplar form, which is God, exclude the derivation of forms from other lower forms whose action produces forms like themselves."[133] All such intermediary causes exercise their own authentic causal power.[134] Through their secondary and instrumental causal-

---

must stand in regard to the species of things as the individual generating agent in nature does to generation, of which he is the direct cause. But generation ceases as soon as the operation of the generative agent ceases. Therefore all the species of things would also cease as soon as the divine operation ceased. So he preserves things in being through his operation" (*SCG* III, 65, no. 4). Cf. *ST* I, 105, 5, co.; *De pot.* 5, 1, ad 18. This, of course, does not mean that God might not allow a particular species to cease to exist or become extinct, any more than it means that God might not allow a particular individual thing to cease to be.

129. "God acts perfectly as first cause: but the operation of nature as second cause is also necessary. Nevertheless God can produce the natural effect even without nature: but he wishes to act by means of nature in order to preserve order in things" (*De pot.* 3, 7, ad 16).

130. "There are certain intermediaries of God's providence; for he governs things inferior by superior, not on account of any defect in his power, but by reason of the abundance of his goodness; so that the dignity of causality is imparted even to creatures" (*ST* I, 22, 3, co.). Cf. *De ver.* 5, 8, ad 11; *SCG* III, 70, no. 7. "God's creative act, for Aquinas, is not an example of divine withdrawal but is, rather, the exercise of divine omnipotence" (William E. Carroll, "Aquinas on Creation and the Metaphysical Foundations of Science," *Sapientia* 54 [1999]: 75).

131. Gilles Emery, "The Immutability of the God of Love and the Problem of Language Concerning the 'Suffering of God,'" in *Divine Impassibility and the Mystery of Human Suffering*, ed. James F. Keating and Thomas Joseph White (Grand Rapids, Mich.: Eerdmans, 2009), 71–72.

132. "God who is pure being is in a fashion the form of all subsistent forms that participate of being but are not their own being" (*De pot.* 6, 6, ad 5). "Every form is from God" (*In de div. nom.* IX, lect. 3, line 98 c.)

133. *De pot.* 3, 8, ad 17. Cf. *ST* I, 65, 4, ad 2; I, 104, 1, co.; I-II, 6, 7, ad 1.

134. "Despite the fact that natural agents are the instruments of higher causes, however, they still possess their own proper actions that follow from their proper forms. Hence, while form as such is not a proper effect of their power, this form as it comes to be in this matter is. Thus the divine ideas do not through their causality exclude natural agency; rather, they facilitate it, for it is through the combined agencies of God and the natural agent that a natural effect is caused—'not so

ity, creatures share in God's providential work of guiding and sustaining creation.[135]

Secondary Causality, Evolution, and the Theology/Science Dialogue   To show how the notion of secondary causality can be useful in the theology/science dialogue on divine action, we will use the example of evolution.[136] The warrants for applying secondary causality to evolution go back to Charles Darwin himself: "Authors of the highest eminence seem to be fully satisfied with the view that each species has been independently created. To my mind it accords better with what we know of the laws impressed on matter by the Creator, that the production and extinction of the past and present inhabitants of the world should have been due to secondary causes, like those determining the birth and death of the individual."[137] Alister McGrath points out that secondary causality is no stranger to present discussions of evolution:

[T]he most widely proposed mechanism which Christian writers have proposed to account for God's involvement in the evolutionary process is the classic notion of secondary causality, particularly as this was developed by Thomas Aquinas in the thirteenth century. For Aquinas, God's causality operates in a number of ways. While God must be considered capable of doing certain things directly, God delegates causal efficacy to the created order. Aquinas understands this notion of secondary causality to be an extension of, not an alternative to, the primary causality of God. Events within the created order can exist in complex causal relationships, without in any way denying their ultimate dependency upon God as final cause. The created order

---

that the same effect is attributed to a natural cause and to the divine power as though part is made by God and part by the natural agent,' Thomas explains, 'but so that in a different way the whole effect is from each: just as the whole same effect is attributed to an instrument and also to the principal agent' (*SCG* III, 70)" (Doolan, "Causality," 409).

135. "Providence ... does not do away with secondary causes but so provides effects that the order of secondary causes falls also under providence. So ... natural effects are provided by God in such a way that natural causes are directed to bring about those natural effects, without which those effects would not happen" (*ST* I, 23, 8, co.). Cf. *ST* I, 104, 2, co.; *SCG* III, 69, no. 29; *Comp.* I, c.130.

136. For the sake of simplicity in this section, "secondary causality" is often used synonymously with "instrumental causality," following the usage of many of the authors quoted here.

137. Darwin, *Origin*, 647. "It accords with what we know of the law impressed on matter by the Creator, that the creation and extinction of forms, like the birth and death of individuals should be the effect of secondary [laws] means. It is derogatory that the Creator of countless systems of worlds should have created each of the myriads of creeping parasites and slimy worms which have swarmed each day of life on land and water on this one globe" (Darwin, *Foundations*, 51). Although Darwin used the language of secondary causality, we might ask how well he really understood the concept. He represents the creator not as a present influence on secondary causes, but as the source of the "laws impressed on matter" at some time in the past. According to Leo Elders, "Darwin had a rather superficial view of philosophical theology: God was imagined as very much external to his work and the opposition between the First Cause and secondary causes was almost total" (Elders, "Background," 44). See also Maurer, "Darwin," 494–95.

thus demonstrates causal relationships which can be investigated by the natural sciences. Those causal relationships can be investigated and correlated—for example, in the form of the "laws of nature"—without in any way implying, still less necessitating, an atheist world-view. God creates a world with its own ordering and processes.[138]

Secondary causality may be helpful in addressing a number of perplexities that arise in the theology/science dialogue about evolution. We can briefly consider two that are closely related. One is whether it makes philosophical sense to say that higher species evolve from lower ones. A second is the often hot-button issue of whether the science of evolution is compatible with the account of creation in Genesis. The flip side of this second issue is the question of whether God's involvement in evolution is compatible with science. The first question will lead us into the second, and the answers to both will involve the principle of secondary causality.

Regarding the first question, Aquinas teaches that an effect cannot be greater than its cause since "every agent acts according as it is in act."[139] Norbert Luyten applies this to evolution: "The fundamental principle in virtue of which traditional philosophy seems to be opposed to evolutionism is that higher perfection cannot come from the lower. This would mean a disproportion between cause and effect and ruin the very principle of causality which maintains precisely that the perfection in the effect can only be understood as derived from the perfection of the cause. This principle is indeed fundamental in philosophy; there can be no question of giving it up, because this would mean to give up the intelligibility of the world and so, finally, to give up thinking."[140]

The theory of evolution would directly contradict this principle if it taught that lower species are the causes of higher ones. This is not, however, what biology teaches. It does not use the philosophical language of causation, but the biological notion of evolution—descent with modification from a common ancestor. It is not clear that "descent from" is equivalent to "cau-

---

138. Alister E. McGrath, "Darwinism," in *The Oxford Handbook of Religion and Science*, ed. Philip Clayton and Zachary Simpson (Oxford: Oxford University Press, 2006), 689–90.

139. *SCG* II, 6, no. 4. "No effect exceeds its cause" (*ST* II-II, 32, 4, obj. 1). "Effects are commensurate with their causes" (*SCG* II, 15, no. 4). "Since every agent acts so far as it is in act, the mode of action must follow the mode of a thing's actual being; the hotter a thing actually is, the more heat it gives. Therefore, anything whose actuality is subject to generic, specific, and accidental determinations must have a power that is limited to effects similar to the agent as such; for every agent produces its like" (*SCG* II, 21, no. 9). Cf. *SCG* II, 16, nos. 3 and 6; II, 41, no. 6.

140. Norbert A. Luyten, "Philosophical Implications of Evolution," in *Ordo rerum: Schriften zur Naturphilosophie, philosophischen Anthropolgie und christlichen Weltanschauung* (Fribourg, Switzerland: Editions Universitaires, 1969), 143.

sation by." Also, biology does not speak of ontologically more or less perfect species, but of biologically more or less complex organisms. Biological complexity cannot readily be equated with ontological perfection. Norbert Luyten argues that "different organisms in biology do not mean the same thing as different essences in philosophy." It is "hard to determine in the realm of organisms where exactly, if at all, we have, philosophically speaking, a really different essence, because we have no adequate knowledge of the essences in their proper intelligibility." Luyten concludes that "it seems difficult for philosophy to oppose evolutionism in virtue of the principle that the higher essence could not be caused by the lower one, because we have no means of determining strictly where these lower and higher essences are to be found."[141]

In the case of human life, however, it might be argued that we do clearly have both an organism of greater complexity biologically and an essence of greater perfection ontologically. It would then seem philosophically impossible to say that this ontologically more perfect organism is the evolutionary effect of less perfect organisms. At the same time, it seems scientifically necessary to include humans in the evolutionary process, given the preponderance of current biological evidence.[142] We can resolve this possible dilemma between philosophy and science by using the notion of instrumental causality.

---

141. Luyten, "Philosophical Implications," 144–45. See also John Deely, "The Philosophical Dimensions of the Origin of Species," *Thomist* 20 (1969): 75–149, 251–342.

142. Not all scientists, however, are satisfied with the adequacy of current evolutionary theory. "I believe that the problems are too severe and too intractable to offer any hope of resolution in terms of the orthodox Darwinian framework" (Michael J. Denton, *Evolution: A Theory in Crisis* [Bethseda, Md.: Adler and Adler, 1986], 16). "I believe the gaps in evolutionary theory are significant and require a serious response from science itself. By serious response, I mean a serious rethinking about the nature of Nature" (Alejandro García-Rivera, "Endless Forms Most Beautiful," *Theology and Science* 5 [2007]: 128). "As to the claim, all too frequently to be found in the 'most authoritative' literature, that the Darwinian evolutionary mechanism (the interplay of chance mutations with environmental pressure) has solved all basic problems, I hold it to be absurd and bordering at times on the unconscionable. While the mechanism in question provoked much interesting scientific research, it left unanswered the question of transition among genera, families, orders, classes, and phyla where the absence of transitional forms is as near-complete as ever. As to the origin of life and especially of consciousness, they are today no less irreducible to physics than they were in Darwin's time" (Jaki, *Chesterton*, 139n2). "Either natural selection can do the work of building organisms from scratch or it cannot. I submit that it cannot, that evolutionary biologists are coming to understand this, and therefore that the problem of design ... remains open and unsolved" (Paul A. Nelson, "Unfit for Survival: The Fatal Flaws of Natural Selection," *Touchstone: A Journal of Mere Christianity* 12, no. 4 [1999]: 64). For contemporary alternatives to Darwinism, see A. Y. Gunter, "Six Scientific Alternatives to Darwinism," in *Back to Darwin: A Richer Account of Evolution*, ed. John B. Cobb (Grand Rapids, Mich.: Eerdmans, 2008), 128–44; Schloss, "Neo-Darwinism," 116–18.

Instrumental causality shows us that an effect may be greater than its immediate cause if that cause is also an instrument of some higher cause. So higher species may be brought forth from lower species if the natural causes of this process are also instrumental causes of a higher principal cause. That higher cause is ultimately God, the universal cause of nature.[143] God's causality is involved not only in the origination of human life but in all stages of evolution, especially those where a certain level of being is considered ontologically inadequate by itself to cause a higher level of being.[144] God's causality does not constitute a miraculous intervention; nor does it negate the real causality of all the natural agents involved in the evolutionary process.[145] In this way, God is most intimately involved in the process of evolution, acting through the natural causes that science studies.[146]

---

143. Aquinas distinguishes between the "particular nature" of each substance which accounts for its characteristic activities and the "universal nature [*natura universalis*]" that belongs to and orders creation as a whole. He describes universal nature as "an active power in some universal principle of nature, for instance in some heavenly body; or again belonging to some superior substance, in which sense God is said by some to be "the Nature Who makes nature [*natura naturans*]" (*ST* I-II, 85, 6, co.). "The intention of universal nature [*intentio naturae universalis*] depends on God, who is the universal author of nature" (*ST* I, 92, 1, ad 1).

144. "One of the objections of Darwin against creationism was that he felt that it implied an unwarranted recourse to miraculous divine interventions. Now, the fact that natural causes do not seem to be able to explain trans-generic evolution does not mean that divine intervention would be miraculous. The First Cause works through nature, preparing the natural milieu for a new species and using the material present in nature. The appearance of new classes or species of living beings is therefore, even with divine intervention, more natural than it might be thought to be" (Elders, "Background," 57). "[A]ll the authors whom we have consulted agree that, for the philosopher, the overall upward trend of evolution cannot be explained entirely by the sole forces of material things and their environment. A scientist may and should explain it that way. The philosopher, who considers a deeper level of causality, needs another factor to make the whole process of evolution intelligible. All our authors agree that this other factor is divine causality" (Joseph Donceel, "Causality and Evolution: A Survey of Some Neo-Scholastic Theories," *New Scholasticism* 39 [1965]: 314–15).

145. "Applied to evolution this would mean that the lower organism has an active role in the production of the higher; that man really has his origin from an animal but under the influence of a higher cause. This higher cause would be the transcendent cause, God" (Luyten, "Philosophical Implications," 146). "No longer need one suppose that God must have added plants here and animals there. Though God could have done so, the evidence is mounting that the resources of the original creation were sufficient for the generation of the successive orders of complexity that make up our world" (Ernan McMullin, "Evolution and Special Creation," *Zygon* 28 [1993]: 328). "The birth of new species is also natural, even though they may be superior to the natures from which they proceed.... The natures of inferior things are dependent on universal nature even in the act of generation. Therefore, although a superior nature is produced from the power of an inferior nature in the generation of a new species, this instigation is still natural, not with respect to the inferior agent considered in itself as inferior, ... but in the measure to which it belongs to the desire of the inferior nature as ordained to the good of the universal nature and to the intrinsic final end of the universe" (De Koninck, "Réflexions," 239–40).

146. "We must further remember that appealing to a transcendent causality wholly extrinsic to the natural factors active in evolution would destroy the value of the evolutionary hypothesis.

In instrumental causality, we also find a principle for answering our second question. A thorough investigation of whether the biblical account of creation is compatible with the science of evolution would, of course, require a careful discussion of the nature of scriptural interpretation. Here we can say simply that the biblical affirmation of God's involvement in the origination of living things may be understood philosophically as the action of a principal cause on instrumental causes. The production of living things is truly God's work, but a work in which the agency of creatures is also involved. Some of the language of Genesis itself suggests this: "Let the earth bring forth vegetation;... Let the earth bring forth all kinds of living creatures" (Genesis 1:11, 24). The reality of God's involvement remains the same, whether the production of living things is understood in terms of the six-day creation account or the theory of evolution.

Regarding the flip side of our second question, a complete explanation of whether it is compatible with science to say that God is somehow involved in the evolutionary process would require a careful account of the nature and limits of scientific methodology. Here we can simply note that while empirical science may (within the limits of its method) offer a complete explanation of evolution in terms of natural (secondary) causes, this does not exclude (beyond the limits of its method) the intimate involvement of God as the transcendent (primary) cause.[147] The International Theological Commission of

---

Hence, the total explanation of evolution, especially when extended to man, will advocate a higher, transcendent causality, which is most intimately connected with the action of the secondary causes: 'We know of enough cases where we meet a complex intertwined causality, and where a double efficiency does not simply stand beside each other, but works in a subordinated relationship. The classic doctrine of instrumentality has sufficiently studied the nature of such a causal subordination. Hence it is conceivable that, in the evolutionary process too, we must admit such a coordination of factors, in which a transcendent factor would cooperate not simply from without but from within with the evolutionary factors at work in the animal series. This means that the transcendent factor must at the same time be immanent, so as to fuse innerly, as it were, with the purely immanent causality of the antecedent' (Norbert Luyten, 'Evolutionisme en wijsbegeerte,' *Tijdschrift voor Philosophie* 16 [1954]: 30). Luyten finally explains that there is only one cause which is at once transcendent and immanent, absolutely immanent because infinitely immanent, the First Cause, God. His creative activity is, in its effects, so intimately intertwined with the secondary causalities, and in its source so far removed above the intramundane activities, that it does not interfere at all with the scientific explanation of evolution. So that the author may conclude that his 'explanation contradicts neither the most solid principles of Thomistic ontology nor the basic assertions of the doctrine of evolution' (ibid., 32)" (Donceel, "Causality and Evolution," 301–2).

147. Benedict Ashley argues that "evolution does not contradict the principle of causality, since when new things emerge, the matter, the energy, and most important, the information necessary to build them are all accounted for in a satisfactory way by current scientific theories." Such a scientific account, however, does not preclude divine involvement: "In any theistic view of evolution the creativity of the created agents is always a participation in the creative action of God" (Ashley, "Causality

the Roman Catholic Church has used this framework of primary and secondary causality in its account of evolution and of the initial emergence of life:

> With respect to the evolution of conditions favorable to the emergence of life, Catholic tradition affirms that, as universal transcendent cause, God is the cause not only of existence but also the cause of causes. God's action does not displace or supplant the activity of creaturely causes, but enables them to act according to their natures and, nonetheless, to bring about the ends he intends. In freely willing to create and conserve the universe, God wills to activate and to sustain in act all those secondary causes whose activity contributes to the unfolding of the natural order which he intends to produce. Through the activity of natural causes, God causes to arise those conditions required for the emergence and support of living organisms, and, furthermore, for their reproduction and differentiation. Although there is scientific debate about the degree of purposiveness or design operative and empirically observable in these developments, they have *de facto* favored the emergence and flourishing of life. Catholic theologians can see in such reasoning support for the affirmation entailed by faith in divine creation and divine providence.[148]

We can understand God's involvement as primary cause in the process of evolution using the analogy of God's involvement in any act of generation. We have seen that, as the cause of new being and of substantial form, God is involved in every substantial change in the natural world, including the production of offspring. As parents are instrumental causes of the being and substantial form of their offspring, so previous generations may be seen as instrumental causes, gradually disposing primary matter for the eduction of a new form in a given generation that might also constitute a new species.[149]

---

and Evolution," 227–28). "The fear is that any causality one attributes to God must, accordingly, be denied to creatures. This is precisely the fear which informs many who defend creation against evolution as well as those who defend evolution against creation: both opposing sides view the general terms of the discourse in the same way. In either case, God and creatures are seen, erroneously, I think, to be causes which, although differing significantly in degree, fall within the same explanatory category. Accordingly, the more one appeals to nature as self-explanatory, the less one appeals to God—or vice versa" (William E. Carroll, "Creation and the Foundations of Evolution," *Angelicum* 87 [2010]: 51).

148. International Theological Commission (ITC), *Communion and Stewardship*, no. 68.

149. "The disposition of matter changes gradually, without the loss of the first form ... until the precise instant when this form is corrupted and the new form ... is generated. Though we may be ignorant of the precise instant that it takes place, this could be a valid description of the transformation of species. Through mutation and natural selection, the disposition and the structure of the DNA gradually changes, until the instant when the new disposition and new structure corresponds to a new substantial form and, consequently, to a new species" (Moreno, "Some Philosophical Considerations," 431). Aquinas himself entertained the possibility that new species might be originated through the causalities of nature under the primary causality of God: "Nothing entirely new was afterwards made by God, but all things subsequently made had in a sense been made before in the work of the six days.... Species, also, that are new, if any such appear, existed beforehand in various active powers; so that animals, and perhaps even new species of animals, are produced" (*ST* I, 73, 1, ad 3).

6

Divine Action and the Causality of Creatures

We have seen how science is breaking out of the confines of causality as understood by Newtonian physics. We have also described how theology, following its example, might engage this broader understanding of contemporary science. Newtonian causality was univocal, the force that moved the atoms. Contemporary causality is analogous, expressed in many different ways in the various sciences.

Analogy is also essential on our language about God. If we speak of God univocally, we reduce God to the level of a creature. By speaking analogously, we preserve both the reality of God and the integrity of the creature. Our task now is to use the analogous notions of causality now emerging in contemporary science, yet so reminiscent of Aquinas and Aristotle, to speak of God's action in the world in a way that diminishes neither God's causality nor the proper causality of creatures.

DIVINE CAUSALITY AND THE MODES OF CREATURELY CAUSALITY

We might classify the modes of creaturely causality into four general types: necessary, contingent, free, and chance. Broadly speaking, creaturely actions are either necessary or contingent, and among contingent acts, some are free, and some are by chance.

We can categorize a particular action in terms of its relation to its cause. If it proceeds from its cause in such a way that it cannot not proceed, it is a necessary effect coming from a necessary cause. Aquinas thought that astronomical events such as eclipses belonged to this category. Given our understanding of contingency in nature, it is hard for us to envision any natural event as absolutely necessary—to think that there are no possible circumstances under which it might not happen. We do, however, tend to see certain laws of nature as necessary (e.g., the conservation of mass-energy).

If an effect proceeds from its cause in such a way that it might not have proceeded, it is a contingent effect coming from a contingent cause. The blossoming of a flower, for instance, is contingent since it might not happen. Aquinas would say that this event is intended in the very nature of the plant. We might say it is genetically programmed, but we would agree with him that it might not happen since some other cause might interfere with it. (A meandering milk cow might eat the bud before it blossoms.) Some contingent events, such as those proceeding from human free will, happen not only contingently but freely. Others are not only contingent but by chance. They are not intended by nature, determined by any genetic code, or chosen by human freedom. They simply happen without any proper cause at all. A diagram of these different categories might look something like figure 6-1.

If Aquinas were asked to which of these categories divine action belongs, he would answer, "None of the above." God's causality transcends all these categories of creaturely action, just as God's being transcends the whole order of creaturely existence. We have already seen in our discussion of primary and secondary causality that no creaturely effect can occur without God's influence. That influence, however, belongs to none of these categories of creaturely causality:

> There is a difference to be noted on the part of the divine will, for the divine will must be understood as existing outside of the order of beings, as a cause producing the whole of being and all its differences. Now the possible and the necessary are differences of being, and therefore necessity and contingency in things and the distinction of each according to the nature of their proximate causes originate from the divine will itself, for he disposes necessary causes for the effects that he wills to be necessary, and he ordains causes acting contingently (i.e., able to fail) for the effects that he wills to be contingent. And according to the condition of these causes, effects are called either necessary or contingent, although all depend on the divine will as on a first cause, which transcends the order of necessity and contingency. This, however, cannot be said of the human will, nor of any other cause, for every other cause already falls under the order of necessity or contingency; hence, either the cause itself must be able to fail or, if not, its effect is not contingent, but necessary. The divine will, on the other hand, is unfailing; yet not all its effects are necessary, but some are contingent.[1]

---

1. *In peri herm.* I, lect. 14, no. 22. Cf.: *In meta.* VI, lect. 1, no. 3 (§1222). "The Thomist ... synthesis was to place God above and beyond the created orders of necessity and contingence: because

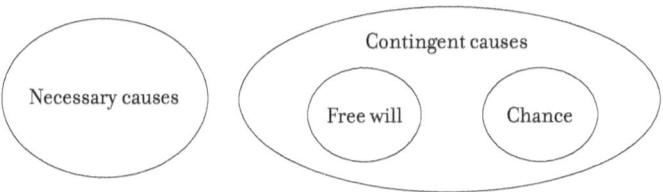

FIGURE 6-1. Categories of Creaturely Causality

A diagram might be useful in illustrating Aquinas's thought here. In figure 6-2, divine causality is portrayed as above or transcending all modes of creaturely causality. It does not distort them, but causes each with precisely its characteristic value, whether necessary, contingent, free, or chance.

If we keep divine transcendence in mind, we will recognize that there can be no contradiction or competition between the causality of God and that of the creature, since God creates the creature's causality. God's causality cannot diminish or distort the causality of the creature since it is its very source.[2]

It is not easy, however, for us to remember divine transcendence. Our natural bent of mind is toward univocal thinking.[3] The notion of secondary causality is therefore not an easy one to grasp. In perhaps one of his greatest understatements, Aquinas observes: "Now, it seems difficult for some people to understand how natural effects are attributed to God and to a natural

---

God is universal cause, his providence must be certain; but because he is a transcendent cause, there can be no incompatibility between terrestrial contingence and the causal certitude of providence" (Bernard Lonergan, *Grace and Freedom: Operative Grace in the Thought of St. Thomas Aquinas* [New York: Herder and Herder, 1971], 79). See also Burrell, *Freedom and Creation*, 122.

2. "It is also evident that, though a natural thing produces its proper effect, it is not superfluous for God to produce it, since the natural thing does not produce it except by divine power" (*SCG* III, 70, no. 6). "[A]n infallibly efficacious cause is only a compulsive cause when it is a particular cause; if it be the universal cause then it grants even the mode of freedom to the secondary cause. In other words God's action and the creature's action are not joint causes as though each cooperated in doing a part.... God's action on our action should be seen according to causal subordination, not coordination, and the whole effect is to be attributed both to the first cause and to the secondary cause" (Thomas Gilby, "Appendix 6," in *Summa theologiae*, by Thomas Aquinas, ed. Thomas Gilby [New York: McGraw-Hill, 1964], 1.82). See also Bernard McGinn, "The Development of the Thought of Thomas Aquinas on the Reconciliation of Divine Providence and Contingent Action," *Thomist* 39 (1975): 741–52.

3. "[T]he endemic tendency of philosophers treating divinity is to assign God a place in the universe, albeit the largest or the first or the most significant" (David B. Burrell, "Divine Action and Human Freedom in the Context of Creation," in *The God Who Acts: Philosophical and Theological Explorations*, ed. Thomas F. Tracy [University Park: Pennsylvania State University Press, 1994], 104).

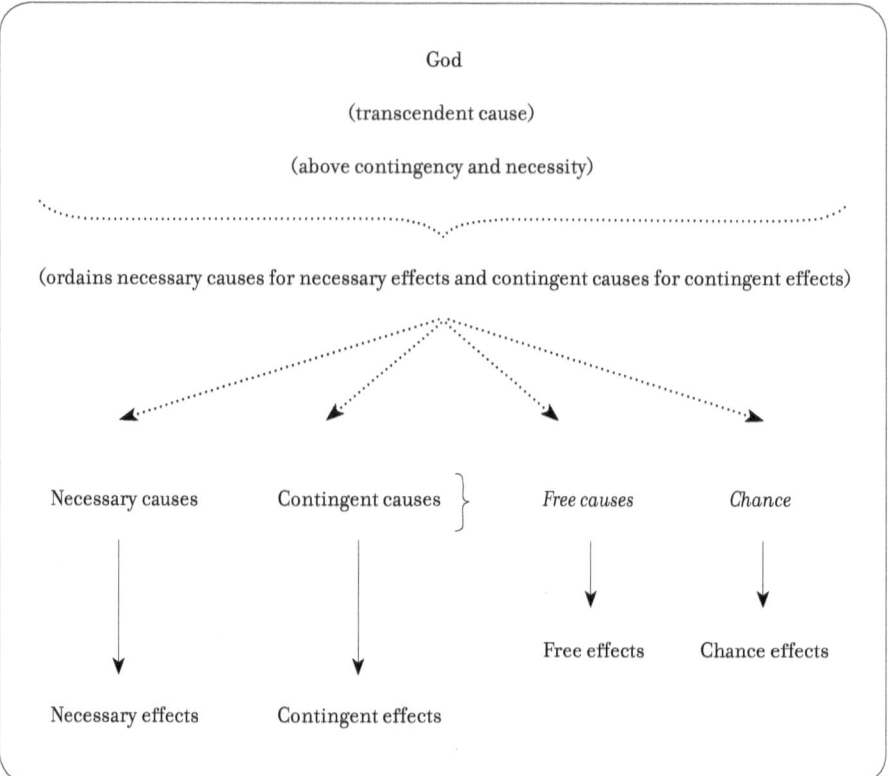

FIGURE 6-2. The Primary Causality of God and the Secondary Causality of Creatures

Note: God, as the source of all actuality, is involved in every production of actuality or being. In exercising his causal influence, God wills not only the things that are actualized but also the way in which they are actualized.

Here, the dotted bracket suggests the transcendent realm of divine causality, as the dotted arrows indicate the transcendent influence of divine causality. The solid arrows indicate how the different categories of natural causes produce the different types of natural effects. The bracket beside "contingent causes" is meant to indicate that "free causes" and "chance" are subsets of contingent causes.

agent."[4] Etienne Gilson elaborates the dilemma: "The problem in the final analysis comes to this. We must hold firmly to two apparently contradictory truths. God does whatever creatures do; and yet creatures themselves do whatever they do. It is a question of understanding how one and the same effect can proceed simultaneously from two different causes: God and the natural agent which produces it. At first sight this seems incomprehensible.

4. SCG III, 70, no. 1.

Most philosophers seem to have cringed before it. They could not see how one action could proceed from two causes."[5]

If we forget divine transcendence, the whole vocabulary of primary and secondary causality loses its meaning. Instances of causality in the world must then be assigned either to a divine cause or to a creaturely cause: they cannot be products of both. If we think of God and creatures as belonging to the same univocal order of causality, any assertion that God can act in the world without distorting or modifying the proper causality of creatures will appear hopelessly incoherent. It would be like saying that, when six men carry a boat, each can carry its entire weight since the causality of one does not affect the causality of another.[6]

Austin Farrer performed a great service for the theological community in retrieving the notion of secondary causality under the name of "double agency."[7] He recognizes that "two agents for the same act would be indeed impossible, were they both agents in the same sense and on the same level." He also sees that God's agency is not like ours and appreciates the mental dilemma this presents to us: "[I]t is true that I am unequipped to think of God's agency otherwise than in terms of my own; it is false that I believe it to be of the same sort."[8] He characterizes double agency as a paradox: "I set myself to illustrate the paradox of double agency ... and to show that so far from being a speculative embarrassment, the paradox involved is the form of practical religious thinking.... The paradox of double agency, creaturely and divine, is all-pervasive."[9]

Farrer's teaching will seem not only paradoxical but completely incoherent if we forget divine transcendence and think of God as one univocal cause among others. This seems to be the dilemma of John Polkinghorne

---

5. Gilson, *Christian Philosophy*, 182. Brian Hebblethwaite notes: "We are dealing here with the ancient problem of the relation between primary and secondary causality, endeavoring to take each seriously and not to confuse one with the other or exalt one at the expense of the other. The relation has always been hard to grasp" (Brian L. Hebblethwaite, "Providence and Divine Action," *Religious Studies* 14 [1978]: 232).

6. "The source of most of the difficulties in grasping an adequate understanding of the relationship between the created order and God is the failure to understand divine transcendence. It is God's very transcendence, a transcendence beyond any contrast with immanence, which enables God to be intimately present in the world as cause. God is not transcendent in such a way that he is 'outside' or 'above' or 'beyond' the world. God is not different from creatures in the way in which creatures differ from one another. We might say that God 'differs differently' from the created order" (Carroll, "Creation and the Foundations," 59–60). See also Carroll, "Aquinas on Creation," 75.

7. See Farrer, *Faith and Speculation*, 65–66, 68, 78, 80, 85, 165.

8. Ibid., 104–5.

9. Ibid., v, 173.

who characterizes Farrer's double agency as an "unintelligible kind of theological *doublespeak*."[10]

If we affirm divine transcendence, we can see that secondary causality neither diminishes the power of God nor distorts that of creatures. God can act through secondary causes, with their character of necessity, contingency, chance, or freedom, without becoming himself just another secondary cause, acting with a univocal necessity, contingency, chance, or freedom. God's causality is not limited or circumscribed by creatures. Nor is the causality of creatures compromised by God's causality: what God wills to be actualized in the world is always actualized, and it is actualized through the mode of secondary causality that God wills—actualized either through necessary causes so that it occurs necessarily, through contingent causes so that it occurs contingently, through free will so that it occurs freely, or by chance so that it occurs spontaneously.[11]

DIVINE ACTION AS UNIVOCAL CAUSALITY

If God were understood as a univocal cause acting among other univocal causes, he could no longer be seen as a primary cause acting through secondary causes. If, in addition, this univocal causality of God were thought to be omnipotent, God would necessarily overpower all other agents, and all worldly events would be due to God's causality alone. The result would be occasionalism. Other agents might appear to be exercising causality, but causal efficacy would really belong to God alone. We have already seen Aquinas's opinion that God's goodness and power would be less manifest if God

---

10. "Although Farrer wrote so extensively and so entrancingly about his notion of double agency, I find it an unintelligible kind of theological *doublespeak*" (John C. Polkinghorne, *The Faith of a Physicist* [Princeton, N.J.: Princeton University Press, 1994], 81–82). "However, some of us feel that the deep obscurity involved in the idea of double agency carries with it the danger that the discussion might turn out to be no more than double talk" (Polkinghorne, "Kenotic Creation," 97). As regards the univocity of divine causality, Polkinghorne quite tellingly embraces a "kenosis of causal status" by which God becomes "a present cause among other causes" (ibid., 104–5). See also Polkinghorne, "Chaos Theory," 244. Some have tried, nonetheless, to reconcile Polkinghorne's views with the secondary causality of Aquinas. See Boyd and Cobb, "Causality Distinction."

11. "God wills whatever is required for a thing that he wills.... But it befits certain things according to the mode of their nature, that they be contingent and not necessary. Therefore God wills that some things be contingent. Now the efficacy of the divine will requires not only that something be that God wills to be, but also that it be as he wills it to be. For, among natural agents as well, when the acting power is strong it assimilates its effect to itself not only as to species but also as to the accidents, which are certain modes of that thing. Therefore the efficacy of the divine will does not remove contingency" (*SCG* I, 85, no. 2). Cf. *Comp.* I, 140; *SCG* III, 72, nos. 2 and 7.

exercised his causality alone rather than through creatures.¹² Aquinas has two words for occasionalism: "stupid" and "impossible."¹³

Aside from the problem of occasionalism, if God were a univocal cause, he would no longer transcend the categories of secondary causality, but would have to belong to one of them. Fundamentally, God would have to be either a necessary or a contingent cause. If God were a necessary cause, all that he wills would have to occur necessarily. Contingency, freedom, and chance would be eliminated from creation.¹⁴ Only a theologian who viewed nature as absolutely determined and human behavior as predestined in such a way as to preclude free will could accept such a consequence.¹⁵

Theologians who conceive God's causality as univocal but consider the elimination of contingency, freedom, and chance to be intolerable must find some way to limit God's causal influence.¹⁶ One solution is simply to assign God to the category of contingent rather than necessary causes. If God is placed there, his causality will be limited by that of creatures, as the contingent causality of any univocal agent is limited by that of other univocal agents. We might see this as the solution of process theology, where God is viewed as a contingent, univocal cause whose causality is consequently limited.¹⁷ Another solution is to say that God limits himself by freely choos-

---

12. See *ST* I, 22, 3, co.; *ST* I, 105, 5, co.

13. "This position is stupid [*stulta*], for it takes away the order of the universe and removes from things their proper operation, and destroys the judgment of sense" (*Sent.* II, 1, 1, 4, co.) "This is impossible [*impossibile*]. First, because the order of cause and effect would be taken away from created things: and this would imply lack of power in the Creator: for it is due to the power of the cause, that it bestows active power on its effect. Secondly, because the active powers which are seen to exist in things, would be bestowed on things to no purpose, if these wrought nothing through them" (*ST* I, 105, 5, co.). Cf.: *De pot.* 3, 7 co.

14. Aquinas clearly sees this consequence in an objection he proposes to one of his arguments: "It would seem that the will is moved of necessity by God. For every agent that cannot be resisted moves of necessity. But God cannot be resisted, because his power is infinite.... Therefore God moves the will of necessity" (*ST* I-II, 10, 4, obj. 1). Cf.: *SCG* III, 94, no. 15.

15. John Calvin and Martin Luther are sometimes pictured as verging on this position because of their views on predestination or the "bondage of the will." William Placher, however, nuances this interpretation, pointing out that their theology includes a much stronger appreciation of divine transcendence than that of some of their followers. See William C. Placher, *The Domestication of Transcendence* (Louisville, Ky.: Westminster John Knox Press, 1996).

16. "[T]he believer will have to admit that there are limits to what God can make of particular providential lines of development without breaking into the structures of creation and suspending operation of its laws.... Recognition of the limitation on providential activity imposed by the present structures of creation need not drive the believer to the opposite conclusion that there is no room for divine action in the world at all" (Hebblethwaite, *Evil, Suffering*, 98).

17. "God is not to be treated as an exception to all metaphysical principles, invoked to save their collapse. He is their chief exemplification" (Whitehead, *Process*, 343). "God cannot guarantee that

ing to restrict his causality to prevent its interfering with the causality of creatures. We might see this as the solution of the theology of divine self-limitation, that we discussed earlier.[18]

Two consequences follow from either of these positions. First, God will be less present to creation if his influence is naturally or voluntarily curtailed in situations where creatures are exercising their own proper causality. Secondly, the effectiveness of God's causality will depend ultimately not upon God but upon creatures.

The first consequence has special implications regarding grace and human freedom. If human freedom is to be preserved, univocal divine causality must in some way be limited, either by God's very nature or by his free decision. This means that God's influence will be less present precisely at those moments that are most important to us, when we make our free decisions. It is precisely at such moments that God must naturally or voluntarily limit himself and, in a sense, step back from us. Such divine abandonment, even in the interest of preserving human freedom, seems contrary to the truth of God's loving concern and providential care for us. It also raises the specter of Pelagianism if our most fundamental choices proceed simply from ourselves either without or with a vastly diminished involvement of God's grace.

The second consequences has implications for divine providence. If God is considered a univocal cause, and his causality is not to overpower that of creatures, God must be consigned (either by God's nature or by God's choice) to the category of contingent rather than necessary causes. The effects of divine causality will then proceed contingently—in such a way that they may or may not occur, depending on the activity of other contingent causes. God may then providentially will the good of creation, but whether his will is accomplished or not will depend on the influence of other causes. Among those other causes we will give special consideration here to chance and human freedom.

God and Chance

There are many opinions on the relationship between God and chance. Some thinkers, such as Jacques Monod, Steven Weinberg, and Richard

---

evil will be overcome simply because he is not the sole agent determining the outcome of the world. It is a joint enterprise involving a vast multiplicity of actualities responding to his cosmic purposes" (Ford, *Lure*, 119).

18. See the subsection "Theology of Divine Limitation" in chapter 3.

Dawkins, contend that worldly contingency simply rules out divine governance.[19] Niels Henrik Gregersen thinks that chance does not exclude, but simply lies beyond the reach of God's providence.[20] Paul Davies believes that God may choose the general laws of nature, but thinks the details are due simply to chance.[21] Kenneth Miller would like to keep chance events within the realm of providence, but thinks that God must simply wait and see what chance, as an autonomous cause, produces.[22] Thomas Tracy also seems to imply that God must wait upon the results of chance.[23]

David Bartholomew has been especially devoted to developing an understanding of the role of chance in the theology of divine action. He finds a new appreciation of chance in contemporary science and invites theologians to see chance as an instrument of divine providence.[24] He is critical of

19. See Monod, *Chance and Necessity*, 44, 112–13; Richard Dawkins, *Climbing Mount Improbable* (New York: Norton, 1996), 223; Richard Dawkins, *The Blind Watchmaker: Why the Evidence of Evolution Reveals a Universe without Design* (New York: Norton, 1996); Steven Weinberg, *Dreams of a Final Theory* (New York: Vintage Books, 1994), 250; Steven Weinberg, "A Designer Universe?" in *Facing Up: Science and Its Cultural Adversaries* (Cambridge, Mass.: Harvard University Press, 2001), 243–46.

20. "On this level of chance, theology should be silent and refrain from talking about Providence. Chance is what simply happens to happen, and theology has no explanation of the happenstance of particulars" (Gregersen, "Providence," 25).

21. "[I]n my view there is no miracle, no crudely-direct teleology, no supernatural tinkering; only the outworking of peculiarly creative and felicitous laws chosen, in my view, by God for these very purposes. And although the general trend of this process is basic to the laws, the actual details of evolution are left to the vagaries of chance" (Paul Davies, "Teleology without Teleology: Purpose through Emergent Complexity," in *Evolutionary and Molecular Biology: Scientific Perspectives on Divine Action*, ed. Robert John Russell, William R. Stoeger, and Francisco J. Ayala [Vatican City State: Vatican Observatory; Berkeley, Calif.: Center for Theology and the Natural Sciences], 162).

22. "So, how is a random, chance process like evolution consistent with the will of a Creator? . . . Would God's purpose have been realized if evolution had turned out a little differently? How can we say for sure? But this much I think is clear: Given evolution's ability to adapt, to innovate, to test, and to experiment, sooner or later it would have given the Creator exactly what He was looking for—a creature who, like us, could know Him and love Him, could perceive the heavens and dream of the stars, a creature who would eventually discover the extraordinary process of evolution that filled His earth with so much life" (K. R. Miller, *Finding*, 238–39).

23. "[I]f the world God has made includes events that are determined neither by created causes nor by God, then the ascription of these events to God as indirect divine acts will need to be qualified accordingly. . . . God's intentional relation to [events] will be more complex, perhaps . . . taking the form of a permissive disjunction ("Let A or B or C come to pass"). . . . This entire structure of possibility, of course, will be ordered by and embraced within God's purposes for creation. In a world of this sort, for example, it could be said that God makes use of both law and chance in establishing the conditions for the evolution of life. As a technique of indirect divine action, ontological chance provides flexibility and a capacity for novelty that a purely deterministic system would lack, but it also entails that God's intentions take a more complex, conditional form" (Thomas F. Tracy, "God and Creatures Acting: the Idea of Double Agency," in *Creation and the God of Abraham*, ed. David B. Burrell, Carlo Coglioti, Janet Soskice, and William R. Stoeger [New York: Cambridge University Press, 2010], 227–28).

24. "Chance has become an integral part of contemporary science but, for the most part, is still not at home in theology. Theology speaks of a purposeful God while chance, by very definition,

a "naive orthodoxy" that would see a contradiction between chance and divine action.[25] He singles out Aquinas as an exception to the theological tendency to depreciate chance: "The weight of theological opinion, St. Thomas Aquinas and his heirs excepted, seems to have regarded chance as the enemy of true religion and, largely, been intent on denying its existence."[26] Like Aquinas, he thinks God exercises a continuous rather than intermittent influence on the world: "To speak of 'interfering' or 'intervening' is to pre-judge the issue. The use of these words implies that creation was an event in the past which set everything up in full working order to be left to run on it own. If creation is a continuing process such language is meaningless. Special providence is thus more accurately regarded as part of the continuing creative act rather than as a distinct and subsequent action of a different kind."[27]

Unlike Aquinas, however, he does not see chance as a secondary cause under the divine influence of God's primary causality. Instead, chance seems to exercise an autonomous causality of its own that may contradict God's intention: "If there is an element of unpredictability, it has to be allowed that things may not turn out as God intended—that the whole thing might go disastrously wrong or never even have got off the ground in the first place. Can we allow that God could fail? ... It does diminish God somewhat if we admit that he could fail at anything he attempted—even though by repetition he would certainly succeed in the end.... It may be that the whole conception of creation was (had to be?) of such stupendous proportions as to tax even the resources of an infinitely powerful God."[28]

This implies a univocal understanding of God and chance that has consequences for divine providence. The outcome of God's action becomes uncertain: "If my thesis that God uses chance is accepted, we cannot avoid the consequence that he appears to be taking risks."[29] Providence becomes pre-

---

seems to signify a total lack of purpose. To suggest the very opposite—that chance lies within the purposes of God—may seem perverse, if not foolhardy, and yet that is precisely what is argued for in this book.... [T]he central purpose of this book is to argue ... that God uses chance. In other words, that the chance we observe in nature is there because God intended it to be so" (Bartholomew, *God, Chance and Purpose*, ix, 174). See also ibid., 187, 192; and Bartholomew, *God of Chance*, 3, 14.

25. Bartholomew, *God, Chance and Purpose*, 241–42.
26. Bartholomew, *God of Chance*, 96. "St. Thomas Aquinas apart, these examples gleaned from many quarters, speak with one voice: God is in charge of everything and chance does not exist" (ibid., 110–11).
27. Ibid., 121.   28. Ibid., 100–101.
29. Bartholomew, *God, Chance and Purpose*, 224.

carious, little more than a possibly favorable product of the law of averages: "So we return to my opening question: 'Is God a risk taker?' In the light of my discussion, this question has to be worded more carefully because we have to distinguish between ultimate goals and short-term deviations. We have seen that determinate ends may be achieved as the result of averaging many random effects or by the interactions within the process. This means that the end of the process may be virtually certain, even though the path to that end is not determined. Is it sufficient to preserve our understanding of God's greatness that he, as it were, gets there in the end—or that he must never put a foot wrong? It seems to me that it is the end that matters and if deviations toward that end deliver side benefits, the net result may be gain."[30]

God and Human Freedom

If the plans of the univocal God can be affected by chance, they are in even greater danger of being thwarted by the free choices of human beings. Maurice Wiles builds this idea into his account of divine action: "God's purpose is fixed and unchanging only in the most general sense. God is affected by our actions in such a way that the particular form of that purpose is changed to take account of them."[31] Arthur Peacocke believes that the presence of human freedom puts God at risk: "In the actual processes of the world, and supremely in human self-consciousness, God is involving himself and expressing himself as creator. However, since human beings have free will we have also to recognize that God put himself 'at risk,' as it were, in creatively evoking in the natural world, beings who have free will and who can transcend their perceived world and shape it in their own way."[32]

Scripture abounds with instances where God's plans appear to get derailed through the free decisions of humans (or angels or demons).[33] Other

---

30. Ibid., 235–36. Ultimately, Bartholomew's understanding of chance affects his concept of God: "If we take the new knowledge about the role of chance in the world seriously, we must either revise our view of God or join those who have abandoned him altogether" (ibid., 226).

31. Wiles, *God's Action*, 51.

32. Arthur R. Peacocke, "Chance and Law in Irreversible Thermodynamics, Theoretical Biology, and Theology," in *Chaos and Complexity: Scientific Perspectives on Divine Action*, ed. Robert John Russell, Nancey Murphy, and Arthur R. Peacocke (Vatican City State: Vatican Observatory; Berkeley, Calif.: Center for Theology and the Natural Sciences, 1995), 140. Cf. Arthur R. Peacocke, "The Cost of New Life," in *The Work of Love: Creation as Kenosis*, ed. John C. Polkinghorne (Grand Rapids, Mich.: Eerdmans, 2001), 27.

33. "When the Lord saw how great was man's wickedness on earth, and how no desire that his heart conceived was ever anything but evil, he regretted that he had made man on the earth, and his heart was grieved" (Gen. 6: 5–6). "How many times I yearned to gather your children together as a

passages, however, seem to proclaim that God's sovereign authority and unconditional love cannot be overcome by the evil plottings of humans or angels.[34] How do we put these passages together? Those of the first kind certainly express a deep truth about God's abiding love for creation and the awesome, sometimes dreadful, power of human freedom. Might those of the second type be a reminder of the transcendence of God? If so, they remind us also of the transcendent nature of divine causality. How should the two kinds of passages shape our theology? If we keep both in mind, we will, in virtue of the second type, be less likely to conceive God metaphysically as a univocal cause acting alongside of others, even as, in virtue of the first type, we deeply appreciate and affirm the fundamental truths expressed in the drama of God's abiding love for his often less than worthy worshipers.

DIVINE ACTION AS TRANSCENDENT CAUSALITY

If we remember divine transcendence, we will be able to speak of God's action in the chance events of nature and the freedom of human beings without depriving either of their contingent character.

God and Chance

As chance gains a new role and importance in empirical science, theologians are invited to reconsider its place in divine action. Viewed as a transcendent cause, God does not deprive chance of its contingent character; nor does chance subvert God's action.[35] Although one secondary cause may hinder the effect of another, no secondary cause can impede the influence of God as the universal primary cause of all things.[36] Chance is not opposed to God and does not exclude God's influence. It is rather, like all creation, a

---

hen gathers her brood under her wings, but you were unwilling!" (Luke 13: 34). Cf. 1 Sam. 15: 29; Mic. 6: 3.

34. "The gifts and the call of God are irreversible" (Rom. 11: 29). "God is not man that he should speak falsely, nor human, that he should change his mind" (Num. 23: 19). Cf. 1 Sam 15: 29; Ps. 50: 21; Ps. 139: 16; Isa. 55: 9.

35. "It pertains to divine providence to produce every grade of being. And thus it has prepared for some things necessary causes, so that they happen of necessity; for others contingent causes, that they may happen by contingency, according to the nature of their proximate causes" (ST I, 22, 4, co.).

36. "There is a difference between universal and particular causes. A thing can escape the order of a particular cause; but not the order of a universal cause. For nothing escapes the order of a particular cause, except through the intervention and hindrance of some other particular cause; as, for instance, wood may be prevented from burning, by the action of water. Since then, all particular causes are included under the universal cause, it could not be that any effect should take place outside the range of that universal cause" (ST I, 22, 2, ad 1). Cf. ST I, 19, 6, ad 3.

product of God's action.[37] God is the primary cause not only of all that happens in the world, but also of the mode of its happening—whether that be by necessity, contingency, freedom, or chance.[38] As God acts through all other secondary causes, so God acts through the secondary causality of chance.

We can affirm that God acts through chance in this way, however, only if we understand God as a transcendent cause, not a univocal cause. Two univocal causes necessarily interfere with or at least affect each other and so cannot produce an effect belonging entirely to both. If two people carry a table, for instance, the effect (the motion of the table) will be divided between them. It will either belong partially to each, if each carries some of the weight, or wholly to one and not at all to the other, if one carries all the weight. A transcendent primary cause, however, may act through a secondary cause to produce an effect that belongs wholly to both. So, a transcendent primary cause can also act through chance (conceived as secondary cause) to produce an effect that belongs wholly to both. A univocal cause cannot work through chance in this way. It can only replace chance—however much the effect may still appear to be the result of chance. (If one person connives to arrange a meeting between two friends, for instance, it may seem like a chance encounter to them, but in reality it will have nothing to do with chance.)

Theologians who locate God's action in the indeterminacy of quantum events seem to treat God as a univocal cause that does not act through chance but simply replaces it, so that the reality of chance dissolves into mere appearance. In this respect, Ian Barbour's comment regarding God's action in quantum events is telling: "What appears to be chance ... may be the very point at which God acts."[39] The event seems to have occurred by chance

---

37. "Nor can the possibility of failure on the part of secondary causes, by means of which the effects of providence are produced, take away the certainty of divine providence.... For God himself operates in all things, and in accord with the decision of his will.... Hence it is appropriate to his providence sometimes to permit defectible causes to fail, and at other times to preserve them from failure" (*SCG* III, 94, no. 16). Cf. *ST* I, 103, 7 ad 3.

38. "God who is the governor of the universe, intends some of his effects to be established by way of necessity, and others contingently. On this basis, he adapts different causes to them; for one group of effects there are necessary causes, but for another, contingent causes. So, it falls under the order of divine providence not only that this effect is to be, but also that this effect is to be contingently, while another is to be necessarily. Because of this, some of the things that are subject to providence are necessary whereas others are contingent and not at all necessary" (*SCG* III, 94, no. 11). Cf. *ST* I, 19, 8, co.; *De ver.* 23, 5, co.

39. Barbour, *Nature*, 27. In the present discussion, we are of course employing the Copenhagen interpretation of quantum mechanics as do the theologians of quantum divine action. At the same time, we recognize that this is only one of the possible interpretations of quantum physics.

but is really the result only of God's determining action. In his theology of divine action, Robert Russell affirms that God acts through nature: "God acts together with nature to determine which quantum outcome becomes actual."[40] He seems to envision this cooperation, however, as the work of two univocal causes, in which the effect is due partly to one and partly to the other, rather than the action of a transcendent primary cause and a creaturely secondary cause, in which the effect would be due wholly to both: "In short, quantum events occur in part because of God's special providence, in part because of natural causality."[41] In the end, however, he attributes quantum events entirely to God's efficient causality: "God can know which potential state will become actual, since *God alone causes it to become actual!* In essence, quantum indeterminism is the result of it being God, not nature, which determines the outcome."[42] Here it seems the indeterminism of quantum chance, as assumed by the Copenhagen interpretation of quantum mechanics, is simply replaced by the divine cause.

Thomas Tracy's careful account of how God might be involved in indeterministic chance also seems to involve a choice of between *God or chance* rather than seeing *God in chance*. In his view, God does not act *through* the secondary causality of chance but *in place of* it: "If the structures of nature in fact include a role for indeterministic chance, then one option for the theologian is to think of God as determining these events. In this case, chance events would be causally undetermined only in their 'horizontal' relations to other finite events, but they would be fully determined by the 'vertical' relationship to God. Note that in determining these finitely undetermined events, God would be acting *directly* in the world's history, rather than indi-

---

40. R. J. Russell, "Quantum Physics," 587.

41. R. J. Russell, "Religion and the Theories," 38. That Russell is envisioning the action of two univocal causes becomes more evident in his assertion that, at a given point in the evolutionary process, God ceases to determine certain quantum events, lest he interfere with the proper causality of creatures: "God acts in all quantum events in the universe until the evolution of organisms capable of even primitive levels of consciousness. God then increasingly refrains from determining the neurophysiological outcomes we associate with conscious choices, leaving room for top-down, mind-brain causality in conscious and self-conscious creatures. This would be one version of the standard 'solution' to the problem of free will: namely, God's voluntary or metaphysically necessary self-limitation, but seen now as a temporal development of the limitations, from minimum to maximum" (R. J. Russell, "Quantum Physics," 592–93).

42. R. J. Russell, "Quantum Physics," 587. "[I]f science claims that there is no complete set of natural causes for a quantum event, then we can argue that the addition of divine causality brings these events to completion without violating these laws or without being equivalent to a natural or secondary cause" (Robert J. Russell, "Religion and the Theories of Science: A Response to Barbour," *Zygon* 31 [1996]: 38). See also R. J. Russell, "Does the 'God Who Acts,'" 90–91.

rectly through secondary causes, but this direct action need not disrupt the causal structures of nature, since chance events, *ex hypothesi,* do not have sufficient secondary causes."[43] What Tracy fails to see is that chance itself, as an intrinsic feature of the real world, may be one of the secondary causes through which God acts. If so, we cannot say, that God's action as described here "does not disrupt the causal structures of nature" if the very indeterminism of nature (chance) is itself part of that causal structure. Such an indeterministic structure of nature, however, is precisely what is proposed in the Copenhagen interpretation of quantum mechanics.

In the accounts of both Russell and Tracy, the quantum event is not a product of the indeterminism of nature (even as a secondary cause), but of the direct and determining action of God. God is not portrayed as working though the indeterminism of nature in such a way that nature maintains its characteristic indeterminism. Instead, quantum chance in the natural world is simply trumped by divine determinism.

Our view of God's involvement in chance events (including quantum events) will be quite different if we view God as a transcendent cause.[44]

---

43. T. F. Tracy, "Creation, Providence," 243–44. "God's action here does not shoulder aside natural processes, interrupting an otherwise closed causal series, because *(ex hypothesi)* the events in question do not have sufficient natural causes. Instead, God actualizes one of the possibilities rooted in, but not already selected by, the past history of the universe" (Thomas F. Tracy, "Special Divine Action and the Laws of Nature," in *Scientific Perspectives on Divine Action: Twenty Years of Challenge and Progress,* ed. Robert John Russell, Nancey Murphy, and William R. Stoeger [Vatican City State: Vatican Observatory; Berkeley, Calif.: Center for Theology and the Natural Sciences, 2008], 252.)

44. It may be useful here to consider the relation between the notion of "quantum chance" as Robert Russell uses the term and the Aristotelian/Thomistic idea of chance that we discussed in chapter 1. Russell distinguishes between classical chance and quantum chance: "I suggest that we now face a more fundamental shift in our discussion of 'law and chance' in light of quantum physics: a shift from chance in classical physics (where chance as mere epistemic ignorance of underlying causal processes precludes NIODA [non-interventionist objective divine action]) to chance in quantum physics (where chance as ontological indeterminism is open to NIODA)" (R. J. Russell, "Quantum Physics," 591). He also distinguishes classical statistics from quantum statistics: "The mathematical form of quantum statistics suggests another important difference from classical statistics. In the latter case we can assume that what we consider to be a chance event is the juxtaposition of two causally-unrelated trajectories (an example is a car crash or winning a lotto ticket). In the case of quantum physics the statistics suggest that no underlying causal explanation can account for the data with its particular form of randomness" (Robert John Russell, "Quantum Physics in Philosophical and Theological Perspective," in *Physics, Philosophy, and Theology: A Common Quest for Understanding,* ed. Robert J. Russell, William R. Stoeger, and George V. Coyne [Vatican City State: Vatican Observatory; Berkeley, Calif.: Center for Theology and the Natural Sciences, 1988], 345–46). Quantum chance also differs from classical chance in terms of predictability: "[Q]uantum chance cannot be due to the mere juxtaposition of causally unrelated, previously undetected, classical trajectories.... Quantum chance is not just accident, the unforeseen (but in principle, predictable) intersection of two causal streams. Quantum events behave as though they were uncaused" (R. J. Russell, "Quantum Physics in Philosophical," 353, 355). Neither Russell's description of "classical chance" nor his ac-

God's transcendent primary causality can act through chance itself as a sort of secondary cause just as it does through other secondary causes. As God is not the immediate cause of effects that occur through other secondary causes, so God is not the direct cause of events that happen by chance. As God does not distort the causality of other secondary causes, neither does God alter the causality of chance. God does not determine the indeterminacy of chance, but acts precisely through that indeterminacy. We might say that God's causality acts precisely through the "noncausality" of chance.

If we apply this understanding of divine causality to the Copenhagen interpretation of quantum mechanics, we will be able to affirm that God acts, not in place of the indeterminism of nature posited by that interpretation, but within it. The Copenhagen interpretation asserts that quantum events are products of the very indeterminism of nature. They occur by chance and require no cause.[45] As primary cause, however, God can act through the indeterminism of nature in its very indeterminism. God can act through quantum chance itself as through a secondary cause to produce the quantum event.[46] It would be as much a mistake to introduce God as the direct

---

count of "classical statistics" precisely coincides with the idea of chance as outlined by Aquinas and Aristotle. In some ways, their idea is more like the "ontological indeterminacy" of quantum chance. For them, chance is not just a name for our ignorance; nor are chance events predictable since they have no proper causes. However much knowledge we might have of a given thing (substance) and of the action that proceeds from it according to its nature, our knowledge will never entail the incidental occurrence that we attribute to chance. Chance bespeaks an objective indeterminacy in nature and an absence of any underlying proper causal explanation. An event is attributed to the "causality" of chance only if it has no proper cause: "It is impossible for that which is accidental to be the proper effect of an active natural principle" (*ST* I, 116, 1 co.). Cf. *In meta.* VI, lect 3 (§1201); *Phys.* II, 5 (197a 12–14); *In phys.* II, lect. 9 (§218). In a sense, this notion of chance involves an even more radical indeterminism than quantum chance, since quantum events are at least statistically predictable and so bespeak an underlying order, even if we can know that order only statistically. Chance also presupposes an ordered series of causes and effects, since every substance acts in accordance with its nature. But chance is precisely a disorder within that ordered series: "Statistics can be applied only to the extent that the material studied has an order. Randomness is open to scientific analysis: but chance, as such, is not. Randomness involves the mathematical; but chance is physical. Chance is a real disorder; but randomness is a disorder only for our logic, accustomed as it is to the non-statistical methods of solving problems" (V. E. Smith, *General*, 206).

45. "[I]n the usual interpretation of the quantum theory, the precise magnitudes of the irregular fluctuations in the results of individual measurements at the atomic level are not supposed to be determined by any kinds of causes at all, either known or unknown" (Bohm, *Causality*, 87). "Nothing in nature determines which of these two possibilities [spin-up or spin-down] will be realized. The outcome is, in the nature of things, random" (Kosso, *Appearance*, 159).

46. "God's will transcends and constitutes the whole hierarchy of created causes, both causes which always and necessarily produce their effects and causes which at times fail to produce their effects. We can say that God causes chance events to be chance events. The role of chance mutations at the genetic level, so important in current evolutionary theory, does not call into question God's creative act" (Carroll, "Creation and the Foundations," 53–54). "This philosophy of action [of

cause of quantum events as to posit God as the direct cause of any event that involves the secondary causality of creatures. To do so would violate not only the physics of the Copenhagen interpretation, which maintains that the quantum event is the result of the very indeterminism of nature, but also the theology of secondary causality, which maintains that God works through secondary causes, not in place of them.

The absence of any natural cause in chance events, including quantum events, does not imply the absence of God's influence. Chance itself is a real feature of the natural world, and as primary cause God acts through all of nature, including the "causality" of chance. All aspects of nature including chance and the indeterminism posited by the Copenhagen interpretation of quantum physics involve the primary causality of the transcendent divine cause.

If God's causality is not excluded from chance events, neither is it excluded from the cumulative effects of such events, such as the generation of new species through the chance events involved in evolution. Robert Russell has affirmed God's action in evolution, using his understanding of God as the determiner of indeterminacies of quantum chance.[47] We have seen, however, that this account of divine action tends to view God as a univocal cause. It is possible, however, to view God's action in evolution as that of a transcendent primary cause acting through chance (including quantum chance) as a secondary cause.[48] This seems to be the approach of the International Theological Commission:

Thomas Aquinas] allows us to recognize that the intervention of God is not an adulteration of natural processes. If the elementary phenomena are by chance, they remain by chance" (Jean-Michel Maldamé, "L'évolution et la question de Dieu," *Revue thomiste* 107 [2007]: 554).

47. "If God acts at the level of the DNA molecule, contributing to genetic variation, then the combined effect of molecular biology/genetics and natural selection on phenotypically expressed genotype can amplify the effects of divine action to the level of organisms, species, and ecosystems, thus influencing the course of evolution. Diametrically contrary to Monod, evolution is precisely what is needed for divine action, hidden in the undergrowth of quantum chance, to realize the divine intentions for the world" (R. J. Russell, "Religion and the Theories," 38).

48. "It is, however, consistent with the thesis that all mutations (and, more generally, all events of evolutionary significance) are due to chance in this Aristotelian sense that God has been guiding evolution—by deliberately causing certain mutations (and other events of evolutionary significance). If God has been doing this, it does not follow that the history of terrestrial life would reveal anything inconsistent with the Darwinian thesis that all mutations are due to chance" (Peter van Inwagen, "The Compatibility of Darwinism and Design," in *God and Design: The Teleological Argument and Modern Science*, ed. Neil A. Manson [London: Routledge, 2003], 361–62). "The combination of chance and necessity, of variation and selection, jointly with the potentialities for self-organization, can be easily seen as the way used by God to bring about the process of evolution" (Artigas, *Mind*, 153).

The current scientific debate about the mechanisms at work in evolution requires theological comment insofar as it sometimes implies a misunderstanding of the nature of divine causality. Many neo-Darwinian scientists, as well as some of their critics, have concluded that, if evolution is a radically contingent materialistic process driven by natural selection and random genetic variation, then there can be no place in it for divine providential causality.... It is important to note that, according to the Catholic understanding of divine causality, true contingency in the created order is not incompatible with a purposeful divine providence. Divine causality and created causality radically differ in kind and not only in degree. Thus, even the outcome of a truly contingent natural process can nonetheless fall within God's providential plan for creation. According to St. Thomas Aquinas: "The effect of divine providence is not only that things should happen somehow, but that they should happen either by necessity or by contingency. Therefore, whatsoever divine providence ordains to happen infallibly and of necessity happens infallibly and of necessity; and that happens from contingency, which the divine providence conceives to happen from contingency" (*Summa theologiae*, I, 22, 4, ad 1). In the Catholic perspective, neo-Darwinians who adduce random genetic variation and natural selection as evidence that the process of evolution is absolutely unguided are straying beyond what can be demonstrated by science. Divine causality can be active in a process that is both contingent and guided. Any evolutionary mechanism that is contingent can only be contingent because God made it so. An unguided evolutionary process—one that falls outside the bounds of divine providence—simply cannot exist because "the causality of God, Who is the first agent, extends to all being, not only as to constituent principles of species, but also as to the individualizing principles.... It necessarily follows that all things, inasmuch as they participate in existence, must likewise be subject to divine providence" (*Summa theologiae* I, 22, 2).[49]

If our affirmation of God's transcendence allows us to maintain that God acts through chance events without depriving them of their character of contingency or indeterminism, it also allows us to see that the presence of chance in the natural world cannot thwart the plan of God's providence. Creation cannot be viewed as a calculated risk on God's part.[50] Though

---

49. International Theological Commission (ITC), *Communion and Stewardship*, no. 69. The production of human life remains a special case since the human substantial form or soul, whether in the evolution of the first human or in the generation of any human, cannot be simply educed from the potency of matter, but must be directy created by God. See ibid., no. 70; *ST* I, 90, 2. See also Norbert A. Luyten, "Die Materie, Quelle des Geistes?" in *Ordo rerum: Schriften zur Naturphilosophie, philosophischen Anthropolgie und christlichen Weltanschauung* [Fribourg, Switzerland: Editions Universitaires, 1969], 368–69); and Luyten, "Philosophical Implications," 147.

50. "At times some have spoken as if creating involved even for God an element of risk, the possibility that what He ultimately intends in the created order might not be achieved. Such a view seems quite incompatible with the data of revelation: God is the Lord whose plan and purpose will certainly be realized" (John H. Wright, "The Eternal Plan of Divine Providence," *Theological Studies* 27 [1966]: 41–42).

events truly happen by chance, God is not left in suspense until they happen since God is the cause both of the event and of the chance mode of its occurrence.

We might be inclined to think that if God is the ultimate cause of everything—of not only all that happens but also of the very mode of its happening—then all worldly events must really happen of necessity; determinism must reign everywhere, and talk of contingency or freedom must be nothing more than a *façon de parler*. To counteract that inclination, we should remember that the very notion of determinism—like the categories of necessity and contingency—belongs to the realm of secondary causes and cannot be applied to the action of the transcendent divine cause.[51] If we apply it to the divine realm, we reduce the ultimate, primary cause to the level of a univocal, secondary cause. We have seen that if we make that reduction, the whole notion of secondary causality becomes incoherent and the transcendent creator becomes a mere manipulator.

Since the categories of necessity, contingency, freedom, and chance belong to the created order, and not to the divine order, Aquinas can say rather dangerous things. He proclaims, for instance, that in relation to God "nothing in the world happens by chance."[52] His statement may be easily misunderstood.[53] If it is taken to mean that the world is in fact determined after

---

51. "[T]he divine will ... transcends the order of necessity and contingency" (*In peri herm.* I, lect. 14, no. 22).

52. "Things are said to be fortuitous as regards some particular cause from the order of which they escape. But as to the order of divine providence, 'nothing in the world happens by chance,' as Augustine declares" (*ST* I, 103, 7, ad 2). Cf. *ST* I, 116, 1, ad 2; *De ver.* 5, 5, ad 5; *In meta.* VI, lect. 3 [§1205]).

53. Aquinas unfortunately seems to invite such misunderstanding by giving, as an example of the relationship between God's primary causality and the secondary causality of creatures, the case of a master who sends two servants to the marketplace, secretly planning for them to meet each other: "So far then as an effect escapes the order of a particular cause, it is said to be casual or fortuitous in respect to that cause; but if we regard the universal cause, outside whose range no effect can happen, it is said to be foreseen. Thus, for instance, the meeting of two servants, although to them it appears a chance circumstance, has been fully foreseen by their master, who has purposely [*scienter*] sent them to meet at the one place, in such a way that the one does not know about the other" (*ST* I, 22, 2, ad 1). Cf. *ST* I, 116, 1, co. The analogy must be rightly understood. It cannot mean that the relationship between the divine primary cause and secondary creaturely causes is just like the relationship between a sneaky, manipulating master and his ignorant servants. If it did, then there would be no true contingency in the world, only the appearance of contingency, just as the meeting seems like a chance event to the servants [*quantum ad eos*], but is really the determined effect of the master's manipulations. This would be contrary to Aquinas's consistent teaching that "it would be contrary to the character of divine providence if nothing were to be fortuitous and a matter of chance" (*SCG* III, 74, no. 2). The key point is that, while we are invited to compare the master of the servants to the universal cause, we are in no way allowed to compare the universal cause to the

all, it contradicts the whole case he has presented for the reality of chance and contingency. We must rather take it to mean that "chance" is a category that applies to secondary causality and does not apply to God. To apply the notion of "chance" to divine action directly is a category mistake. God's causality is not itself chance; nor can chance interfere with it. If we look at what is happening in the world directly in relation to divine causality, therefore, we cannot use the word "chance." So we may say that directly in relation to God, nothing in the world happens by chance.[54] By the same token, since "necessity" is also a category of secondary causes, we would have to say that directly in relation to God, nothing in the world happens by necessity.[55] If we consider such events in their full context, however, including both the primary causality of God and the secondary causality of creatures, we can affirm that worldly events do happen by necessity, contingency, freedom, or chance, just as God intends them to occur.

Since contingent causes cannot impede God's causality, all that God wills happens unfailingly. Among secondary causes, one that produces its effect unfailingly, in such a way that the effect cannot not happen, is seen as a necessary cause producing a necessary effect. If we placed God on the same level

---

master. This is in accord with Aquinas's teaching that, "although it may be admitted that creatures are in some way like God, it must nowise be admitted that God is like creatures" (*ST* I, 4, 3, ad 4). Furthermore, we are invited to compare the master to the universal cause in one respect only: just as the master might directly intend an event (the meeting) that is merely incidental to the intention of the servants, so the universal cause (God) may directly intend a chance event that is only incidental to the intention of secondary causes (creatures). The crucial difference is that the effect of the master's manipulations (the meeting) is not truly a chance event no matter how much it may look like one to the servants, since it has a natural cause, the master himself. The effect of divine providence, however, may truly be a chance event that has no natural "cause" other than chance itself. The master cannot truly act "through chance" since his causality is univocal. His free action, in sending the servants, belongs to the creaturely category of "freedom," and cannot pretend to work through the category of "chance" without distorting that category—changing "chance" into "manipulation." The divine cause, transcending all creaturely categories of causality, can truly act through the causality of chance (as a secondary cause) to produce a genuinely chance event.

54. "It follows then that everything which occurs here insofar as it is related to the first divine cause, is found to be ordained by it and not to be accidental, although it may be found to be accidental in relation to other causes. This is why the Catholic faith says that nothing in the world happens by chance or fortuitously, and that everything is subject to divine providence" (*In meta.* VI, lect. 3 [§1216]). "Thus, some good or evil may happen to man that is fortuitous in relation to himself, and in relation to the celestial bodies, and in relation to the angels, but not in relation to God. Indeed, in relation to him, nothing can be a matter of chance and unforeseen, either in the sphere of human affairs or in any matter" (*SCG* III, 92, no. 5).

55. Aquinas does sometimes use the word "necessary" when speaking of God's being, as he uses the word "free" to characterize God's action. He makes it clear, however, that such uses are analogous and that, when employed in these contexts, the terms do not have the same (univocal) meaning they bear when applied to secondary causes. See *ST* I, 2, 3, co.; I, 13, 5, co.; I, 19, 3, co.

as secondary causes, the same would apply to divine causality: God would be a necessary cause producing only necessary effects. The world would then be devoid of contingency, freedom, and chance. Remembering divine transcendence, we will be able to confess both that the effect intended by God does unfailingly occur since no creaturely cause can impede divine causality and that the effect unfailingly occurs precisely in the way that God intends it to occur, whether by necessity, contingency, freedom, or chance: "The effect of divine providence is not only that things should happen somehow; but that they should happen either by necessity or by contingency. Therefore whatsoever divine providence ordains to happen infallibly and of necessity happens infallibly and of necessity; and that happens from contingency, which the plan of divine providence conceives to happen from contingency."[56]

God and Human Freedom

The reality of human freedom presents a particular challenge in speaking about God's causality. Can humans be truly free if God's omnipotent causality is involved in their every action? Theologians who see divine and creaturely action univocally must answer this question negatively. If we affirm divine transcendence, however, the answer comes out differently.[57]

Since our actions are part of creation, we should not expect them to be exempt from the general pattern of creaturely action which always involves God's causality. Since God is the first source of all being and actuality, we cannot think that we are absolutely the "first causes" of our free actions; nor can we reasonably maintain that such autonomy of action is essential to our freedom. Rather, we should recognize that, as God is involved in all creaturely activity without depriving it of its essential character, so God is involved in our free actions without depriving them of their freedom. Aquinas explains: "Free will is the cause of its own movement, because by his free will man moves himself to act. But it does not of necessity belong to liberty that what is free should be the first cause of itself, as neither for one thing

---

56. *ST* I, 22, 4, ad 1. Cf. *De ver.* 6, 3, ad 3.
57. "It may be objected, however, that if divine providence is the *per se* cause of everything that happens in this world, at least of good things, it would look as though everything takes place of necessity: first on the part of his knowledge, for his knowledge cannot be fallible, and so it would seem that what he knows happens necessarily; secondly, on the part of his will, for the will of God cannot be inefficacious; it would seem, therefore, that everything he wills happens of necessity. These objections arise from judging of the cognition of the divine intellect and the operation of the divine will in the way in which these are in us, when in fact they are very dissimilar" (*In peri herm.* I, lect. 14, no. 17–18).

to be cause of another need it be the first cause. God therefore is the first cause, who moves causes both natural and voluntary. And just as by moving natural causes he does not prevent their acts being natural, so by moving voluntary causes he does not deprive their actions of being voluntary; but rather is he the cause of this very thing in them: for he operates in each thing according to its own nature."[58]

As primary cause, God transcends all categories of creaturely causality. God is the source not only of the being of things but also of their mode of being, whether necessary or contingent or free or chance.[59] Our actions are free not despite God's involvement but precisely because of it.[60] Without

---

58. ST I, 83, 1, ad 3. Cf. SCG III, 149, no. 3; ST I-II, 10, 4, co.; ST I-II, 10, 4, ad 1; ST I-II, 6, 1, ad 3; De pot. 3, 7, ad 13; De malo 3, 3, co.; SCG III, 148, no. 3; ST I-II, 9, 4, ad 1. See also Burrell, "Creator/Creatures Relation," 184–85; Te Velde, Participation, 182–83; and Freddoso, "God's General Concurrence," 132.

59. See In peri herm. I, lect. 14, nos. 19–22. "If the Thomist solution to the reconcilability of finite free action and divine causal power is to work, then both for the sake of creaturely contingency and the maintenance of the divine status, God cannot be inserted into the world's causal chains; the divine causal influence, as ex nihilo, cannot and must not be thought of as univocal with other causes. As in all other things, God is not to be conceived of as a 'cause' in the categorical sense; he does not belong to any categories precisely because he is the 'cause' of them all" (John C. Yates, The Timelessness of God [Lanham, Md.: University Press of America, 1990], 255).

60. Aquinas's position on the relation between the divine will and human freedom is quite different from what has become known as the "compatibilist" position. Compatibilism sees our will as in fact determined either by natural causes or by God, conceived as a univocal, necessary cause producing a necessary effect. Human "freedom" then consists simply in the fact that we do not know that our will is really determined. This ignorance on our part is thought to make the actual determinism of our will "compatible" with freedom. Both "freedom" and "determinism" are certainly used in some pickwickian sense here, if this argument is not a flat contradiction in terms. The contradiction consists in calling human action "free" while simultaneously viewing it as the necessary effect of a univocal cause (either God, conceived as a univocal and necessary cause, or nature, conceived as a univocal and deterministic cause). Aquinas's account of human freedom in relation to divine causality is quite different. God is the primary cause both of our action and of the mode that action (as free). The free character of our action does not arise (as in compatibilism) from our ignorance of the fact that God, as a univocal cause, has really produced our action necessarily. It arises instead from God's very intention that our act be produced freely (and not necessarily or by chance). In compatibilism, apart from our (epistemological) ignorance, we could not say that we act freely. In Aquinas's account, apart from God's (ontological) action, we could not truly act freely. Aquinas is quite clear on the uniqueness of the divine transcendent cause in this context, and his explanation is worth citing at length: "But there is a greater difficulty with regard to providence, because divine providence cannot fail; for these two statements are incompatible, namely, that something is foreknown by God, and that it does not come to pass. Hence it seems that, once providence is posited, its effect follows of necessity. But it must be noted that an effect and all of its proper accidents depend on one and the same cause; for just as a man is from nature, so also are his proper accidents, such as risibility and susceptibility to mental instruction.... Now being as being has God himself as its cause. Hence just as being itself is subject to divine providence, so also are all the accidents of being as being, among which are found necessity and contingency. Therefore it belongs to divine providence not only to produce a particular being but also to give it contingency or

God's causality, we could produce no act at all.[61] God's action does not diminish, but creates, preserves, and empowers our freedom.[62]

SUMMARY

God's causality cannot interfere with the causality of creatures since it is the very source of their causality. As the origin of the very being of the creature, God is the cause of the substantial form of the creature, by which it is such a creature, and also the cause of the being and actuality of whatever the creature produces in virtue of being such a creature, that is, in virtue of its own proper causality. Should one creature produce another, as in the case of generation, God is the cause, together with the creature—God as the

---

necessity; for insofar as God wills to give contingency or necessity to anything, He has prepared for it certain intermediate causes from which it follows either of necessity or contingently. Hence the effect of every cause is found to be necessary insofar as it comes under the control of providence. And from this it follows that this conditional proposition is true: 'If anything is foreknown by God, it will be.' However, insofar as any effect is considered to come under a proximate cause, not every effect is necessary; but some are necessary and some contingent in proportion to their cause. For effects are likened in their nature to their proximate causes, but not to their remote cause, whose state they cannot attain. It is evident, then, that when we speak of divine providence we must say that this thing is foreseen by God not only insofar as it is but also insofar as it is either contingent or necessary. Therefore, just because divine providence is held to exist, it does not follow ... that every effect happens of necessity, but only that it must be either contingent or necessary. In fact this applies solely in the case of this cause, i.e., divine providence, because the remaining causes do not establish the law of necessity or contingency, but make use of this law established by a higher cause. Hence the only thing that is subject to the causality of any other cause is that its effect be. But that it is be either necessary or contingent depends on a higher cause, which is the cause of the being as being, and the one from which the order of necessity and of contingency originates in the world" (*In meta.* VI, lect. 3 [§1218–22]). For further discussions of compatibilism, see Brian J. Shanley, "Beyond Libertarianism and Compatibilism: Thomas Aquinas on Created Freedom," in *Freedom and the Human Person*, ed. Richard Velkley (Washington, D.C.: The Catholic University of America Press, 2007), 70–89; Gregersen, "Divine Action, Compatibilism," 217–18; and T. F. Tracy, "Divine Action, Created Causes," 92–102.

61. "God moves man's will, as the Universal Mover, to the universal object of the will, which is good. And without this universal motion, man cannot will anything" (*ST* I-II, 9, 6, ad 3). Cf. *SCG* III, 89, no. 5; *ST* I-II, 109, 2, ad 1; *ST* I-II, 6, 7, ad 3. "[God's] active presence is not an impediment to finite freedom in contestation with it but is the root, the very creative ground of created freedom and its exercise" (Hill, "The Implicate World," 88). See also Burrell, *Freedom and Creation*, 90–91.

62. "It is proper to divine providence to use things according to their own mode. Now, the mode of acting peculiar to each thing results from its form, which is the source of motion. Now, the form whereby an agent acts voluntarily is not determined, for the will acts through a form apprehended by the intellect, since the apprehended good moves the will as its object. Now the intellect does not have one form determined to an effect; rather, it is characteristic of it to comprehend a multitude of forms. And because of this the will can produce effects according to many forms. Therefore, it does not pertain to the character of providence to exclude liberty of will" (*SCG* III, 73, no. 3). Cf. *SCG* III, 88, no. 5; *SCG* III, 88, no. 3–4, 6; III, 92, no. 4; III, 148, no. 2; *ST* I, 105, 4, co.; *ST* I, 104, 4, ad 1, ad 3; I-II, 6, 7, co. See also Burrell, *Freedom and Creation*, 122–23.

cause of its being, and the creature as the cause of its coming to be. Should a creature produce any act whatever, from the slightest unintentional gesture to the most profound moral act, God is the primary cause and the creature is the secondary and instrumental cause of whatever actuality the act entails.[63] God is involved in every creaturely act, not as negating or interfering with the proper causality of the creature, but as its very source.

63. See *SCG* III, 67 and *De Pot.* 3, 7.

7

Providence, Prayer, and Miracles

We have shown how an expanded notion of causality, suggested by developments in contemporary science and retrieving consonant elements of the understanding of causality in the thought of Aristotle and Thomas Aquinas, can be applied to the question of divine action in a way that preserves both the integrity of divine action and the proper causality of creatures. We will now use this understanding of causality to address three central issues in the theology of divine action: providence, prayer, and miracles.

In many ways, our entire discussion of divine action thus far has been a meditation on divine providence, since it is especially through God's intimate involvement as First Cause in the action of his creatures, as secondary and instrumental causes, that God guides and governs his creation toward the fulfillment of his providential plan. There is one aspect of providence, however, that we have intentionally neglected thus far so that it might be given special consideration now against the understanding of divine action that we have outlined. This is the relation of God's providential action to the reality of evil and suffering in creation.

The practice of prayer also invites a special consideration of the relation between the causality of God and creatures. We sometimes picture prayer, especially petitionary prayer, as an action on our part that draws a divine response. This certainly corresponds to some scriptural admonitions: "Ask and it will be given to you; seek and you will find; knock and the door will be opened to you" (Matthew 7:7). But Scripture also teaches: "Your Father knows what you need before you ask him" (Matthew 6:8). Does the initiative in prayer belong to God or to us? Should prayer be seen as a creaturely action that provokes a divine response, so that the initiator of the action is the creature who prays? Or should our account of prayer maintain the primary causality of the Creator and the secondary causality of creatures?

The notion of miracle suggests that God might act in the world not only in and through the causality of creatures and the laws of science that describe this, but also beyond their causality. The question of miracles was in some ways the fundamental issue that jump-started the discussion of divine action in contemporary theology. How should we characterize miraculous divine action, and how does it relate to the practice, methodology, and worldview of empirical science?

PROVIDENCE AND EVIL

The presence of evil and suffering in the world raises a question for any theology that proclaims a God of love.[1] It is a question, however, that no theology can answer or "solve." Christian theology affirms the reality of Creator and creation. To bring something forth from nothing, the Creator must be infinitely powerful.[2] To do so freely, bespeaks unbounded goodness and love.[3] In affirming the reality of creation, theology cannot neglect the presence of evil and suffering. Yet, one cannot juxtapose the reality of God and the presence of evil without raising the question, "Why?"—the very cry of Jesus from the cross: "My God, my God, why have you forsaken me?" (Mark 15:34). For the Christian, the only answer to evil and suffering lies there in the cross, in that divine response to human evil through the death and resurrection of Christ. That answer, however, is not a logical solution, but a mystery.

Charles Journet once said that "the aim of the theologian dealing with a mystery is to do away with phrases which diminish the mystery."[4] Any theo-

---

1. Here we can discuss the problem of theodicy only briefly as it touches on the question of divine action. For a more thorough treatment, see B. Davies, *The Reality of God*; David B. Burrell, *Deconstructing Theodicy: Why Job Has Nothing to Say to the Puzzle of Suffering* (Grand Rapids, Mich.: Baker Academic, 2008); Nancey Murphy, Robert John Russell, and William Stoeger, eds., *Physics and Cosmology: Scientific Perspectives on the Problem of Natural Evil* (Vatican City State: Vatican Observatory; Berkeley, Calif.: Center for Theology and the Natural Sciences, 2007); Gustavo Gutiérrez, *On Job: God-Talk and the Suffering of the Innocent*, trans. Matthew J. O'Connell (Maryknoll, N.Y.: Orbis Books, 1987); and Laurent Sentis, *Saint Thomas d'Aquin et le mal. Foi chrétienne et théodicée* (Paris: Beauchesne, 1992).

2. "Although to create a finite effect does not show an infinite power, yet to create it from nothing does show an infinite power" (*ST* I, 45, 5, ad 3).

3. See *ST* I, 19, 2, ad 2; I, 19, 3; I, 20, 2.

4. Charles Journet, *The Meaning of Evil* (New York: J. P. Kennedy and Sons, 1963), 14. In Thomas Tracy's insightful phrase: "Christianity, after all, is first and foremost a religion of redemption, not of

logical response to evil, therefore, must diminish neither the reality of God nor the reality of sin and suffering. We have theological reasons, given in Scripture and tradition, to affirm the infinite power and goodness of God. We cannot abandon those affirmations in addressing the question of evil and suffering. Aquinas himself sees that the easiest "answer" to the problem of suffering (if one wanted an easy answer) would be simply to deny the reality of God: "It seems that God does not exist; because if one of two contraries be infinite, the other would be altogether destroyed. But the word 'God' means that He is infinite goodness. If, therefore, God existed, there would be no evil discoverable; but there is evil in the world. Therefore God does not exist."[5] Aquinas rejects such easy solutions and embraces, instead, the mystery of divine goodness that exceeds human understanding: "This is part of the infinite goodness of God, that He should allow evil to exist, and out of it produce good."[6] Though his statement is clear, it is hardly a "solution." If anything, it provokes more questions such as *"Why* does God allow evil to exist?" and *"How* does God produce good out of it?" Perhaps, though, his words are meant not to provide a solution, but to invoke a mystery.[7] In discussing the relation between evil and God's providential action, our aim will not be to find a solution to the problem of suffering, but to provide whatever insight we can, while denying neither the being of God nor the reality of evil.

Evil and Univocal Divine Causality

Not all theologians follow this approach, especially those who see God as a univocal cause. Some try to solve the problem of evil by limiting the

---

explanation" (T. F. Tracy, "Evolutionary Theologies," 115). See also Andrew Moore, "Not Explanation but Salvation: Scientific Theology, Christology, and Suffering," *Modern Theology* 22 (2006): 65–83.

5. *ST* I, 2, 3, obj. 1.
6. *ST* I, 2, 3, ad 1.
7. "St. Thomas's account of evil ... does not seek to explain the evil in the world. When we speak of God we do not clear up a puzzle; we draw attention to a mystery" (McCabe, *God and Evil*, 128). After examining various approaches to the question of God and human suffering, Edward Schillebeeckx remarks: "I think at this point it would be good to resort to Thomas Aquinas. True, in reality he is seldom understood and little studied.... However, he does seem to me one of the few people who can give us some reasonably satisfactory viewpoints which at the same time leave all the darkness in its incomprehensibility.... Thomas expresses deep insights into life which, without making the history of human suffering understandable in theory—i.e., without harmonizing it with God's Goodness or our positive humanity—, nevertheless point to the unfathomable depths in which they have to be put. On the one hand is the incomprehensible depth of the mystery of God, and on the other hand the negative depth of what finitude and freedom can involve" (Edward Schillebeeckx, *Christ: The Experience of Jesus as Lord* [New York: Crossroad Publishing Co., 1983], 728–29).

scope of God's action in the world; others, by making God himself subject to suffering. Among those who teach that God's action is limited, some see this limitation as the result of a free divine decision; others, as an inherent characteristic of God's being or of God's confrontation with the causality of creatures. We can look briefly at these approaches before considering that of Aquinas.

Evil and Divine Limitation   John Polkinghorne exemplifies the position that God's limitation is the result of a free divine decision: "It has been an important emphasis in much recent theological thought about creation to acknowledge that by bringing the world into existence God has self-limited divine power by allowing the other truly to be itself.... Not all that happens is in accordance with God's will because God has stood back, making metaphysical room for creaturely action."[8] Here, God is clearly conceived as a univocal cause who must limit his causality to make "room" for the causality of creatures. Apart from such self-limitation, God would be a "Cosmic Tyrant."[9]

Voluntary divine self-limitation raises a number of questions. The first is whether or not God's decision to limit himself is reversible. If it is, then one can ask why God does not reverse it and act to alleviate the suffering of creation.[10] If the decision is (somehow) not reversible, then one may question whether the decision is justified, given the evil that follows upon it.[11] If the decision seems unjustified, theologians are left with a new ques-

---

8. Polkinghorne, *Belief in God*, 13. See also Polkinghorne, *Science and Providence*, 59–68.

9. Polkinghorne, *Belief in God*, 14.

10. "Either the kenotic God retains omnipotence or not. In the first case, kenosis seems artificial and unconvincing because it is merely a reversible divine decision rather than a fundamental and inescapable feature of divine creation. That is, if God deliberately embraces self-limitation for the sake of allowing moral and spiritual life to flower, then there ought to be nothing to prevent God from making exceptions as needed. Kenosis in this sense does nothing to protect the humanly recognizable goodness of God.... If kenosis is a matter of deliberate divine self-limitation through which omnipotence perseveres, then it is no longer truly binding and thus unconvincing as an explanation of divine silence in response to needless suffering in nature" (Wesley J. Wildman, "Incongruous Goodness, Perilous Beauty, Disconcerting Truth: Ultimate Reality and Suffering in Nature," in *Physics and Cosmology: Scientific Perspectives on the Problem of Natural Evil*, ed. Nancey Murphy, Robert John Russell, and William Stoeger [Vatican City State: Vatican Observatory; Berkeley, Calif.: Center for Theology and the Natural Sciences, 2007], 289–90).

11. "It is far from clear, however, that the autonomy and integrity of the natural order is, in itself, a *great enough good* to justify all the misery and loss that results from events running their course untouched" (Thomas F. Tracy, "The Lawfulness of Nature and the Problem of Evil," in *Physics and Cosmology: Scientific Perspectives on the Problem of Natural Evil*, ed. Nancey Murphy, Robert John Russell, and William Stoeger [Vatican City State: Vatican Observatory; Berkeley, Calif.: Center for

tion—not "Why does the all-powerful God not do away with evil?" but "Why would the all-powerful God decide to render himself incapable of dealing with evil?"

The second option is to see divine limitation not as the result of God's choice, but as an inherent characteristic of God's being or of God's confrontation (as one, univocal, contingent cause) with the causality of creatures. This certainly solves the problem of evil: God is not responsible for the world's misfortunes, since they simply lie beyond his control. Process theology sees God's power as inherently limited, as Ian Barbour points out: "Process thought is distinctive in holding that limitations of divine knowledge and power arise from metaphysical necessity rather than from voluntary self-limitation."[12] Divine limitation is also affirmed by many participants in the theology/science dialogue, who see God as a univocal cause whose causality is somehow constricted by that of creatures. Nancy Murphy, for instance, limits God's causality in the physical world to the sphere of quantum indeterminacy where it cannot interfere with creaturely causes. She views this as a kind of bonus when the question of theodicy arises: "Those of us who argue for the locus of divine action at the quantum level have been accused of allowing too little scope for special divine acts. This criticism, though, becomes a strength when confronting the problem of evil."[13] Francisco Ayala argues that science has solved the problem of evil by removing divine influence from natural causes: "Theologians in the past struggled with the issue of dysfunction because they thought it had to be attributed to God's design. Science, much to the relief of many theologians, provides an explanation that convincingly attributes defects, deformities and dysfunctions to natural causes."[14]

Theology and the Natural Sciences, 2007], 163). As justification for God's decision and the consequent presence of evil, Polkinghorne offers the "free will defense" (the possibility of evil in the interest of creaturely freedom) and the "free process defense" (the possibility of suffering in the interest of genuine creaturely causality and contingency). See Polkinghorne, *Belief in God*, 13–14; and Polkinghorne, *Science and Providence*, 66.

12. Ian G. Barbour, "God's Power: A Process View," in *The Work of Love: Creation as Kenosis*, ed. John Polkinghorne (Grand Rapids, Mich.: Eerdmans, 2001), 12.

13. Murphy, "Science and the Problem," 141.

14. Ayala, "Intelligent Design," 29. "What about earthquakes, storms, floods, droughts, and other physical catastrophes? Enter modern science into the theologian's reasoning. Physical events are built into the structure of the world itself.... As floods and drought were a necessary consequence of the fabric of the physical world, predators and parasites, dysfunctions and diseases were a consequence of the evolution of life. They were *not* a result of deficient or malevolent design: the features of organisms were not *designed* by the Creator" (Ayala, *Darwin's Gift*, 4–5). Darwin himself

Although divine limitation may seem to solve the problem of evil, it raises other theological difficulties. A limited God cannot be regarded as the creator, the source of all being, if some aspects of creation lie beyond the scope of its influence. Nor can such a God promise eschatological fulfillment if it is only a univocal cause, whose plans may be thwarted by others. This is the situation of process theology, as Lewis Ford notes: "Process theism, by relinquishing the claim that God could completely control the world in order to overcome the problem of present evil, cannot have this traditional assurance about the future.... God cannot guarantee that evil will be overcome simply because he is not the sole agent determining the outcome of the world. It is a joint enterprise involving a vast multiplicity of actualities responding to his cosmic purposes."[15] Keith Ward seems to recognize this eschatological constraint even as he accepts the notion of a limited God: "I suggest rejecting the idea that God can do absolutely anything at all. But we can still call God 'omnipotent' because God is the only source of all other beings, and because there is no other possible being that has greater power than God. We may be sure that such a God will not only create a universe for the sake of the goods it contains, but will also act within the created universe to ensure the eventual fulfillment of the divine purpose. However, the nature of any universe that God wills is such that there will be definite constraints on the actions of a God who acts through the persuasion of love rather than through irresistible power."[16] If the "purpose of the one who accomplishes all things according to the intention of his will" (Ephesians 1:11) becomes subject to "definite constraints," then the eschatological "plan for the fullness of times" (Ephesians 1:10) becomes no more than one possible scenario for the world's future. Christian revelation, however, proclaims not just the possibility, but the certainty of the triumph of good over evil: "He will wipe every tear from their eyes, and there shall be no more death or mourning, wailing or pain, for the old order has passed away" (Revelation 21:4).

---

once entertained an argument similar to Ayala's, but found it less than satisfactory: "I am inclined to look at everything as resulting from designed laws, with the details, whether good or bad, left to the working out of what we may call chance. Not that this notion *at all* satisfies me. I feel most deeply that the whole subject is too profound for the human intellect" (Charles Darwin, "Letter to Asa Gray, May 22, 1860," in *The Life and Letters of Charles Darwin*, ed. Francis Darwin [New York: D. Appleton and Co., 1897], 2.104).

15. Ford, *Lure*, 119. See also Barbour, "God's Power," 18.
16. Keith Ward, *God, Faith and the New Millennium: Christian Belief in an Age of Science* (Oxford: Oneworld Publications, 1998), 102.

Evil and Divine Suffering   Apart from the question of divine limitation, some theologians seek to solve the problem of evil by making God subject to suffering. Here we might think of Whitehead's famous description of God as "the fellow sufferer who understands."[17] The image of divine suffering has a certain appeal in its evocation of divine compassion, but in the end it has little power to mitigate the problem of *creaturely* suffering.

This becomes clear if we consider Paul Fiddes's description of the suffering God: "[O]ut of his desire for his creatures he chooses to suffer, and because he chooses to suffer, he is not ruled by suffering; it has no power to overwhelm him because he has made the alien thing his own. He fulfills his own being *through* suffering, since he can only become more truly himself through suffering with the world."[18] Such suffering may be quite noble, but it has little to do with us. We do not usually "choose" our sufferings and would just as soon do without them (thank you). Suffering cannot "overwhelm" Fiddes's God, but it can overwhelm us, as is evident in the human cry of Jesus from the cross (Mark 15:34). Fiddes's God "fulfills his own being through suffering," while our suffering often seems like the very annihilation of our being. There is small comfort for us in the quite alien suffering of this God. A suffering *divinity* seems to have little to do with us in our suffering *humanity*.

The traditional understanding of divine suffering, however, does have to do with us. If properly understood in terms of the sufferings of Christ, the confession that "God suffers" is a central tenet of Christian faith. Since Jesus is truly God and since he truly suffered, Christians must say that God suffered on the cross.[19] Christ also suffers in us since we are one with him in his Mystical Body, the Church.[20] As Aquinas explains, the sufferings of the members of Christ's Body are truly the sufferings of Christ: "'I make up those things which are lacking from the suffering of Christ' [Colossians 1:24] that is, [from the suffering] of the whole Church whose head is

---

17. Whitehead, *Process*, 351.
18. Paul S. Fiddes, *The Creative Suffering of God* (Oxford: Clarendon Press, 1988), 108–9. "I propose that a God who creates 'out of love' has needs to be satisfied.... We can say that in the transforming power of love God uses even suffering to fulfill God's own being, becoming more truly who and what God is" (Paul S. Fiddes, "Creation Out of Love," in *The Work of Love: Creation as Kenosis*, ed. John Polkinghorne [Grand Rapids, Mich.: Eerdmans, 2001], 169, 173).
19. See *ST III*, 16, 4, co.
20. "As a natural body is one, though made up of various members, so the whole Church, which is the Mystical Body of Christ, is reckoned as one person with its head, who is Christ" (*ST* III, 49, 1, co.). Cf. *ST* III, 48, 2, ad 1; *Sent.* 22, 3, 3, qc. 3, *exp.*, line 21 c.

Christ.... For this was lacking, that as Christ suffered in his own body, so he would suffer in Paul, his member, and similarly in others."[21] All of these statements point to a God who suffers *as we do,* a God who suffers in the *humanity* of Christ and the *humanity* of his followers.

The God proposed by Whitehead and Fiddes does not so much suffer *in his people* as *in reaction to* them when human suffering causes him to experience distress. A God who merely experiences a sympathetic sadness *in his own being* at the distress of his people, however, is much less lovingly engaged with them than the God who empathetically identifies with them *in their own being* and so makes their suffering his own. After all, Jesus did not say, "Saul, Saul, why are you persecuting *them* (and upsetting me)?" but "Saul, Saul, why are you persecuting me?" (Acts 9:4). Nor did he say, "You were hungry, and I grieved for you," but "I was hungry . . . I was thirsty" (Matthew 25:35). Aquinas comments: "'Hence whatever you do to one of these least of my brothers, you do to me' [Matthew 25:40], ... because the head and the members are one body."[22] A God who reacts to creaturely suffering by weeping *his own tears* does not seem like the God who will ultimately wipe away *"every tear."*[23]

Evil and Transcendent Divine Causality

Aquinas addresses the question of God and evil in his teaching on divine providence. Since God is the universal creator, all things require his providential care.[24] To Aquinas, it would be senseless to say that God sustains all things in being if one did not also say that God is providentially involved in all that they do and in all that happens to them: "Suppose someone says that God takes care of these singulars to the extent of preserving them in being, but not in regard to anything else; this is utterly impossible. In fact, all other events that occur in connection with singulars are related to their preservation or corruption. So, if God takes care of singulars as far as their

---

21. *Super ad Col.* 1, lect. 6 [line 55 c.].
22. *Super ev. matt.* 25, lect. 3 [line 450 c.].
23. Revelation 21:4. For a more complete presentation of such arguments, see Thomas G. Weinandy, *Does God Suffer?* (South Bend, Ind.: University of Notre Dame Press, 2000); Dodds, *Unchanging*; Michael J. Dodds, "Thomas Aquinas, Human Suffering, and the Unchanging God of Love," *Theological Studies* 52 (1991): 330–44; and Herbert McCabe, "The Involvement of God," *New Blackfriars* 66 (1985): 464–76.
24. "God is the cause not indeed only of some particular kind of being, but of the whole universal being.... Wherefore, as there can be nothing which is not created by God, so there can be nothing which is not subject to His government" (*ST* I, 103, 5, co.). Cf. *ST* I, 22, 2, co.; 103, 6, co.; *SCG* III, 64, no. 40.

preservation is concerned, he takes care of every contingent event connected with them."[25]

Aquinas rejects any approach to the question of God and evil that would limit God's providential involvement. He is aware of a variety of such arguments, some of which sound very similar to the arguments we have seen among contemporary theologians. Some say that nothing can be under the guidance of divine providence since everything happens by chance.[26] Others allow that not all things happen by chance, but exclude providence from those that do.[27] Some deny chance altogether and maintain that, since everything in the world happens by necessity, divine guidance is simply not needed.[28] Some are willing to include incorruptible substances under God's care, but not corruptible substances.[29] Others allow that providence might extend to the preservation of species, but not to individuals.[30] Then there are some who think that no evil, whether moral or natural, can fall under the influence of providence.[31]

To all such arguments, Aquinas answers that all things must fall under God's providence since God is the universal cause of being: "If these contingent events are traced back further to the highest, divine cause, it will be impossible to find anything that lies outside its sphere of influence, since its causality extends to all things insofar as they are beings."[32] He concludes: "Foolish [*stulta*] therefore was the opinion of those who said that the corruptible lower world, or individual things, or that even human affairs, were not subject to the Divine government."[33]

Aquinas follows Augustine in characterizing evil not an actuality in itself, but as the privation or lack of an actuality that should be present (the lack of sight, for instance, in a being that should be capable of seeing).[34] He applies this understanding to both natural and moral evils.

Natural evil is part of the structure of creation, since creation includes beings that are capable of failure (such as the flower that blossoms today and withers tomorrow). The failure or corruption of such a being is a "natural evil" (*malum naturae*).[35] If there were no such contingent beings, there

25. *SCG* III, 75, no. 7.
26. See *Sent.* I, 39, 2, 2, co.; *SCG* III, 64, no 13; *ST* I, 103, 1, co.
27. *ST* I, 22, 2, obj. 1.
28. *ST* I, 22, 2, obj. 3.
29. *ST* I, 22, 2, co.; ad 2.
30. See *De ver.* 5, 6, co.; *ST* I, 22, 2, obj. 5.
31. *ST* I, 22, 2, obj. 2; obj. 4.
32. *In meta.* VI, lect. 3 (§1215).
33. *ST* I, 103, 5, co.
34. "Evil is the absence of the good which is natural and due to a thing" (*ST* I, 49, 1, co.).
35. *Sent.* I, 39, 2, 2, co.

could be no creaturely causality. For causality implies change, and change always involves the corruption of one thing and the generation of another.[36] The world would be less perfect if it did not contain contingent creatures.[37] God intends the good of the universe and so preserves the nature of each creature, including the defectibility of the defectible creature.[38] In affirming that God wills the universal good, we may say that God allows the natural evil of the corruption of the contingent creature without directly intending it, directing the corruption of one creature toward some other natural good.[39] So, the death or corruption of one creature entails the life or generation of another, as "the death of the fly is the life of the spider."[40]

Aquinas's arguments here have a remarkable consonance with Keith Ward's account of evolution: "The metaphor of a war of nature here gives way to a different metaphor; that of a developing emergent whole, with increasingly complex and beautiful co-adaptedness among organic life-forms, and

---

36. "If the inclination to generate its like were taken away from fire (from which inclination there results this particular evil which is the burning up of combustible things), there would also be taken away this particular good which is the generation of fire and the preservation of the same according to its species.... In the order of nature, there would not be the generation of one thing unless there were the corruption of another. So, if evil were totally excluded from the whole of things by divine providence, a multitude of good things would have to be sacrificed.... Therefore evil should not be totally excluded from things by divine providence" (*SCG* III, 71, nos. 5–6). Cf. *Sent.* I, 46, 1, 3, ad 6.

37. "Since God, then, provides universally for all being, it belongs to His providence to permit certain defects in particular effects, that the perfect good of the universe may not be hindered, for if all evil were prevented, much good would be absent from the universe. A lion would cease to live, if there were no slaying of animals; and there would be no patience of martyrs if there were no tyrannical persecution" (*ST* I, 22, 2, ad 2). Cf.: *Sent.* I, 39, 2, 2, co.; 46, 1, 3, ad 6; SCG III, 71, no. 3.

38. "Any prudent man will endure a small evil in order that a great good will not be prevented. Any particular good, moreover, is trifling in comparison with the good of universal nature. Again, evil cannot be kept from certain things without taking away their nature, which is such that it may or may not fail; and while this nature may harm something in particular, it nevertheless gives some added beauty to the universe. Consequently, since God is most prudent, his providence does not prevent evil, but allows each thing to act as its nature requires it to act" (*De ver.* 5, 4, ad 4).

39. "Good and evil are subject to divine providence, evil as foreknown and ordered to something, but not as itself intended by God; the good, however, as intended" (*Sent.* I, 39, 2, 2, co.). "It belongs to providence to direct each thing to its end and take away impediments, preserving, however, the nature of the thing directed to the end, from whose defectible condition evils arises, and not from the divine intention, which ordains these evils toward the good" (*Sent.* I, 39, 2, 2, ad 1). Although natural evil is not directly intended by God, Aquinas thinks that God can still in some sense be considered its cause since such evil is incidental to the creation and order of the whole universe that God does will: "God wills no good more than He wills His own goodness; yet He wills one good more than another.... The evil of natural defect, or of punishment, He does will, by willing the good to which such evils are attached. Thus in willing justice He wills punishment; and in willing the preservation of the natural order, He wills some things to be naturally corrupted" (*ST* I, 19, 9, co.). Cf. *ST* I, 49, 2, co.; *Sent.* I, 46, 1, 4, co.

40. *Sent.* I, 39, 2, 2, co.

which pictures nature as expressing a continuous growth in harmonious complexity. Instead of selfish genes, ruthlessly competing, Darwin sees a finely balanced interplay of forms within an emergent totality, generating new states of organization and beauty. This change of metaphor reflects a change that has also taken place in physics, from the atomism of Newton to the interconnected fields of energy that characterize relativity theory. In biology, the model of isolated units in competition has for some time now been opposed by a model of a unified web of interrelated and intricately balanced forces. On the newer, more holistic, picture, suffering and death are inevitable parts of a development that involves improvement through conflict and generation of the new. But suffering and death are not the predominating features of nature. They are rather necessary consequences or conditions of a process of emergent harmonization which inevitably discards the old as it moves on to the new."[41]

Moral evil presents a greater dilemma for theology than natural evil. It consists in the lack of some due perfection (such as justice) in the free action of some agent (human or angelic). This is the evil of sin or, in Aquinas's terminology, the "evil of fault" *(malum culpae)*.[42] Aquinas is careful to point out that God is in no way the cause of this evil: "God wills no good more than he wills His own goodness.... Hence he in no way wills the evil of sin, which is the privation of right order toward the divine good."[43] Since moral evil essentially involves not actuality but privation, God's action, as the first cause of all actuality, is not required or involved in its production. Rather, a human being (or angel) is the "first cause" of that lack or negation of being.[44] With a kind of metaphysical scalpel, Aquinas dissects the act of

---

41. Ward, *God, Chance,* 87. Thomas Tracy also seems implicitly to acknowledge the truth of Aquinas's insights in his account of evil and evolution. See T. F. Tracy, "Evolutionary Theologies," 114.

42. "We may speak of the evil of fault [*malum culpae*], which is found in that which is not determined [by nature] to one action, as all things that act from free will" (*Sent.* II, 1, 1, ad 3).

43. *ST* I, 19, 9, co. Cf. *De malo* 3, 1, co.

44. "The first cause of the defect of grace is on our part; but the first cause of the bestowal of grace is on God's" (*ST* I-II, 112, 3, ad 2). "Nothing other than the will is the direct cause of human sin" (*De malo* 3, 3, co.). "Although God is the cause of the will, making it from nothing, it does not have this 'being from nothing' from another, but from itself, and therefore the defect that follows it, according as it is from nothing, does not need to be reduced to any higher cause" (*Sent.* II, 37, 2, 1, ad 2). "[H]ere we have finitude, as it were, as 'the first cause.' As soon as there are *creatures*, there is the *possibility* (not the necessity) of a negative and original *initiative of finitude*, if I can put it that way.... For Thomas, it is a senseless philosophical undertaking to look for a particular cause, a ground or motive for evil and suffering in God; these do not necessarily follow from our finitude, but they do draw their fundamental possibility from there" (Schillebeeckx, *Christ,* 728–29). "Creatures are indeed capable of an utterly initiatory role, but it will not be one of acting but of failing to

sin, arguing that, to the extent that it is an act and has actuality, it must—like all actuality—have its source in God. Precisely to the extent that it is in act, however, it is not evil since evil consists in privation. To the extent that it is privation, or evil or sin, it has its source in the creature.[45]

On the relationship between sin and the divine will, Aquinas argues that God neither wills such evil to be (since then God would be the cause of sin) nor wills it not to be (since then it could not be), but wills to permit it to be.[46] This permission of evil is not contrary to divine goodness.[47] God wills to allow creatures to use their freedom in accordance with their nature, and this includes at least the possibility of moral evil. Such evil is contrary to God's will and certainly contrary to the divine law, but it is not contrary to divine providence in the sense of being able to frustrate God's providential plan for all things. If a particular action departs from God's providence in one way, it remains under it in another.[48]

---

act, of 'refusing' to enter into the process initiated by actively willing 'the good'" (Burrell, *Freedom and Creation*, 90–91).

45. "The effect of the deficient secondary cause is reduced to the first nondeficient cause as regards what it has of being and perfection, but not as regards what it has of defect; just as whatever there is of motion in the act of limping is caused by the motive power, whereas what there is of obliqueness in it does not come from the motive power, but from the curvature of the leg. And, likewise, whatever there is of being and action in a bad action, is reduced to God as the cause; whereas whatever defect is in it is not caused by God, but by the deficient secondary cause" (*ST* I, 49, 2, ad 2). Cf. *ST* I-II, 80, 1, co.; ad 3; *De malo* 3, 2, co.; *Sent.* II, 37, 2, 2, co.

46. "The statements that evil exists, and that evil exists not, are opposed as contradictories; yet the statements that anyone wills evil to exist and that he wills it not to be, are not so opposed; since both are affirmative. God therefore neither wills evil to be done, nor wills it not to be done, but wills to permit evil to done; and this is a good" (*ST* I, 19, 9, ad 3).

47. "To do evil is in no way proper to those who are good. To do evil for the sake of a good is blameworthy in a man, and cannot be attributed to God. On the other hand, to direct evil to a good is not opposed to one's goodness. Hence permitting evil in order to draw some good from it can be attributed to God" (*De ver.* 5, 4, ad 10).

48. "Something may fall outside the order of any particular active cause, but not outside the order of the universal cause; under which all particular causes are included: and if any particular cause fails of its effect, this is because of the hindrance of some other particular cause, which is included in the order of the universal cause.... Since, then, the will of God is the universal cause of all things, it is impossible that the divine will should not produce its effect. Hence that which seems to depart from the divine will in one order, returns into it in another order: as does the sinner who by sin falls away from the divine will as much as lies in him, yet falls back into the order of that will, when by its justice he is punished" (*ST* I, 19, 6, co.). Cf. *ST* I, 103, 7, co. Although Aquinas here associates suffering with punishment, he is not unaware of the problem of innocent suffering and in fact devotes a whole book to it: "Now in this book the author proceeds to demonstrate his proposition from the supposition that natural things are governed by divine providence. Now what especially seems to impugn God's providence where human affairs are concerned is the affliction of just men, for although it seems at first sight unreasonable and contrary to providence that good things should sometimes happen to bad men, it can be excused in one way or another as the result of divine mercy.

There is a special place for human beings in God's providential plan: "There is one orderly plan in accord with which rational creatures are subjected to divine providence, and another by means of which the rest of creatures are ordered."[49] Humans are not simply cogs in the larger wheels of creation. To explain human destiny merely in terms of the workings of the larger universe would be utterly inadequate.[50] What befalls a human being has a significance and value for the person beyond considerations of other things in nature. Aquinas explains the difference with a rather vivid example, affirming that both "brute animals" and humans are subject to God's providence, but in different ways:

> Brutes and their acts, taken even individually, fall under God's providence but not in the same way in which men and their actions do. For providence is exercised over men even as individuals for their own sake.... Hence the evil that happens to a brute is not ordered to the good of the brute but to the good of something else, just as the death of an ass is ordered to the good of a lion or that of a wolf. But the death of a man killed by a lion is directed not merely to the good of the lion, but principally to the man's punishment or to the increase of his merit; for his merit can grow if he accepts suffering.[51]

But that just men should be afflicted without cause seems to undermine totally the foundation of providence. Therefore, there are proposed for the intended discussion as a kind of theme the many grave afflictions of a certain man, perfect in every virtue, named Job" (*Super iob*, Prologue).

49. *SCG* III, 111, no. 1. Cf. *SCG* III, 112, no. 1. On the special place of humans in the cosmos, see also Jean-Michel Maldamé, *Le Christ et le cosmos: Incidence de la cosmologie moderne sur la théologie* (Paris: Desclée, 1993); and Maldamé, *Le Christ pour l'univers*.

50. "A different order of providence is required for human affairs than is required for brutes. Consequently, if the ordering of human affairs were only that proper to brutes, human affairs would seem to be entirely without providence. Yet, that order is sufficient for the providence of brutes" (*De ver.* 5, 6, ad 3). "The suffering of a man is the suffering of a person, of a whole. Here he is considered no longer as part of the universe, but insofar as he is a person he is considered as a whole, a universe to himself; to suffer that pain as part of the universe in the perspective of nature or of the world taken as God's work of art, does not do away with the fact that as far as the person is concerned it is an utter anomaly" (Jacques Maritain, *Saint Thomas and the Problem of Evil* [Milwaukee, Wis.: Marquette University Press, 1942], 12).

51. *De ver.* 5, 6, co. Aquinas certainly sees animal life as providentially ordered toward human life, allowing humans to make use of animals: "For animals are ordered to man's use in the natural course of things, according to divine providence. Consequently, man uses them without any injustice, either by killing them or by employing them in any other way" (*SCG* III, 112, no. 12). This human ascendancy, however, does not permit acts of "cruelty against brute animals" (ibid., no. 13). On the contrary, humans may have compassion for animals: "Since the passion of pity is caused by the afflictions of others; and since it happens that even irrational animals are sensible to pain, it is possible for the affection of pity to arise in a man with regard to the sufferings of animals. Now it is evident that if a man practice a pitiful affection for animals, he is all the more disposed to take pity on his fellow-men" (*ST* I-II, 102, 6, ad 8). Cf. *ST* I, 96, 1, co.; *De pot.* 5, 9; *Sent.* IV, 48, 2, 5. Andrew Linzey criticizes Aquinas for his anthropocentric view of the relation between humans and animals. See Andrew Linzey, *Why Animal Suffering Matters: Philosophy, Theology, and Practical Ethics* (New

Every human person has a transcendent value as an individual, not merely as a member of a species.[52] God guides humans in their actions in a special way, since their actions, unlike those of other living things, do not proceed simply from their nature, but from free will.[53] They share in a special way in God's loving care.[54] Through God's providential care for them in this life, they are led to eternal life in love and friendship with God.[55]

York: Oxford University Press, 2009), 12–15. H. Paul Santmire is also wary of Aquinas's anthropocentrism. See Paul Santmire, *The Travail of Nature: The Ambiguous Ecological Promise of Christian Theology* (Minneapolis, Minn.: Fortress, 1985), 84–95. Willis Jenkins admits that "Thomas seems relatively unconcerned for a theodicy of natural evil," yet he finds in him a "strikingly nonanthropomorphic ethical purchase to a hierarchy of being: if it is true that God loves all creatures, and some are loved more than others on the basis of their likeness to God, and that the whole order of creation represents the divine goodness better than any single creature, then it follows that more is owed by justice to the whole of creation. There is then in Thomas the principle of ecocentrism: let us be concerned with whole earth systems, with keystone habitats, biomes, and ecosystems, for these are more representative of God than single species or particular entities" (Willis Jenkins, "Biodiversity and Salvation: Thomistic Roots for Environmental Ethics," *Journal of Religion* 83 [2003]: 415–16). See also Patrick Halligan, "The Environmental Policy of Saint Thomas Aquinas," *Environmental Law* 19 (1989): 767–806.

52. "Each thing is ordered to its action by God according to the way in which it is subordinated to divine providence. Now a rational creature exists under divine providence as being governed and provided for in himself, and not simply for the sake of his species, as is the case with other corruptible creatures. For the individual that is governed only for the sake of the species is not governed for its own sake, but the rational creature is governed for his own sake.... And so only rational creatures receive direction from God in their acts, not only for the species but for the individual" (*SCG* III, 113, no. 1). Cf. *De ver.* 5, 5, co.; *SCG* I, 113, no. 2.

53. "Divine providence extends to all singular things, even to the least. In the case of those beings, then, whose actions take place apart from the inclination appropriate to their species, it is necessary for them to be regulated in their acts by divine providence, over and above the direction which pertains to the species. But many actions are evident, in the case of the rational creature, for which the inclination of the species is not enough. The mark of this is that such actions are not alike in all, but differ in various cases. Therefore, the rational creature must be directed by God in his acts, not only specifically but also individually.... The governing of the acts of a rational creature, insofar as they are personal acts, pertains to divine providence" (*SCG* III, 113, no. 3, no. 5). Cf. *ST* I, 22, 2, ad 5; I, 48, 5, co.; I-II, 114, 1, co.

54. "The governance of providence stems from the divine love whereby God loves the things created by Him. In fact, love consists especially in this, 'that the lover wills the good for his loved one.' So the more that God loves things, the more do they fall under his providence.... It may then be gathered from this, that he loves intellectual substances best. Therefore, their acts of will and choice fall under his providence" (*SCG* III, 90, no. 6). Cf. *ST* I-II, 91, 2, co.

55. "Now the created rational nature alone is immediately subordinate to God, since other creatures do not attain to the universal, but only to something particular, while they partake of the Divine goodness either in 'being' only, as inanimate things, or also in 'living,' and in 'knowing singulars,' as plants and animals; whereas the rational nature, inasmuch as it apprehends the universal notion of good and being, is immediately related to the universal principle of being. Consequently the perfection of the rational creature consists not only in what belongs to it in respect of its nature, but also in that which it acquires through a supernatural participation of Divine goodness. Hence ... man's ultimate happiness consists in a supernatural vision of God: to which vision man cannot attain unless he be taught by God.... Now man acquires a share of this learning, not indeed all at once, but by little and little, according to the mode of his nature.... Hence in order that a man

Aquinas's arguments reflect a fundamentally positive view of creation. If evil is a privation of the good, goodness must always have ontological precedence over it.[56] In fact, the very presence of evil in the world may be used as an argument for the existence of God: "Now, with these considerations we dispose of the error of those who, because they noticed that evils occur in the world, said that there is no God. Thus, Boethius introduces a certain philosopher who asks: 'If God exists, whence comes evil?' But it could be argued to the contrary: 'If evil exists, God exists.' For, there would be no evil if the order of good were taken away, since its privation is evil. But this order would not exist if there were no God."[57]

Aquinas's arguments do not solve the problem of God and suffering. They do, however, have the merit of denying neither the being of God nor the reality of evil. At the same time, they point us toward God's own providential answer to evil, revealed in the cross of Christ. It seems theology can go no further than this, although it can fall far short if it diminishes either the transcendent being of God or the evident reality of evil.

PRAYER

Prayer, especially petitionary prayer, seems essentially related to divine action.[58] Prayer was therefore a problem for the Newtonian worldview in which there seemed to be no room for such action. With the new theories of contemporary science, theology has found new ways for speaking of God's action in the world. These take two fundamental forms. The first uses the indeterminism of certain interpretations of contemporary science as a place where God may act in the world without interfering with other causes. It implicitly views God as a univocal cause capable of such interference. The second sees God as a transcendent cause who does not interfere with natural causes because he is the very source of their causality. It utilizes the expanded understanding of causality suggested by contemporary theories of

---

arrive at the perfect vision of heavenly happiness, he must first of all believe God, as a disciple believes the master who is teaching him" (*ST* II-II, 2, 3, co.).

56. "There is nothing wholly evil in the world, for evil is ever founded on good.... Therefore something is said to be evil through escaping from the order of some particular good. If it wholly escaped from the order of Divine government, it would wholly cease to exist" (*ST* I, 103, 7, ad 1).

57. *SCG* III, 71, no. 10.

58. "It is of primary importance, however, for Jewish and Christian theology to encompass divine action; if God is unable to act, then even petitionary prayer is useless: there is simply no way for God to 'give us our daily bread'" (Nicholas Saunders, "Does God Cheat at Dice? Divine Action and Quantum Possibilities," *Zygon* 35 [2000]: 518).

science to explore the relationship between the transcendent causality of God and the natural causality of creatures. Both approaches speak of the relation between prayer and divine action, but in quite different ways.

Prayer and Univocal Divine Causality

As a univocal cause, God might be said to respond to prayer in the way a good friend or neighbor would respond to a call for help. As the neighbor must first be roused to action, so God is viewed as reacting or responding to our prayerful initiatives. As the neighbor might use certain tools to render assistance, so God may employ the indeterminacy of quantum mechanics or chaos theory as a medium through which to render hope, comfort, and perhaps even physical healing. Keith Ward explains that "in most cases divine action will be a causal influence that works within the parameters of probabilistic physical law. God might console me when I am in trouble, or might heal someone in answer to my prayer. This can happen without breaking any laws of nature."[59]

Since God's response will be limited to whatever action is possible within that indeterministic realm, however, it may not be as immediate or effective as even God might wish. Timothy Sansbury points out the liabilities of using quantum indeterminacy to explain how God might respond to prayer: "In most cases, instantaneous or near-instantaneous divine action will be impossible if quantum mechanics, with or without chaotic amplifiers, is the means of (responsive) divine actions.... The processes that could translate quantum determinations into specific macroscopic events must be extremely delicate to respond to a limited set of quantum events, and therefore even slight interference should be expected to disrupt or even destroy the process before it reaches its intended conclusion."[60] Some theologians see this limitation on divine action as an advantage in preserving the proper causality of creatures and addressing the problem of evil.[61] Others, such as John Houghton, find it theologically inadequate: "While not wishing to underestimate the value of this new perspective, however, I would wish to emphasise that it cannot provide anything like the whole story. To think of God operating in the margins or being limited to restricted manoeuvres is not an adequate picture of his activity."[62]

---

59. Ward, *God, Faith,* 89. See also Polkinghorne, *Science and Providence,* 31; and Peacocke, "Emergence, Mind," 274–75.

60. Sansbury, "False Promise," 117.

61. See, for example, Murphy, "Science and the Problem," 141.

62. John Houghton, "What Happens When We Pray," *Science and Christian Belief* 7 (1995): 11.

Prayer and Transcendent Divine Causality

When we look at prayer in relation to the transcendent God, a different picture emerges. God is the first source of all of our actions, including prayer. The initiative of prayer lies not with us, but with God. Far from worrying about a possible lag time between our prayerful request and God's response, we find that our prayer itself is already a sign of God's action in us. The fundamental dynamic of prayer is not that we pray first and then God responds, but that God prays in us: "In the same way, the Spirit too comes to the aid of our weakness; for we do not know how to pray as we ought, but the Spirit itself intercedes with inexpressible groanings" (Romans 8:26). As C. S. Lewis observes: "God and man cannot exclude one another, as man excludes man, at the point of junction, so to call it, between Creator and creature; the point where the mystery of creation—timeless for God and incessant in time for us—is actually taking place. 'God did (or said) it' and 'I did (or said) it' can both be true.... The deeper the level within ourselves from which our prayer, or any other act, wells up, the more it is His, but not at all the less ours. Rather, most ours when most His."[63]

Beginning with God's transcendent causality also reminds us of the importance of prayer. We might think of prayer as a kind of secondary cause under the influence of God's primary causality. We have seen how God acts through secondary causes in the natural world. God keeps us alive, for instance, through the instrumentality of the food we eat and the air we breathe. It would be unreasonable for us, however much we may believe in God's infinite power, to think that we do not need food or air since God could keep us alive without them. God wills to act through secondary causes. If prayer is also a secondary cause, then just as God keeps us alive through food and air, there may be good things that God intends to accomplish in the world precisely through our prayer. As the good of life that God wills for us might be lost if we did not make use of the secondary causality of food, so the spiritual or physical good that God wishes to accomplish through prayer may remain undone if we fail to employ the secondary causality of prayer. In this way, prayer is not superfluous, but essential to our spiritual life, just as food and air are essential to physical life. All are in some way secondary causes, as Aquinas explains:

---

63. C. S. Lewis, *Letters to Malcolm: Chiefly on Prayer* (New York: Harcourt Brace Jovanovich: 1964), 68–69.

The cause of some things that are done by God is prayers and holy desires. For divine providence does not exclude other causes; rather, it orders them so that the order which providence has determined within itself may be imposed on things. And thus secondary causes are not incompatible with providence; instead, they carry out the effect of providence. In this way, then, prayers are efficacious before God, yet they do not destroy the immutable order of divine providence, because this individual request that is granted to a certain petitioner falls under the order of divine providence. So it is the same thing to say that we should not pray in order to obtain something from God, because the order of his providence is immutable, as to say that we should not walk in order to get to a place, or eat in order to be nourished; all of which are clearly absurd.[64]

Considering prayer as a secondary cause reminds us that the purpose of prayer is not to change God but to change us. As secondary causes in nature do not change the divine causality that works through them, but are rather moved by it, so prayer is not meant to change God, but to transform us.[65] Since God loves us constantly with an infinite love, we cannot think that our prayer is what awakens God's love and concern for us. When we pray, what changes is not God's love, but ours. We come to see our need for God more clearly, surrender more completely, and so become more and more transformed into God's likeness. Aquinas illustrates this, using an image from Pseudo-Dionysius of a "chain of abundant light hanging from the highest heaven and descending to the earth":

If we take hold of this chain and move ourselves hand over hand toward the top, we will seem to pull the chain downwards, but really we will not bring it down.... Rather we ourselves will be raised into the greater splendor of that luminous chain.... Before all acts, but most especially before theological work, it is beneficial for us

---

64. *SCG* III, 96, no. 8. "[C]ertain effects will result by divine ordination by means of these prayers, just as they do by means of other causes. So, it will be the same thing to exclude the effect of prayer as to exclude the effect of all other causes. But if the immutability of the divine order does not take away their effects from other causes, neither does it remove the efficacy of prayers. Therefore prayers retain their power; not that they can change the order of eternal disposition, but rather as they themselves exist under such order" (*SCG* III, 96, no. 14). Cf. *ST* I, 23, 8, co. On prayer and secondary causality, see also Richard Kocher, *Herausgeforderter Vorsehungsglaube. Die Lehre von der Vorsehung im Horizont der gegenwärtigen Theologie* (St. Ottilien: EOS Verlag, 1993), 296–301; and Joseph Bobik, *Veritas Divina: Aquinas on Divine Truth* (South Bend, Ind.: St. Augustine's Press, 2001), 62–64.

65. "Prayer is not established for the purpose of changing the eternal disposition of providence" (*SCG* III, 95, no. 1). "Nothing prevents some particular order, due to an inferior cause, from being changed though the efficacy of prayers, under the operation of God, who transcends all causes, and thus is not confined under the necessity of any order of cause; on the contrary, all the necessity of the order of an inferior cause is confined under him as being brought into being by him. So, insofar as something in the order of inferior causes established by God is changed through prayer, God is said to turn or to repent; not in the sense that his eternal disposition is changed, but that some effect of his is changed" (*SCG* III, 96, no. 15).

to begin with prayer, not as if we were to draw down divine power which is everywhere present and nowhere contained, but as drawing and uniting ourselves to him through recollection and supplication.[66]

MIRACLES

The question of miracles or "special divine action" has been a particular focus in the dialogue between science and theology. Ever since Hume defined a miracle as a "violation of the laws of nature," many have considered the practice of science to be incompatible with the affirmation of miracles.[67] Now that science has developed a less deterministic view of the world, a reconciliation seems possible. This can be achieved in two ways: either by making direct, theological use of certain interpretations of contemporary science or by employing the new understanding of causality emerging from contemporary science. We will look at these two ways, but first we will have to find an adequate definition of miracle and consider some objections to miracles.

The *Oxford English Dictionary* defines miracle as: "A marvelous event occurring within human experience, which cannot have been brought about by human power or by the operation of any natural agency, and must therefore be ascribed to the special intervention of the Deity or of some supernatural being; chiefly, an act (e.g., of healing) exhibiting control over the laws of nature, and serving as evidence that the agent is either divine or is specially favored by God."[68] The *American Heritage Dictionary* has a similar definition: "An event that appears inexplicable by the laws of nature and so is held to be supernatural in origin or an act of God."[69] Both definitions invoke some reference to nature as part of the meaning of "miracle." The first notes that a

---

66. *In de div. nom.* III, lect. un. (§239, 243–44). Cf. *SCG* III, 119, no. 4.
67. "A miracle is a violation of the laws of nature, and as a firm and unalterable experience has established these laws, the proof against a miracle, from the very nature of the fact, is as entire as any argument from experience can possibly be imagined" (Hume, *An Enquiry*, 120). Maurice Wiles seems a devoted disciple of Hume in his comment on miracles: "We need a word for the concept of an event directly caused by God that conflicts with normally experienced regularities of the world's working, even if we decide that it is not only a null set but a logically incoherent concept. I would prefer to keep the word 'miracle' for that concept and say that miracle, so understood, should have no place in Christian theology" (Maurice Wiles, "Divine Action: Some Moral Considerations," in *The God Who Acts: Philosophical and Theological Explorations*, ed. Thomas F. Tracy [University Park: Pennsylvania State University Press, 1994], 26).
68. *The Oxford English Dictionary: Second Edition*, ed. J. A. Simpson and E. S. C. Weiner (Oxford: Clarendon Press, 1989), 9.835–36.
69. *The American Heritage Dictionary of the English Language*, 4th ed. (New York: Houghton Mifflin Company, 2000).

miracle is not "ascribable to ... the operation of any natural force;" the second, that it is not "explicable by the laws of nature." Both also make reference to God. The first mentions a "divine agency," and the second, an "act of God." We may perhaps see a tacit rejection of Hume's definition in the fact that neither speaks of a violation of nature or the laws of nature. It seems, then, that the contemporary understanding of miracle involves some relation to God (or at least the supernatural) and to nature, but does not imply a violation of nature.

These parameters are similar those proposed by Keith Ward: "Many theists will wish to speak of ... 'miracles' as points at which physical structures transcend their normal modes of operation, having been united in a special way with their spiritual basis and goal.... [M]iracles are occasions when normal physical regularities are modified by a more overt influence of the underlying spiritual basis of all beings."[70] The parameters are also similar to Aquinas's understanding of miracle: "The word 'miracle' is derived from admiration, which arises when an effect is manifest, whereas its cause is hidden.... Now a miracle is so called as being full of wonder, as having a cause absolutely hidden from all; and this cause is God. Wherefore those things which God does outside those causes which we know are called miracles."[71] As in our contemporary definition, Thomas references God and nature. He sees miracles not as a violation of nature or against (*contra*) nature, but rather "outside" or "beyond" (*praeter*) nature.[72] Since a miracle is beyond the whole order of nature, God alone can be its author.[73]

Objections to Miracles

We have already discussed how the notion of divine action became problematic with the narrowing of causality in modern science. Given its meth-

---

70. Ward, *God, Chance*, 83. Ward also criticizes Hume's definition: "[Miracles] are not well described as 'violations of laws of nature,' a description chosen by the philosopher David Hume precisely because it helped to make miracles seem immoral and irrational" (ibid.).

71. *ST* I, 105, 7, co. Cf. *Sent.* II, 18, 1, 3, co.; ad 2; *De pot.* 6, 2, co.; *SCG* III, 101, no. 1.

72. "Since the order of nature is given to things by God; if He does anything outside [*praeter*] this order, it is not against [*contra*] nature" (*ST* I, 105, 6, ad 1). Elsewhere, Aquinas explains the "customary" division of miracles into things done "above," "against [*contra*]" or "without" nature (*De pot.* 6, 2, ad 3) and explains how, fundamentally considered, miracles may not be "against nature" (*De pot.* 6, 1, ad 1).

73. "True miracles cannot be wrought save by divine power: because God alone can change [*mutare*] the order of nature; and this is what is meant by a miracle" (*ST* III, 43, 2, co.). "Now the most hidden cause and the furthest removed from our senses is God who works most secretly in all things; wherefore those effects are properly called miracles which are produced by God's power

od, science must look for explanations of events only among natural causes. When its methodological assumptions are transformed into metaphysical principles, the world becomes a deterministic nexus of causes. It is then impossible for a divine cause, itself understood as fundamentally univocal with natural causes, to insert itself. New possibilities for speaking of divine action emerged with the theories of contemporary science and the broadened understanding of causality that they entailed.

Some theologians, however, still seem to operate out of the presuppositions of modern science in their discussion of miracles. John Macquarrie, for instance, thinks that the "traditional conception of miracle is irreconcilable with our modern understanding of both science and history."[74] Arthur Peacocke, though well aware of developments of contemporary science, expresses a similar concern: "Our current perception of the world as a closed nexus of events renders the idea of God 'intervening' in the world to rupture its God-given regularities as incoherent."[75] Paul Davies explains why miracles are distasteful to the scientific community: "The religious person, who is comfortable with the notion of God's activity and sees God's work all around him every day, finds nothing incongruous about miraculous events because they are simply another facet of God's action in the world. In contrast the scientist, who prefers to think of the world as operating according to natural laws, would regard a miracle as 'misbehavior,' a pathological event which mars the elegance and beauty of nature. Miracles are something most scientists would rather do without."[76]

In addition to objections to miracles based on science (or scientism), there are also theological objections. To John Macquarrie, if "miracle in the sense of supernatural intervention is irreconcilable with science and history, it is also objectionable theologically."[77] The strongest objection arises in theodicy, as Brian Hebblethwaite notes: "If it really is God's way to inter-

---

alone on things which have a natural tendency to the opposite effect or to a contrary mode of operation" (*De pot.* 6, 2, co.). Cf. *ST* I, 110, 4, co.

74. John Macquarrie, *Principles of Christian Theology* (New York: Charles Scribner's Sons, 1977), 248. His comment is reminiscent of Rudolph Bultmann: "It is impossible to use electric light and the wireless and to avail ourselves of modern medical and surgical discoveries, and at the same time to believe in the New Testament world of spirits and miracles" (Rudolf Bultmann, "New Testament and Mythology," in *Kerygma and Myth: A Theological Debate*, ed. Hans Werner Bartsch, trans. Reginald H. Fuller [New York: Harper and Row, 1961], 5).

75. Peacocke, "Problems," 2–3.

76. Paul Davies, *God and the New Physics* (New York: Simon and Schuster, 1983), 197.

77. Macquarrie, *Principles*, 249.

vene miraculously to bring about his purposes in nature, history and individual life, then why does he not do so more often and to greater effect? ... To suppose that he does so just occasionally would be to raise all the problems which perplex believers as they reflect on the problem of evil, about why God does not intervene more often."[78] Since we have already considered theodicy in our discussion of divine providence, we will not return to it here. Beyond theodicy, there is a concern that, by admitting God's miraculous action in the world, one might turn God into just one cause among others—and rather a meddlesome one at that.[79]

Miracles and the New Theories of Science

The new theories of science have led, as we have seen, not only to a new sense of indeterminacy and openness in nature, but to a renewed appreciation of the method of science and its limits. The deterministic worldview of classical science, for instance, is recognized as a product of scientism rather than science itself. The rejection of miracles is also a product of scientism, as Stanley Jaki points out: "So-called 'liberal' Christians have for some time turned their back on miracles as unworthy of a Christianity that has come of age. By this they mean the age of science. Biblical miracles have been the principal target of their demythologization of the gospel story in particular. What they mean by demythologization consists in the naturalization of biblical reports about miracles, a procedure in which they make much of science. Only some keener eyes noticed that Bultmann, the chief of demythologizers, invoked not science but scientism when he declared that the coming of electromagnetism had once and for all discredited belief in miracles."[80]

Once scientism is laid to rest, miracles are not incompatible with science. Richard Swinburne argues that "the doctrine that God intervenes in the natural order from time to time to answer prayers in the ways most expedient for us is not at odds with our knowledge of the natural world."[81] Steven Dale Crain agrees: "The practice of science is compatible with single

---

78. Hebblethwaite, *Evil, Suffering*, 93, 97. See also R. A. Ellis, "Can God Act," 100.
79. "[T]he direct interventionist view of divine providence seems to treat God's purposive causal activity as one causal factor among others, bringing about the things that happen in the world. This seems to reduce God to one more piece of the world, one more power at work among others" (Hebblethwaite, *Evil, Suffering*, 93). David Jenkins thinks that a God who works miracles must be "a meddling demigod, a moral monster and a contradiction of himself" (Jenkins, *Anglicanism*, 21–22).
80. Jaki, *Means*, 182.
81. Richard Swinburne, *Providence and the Problem of Evil* (Oxford: Clarendon Press, 1998), 118.

Providence, Prayer, and Miracles • 251

events going unexplained scientifically, be they, for example, miraculous healings, or indeed even resurrections from the dead, because a universe whose natural laws are only occasionally interrupted still in general exhibits law-like behavior, so that general classes of phenomena remain open to scientific investigation."[82] William Alston also thinks that "particular divine actions would not jeopardize, or otherwise adversely affect, anything fundamental to science."[83]

Certain interpretations of contemporary science seem especially compatible with miracles as they break free from the closed causal nexus of classical Newtonian science. Some theologians have used these interpretations directly in their discussion of miracles. The interpretations provide a locus of indeterminism in the natural world where miraculous action might take place without interfering with natural causes.[84] We will not give a lengthy account of their arguments here since we have already seen them in the context of our more general discussion of how theologians have used the interpretations of the theories of contemporary science to speak of divine action. The criticisms we raised in that context would apply also to the more specific question of miracles. Briefly, the very fact that one would search for "room" in the world for miraculous divine action shows that one is considering God's causality to be univocal with that of creatures and so liable to interfere with them. Also, if God's causality is limited to the realms of indeterminism in the natural world, opportunities for miraculous action are greatly diminished.[85] Even those limited opportunities may dry up if the present theories of science change and the ontological indeterminism that they postulate disappears.[86] Given such limitations and liabilities, it may

---

82. Crain, "Divine Action," 48.
83. William P. Alston, "Divine Action: Shadow or Substance?" in *The God Who Acts: Philosophical and Theological Explorations,* ed. Thomas F. Tracy (University Park: Pennsylvania State University Press, 1994), 49.
84. See, for instance, the account of "extraordinary acts of God" in Murphy, "Buridan's."
85. "The loss of interventionist miracles is a hard cost to pay for traditional theists. But after a period when it seemed impossible to many to maintain any account of divine action, it is encouraging to have found a framework that allows one to speak of divine action in at least some spheres, as I have done, without conflicting with scientific results or methods. Emergence provides a way for theists to speak of the response of agents to the divine while remaining consistent with the scientific study of natural history" (Clayton, "Emergence from Physics," 682). "Theological claims for divine action in the natural world are much more difficult to maintain than those that talk about God's influencing the thoughts, wishes, or decisions of an individual person" (Clayton, *God and Contemporary,* 190). See also Murphy, "Science and the Problem," 141.
86. "If (and only if) downward mental causation is a viable notion, God could bring about

be preferable in discussing miracles to use the new notions of causality that contemporary science suggests rather than the particular interpretations of scientific theories themselves.

Miracles and the New Causality of Science

The new modes of causality implied in the theories of contemporary science can be helpful in addressing the question of miracles or special divine action. We have seen that these new modes hearken back to certain "older" modes of causality in the philosophy of Aristotle and Thomas Aquinas. These include God's causality as the first efficient, formal exemplar, and final cause of all things. We will look at how each of these modes of causality can help us to understand miraculous divine action.

We have described how God's primary efficient causality does not interfere with, but is rather the source of the secondary causality of creatures. The same framework of primary and secondary causality will allow us to see the relation of God's miraculous action to the causality of creatures and the laws of nature. It can also help us to understand why, in acting directly in the natural world, God does not become just another natural cause or contradict his own causality as creator.

Aquinas knew nothing of the closed causal nexus of Newtonian science, but he was aware of an argument, attributed to Anaxagoras, that led to the same conclusion: "Natural forms which are the principles of natural actions cannot be influenced, nor their actions hindered by any supernatural cause; so that nothing can happen contrary to the course of nature, which is unchangeably regulated by these corporeal causes."[87] If we change the terms "natural forms" and "corporeal causes" to "laws of nature," we have precisely the argument attributed to modern science against the possibility of miracles. Aquinas thought that Anaxagoras's error sprang from his contention that "corporeal things do not derive their existence from any higher cause." Having failed to see that the existence of natural things was due to a higher cause, Anaxagoras could not understand how their operation might be in-

---

changes in individuals' subjective dispositions without negating the laws that we know to hold in physics and biology" (Clayton, "Natural Law," 627). "If humans have a purely spiritual soul associated with their body, one that can influence events in the physical world, then there is in principle no difficulty with a spiritual being such as God influencing events in the physical world.... If physicalism (whether 'reductionist' or not) wins this battle, I will argue, the most hopeful means for making sense of divine causation will be removed" (Clayton, *God and Contemporary*, 234–35). See also Clayton, *Mind*, 189.

87. *De pot.* 6, 1, co.

fluenced by such a cause. Only if one recognizes God as the first cause of all being, can one admit his influence in the operations of secondary causes.[88]

In addition to causing the natural actions of secondary causes, God can also "act independently of the course of nature in the production of particular effects."[89] Through such action, God may produce effects that are beyond the power of nature.[90] He may also restrain secondary causes from producing their normal effects or produce those same effects directly by his causal power alone.[91] In addition, he may use secondary causes, such as the saints, as his instruments in working miracles.[92]

In all of these actions, God's influence is not contrary to nature: "Since God is the primary agent, all things that come after Him are like instruments for Him. But instruments are made for the purpose of subserving the action of the principal agent, while being moved by him.... This is why it is not contrary to the nature of an instrument for it to be moved by a principal agent, but, rather, is most fitting for it. Therefore, it is not contrary to nature when created things are moved in any way by God; indeed, they were so made that they might serve Him."[93] Aquinas argues that God's action cannot be against nature, since he is the author of nature: "Since the order of nature is given to things by God; if he does anything outside [*praeter*] of this order, it is not against [*contra*] nature."[94] Even if God did something beyond the entire capacity of nature, it would not be against nature. Aquinas explains this with an argument that is admittedly steeped in medieval cosmology: "By the power of God something can occur that is contrary to universal nature which is dependent on the power of the heavens; without being contrary to nature simply, since it will be in accord with the supremely universal nature, dependent on God in relation to all creatures."[95] Vincent Guagliardo suggests that we can update this argument quite easily by changing the phrase "power of the heavens" to "laws of physics": "Now Aquinas is speaking in terms of ancient cosmology. But if we make the appropriate 'cosmological shift,' it would seem that the same principle might obtain: ... 'By the power of God something can occur that is contrary to universal nature which is dependent

---

88. *De pot.* 6, 1, co.
89. *De pot.* 6, 1, co. "As God can imprint form immediately in matter, it follows that he can move any body whatever in respect to any movement whatever" (*ST* I, 105, 2, co.).
90. *De pot.* 6, 1, co.
91. See *SCG* III, 96, no. 14; III, 99, nos. 2 and 7; *ST* I, 105, 1, ad 3; I, 105, 2, co.; I, 109, 1, co.
92. *De pot.* 6, 4, co.
93. *SCG* III, 100, no. 3.
94. *ST* I, 105, 6, ad 1. Cf. *SCG* III, 100, no. 2.
95. *De pot.* 6, 1, ad 1.

on the power of the heavens [read: laws of physics]; without being contrary to nature simply, since it will be in accord with the supremely universal nature, dependent on God in relation to all creatures.'"[96] William Alston offers similar arguments:

> It will be noted that I have thus far abstained from speaking of God's specific acts in the world as divine "intervention" or "interferences." Though this terminology may be, strictly speaking, accurate, in that I am thinking of God as providing a causal input that alters how things would have gone had only natural factors been operative, still it has the unfortunate implication that the normal procedure is the purely natural one and that divine action involves a departure from that norm. From the point of view of the Christian tradition, it is much better to think of the normal as God's usual way of dealing with His creation, which involves both purely natural causation, much of the time, and special divine causal inputs some of the time. One is no more untoward or "interfering" or "interventionist" than another. After all, this is God's creation. Talk of divine "intervention" stems from a deist picture of God as "outside" His creation, making quick forays or incursions from time to time and then retreating to His distant observation post.[97]

In acting miraculously in nature, God does not become a univocal or secondary cause himself, since his action transcends the whole order of secondary causes.[98] Nor does God act against his own causality or intention as the primary cause, the author of nature, as Aquinas notes: "If we consider the order of things depending on the first cause, God cannot do anything against this order; for if he did so, he would act against his foreknowledge, or his will or his goodness. But if we consider the order of things depending on any secondary cause, thus God can do something outside such order; for he is not subject to the order of secondary causes, but on the contrary this order is subject to him as proceeding from him not by a natural necessity, but by the choice of his own will; for he could have created another order of things. Wherefore God can do something outside this order when he chooses, for instance by producing the effects of secondary causes without them

---

96. Vincent Guagliardo, "Nature and Miracle," *CTNS Bulletin* 10, no. 2 (1990): 17–18.
97. Alston, "Divine Action: Shadow," 45.
98. See *In peri herm.* I, lect. 14, no. 22. William Alston observes: "In what respects does bringing about particular effects in the world reduce God to the level of creatures? It will certainly imply that both He and creatures are engaged in bringing about states of affairs; that is, they are both agents. But it is a mere rhetorical flourish to say that this puts Him on our level. Obviously there is a world of difference, all the difference there can be, between an infinite-source-of-all-being bringing about X, and you or me bringing about X. The fact that we are both engaged in bringing about something should not panic us into denying the differences between creator and creature that the Christian tradition has insisted on. In short, I see no merit whatsoever in these allegations" (Alston, "Divine Action: Shadow," 53).

Providence, Prayer, and Miracles • 255

or by producing certain effects to which secondary causes do not extend."[99] Aquinas uses the analogy of an artist to show that in performing miracles God does not act against either nature or himself: "The whole of nature is like an artifact of the divine artistic mind. But it is not contrary to the essential character of an artist if he should work in a different way on his product, even after he has given it its first form. Neither, then, is it against nature if God does something to natural things in a different way from that to which the course of nature is accustomed."[100]

These arguments hinge on seeing God as a transcendent rather than a univocal cause. When a univocal agent causes something to move in a way that is contrary to its natural tendency, the result is what Aquinas calls "violent motion" (movement contrary to the nature of the substance) as distinct from "natural motion" (movement in accordance with or flowing from the nature of the substance). In his cosmology, the motion of a rock when thrown "upward" would be violent, since the natural tendency of heavy things is to move "downward" toward the earth at the center of the cosmos. The categories of "violent" and "natural" motion are, of course, quite foreign to our understanding of the world. We do not find a natural tendency in things to go "up" or "down." In fact, there is no absolute "up" or "down" in our universe. Still we do affirm that things have characteristic behaviors that we may describe through the laws of science. If a thing should move in a way contrary to those laws, we would say that its motion is unnatural, an aberration of the laws of nature as we have formulated them. But is an event that seems contrary to the laws of nature as we know them contrary to nature as such?

To answer this, we would have to ask the further question of why things move at all or why they should have characteristic patterns of action in the first place that can then be described by scientific laws.[101] Whatever an-

---

99. *ST* I, 105, 6, co. "Whatever is done by God in created things is not contrary to nature, even though it may seem to be opposed to the proper order of a particular nature" (*SCG* III, 100, no. 2). Keith Ward notes: "Many of these particular divine acts, though not all, may be termed 'miracles.' They are not violations of immutable laws of nature—a picture which makes one think they are both immoral (instances of law-breaking) and irrational (since the laws should have been better designed in the first place). They are law-transcending events which manifest the basis or goal of the physical world in a wider spiritual realm. They show the power of Spirit to relate matter to itself so as to transcend normal material patterns of interaction, and establish a new interaction between the material and the spiritual" (Keith Ward, *Religion and Creation* [Oxford: Clarendon Press, 1996], 313).

100. *SCG* III, 100, no. 6.

101. "When the great variety of natural phenomena has been classified scientifically, their laws noted, we are still left with the question of their radical source, the ultimate accountability of all such phenomena.... It does not make much difference what name is applied. The important thing

swers we come up with, we must eventually say that they act the way they do "because of the kinds of things they are." And if we ask why a particular object is this type of thing rather than something else, we must name some principle such as substantial form as the explanation.[102] If we then ask why the world should be configured into natural types according to such forms, or why there should be such forms at all, we push the question back to Aquinas's discussion of God as the transcendent cause of such forms.[103]

Once the question is pushed that far, however, we can reverse the order of inquiry, and ask about the character of the action of that transcendent cause in the world. We will then be in a position to understand Aquinas's argument that, however God acts in the world, God's action cannot be a violation of nature since God is the transcendent source of the forms that make the things we find in the world to be the kinds of things they are, and so to act in the characteristic ways that they do, and so to manifest the consistent behaviors that we can then describe in our laws of science.

Aquinas did not speak of "laws of science," but of the natural movements of substances. In his cosmology, the natural motions of earthly substances are derived from the motions of heavenly bodies. If one earthly substance acted on another, it might cause an unnatural motion. If, for instance, someone threw a rock "up," when its natural tendency was to go "down," the result would be violent or unnatural motion. If a heavenly body caused an earthly substance to go "up," however, the motion would not be unnatural since the heavenly body is the source of the natural motion of the object. To illustrate this, Aquinas uses the example of the tides, in which the moon causes the

---

is that we must in the last analysis acknowledge a certain *internal spontaneity* in all things from the smallest to the largest in the universe" (Weisheipl, "Concept of Nature," 9). Nancey Murphy seems to be on this same trail of reasoning: "My own speculations in this area have led me to a position closer to Aristotle's and Thomas's than to Newton's: entities in the world behave the way they do because of innate powers and tendencies. The regularities that we observe are a result of these intrinsic tendencies, not of transcendent laws. I have argued that just such a radical reconception of the nature of matter and of causation is needed in order to solve the problem of divine action. This is clearly a topic that needs much further consideration, and ... may be the most important issue to explore in order to understand God's relation to nature" (Nancey Murphy, "Scientific Cosmology: A New Challenge to Theology," in *Science and Theology: Ruminations on the Cosmos*, ed. Chris Impey and Catherine Petry [Vatican City State: Vatican Observatory, 2003], 121).

102. "Since everything acts in so far as it is actual ... and since every being is actual through form, it is necessary for the operation of a thing to follow its form" (*SCG* III, 97, no. 4.)

103. "Therefore He [God] is the cause of action not only by giving the form which is the principle of action, as the generator is said to be the cause of movement in things heavy and light; but also as preserving the forms and powers of things" (*ST* I, 105, 5, co.). Cf. *ST* I, 104, 1, co.; *SCG* II, 21, no. 5. See also O'Rourke, "Aristotle and the Metaphysics," 23–24; and Weisheipl, "Concept of Nature," 18–19.

water to move up on the beach, when its natural tendency is to go down. If the influence of a planetary agent does not render such motion unnatural, neither does the influence of God. Since God is the source of all actuality, God's action can never cause a creaturely action that is contrary to nature:

> In natural things something may happen outside this natural order in two ways. It may happen by the action of an agent which did not give them their natural inclination; as for example when a man moves a heavy body upward, which does not owe to him its natural inclination to move downward; and that would be against nature. It may also happen by the action of the agent on whom the natural inclination depends; and this is not against nature, as is clear in the ebb and flow of the tide, which is not against nature; although it is against the natural movement of water in a downward direction; for it is owing to the influence of a heavenly body, on which the natural inclination of lower bodies depends. Therefore since the order of nature is given to things by God; if He does anything outside this order, it is not against nature.[104]

In addition to primary and secondary causality, the notions of formal and final causality can also be useful in the discussion of miracles. The new modes of causality of contemporary science, especially in theories of emergence, lead us back to Aquinas's notion of formal causality. The idea of intrinsic formal causality, or substantial form, allows us to account for the being of the whole and so ground the top-down causality often discussed in theories of emergence. The idea of the extrinsic or exemplar formal cause points us toward God as the ultimate source of the substantial forms of all things. Aquinas employs this idea of God as exemplar cause in his discussion of miracles:

> Although the order implanted in things by divine providence represents in its own way divine goodness, it does not represent it perfectly, because the goodness of a creature does not attain to equality with divine goodness. But that which is not perfectly represented by a given copy may again be represented in another way besides this one. Now, the representation in things of the divine goodness is the end for the production of things by God. . . . Therefore the divine will is not limited to this particular order of causes and effects in such a manner that it is unable to will to produce immediately an effect in things here below without using any other causes.[105]

Aquinas also uses the idea of final causality in his discussions of miracles. The universe is ordered to the goodness of God as its ultimate end or final cause. Each thing is directed by its nature toward a particular end that is

---

104. *ST* I, 105, 6, ad 1. Cf.: *SCG* III, 100, no. 4–5; *De pot.* 6, 1, ad 17.
105. *SCG* III, 99, no. 6.

a reflection and participation of the transcendent goodness of God. Human beings are directed in a special way toward that end, since God wills them to share in his own life.[106] God's miraculous action is also explained in terms of this final causality: "When God does anything contrary to the course of nature, the whole order of the universe is not subverted, but the course resulting from the relation between one particular thing and another. Hence it is not unfitting if at times something is done contrary to the course of nature for man's spiritual welfare which consists in his being ordered to the last end of the universe."[107] Sometimes, we may see such action as a manifestation of God's power: "He does this at times to manifest his power. For it can be manifested in no better way, that the whole of nature is subject to the divine will, than by the fact that sometimes he does something outside the order of nature. Indeed, this makes it evident that the order of things has proceeded from him, not by natural necessity, but by free will."[108] This manifestation of power, however, is itself ordered to the final end of sharing the knowledge of himself with his creatures: "Nor should this argument, that God does a thing in nature in order to manifest himself to the minds of men, be regarded as of slight importance, because we showed above that all corporeal creatures are, in a sense, ordered to intellectual nature as an end; moreover, the end of this intellectual nature is divine knowledge.... So it is not astonishing that some change is made in corporeal substance in order to make provision for the knowing of God by intellectual nature."[109]

106. See *ST* I, 10, 3, co.; I, 24, 2, co.; I, 114, 2, co.
107. *De pot.* 6, 1, ad 21. Cf. *De pot.* 6, 1, ad 7.
108. *SCG* III, 99, no. 9.
109. *SCG* III, 99, no. 10. On the divine purpose in the miracles of Christ, see *ST* III, 43, 1, co. Keith Ward also sees the role of final causality in miracles: "In miracles, God does not 'interfere' in a closed physical process. God perfects the physical process, showing what the ultimate divine purpose is. Every authentic miracle has such a disclosive function, transforming matter to be a sacrament of spirit" (Ward, *Religion and Creation*, 314).

Conclusion

THE CAUSALITY OF LOVE

Our discussion has been concerned fundamentally with two approaches to divine action that have become possible, in some way, through contemporary science. One directly employs certain interpretations of the theories of contemporary science. The other uses not so much those interpretations as the understanding of causality that arises from them.

We have seen that our idea of divine action is closely tied to our notion of causality and that the ways we think about causality affect the ways we can talk about God's action. Our idea of causality, however, has been profoundly influenced by empirical science. Before the Scientific Revolution, a rich account of causality was available to theologians, especially in the philosophy of Thomas Aquinas who developed Aristotle's notions of material, formal, efficient and final causality. Modern Newtonian science reduced causality to one type: the force that moves the atoms. Since what we can say about divine action is closely tied to what we think about causality, the discussion of divine action inevitably became locked into the narrow notions of causality of modern science. Ultimately it seemed that God could not act in the world at all. Any act of God would interfere with the proper causality of creatures. There was simply no "room" in the cosmos for God's action.

Through certain interpretations of the theories of contemporary science, our ideas about causality have again expanded. Quantum mechanics and chaos theory have once more found a place for chance and indeterminism in the cosmos. Biology explains the features of organisms in terms of their purpose, employing the notion of final causality. The theory of emergence finds application in cognitive science, biology, chemistry and physics. Looking to the structure of the whole to explain the behavior of the part, it evokes the notion of formal causality.

The developments of contemporary science have accordingly opened two new approaches to divine action. One is to employ the developments themselves (or certain interpretations of the theories associated with them) to speak of divine action. So the indeterminism of the Copenhagen interpretation of quantum mechanics and of certain readings of chaos theory have been seen as a place where God can act in the world without interfering with the order of nature. The top-down causality of emergence has also been used to model divine action. The presence of design, whether in cosmology in some versions of the anthropic principle or in biology in some approaches to evolution, has likewise been taken as a pointer to God's action in the world.

We have seen how this approach has proved a rich source of theological reflection. At the same time, we have discovered its limitations and liabilities. Its accounts of divine action always depend on particular interpretations of science and so can only be as permanent as those interpretations. To the extent that it introduces God's causality into areas of the natural world that science has not yet explained, it is in danger of falling into cahoots with that ever sadly retreating deity known as the god of the gaps. It also betrays an implicit tendency to see God as a univocal cause. This is especially evident in its concern to find a realm of nature, such as the indeterminism of chaos theory or quantum mechanics, in which God can act without interfering with the causality of creatures.

The second approach seems to overcome these liabilities. In exploring the new modes of causality that arise in contemporary science, it retrieves elements of the philosophy of Aristotle and Thomas Aquinas. It allows us to maintain God's transcendence while affirming his immanence in creation as final, exemplar, and efficient cause. Far from interfering with created causes, God's influence as primary cause is found to be essential to them in the exercise of their proper activity as secondary causes. God's action does not hinder or distort the reality of chance or freedom, but is the very source of these modes of creaturely causality. Even when God acts miraculously beyond the normal patterns of nature, his action cannot be regarded as against nature, since the fundamental order of nature is always towards God as First Cause. Through this second approach we can unlock the notion of divine action and affirm God's intimate presence and providential care for all things.

We can also recognize God's action as the causality of love. God is not one cause among others but the transcendent cause of all, and the source of his causality is nothing other than his gratuitous love.[1] Before any creature came to be, this love was eternally shared in the triune life of Father, Son and Holy Spirit. The act of creation did not spring from any need on God's part, but from that abundant love which gave rise to a dynamic world of creatures that share in God's own causality. As Etienne Gilson notes: "The universe, as represented by St. Thomas, is not a mass of inert bodies passively moved by a force which passes through them, but a collection of active beings each enjoying the efficacy delegated to it by God along with actual being. At the first beginnings of a world like this, we have to place not so much a force being exercised as an infinite goodness being communicated. Love is the unfathomable source of all causality."[2] At the heart of creation, there is not the aching need of eros, but the sheer gift of agape.[3] The creator acts not for his own fulfillment, but only for the good of his creatures: "Some things are ... imperfect agents, and to these it belongs to intend, even while acting, the acquisition of something. But it does not belong to the First Agent, who is agent only, to act for the acquisition of some end; He intends only to communicate His perfection, which is His goodness."[4]

In creation, God is the exemplar cause, making creatures that are like himself, not only in their being but also in their action: "Because of his goodness, God communicates his perfections to creatures according to their capacity. Consequently, he shares his goodness with them, not only so that they will be good and perfect themselves, but also so that they can, with God's help, give perfection to others. Now, to give perfection to other creatures is the most noble way of imitating God."[5] By acting, the creature attains its proper perfec-

---

1. See *ST* I, 19, 3–5; I, 20, 2.   2. Gilson, *Christian Philosophy*, 183.
3. See Hill, "Two Gods of Love."
4. *ST* I, 44, 4, co. "To act from need belongs only to an imperfect agent, which by its nature is both agent and patient. But this does not belong to God, and therefore he alone is the most perfectly liberal giver, because he does not act for his own profit, but only for his own goodness" (*ST* I, 44, 4, ad 1). "God is operative at the heart of all creaturely activity but without being acted upon by creatures in return in such wise as to gain something previously lacking to him" (Hill, "The Implicate World," 87).
5. *De ver.* 9, 2, co. "Again, a thing must first be perfect in itself before it can cause another thing, as we have said already. So, this final perfection comes to a thing in order that it may exist as the cause of others. Therefore, since a created thing tends to the divine likeness in many ways, this one whereby it seeks the divine likeness by being the cause of others takes the ultimate place" (*SCG* III, 21, no. 8). "It [the argument that creatures do not have their own proper actions] is also opposed to God's goodness which is self-communicative: the result being that things were made like God not

tion, which is a participation in the perfection of the creator.[6] Each creature, by acting according to its nature, imitates the perfection of God.[7]

The creator of the universe is not in competition with his creatures, but is rather the source of their proper actions. Aquinas sees not competition but compassion as the font of all God's works.[8] God is not distant, but intimately present in the being and action of each creature. His action is not called "intervention" since that term fails to represent the intimacy of his presence.[9] Every creature in its being and action is a sign of God's contin-

---

only in being but also in acting" (*De pot.* 3, 7, co.). "The form of the first agent, who is God, is nothing else than his goodness. This, then, is the reason why all things were made: that they might be assimilated to the divine goodness" (*Comp.* I, 101). "All movements and operations of every being are seen to tend to what is perfect. Perfect signifies what is good, since the perfection of anything is its goodness. Hence every movement and action of anything whatsoever tends towards good. But all good is a certain imitation of the supreme Good, just as all being is an imitation of the first Being. Therefore the movements and actions of all things tend toward assimilation with the divine goodness" (*Comp.* I, 103). Cf.: *ST* I, 4, 3, co.; *SCG* III, 70, no. 7

6. See *ST* I, 6, 1, co.

7. "Created things attain to the divine likeness by their operations in different ways, as they also represent it in different ways conformably to their being. For each of them acts in a manner which corresponds to its being. Therefore, as all creatures in common represent the divine goodness to the extent that they exist, so by their actions they all in common attain to the divine likeness in the conservation of their being and in the communication of their being to others. For every creature endeavors, by its activity, first of all to keep itself in perfect being, so far as this is possible. In such endeavor it tends, in its own way, to an imitation of the divine permanence. Secondly, every creature strives, by its activity to communicate its own perfection, in its own fashion, to another; and in this it tends toward an imitation of the divine causality" (*Comp.* I, 103).

8. "So in every work of God, viewed at its primary source, there appears compassion. In all that follows, the power of compassion remains and works indeed with even greater force, as the influence of the first cause is more intense than that of second causes" (*ST* I, 21, 4, co.).

9. "Yet the thought of God intervening in the created order (or intruding into it) is an exceedingly odd one. It would not be so if we took God to be an agent akin to a human being (albeit an invisible agent) living alongside the world and observing it from outside. Such an agent might well be thought of as able to intervene, just as I can be thought of as able to intervene in a brawl. Yet God ... is not such an agent. I take God to be the cause of the existence of everything other than himself, and it seems hard to see how God, so understood, can be thought of as literally able to intervene in or to interfere with what he brings about. For something can only intervene by entering into a situation from which it is first of all absent, while God, as I am conceiving of him, cannot be thought to be absent from anything he creates. If God makes the universe to be (at any time), then God is creatively present to everything at all times—as making it to be and to be as it is. From this it seems to follow that God cannot intervene in the world. He is, as creative cause, already in everything at the outset.... Talk about God as intervening has to presuppose that there is commonly a serious absence of God from created things. Yet if God is (in my sense) indeed the Creator of all things, then he is never absent from any of them" (Brian Davies, *The Reality of God and the Problem of Evil* [New York: Continuum, 2006], 75). "And if we strive to remain faithful to 'the distinction' of God from the world, we will realize that we are unable to find an image for the interaction of creatures with their creator, since one of the terms is not an object in the world but the source of all that the other is. Yet it is this very fact which suggests a model for their interaction: that of lover and beloved" (Burrell, *Freedom and Creation*, 128).

ued action in the world, since none could exist or act apart from his abiding influence as the source of all being and actuality.[10]

We share in a unique way in God's action in the world and so in his providence: "Now among all others, the rational creature is subject to Divine providence in the most excellent way, in so far as it partakes of a share of providence, by being provident both for itself and for others."[11] The philosophical teaching that we are secondary causes finds its true depth in the theological truth that we are partners with God in his providential action: "In another way one is said to be helped by a person through whom he carries out his work, as a master through a servant. In this way, God is helped by us; inasmuch as we execute his orders, according to 1 Corinthians 3:9, 'We are God's coadjutors.' Nor is this on account of any defect in the power of God, but because he employs intermediary causes, in order that the beauty of order may be preserved in the universe; and also that he may communicate to creatures the dignity of causality."[12]

It is through our action that God manifests his love to the world, as Leo Thomas notes: "We have not begun to realize the dignity that is ours, a dignity that carries a very remarkable responsibility. Our eyes are the eyes that God uses to weep for the pain of the world. Our emotions are the emotions God uses to have compassion upon his people. Our hands are the hands God uses to bestow his healing blessing upon those in need. If we do not weep, some people will never know God cares. If we do not lay our hand on others in a gesture of acceptance, some will never experience healing in this world. We have the ability to let God use us to build up his kingdom; we also have the freedom to refuse, and thus hinder the coming of God's kingdom. This is the mystery of the Incarnation: God will establish his presence in the world though the weakness and limitations of sinful humanity."[13]

The God who is the efficient and exemplar cause of all things, creating them in his likeness and present in all their actions, is also the final cause drawing all creation to its fulfillment in him. Each creature, through its action, seeks to share God's goodness according to the capacity of its particu-

---

10. "The natural laws of motion, and its communication from being to being, imitate the primitive creative effusion from God. The efficacy of second causes is but the counterpart of his fecundity" (Gilson, *Christian Philosophy*, 184). See also Schulte, "Wie ist Gottes," 144–45.
11. *ST* II, 91, 2, co.   12. *ST* I, 23, 8, ad 2.
13. Leo Thomas, with Jan Alkire, *Healing Ministry: A Practical Guide* (Kansas City, Mo.: Sheed and Ward, 1994), 12.

lar nature.¹⁴ If God's love reaches out to all, it reaches out most especially to his human creation for whom God wills nothing less than his own goodness:

> One [love] is common, whereby God loves all things that are, and thereby gives things their natural being. But the second is a special love, whereby he draws the rational creature above the condition of its nature to a participation of the divine good; and according to this love he is said to love anyone simply, since it is by this love that God simply wishes the eternal good, which is himself, for the creature.¹⁵

The triune God who created all things leads his human creation through the redemptive act of the Son and the gift of the Spirit to its ultimate completion in the heart of God: "Nothing in this life can fulfill man's desire, nor can any creature satisfy his longing. For God alone can satisfy and infinitely surpass his desire. And thus it is that he does not rest unless in God. As Augustine says: 'You have made us, Lord, for yourself, and our heart is restless until may rest in you.'"¹⁶ Ultimately, to tell the story of divine action, we must use the language of love:

> A lover is placed outside himself, and made to pass into the object of his love, inasmuch as he wills good to the beloved; and works for that good by his providence even as he works for his own. Hence Dionysius says: "On behalf of the truth we must make bold to say even this, that He Himself, the cause of all things, by His abounding love and goodness, is placed outside Himself by His providence for all existing things."¹⁷

---

14. See *ST* I, 44, 4, ad 3; Q. 6, 1, ad 2; *Sent.* II, 1, 2, 2, co.; IV, 49, 1, 2, qc. 2; *De ver.* Q. 21, 2, co.; *Super ad hebr.* XI, lect. 2 (§575).
15. *ST* I-II, 110, 1, co. Cf.: *SCG* III, 95, no. 5.
16. *Super sym. apos.* ar. 12, "vitam aeternam."
17. *ST* I, 20, 2, ad 1.

Glossary

ACCIDENT An incidental aspect of a substance; that which is not of the essence (e.g., the color of a dog).

CAUSE That upon which something depends for its being or becoming.

CHANGE The transformation of some thing. Change may be accidental (when a substance remains what it is but is altered incidentally in size, quality, or location) or substantial (when a substance ceases to be what it is and becomes something else).

EFFICIENT CAUSE That which acts; the primary source of change; the agent or producer of an effect (e.g., the batter who hits the ball).

ELEMENT A first component of a thing, which in some way subsists in that thing, and is not itself reducible to more basic components of a given order. In the biological order, for example, the cell is an element (basic building block) of the body; in chemistry, hydrogen and oxygen are elements of water; in physics, the proton is an element of the atom, and, on a deeper level, the quark is an element of the proton.

FINAL CAUSE That for the sake of which something is done (e.g., the money that the employee works for).

FORM/FORMAL CAUSE A formal cause may be intrinsic or extrinsic. As an intrinsic cause, a form is that by which a thing is what it is. Accidental form is that by which a substance has a certain incidental characteristic (e.g., the shape by which the marble is a statue of Lincoln). Substantial form is that by which the substance is the kind of thing that it is (e.g., that by which a duck is a duck). As an extrinsic cause, a form is the exemplar—the model according to which something is made, as the idea of the statue in the mind of the sculptor.

INSTRUMENTAL CAUSE An efficient cause that acts under the influence of another efficient cause (the principal cause) to produce an effect that belongs wholly to both causes and exceeds the capacity of the instrumental cause acting alone (e.g., the chalk that makes intelligible marks on the blackboard when used by a teacher).

MATTER/MATERIAL CAUSE That out of which something is made; the passive principle of change which endures through a given change. In accidental change, the matter is a substance (e.g., the marble that remains marble when it is made into a statue). In substantial change, the matter is primary matter (the mere possibility-of-being-something-or-other that endures when a single, unified substance ceases to be what it is and becomes something else—when, for example, a dog dies and becomes the various substances that make up the carcass).

NATURE   The substantial form and primary matter of a thing, considered together as the source its spontaneous action. The substantial form, in making a thing to be what it is, is also the principle of its characteristic activity. For example, ducks quack and dogs bark because of their respective natures. Primary matter also explains an aspect of the thing's activity since the thing can cease to be what it is and become something else in virtue of its "possibility of being" something else.

PRIMARY CAUSE   See *Secondary cause*.

PRINCIPAL CAUSE   See *Instrumental cause*.

PRINCIPLE   That from which something proceeds in any way at all. "Principle" is a broader notion than "cause" (that from which something proceeds with dependency), and "cause" is a broader notion than "element" (that from which something proceeds materially, as a basic component).

QUANTUM EVENT   An occurrence involving elementary particles (e.g., photons, electrons) which results in their reduction from an indeterminate to a determinate state. "An example of a quantum event is the detection of an electron in a certain position. The position variable of the electron assumes a determined value in the course of the interaction between the electron and an external system, and the quantum event is the 'manifestation' of the electron in a certain position."[1]

SECONDARY CAUSE   An efficient cause that acts under the influence of another efficient cause (the primary cause) to produce an effect that belongs wholly to both causes and is proportionate to the nature of the secondary cause, but which the secondary cause could not produce apart from the primary cause (e.g., the orchestra members who, as secondary causes, produce the sounds of a symphony under the influence of the conductor as primary cause).

SUBSTANCE   An existing thing (e.g., a dog).

UNIVOCAL CAUSE   An efficient cause that acts with another efficient cause of the same order to produce some effect. Since they belong to the same order, their effect belongs only partly to each, and one may interfere with the causality of the other. When two men carry a table, for instance, they act as univocal causes. Each is only partly responsible for the motion of the table, and the causality of one may interfere with that of the other. The more weight one lifts, for instance, the less weight there is for the other to lift. (See *ST* I, 105, 5, ad 2.) In a second sense, "univocal cause" means a cause belonging to the same species as its effect, as a parent and its offspring in biological reproduction. (See *ST* I, 4, 2, co.). In this book, the term is generally used in the first sense.

---

1. "Relational Quantum Mechanics," in the "Stanford Encyclopedia of Philosophy," available at *http://plato.stanford.edu/entries/qm-relational* (accessed January 20, 2011). In this book, I follow Robert Russell's assumption that quantum events occur not just in science laboratories, but everywhere in the universe. See R. J. Russell, "Special Providence and Genetic Mutation," 204n39, 214; Wegter-McNelly, "Atoms," 100, 102; and Barbour, *Nature*, 27.

Bibliography

WORKS BY THOMAS AQUINAS

Commentarium in Aristotelis libros Peri hermeneias. Turin and Rome: Marietti, 1955. [English translation: *Commentary on Aristotle's On Interpretation.* In *Aristotle: On Interpretation. Commentary by St. Thomas and Cajetan.* Translated by Jean T. Oesterle. Milwaukee, Wis.: Marquette University Press, 1962.]

Compendium theologiae. Vol. 42 of *Opera omnia.* Rome: Typographia polyglotta, 1979, 83–191. [English translation: *Aquinas's Shorter Summa: St. Thomas's Own Concise Version of His Summa Theologica.* Translated by Cyril Vollert. Manchester, N.H.: Sophia Institute Press, 2002.]

De ente et essentia. Vol. 43 of *Opera omnia.* Rome: Typographia polyglotta, 1976, 369–81. [English translation: *On Being and Essence.* In *Selected Writings of St. Thomas Aquinas.* Translated by Robert P. Goodwin. New York: Bobbs-Merrill Company, 1965, 29–67.]

De principiis naturae. Vol. 43 of *Opera omnia.* Rome: Typographia polyglotta, 1976, 39–47. [English translation: *The Principles of Nature.* In *Selected Writings of St. Thomas Aquinas.* Translated by Robert P. Goodwin. New York: Bobbs-Merrill, 1965, 7–28.]

Expositio et lectura super epistolas Pauli apostoli. 2 vols. Turin and Rome: Marietti, 1953.

Expositio super Iob ad litteram. Vol. 26 of *Opera omnia.* Rome: Typographia polyglotta, 1965. [English translation: *The Literal Exposition on Job: A Scriptural Commentary Concerning Providence.* Translated by Anthony Damico. Atlanta, Ga.: Scholars Press, 1989.]

Expositio super librum Boethii De Trinitate. Edited by B. Oecker. Leiden: E. J. Brill, 1959. [English translation of Questions 5–6: *The Division and Method of the Sciences.* Translated by Armand Maurer. Toronto: Pontifical Institute of Mediaeval Studies, 1963.]

Expositio super symbolo apostolorum. Vol. 4 of *Opuscula omnia.* Edited by P. Mandonnet. Paris: Lethielleux, 1927.

In Aristotelis librum De anima commentarium. Vol. 45/1 of *Opera omnia.* Rome: Typographia polyglotta, 1984. [English translation: *Commentary on Aristotle's De Anima in the Version of William of Moerbeke and the Commentary of St. Thomas Aquinas.*

Translated by Kenelm Foster and Silvester Humphries. London: Routledge and Kegan Paul, 1951.]

In librum beati Dionysii De divinis nominibus expositio. Turin and Rome: Marietti, 1950.

In Metaphysicam Aristotelis commentaria. Turin and Rome: Marietti, 1926. [English translation: *Commentary on the Metaphysics of Aristotle.* 2 vols. Translated by John Rowan. Chicago: Regnery Press, 1961.]

In octo libros Physicorum Aristotelis expositio. Turin and Rome: Marietti, 1965. [English translation: *Commentary on Aristotle's Physics.* Translated by Richard Blackwell, Richard J. Spath, and W. Edmund Thirlkel. New Haven, Conn.: Yale University Press, 1963.]

Quaestio disputata de anima. Edited by J. Robb. Toronto: Pontifical Institute of Mediaeval Studies, 1968. [English translation: *Questions on the Soul.* Translated by James H. Robb. Milwaukee, Wis.: Marquette University Press, 1984.]

Quaestio disputata de spiritualibus creaturis. Edited by L. Keeler. Rome: Università Gregoriannae, 1937.

Quaestiones disputatae de malo. Vol. 23 of *Opera omnia.* Rome: Typographia polyglotta, 1982. [English translation: *On Evil.* Translated by John A. Oesterle and Jean T. Oesterle. South Bend, Ind.: University of Notre Dame Press, 1995.]

Quaestiones disputatae de potentia. Turin and Rome: Marietti, 1965. [English translation: *On the Power of God.* Translated by the English Dominican Fathers. Westminster, Md.: Newman Press, 1952.]

Quaestiones disputatae de veritate. Vol. 22/1–3 of *Opera omnia.* Rome: Typographia polyglotta, 1972–1976. [English translation: *Truth.* 3 vols. Translated by R. Mulligan et al. Chicago: Regnery Press, 1952–54.]

Quaestiones quodlibetales. Turin and Rome: Marietti, 1949.

Responsio ad magistrum Ioannem de Vercellis de 43 articulis in *Opuscula theologica* (Turin and Rome: Marietti, 1954), 1.211–18.

Scriptum super libros Sententiarum. Edited by S. E. Fretté and P. Maré. Vols. 7–11 of *Opera omnia.* Paris: Vivès, 1882–1889.

Summa contra gentiles. 3 vols. Turin and Rome: Marietti, 1961. [English translation: *On the Truth of the Catholic Faith: Summa Contra Gentiles.* 4 vols. Translated by Anton C. Pegis et al. Garden City, N.Y.: Image Books, 1955–1957.]

Summa theologiae. Rome: Editiones Paulinae, 1962. [English translation: *Summa Theologica.* 3 vols. Translated by the Fathers of the English Dominican Province. New York: Benziger Bros., 1946.]

Super evangelium S. Matthaei lectura. Turin and Rome: Marietti, 1951.

Super librum De causis expositio. Edited by H. D. Saffrey. Fribourg-Louvain: Société Philosophique, 1954. [English translation: *Commentary on the Book of Causes.* Translated by Vincent A. Guagliardo, Charles R. Hess, and Richard C. Taylor. Washington, D.C.: The Catholic University of America Press, 1996.]

GENERAL BIBLIOGRAPHY

Albertson, James S. "Instrumental Causality in St. Thomas." *New Scholasticism* 38 (1954): 409–35.

Alexander, Samuel. *Space, Time, and Deity: The Gifford Lectures, 1916–1918*. 2 vols. London: Macmillan and Co., 1920.

Allen, Paul L. *Ernan McMullin and Critical Realism in the Science-Theology Dialogue*. Burlington, Vt.: Ashgate, 2006.

Alston, William P. "Divine Action: Shadow or Substance?" In *The God Who Acts: Philosophical and Theological Explorations*, edited by Thomas F. Tracy, 41–63. University Park: Pennsylvania State University Press, 1994.

The American Heritage Dictionary of the English Language: Fourth Edition. New York: Houghton Mifflin Company, 2000.

Appleyard, Bryan. *Understanding the Present: Science and the Soul of Modern Man*. New York: Doubleday, 1992.

Aristotle, *Categories*. In *The Basic Works of Aristotle*. Edited by Richard McKeon. New York: Random House, 1941.

———. *Metaphysics*. In *The Basic Works of Aristotle*. Edited by Richard McKeon. New York: Random House, 1941.

———. *On Generation and Corruption*. In *The Basic Works of Aristotle*. Edited by Richard McKeon. New York: Random House, 1941.

———. *On the Parts of Animals*. In *The Basic Works of Aristotle*. Edited by Richard McKeon. New York: Random House, 1941.

———. *On the Soul*. In *The Basic Works of Aristotle*. Edited by Richard McKeon. New York: Random House, 1941.

———. *Physics*. In *The Basic Works of Aristotle*. Edited by Richard McKeon. New York: Random House, 1941.

Artigas, Mariano. *The Mind of the Universe: Understanding Science and Religion*. Philadelphia: Templeton Foundation Press, 2000.

Ashley, Benedict. "Causality and Evolution." *Thomist* 36 (1972): 199–230.

Augros, Robert M. "Nature Acts for an End." *Thomist* 66 (2002): 535–75.

Auletta, Gennaro. "Science, Philosophy and Religion Today: Some Reflections." *Theology and Science* 5 (2007): 267–87.

Austriaco, Nicanor Pier Giorgio. "The Intelligibility of Intelligent Design." *Angelicum* 86 (2009): 103–11.

Ayala, Francisco J. "The Autonomy of Biology as a Natural Science." In *Biology, History, and Natural Philosophy*, edited by Allen D. Breck and Wolfgang Yourgrau, 1–16. New York: Plenum Press, 1972.

———. "Darwin's Devolution: Design without Designer." In *Evolutionary and Molecular Biology: Scientific Perspectives on Divine Action*, edited by Robert John Russell, William Stoeger and Francisco Ayala, 101–16. Vatican City State: Vatican Observatory; Berkeley, Calif.: Center for Theology and the Natural Sciences, 1998.

———. "The Evolution of Life: An Overview." In *Evolutionary and Molecular Biology: Scientific Perspectives on Divine Action,* edited by Robert John Russell, William Stoeger, and Francisco Ayala, 21–57. Vatican City State: Vatican Observatory; Berkeley, Calif.: Center for Theology and the Natural Sciences, 1998.

———. "Teleological Explanations in Evolutionary Biology." In *Nature's Purposes: Analyses of Function and Design in Biology,* edited by Colin Allen, Marc Bekoff, and George Lauder, 29–49. Cambridge, Mass.: MIT Press, 1998.

———. "Intelligent Design: The Original Version." *Theology and Science* 1 (2003): 9–32.

———. *Darwin and Intelligent Design.* Minneapolis, Minn.: Fortress Press, 2006.

———. *Darwin's Gift to Science and Religion.* Washington, D.C.: Joseph Henry Press, 2007.

———. "From Paley to Darwin: Design to Natural Selection." In *Back to Darwin: A Richer Account of Evolution,* edited by John B. Cobb, 50–75. Grand Rapids, Mich.: Eerdmans, 2008.

———. "Reduction, Emergence, Naturalism, Dualism, Teleology: A Précis." In *Back to Darwin: A Richer Account of Evolution,* edited by John B. Cobb, 76–87. Grand Rapids, Mich.: Eerdmans, 2008.

Ayala, Francisco J., et al. *Science, Evolution, and Creationism.* Washington, D.C.: National Academies Press, 2008.

Bacon, Francis. *The New Organon.* In James Spedding, Robert Leslie Ellis, and Douglas Denon Heath, eds., *The Works of Francis Bacon,* 4.39–248. London: Longman and Co., 1858.

———. *Of the Dignity and Advancement of Learning.* In James Spedding, Robert Leslie Ellis, and Douglas Denon Heath, eds., *The Works of Francis Bacon,* 4.:275–498. London: Longman and Co., 1858.

———. *The Proficience and Advancement of Learning: Divine and Humane.* In James Spedding, Robert Leslie Ellis, and Douglas Denon Heath, eds., *The Works of Francis Bacon,* 3.259–491. London: Longman and Co., 1857.

Barbour, Ian G. *Religion in an Age of Science.* San Francisco: HarperSanFrancisco, 1990.

———. "God's Power: A Process View." In *The Work of Love: Creation as Kenosis,* edited by John Polkinghorne, 1–20. Grand Rapids, Mich.: Eerdmans, 2001.

———. *Nature, Human Nature, and God.* Minneapolis: Fortress Press, 2002.

———. "Indeterminacy, Holism, and God's Action." In *God's Action in Nature's World: Essays in Honor of Robert John Russell,* edited by Ted Peters and Nathan Hallanger, 113–25. Aldershot, U.K.: Ashgate, 2006.

Barrow, John D., and Frank J. Tipler. *The Anthropic Cosmological Principle.* Oxford: Oxford University Press, 1986.

Bartholomew, David J. *God of Chance.* London: SCM Press, 1984.

———. *God, Chance and Purpose: Can God Have It Both Ways?* New York: Cambridge University Press, 2008.

Behe, Michael J. "Darwin's Breakdown: Irreducible Complexity and Design at the Foundation of Life." *Touchstone: A Journal of Mere Christianity* 12, no. 4 (1999): 39–43.
———. "Evidence for Design at the Foundation of Life." In *Science and Evidence for Design in the Universe*, edited by Michael J. Behe, William A. Dembski, and Stephen C. Meyer, 113–49. San Francisco: Ignatius Press, 2000.
———. "The Modern Intelligent Design Hypothesis: Breaking Rules." In *God and Design: The Teleological Argument and Modern Science*, edited by Neil A. Manson, 277–91. London: Routledge, 2003.
———. *Darwin's Black Box: The Biochemical Challenge to Evolution*. New York: Free Press, 2006.
———. *The Edge of Evolution: The Search for the Limits of Darwinism*, New York: Free Press, 2007.
Bielfeldt, Dennis. "Nancey Murphy's Nonreductive Physicalism." *Zygon* 34 (1999): 619–28.
———. "Can Western Monotheism Avoid Substance Dualism?" *Zygon* 36 (2001): 153–77.
Bobik, Joseph. *Aquinas on Matter and Form and the Elements*. South Bend, Ind.: University of Notre Dame Press, 1997.
———. *Veritas Divina: Aquinas on Divine Truth: Some Philosophy of Religion*. South Bend, Ind.: St. Augustine's Press, 2001.
Boeri, Marcelo D. "Chance and Teleology in Aristotle's Physics." *International Philosophical Quarterly* 35 (1995): 87–96.
Bohm, David. *Causality and Chance in Modern Physics*. Philadelphia: University of Pennsylvania Press, 1971.
Boland, Vivian. *Ideas in God according to Saint Thomas Aquinas: Sources and Synthesis*. Leiden: Brill, 1996.
Booth, Edward. "The Dialogue of Metaphysics and Religion with Natural Science: Continental Examples." *New Blackfriars* 83 (2002): 160–72.
Boyd, Craig A., and Aaron D. Cobb. "The Causality Distinction, Kenosis, and a Middle Way: Aquinas and Polkinghorne on Divine Action." *Theology and Science* 7 (2009): 391–406.
Brecha, Robert J. "Schrödinger's Cat and Divine Action: Some Comments on the Use of Quantum Uncertainty to Allow for God's Action in the World." *Zygon* 37 (2002): 909–24.
Brierley, Michael W. "The Potential of Panentheism for Dialogue between Science and Religion." In *The Oxford Handbook of Religion and Science*, edited by Philip Clayton and Zachary Simpson, 635–51. Oxford: Oxford University Press, 2006.
Brisson, Luc. "Plato's Natural Philosophy and Metaphysics." In *A Companion to Ancient Philosophy*, edited by Mary Louise Gill and Pierre Pellegrin, 212–31. Malden, Mass.: Blackwell, 2006.

Brooke, John Hedley. *Science and Religion: Some Historical Perspectives.* Cambridge: Cambridge University Press, 1991.

———. "Einstein, God, and Time." *Zygon* 41 (2006): 941–54.

Brümmer, Vincent. "Farrer, Wiles, and the Causal Joint." *Modern Theology* 8 (1992): 1–14.

Bultmann, Rudolf. *Jesus Christ and Mythology.* New York: Charles Scribner's Sons, 1958.

———. "Bultmann Replies to His Critics." In *Kerygma and Myth: A Theological Debate,* edited by Hans Werner Bartsch and translated by Reginald H. Fuller, 191–211. New York: Harper and Row, 1961.

———. "New Testament and Mythology." In *Kerygma and Myth: A Theological Debate,* edited by Hans Werner Bartsch and translated by Reginald H. Fuller, 1–44. New York: Harper and Row, 1961.

Bunge, Mario. "Survey of the Interpretations of Quantum Mechanics." *American Journal of Physics* 24 (1956): 272–86.

———. *Causality and Modern Science.* New York: Dover Publications, 1979.

———. *Chasing Reality: Strife over Realism.* Toronto: University of Toronto, 2006.

Burrell, David B. *Analogy and Philosophical Language.* New Haven, Conn.: Yale University Press, 1973.

———. *Freedom and Creation in Three Traditions.* South Bend, Ind.: University of Notre Dame Press, 1993.

———. "Divine Action and Human Freedom in the Context of Creation." In *The God Who Acts: Philosophical and Theological Explorations,* edited by Thomas F. Tracy, 103–9. University Park: Pennsylvania State University Press, 1994.

———. "Aquinas and Islamic and Jewish Thinkers." In *The Cambridge Companion to Aquinas,* edited by Norman Kretzmann and Eleonore Stump, 60–84. Cambridge: Cambridge University Press, 1999.

———. "Analogy, Creation, and Theological Language." *Proceedings of the American Catholic Philosophical Association* 74 (2000): 35–52.

———. "Creator/Creatures Relation: 'The Distinction' vs. 'Onto-theology.'" *Faith and Philosophy* 25 (2008): 177–89.

———. *Deconstructing Theodicy: Why Job Has Nothing to Say to the Puzzle of Suffering.* Grand Rapids, Mich.: Baker Academic, 2008.

Burtt, Edwin A. *The Metaphysical Foundations of Modern Physical Science.* Garden City, N.Y.: Doubleday, 1954.

Carr, Bernard. "Cosmology and Religion." In *The Oxford Handbook of Religion and Science,* edited by Philip Clayton and Zachary Simpson, 139–55. Oxford: Oxford University Press, 2006.

Carroll, William E. "Galileo, Science, and the Bible." *Acta Philosophica* 6, no. 1 (1997): 5–37.

———. "Aquinas on Creation and the Metaphysical Foundations of Science." *Sapientia* 54 (1999): 69–91.

———. "Thomas Aquinas, Creation, and Big Bang Cosmology." In *Science and Theology: Ruminations on the Cosmos,* edited by Chris Impey and Catherine Petry, 1–18. Vatican City State: Vatican Observatory, 2003.

———. *Galileo: Science and Faith.* London: Catholic Truth Society, 2009.

———. "Creation and the Foundations of Evolution." *Angelicum* 87 (2010): 45–60.

Carter, Brandon. "Large Number Coincidences and the Anthropic Principle in Cosmology." In *Confrontation of Cosmological Theories with Observational Data: Symposium no. 63 (Copernicus Symposium II) held in Cracow, Poland, 10–12 September, 1973,* edited by M. S. Longair, 291–98. Boston: D. Reidel,1974.

Charlton, William. "Appendix: Did Aristotle Believe in Prime Matter?" In *Aristotle's Physics, Books I–II.* Edited by William Charlton, 129–45. Oxford: Clarendon Press, 1970.

Chesterton, G. K. *Saint Thomas Aquinas: The Dumb Ox.* Garden City, N.Y.: Doubleday, 1960.

Clarke, William Norris. "The Limitation of Act by Potency: Aristotelianism or Neoplatonism?" *New Scholasticism* 26 (1952): 167–94.

———. "Is a Natural Theology Still Possible Today?" In *Physics, Philosophy, and Theology: A Common Quest for Understanding,* edited by Robert J. Russell, William R. Stoeger, and George V. Coyne, 103–23. Vatican City State: Vatican Observatory; Berkeley, Calif.: Center for Theology and the Natural Sciences, 1988.

———. *The One and the Many: A Contemporary Thomistic Metaphysics.* South Bend, Ind.: University of Notre Dame Press, 2001.

Clayton, Philip. *God and Contemporary Science.* Edinburgh: Edinburgh University Press, 1997.

———. "The Impossible Possibility: Divine Causes in the World of Nature." In *God, Life, and the Cosmos,* edited by Ted Peters, Muzaffar Iqbal, and Syed Nomanul Haq, 249–80. Aldershot, U.K.: Ashgate, 2002.

———. *Mind and Emergence: From Quantum to Consciousness.* Oxford: Oxford University Press, 2004.

———. "Natural Law and Divine Action: The Search for an Expanded Theory of Causation." *Zygon* 39 (2004.): 615–36.

———. "Panentheism in Metaphysical and Scientific Perspective." In *In Whom We Live and Move and Have Our Being: Panentheistic Reflections on God's Presence in a Scientific World,* edited by Philip Clayton and Arthur Peacocke, 73–91. Grand Rapids, Mich.: Eerdmans, 2004.

———. "Conceptual Foundations of Emergence Theory." In *The Re-Emergence of Emergence: The Emergentist Hypothesis from Science to Religion,* edited by Philip Clayton and Paul Davies, 1–31. New York: Oxford University Press, 2006.

———. "Emergence from Physics to Theology: Towards a Panoramic View." *Zygon* 41 (2006): 675–87.

———. "The Emergence of Spirit: From Complexity to Anthropology to Theology." *Theology and Science* 4 (2006): 291–307.

———. *Adventures in the Spirit: God, World, Divine Action*, edited by Zachary Simpson. Philadelphia: Fortress Press, 2008.

———. "Toward a Theory of Divine Action That Has Traction." In *Scientific Perspectives on Divine Action: Twenty Years of Challenge and Progress*, edited by Robert John Russell, Nancey Murphy, and William R. Stoeger, 85–110. Vatican City State: Vatican Observatory; Berkeley, Calif.: Center for Theology and the Natural Sciences, 2008.

Cobb, John B. *A Christian Natural Theology.* Philadelphia: Westminster Press, 1965.

———. "Natural Causality and Divine Action." In *God's Activity in the World: The Contemporary Problem*, edited by Owen C. Thomas, 101–16. Chico, Calif.: Scholars Press, 1983.

Code, Alan. "The Priority of Final Causes over Efficient Causes in Aristotle's *Parts of Animals.*" In *Aristotelische Biologie: Intentionen, Methoden, Ergebnisse*, edited by Wolfgang Kullmann and Sabine Föllinger, 127–43. Stuttgart: Franz Steiner, 1997.

Cohen, Sheldon M. *Aristotle on Nature and Incomplete Substance.* Cambridge: Cambridge University Press, 1996.

Collins, James. *God in Modern Philosophy.* Chicago: Henry Regnery, 1959.

Collins, John. "Science and the Denial of the Miraculous: Another Look." *Perspectives in Religious Studies* 10 (1983): 123–33.

Collins, Robin. "Evidence for Fine-Tuning." In *God and Design: The Teleological Argument and Modern Science*, edited by Neil A. Manson, 178–99. London: Routledge, 2003.

Connell, Richard. *Substance and Modern Science.* Houston: Center for Thomistic Studies, 1988.

Cooper, John W. *Panentheism: The Other God of the Philosophers: From Plato to the Present.* Grand Rapids, Mich.: Baker Books, 2006.

Copleston, Frederick. *A History of Philosophy.* 9 vols. Garden City, N.Y.: Doubleday, 1985.

Coveney, Peter, and Roger Highfield. *Frontiers of Complexity: The Search for Order in a Chaotic World.* New York: Fawcett Columbine, 1995.

Craig, William Lane. *God, Time, and Eternity.* Dordrecht, The Netherlands: Kluwer, 2001.

———. "Design and the Anthropic Fine-Tuning of the Universe." In *God and Design: The Teleological Argument and Modern Science*, edited by Neil A. Manson, 155–77. London: Routledge, 2003.

Crain, Steven Dale. "Divine Action in a World of Chaos." *Faith and Philosophy* 14 (1997): 41–61.

Cross, Frank Leslie, and Elizabeth A. Livingstone, eds. *The Oxford Dictionary of the Christian Church.* 3rd ed. rev. Oxford: Oxford University Press, 2005.

Dalferth, Ingolf U. "The Historical Roots of Theism." In *Traditional Theism and Its Modern Alternatives*, edited by Svend Andersen, 15–43. Aarhus: Aarhus University Press, 1994.

Darwin, Charles. *The Autobiography of Charles Darwin*. Edited by Nora Barlow. New York: Norton, 1958.

———. *The Foundations of the Origin of Species. Two Essays Written in 1842 and 1844 by Charles Darwin*. Edited by Francis Darwin. Cambridge: Cambridge University Press, 1909.

———. *The Life and Letters of Charles Darwin*. 2 vols. Edited by Francis Darwin. New York: D. Appleton and Co., 1897.

———. *More Letters of Charles Darwin: A Record of His Work in a Series of Hitherto Unpublished Letters*. 2 vols. Edited by Francis Darwin and A. C. Seward. New York: D. Appleton and Co., 1903.

———. "Notebook N [1838–1839]." In *Charles Darwin's Notebooks, 1836–1844: Geology, Transmutation of Species, Metaphysical Enquiries, by Charles Darwin*, edited by Paul H. Barrett, Peter J. Gautrey, Sandra Herbert, David Kohn, and Sydney Smith, 561–96. Ithaca, N.Y.: Cornell University Press, 1987.

———. *The Origin of Species*. New York: Modern Library, 1998.

Davies, Brian. *The Thought of Thomas Aquinas*. New York: Oxford University Press, 1992.

———. *An Introduction to the Philosophy of Religion*. Oxford: Oxford University Press, 1993.

———. "God and Evil: A Dialogue." *New Blackfriars* 85 (2004): 270–89.

———. *The Reality of God and the Problem of Evil*. New York: Continuum, 2006.

Davies, Paul. *God and the New Physics*. New York: Simon and Schuster, 1983.

———. "Teleology without Teleology: Purpose through Emergent Complexity." In *Evolutionary and Molecular Biology: Scientific Perspectives on Divine Action*, edited by Robert John Russell, Willliam R. Stoeger, and Francisco J. Ayala, 151–62. Vatican City State: Vatican Observatory; Berkeley, Calif.: Center for Theology and the Natural Sciences, 1998.

———. "The Physics of Downward Causation." In *The Re-Emergence of Emergence: The Emergentist Hypothesis from Science to Religion*, edited by Philip Clayton and Paul Davies, 35–52. New York: Oxford University Press, 2006.

Dawkins, Richard. *The Blind Watchmaker: Why the Evidence of Evolution Reveals a Universe without Design*. New York: Norton, 1996.

———. *Climbing Mount Improbable*. New York: Norton, 1996.

———. *The God Delusion*. New York: Houghton Mifflin, 2006.

Deacon, Terrence W. D. "Response [to Philip Clayton]." *CTNS Bulletin* 20, no. 4 (2000): 26–27.

———. "Emergence: The Hole at the Wheel's Hub." In *The Re-emergence of Emergence: The Emergentist Hypothesis from Science to Religion*, edited by Philip Clayton and Paul Davies, 111–50. New York: Oxford University Press, 2006.

Decaen, Christopher. "Elemental Virtual Presence in St. Thomas." *Thomist* 64 (2000): 271–300.

de Duve, Christian. *Blueprint for a Cell: The Nature and Origin of Life*. Burlington, N.C.: Neil Patterson, 1991.

———. *Vital Dust: Life as a Cosmic Imperative*. New York: BasicBooks, 1998.

———. *Life Evolving: Molecules, Mind, and Meaning*. New York: Oxford University Press, 2002.

Deely, John. "The Philosophical Dimensions of the Origin of Species." *Thomist* 20 (1969): 75–149, 251–342.

De Koninck, Charles. "Thomism and Scientific Indeterminacy." *Proceedings of the American Catholic Philosophical Association* 12 (1936): 58–76.

———. "Réflexions sur le problème de l'indéterminisme." *Revue Thomiste* 43 (1937): 227–52.

———. *The Hollow Universe*. London: Oxford University Press, 1960.

Dembski, William A. *The Design Inference: Eliminating Chance through Small Probabilities*. New York: Cambridge University Press, 1998.

———. *Intelligent Design: The Bridge between Science and Theology*. Downers Grove, Ill.: InterVarsity, 1999.

———. "Signs of Intelligence: A Primer on the Discernment of Intelligent Design." *Touchstone: A Journal of Mere Christianity* 12, no. 4 (1999): 76–84.

———. "Introduction: What Intelligent Design Is Not." In *Signs of Intelligence: Understanding Intelligent Design*, edited by William A. Dembski and James M. Kushiner, 7–23. Grand Rapids, Mich.: Brazos Press, 2001.

———. *No Free Lunch: Why Specified Complexity Cannot Be Purchased without Intelligence*. Lanham, Md.: Rowman and Littlefield, 2002.

———. *The Design Revolution: Answering the Toughest Questions about Intelligent Design*. Downers Grove, Ill.: InterVarsity Press, 2004.

———. "In Defense of Intelligent Design." In *The Oxford Handbook of Religion and Science*, edited by Philip Clayton and Zachary Simpson, 715–31. Oxford: Oxford University Press, 2006.

Denton, Michael J. *Evolution: A Theory in Crisis*. Bethseda, Md.: Adler and Adler, 1986.

———. *Nature's Destiny: How the Laws of Biology Reveal Purpose in the Universe*. New York: Free Press, 1998.

Descartes, René. *Discourse on Method*. In *Discourse on Method and Meditations*. Translated by Laurence J. Lafleur. New York: Bobbs Merrill, 1977.

DeSchrijver, Georges. "Religion and Cosmology at the End of the 20th Century." *CTNS Bulletin* 14, no. 1 (1994): 1–15.

Desmond, Adrian, and James Moore. *Darwin*. New York: Warner Books, 1992.

Dewan, Lawrence. "St. Thomas and the Distinction between Form and Esse in Caused Things." *Gregorianum* 80 (1999): 353–70.

———. "Faith and Reason from St. Thomas Aquinas's Perspective." *Science et Esprit* 58, no. 2 (2006): 113–23.

———. "Saint Thomas and the Principle of Causality." In *Form and Being: Studies in*

Thomistic Metaphysics, by Lawrence Dewan, 61–80. Washington, D.C.: The Catholic University of America Press, 2006.

———. *St. Thomas and Form as Something Divine in Things*. Milwaukee: Marquette University Press, 2007.

Dickson, William Michael. *Quantum Chance and Non-locality: Probability and Non-locality in the Interpretations of Quantum Mechanics*. New York: Cambridge University Press, 1998.

Dilley, Frank B. "Does the 'God Who Acts' Really Act?" In *God's Activity in the World: The Contemporary Problem*, edited by Owen C. Thomas, 45–60. Chico, Calif.: Scholars Press, 1983.

Dirac, Paul Adrien Maurice. "The Physicist's Picture of Nature." *Scientific American* 208, no. 5 (1963): 45–53.

The Documents of Vatican II. Edited by Austin P. Flannery. New York: Pillar Books, 1975.

Dodds, Michael J. "Thomas Aquinas, Human Suffering, and the Unchanging God of Love." *Theological Studies* 52 (1991): 330–44.

———. "Ultimacy and Intimacy: Aquinas on the Relation between God and the World." In *Ordo Sapientiae et Amoris: Hommage au Professeur Jean-Pierre Torrell, O.P.*, edited by Carlos-Josaphat Pinto de Oliveira, 211–27. Fribourg, Switzerland: Editions Universitaires, 1993.

———. "Science, Causality, and Divine Action: Classical Principles for Contemporary Challenges." *CTNS Bulletin* 21, no. 1 (2001): 3–12.

———. *The Unchanging God of Love: Thomas Aquinas and Contemporary Theology on Divine Immutability*. Washington, D.C.: The Catholic University of America Press, 2008.

———. "Hylomorphism and Human Wholeness: Perspectives on the Mind-Brain Problem." *Theology and Science* 7 (2009): 141–62.

———. "Unlocking Divine Causality: Aquinas, Contemporary Science, and Divine Action." *Angelicum* 86 (2009): 67–86.

Donceel, Joseph. "Causality and Evolution: A Survey of Some Neo-Scholastic Theories." *New Scholasticism* 39 (1965): 295–315.

Doolan, Gregory T. "The Causality of the Divine Ideas in Relation to Natural Agents in Thomas Aquinas." *International Philosophical Quarterly* 44 (2004): 393–409.

———. *Aquinas on the Divine Ideas as Exemplar Causes*. Washington, D.C.: The Catholic University of America Press, 2008.

Doran, Chris. "Implicit Presuppositions Made Explicit: A Critical Appraisal of the Theology of Intelligent Design as Found in the Work of William Dembski." Ph.D. diss., Graduate Theological Union, Berkeley, Calif., 2007.

———. "Intelligent Design: It's Just Too Good to be True." *Theology and Science* 8 (2010): 223–37.

Dowd, Sharon. "Is Whitehead's God the 'God Who Acts'?" *Perspectives in Religious Studies* 9 (1982): 157–70.

Drees, Willem B. *Beyond the Big Bang: Quantum Cosmologies and God*. LaSalle, Ill.: Open Court, 1990.

———. "Gaps for God?" In *Chaos and Complexity: Scientific Perspectives on Divine Action*, edited by Robert John Russell, Nancey Murphy, and Arthur R. Peacocke, 223–37. Vatican City State: Vatican Observatory; Berkeley, Calif.: Center for Theology and the Natural Sciences, 1995.

Dubarle, Dominique. "Causalité et finalité chez saint Thomas et au niveau des sciences modernes de la nature." In *Il cosmo e la scienza*, edited by D. Dubarle, W. Wallace, J. Meurers, et al. Atti del congresso internazionale Tommaso d'Aquino nel suo settimo centenario, no. 9, 9–25. Naples: Edizioni Domenicane Italiane, 1975.

Dulles, Avery. "God and Evolution." *First Things* 176 (2007): 19–24.

Dupré, John. "It Is Not Possible to Reduce Biological Explanations to Explanations in Chemistry and/or Physics." In *Contemporary Debates in Philosophy of Biology*, edited by Francisco J. Ayala and Robert Arp, 32–47. Chichester, U.K.: Wiley-Blackwell, 2010.

Ecklund, Elaine Howard. *Science vs. Religion: What Scientists Really Think*. New York: Oxford University Press, 2010.

Eddington, Arthur Stanley. *The Nature of the Physical World*. New York: Macmillan, 1929.

———. *The Philosophy of Physical Science*. New York: Macmillan, 1939.

Edwards, Denis. *How God Acts: Creation, Redemption, and Special Divine Action*. Minneapolis: Fortress Press, 2010.

Einstein, Albert. *Out of My Later Years*. New York: Wisdom Library, 1950.

———. *Ideas and Opinions*. Translated by Sonja Bargmann. New York: Bonanza Books, 1954.

Elders, Leo J. "The Philosophical and Religious Background of Charles Darwin's Theory of Evolution." *Doctor Communis* 37 (1984): 32–67.

———. *The Metaphysics of Being of St. Thomas Aquinas in a Historical Perspective*. New York: Brill, 1993.

El-Hani, Charbel Niño, and Antonio Marcos Pereira. "Higher-Level Descriptions: Why Should We Preserve Them?" In *Downward Causation: Minds, Bodies and Matter*, edited by Peter Bogh Andersen, Claus Emmeche, Niels Ole Finnemann, and Peder Voetmann Christiansen, 118–42. Aarhus: Aarhus University Press, 2000.

Ellis, George F. R. *Before the Beginning: Cosmology Explained*. New York: Boyars/Bowerdean, 1993.

———. "The Theology of the Anthropic Principle." In *Quantum Cosmology and the Laws of Nature: Scientific Perspectives on Divine Action*, edited by Robert John Russell, Nancey Murphy, and C. J. Isham, 367–405. Vatican City State: Vatican Observatory; Berkeley, Calif.: Center for Theology and the Natural Sciences, 1993.

———. "Physics, Complexity, and the Science-Religion Debate." In *The Oxford*

Handbook of Religion and Science, edited by Philip Clayton and Zachary Simpson, 751–66. Oxford: Oxford University Press, 2006.

———. "Science, Complexity, and the Natures of Existence." In *Evolution and Emergence: Systems, Organisms, Persons,* edited by Nancey Murphy and William R. Stoeger, 113–40. New York: Oxford University Press, 2007.

Ellis, Robert Anthony. "Can God Act in History? A Whiteheadian Perspective." Ph.D. diss., University of Oxford, 1984.

Emery, Gilles. *Trinity in Aquinas.* Ypsilanti, Mich.: Sapientia Press, 2002.

———. "The Personal Mode of Trinitarian Action in Saint Thomas Aquinas," *Thomist* 69 (2005): 31–77.

———. *The Trinitarian Theology of Saint Thomas Aquinas.* New York: Oxford University Press, 2007.

———. "The Immutability of the God of Love and the Problem of Language Concerning the 'Suffering of God.'" In *Divine Impassibility and the Mystery of Human Suffering,* edited by James F. Keating and Thomas Joseph White, 27–76. Grand Rapids, Mich.: Eerdmans, 2009.

Erbrich, Paul. "The Problem of Creation and Evolution." In *Creation and Evolution: A Conference with Pope Benedict XVI in Castel Gandolfo,* edited by Stephan Otto Horn and Sigfried Wiedenhofer, 70–83. San Francisco: Ignatius Press, 2008.

Farrer, Austin. *Faith and Speculation.* Edinburgh: T. & T. Clark, 1988.

Feynman, Richard P. *The Character of Physical Law.* Cambridge, Mass.: M.I.T. Press, 1987.

Fiddes, Paul S. *The Creative Suffering of God.* Oxford: Clarendon Press, 1988.

———. "Creation Out of Love." In *The Work of Love: Creation as Kenosis,* edited by John Polkinghorne, 167–91. Grand Rapids, Mich.: Eerdmans, 2001.

Finance, Joseph de. *Etre et agir dans la philosophie de saint Thomas.* Rome: Presses de l'Université Grégorienne, 1965.

Fine, Arthur. *The Shaky Game: Einstein, Realism and the Quantum Theory.* Chicago: University of Chicago Press, 1997.

Ford, Lewis S. *The Lure of God: A Biblical Background for Process Theism.* Philadelphia: Fortress Press, 1978.

Frank, Patrick. "On the Assumption of Design." *Theology and Science* 2 (2004): 109–30.

Freddoso, Alfred. "God's General Concurrence with Secondary Causes: Why Conservation Is Not Enough." *Philosophical Perspectives* 5 (1991): 553–85.

———. "God's General Concurrence with Secondary Causes: Pitfalls and Prospects." *American Catholic Philosophical Quarterly* 68 (1994): 131–56.

Galileo Galilei. *The Assayer.* In *Discoveries and Opinions of Galileo.* Translated by Stillman Drake, 231–80. Garden City, N.Y.: Doubleday, 1957.

———. *Letter to the Grand Duchess Christina.* In *Discoveries and Opinions of Galileo.* Translated by Stillman Drake, 173–216. Garden City, N.Y.: Doubleday, 1957.

García-Rivera, Alejandro. "Endless Forms Most Beautiful." *Theology and Science* 5 (2007): 125–35.

———. *The Garden of God: A Theological Cosmology.* Minneapolis, Minn.: Fortress Press, 2009.

George, Marie I. "On the Tenth Anniversary of Barrow and Tipler's Anthropic Cosmological Principle: Thomistic Reflections on Anthropic Principles." *American Catholic Philosophical Quarterly* 72 (1998): 39–58.

Gilby, Thomas. "Appendix 6." In *Summa theologiae*, by Thomas Aquinas. Edited by Thomas Gilby, 67–87. New York: McGraw-Hill, 1964.

Gilkey, Langdon. *Reaping the Whirlwind: A Christian Interpretation of History.* New York: Seabury, 1976.

———. "Cosmology, Ontology and the Travail of Biblical Language." In *God's Activity in the World: The Contemporary Problem*, edited by Owen C. Thomas, 29–44. Chico, Calif.: Scholars Press, 1983.

Gill, Mary Louise. *Aristotle on Substance: The Paradox of Unity.* Princeton, N.J.: Princeton University Press, 1989.

Gilson, Etienne. *The Spirit of Medieval Philosophy.* New York: Scribner, 1936.

———. *The Christian Philosophy of St. Thomas Aquinas.* Translated by L. K. Shook. New York: Random House, 1956.

———. *From Aristotle to Darwin and Back Again: A Journey in Final Causality, Species and Evolution.* Translated by John Lyon. South Bend, Ind.: University of Notre Dame Press, 1984.

———. *Thomist Realism and the Critique of Knowledge.* Translated by Mark A. Wauck. San Francisco: Ignatius Press, 1986.

———. *Methodical Realism.* Translated by Philip Trower. Front Royal, Va.: Christendom Press, 1990.

Gilson, Etienne, and Jacques Maritain. *Deux approches de l'être: Correspondance 1923–1971.* Edited by Géry Prouvost. Paris: Vrin, 1991.

Gingerich, Owen. "Let There Be Light: Modern Cosmogony and Biblical Creation." In *Is God a Creationist? The Religious Case against Creation-Science*, edited by Roland Mushat Frye, 119–37. New York: Charles Scribner's Sons, 1983.

———. *Space, Time, and Beyond: The Place of God in the Cosmos.* Valparaiso, Ind.: Valparaiso University Press, 1993.

———. "Dare a Scientist Believe in Design?" In *Science and Theology: Ruminations on the Cosmos*, edited by Chris Impey and Catherine Petry, 35–55. Vatican City State: Vatican Observatory, 2003.

Gleick, James. *Chaos: Making a New Science.* New York: Penguin Books, 1988.

———. "Chaos and Beyond." In *Chaos: the New Science*, edited by John Holte, 119–27. Saint Peter, Minn.: Gustavus Adolphus College, 1993.

Goodenough, Ursula, and Terrence W. Deacon. "From Biology to Consciousness to Morality." *Zygon* 38 (2003): 801–19.

Goris, Harm J. M. J. *Free Creatures of an Eternal God: Thomas Aquinas on God's Infallible Foreknowlege and Irresistible Will.* Leuven: Peeters, 1996.

Goyette, John. "Substantial Form and the Recovery of an Aristotelian Natural Science." *Thomist* 66 (2002): 519–33.

Granger, E. Herbert. "Aristotle and the Concept of Supervenience." *Southern Journal of Philosophy* 31 (1993): 161–78.

Graves, Mark. *Mind, Brain, and the Elusive Soul: Human Systems of Cognitive Science and Religion.* Aldershot, U.K.: Ashgate, 2008.

Green, Richard. *The Thwarting of Laplace's Demon: Arguments against the Mechanistic World-View.* New York: St. Martin's Press, 1995.

Greene, Brian. *The Elegant Universe: Superstrings, Hidden Dimensions and the Quest for the Ultimate Theory.* New York: Vintage Books, 1999.

Greene, John C. *Darwin and the Modern World View.* Baton Rouge: Louisiana State University Press, 1974.

Gregersen, Niels Henrik. "Providence in an Indeterministic World." *CTNS Bulletin* 14, no. 1 (1994): 16–31.

———. "Complexity: What Is at Stake for Religious Reflection." In *The Significance of Complexity: Approaching a Complex World through Science, Theology and the Humanities,* edited by Kees van Kooten Niekerk and Hans Buhl, 135–65. Aldershot, U.K.: Ashgate, 2004.

———. "Three Varieties of Panentheism." In *In Whom We Live and Move and Have Our Being: Panentheistic Reflections on God's Presence in a Scientific World,* edited by Philip Clayton and Arthur Peacocke, 19–35. Grand Rapids, Mich.: Eerdmans, 2004.

———. "The Complexification of Nature: Supplementing the Neo-Darwinian Paradigm?" *Theology and Science* 4 (2006): 5–31.

———. "Divine Action, Compatibilism, and Coherence Theory: A Response to Russell, Clayton, and Murphy." *Theology and Science* 4 (2006): 215–28.

———. "Emergence and Complexity." In *The Oxford Handbook of Religion and Science,* edited by Philip Clayton and Zachary Simpson, 767–83. Oxford: Oxford University Press, 2006.

———. "Special Divine Action and the Quilt of Laws: Why the Distinction between Special and General Divine Action Cannot Be Maintained." In *Scientific Perspectives on Divine Action: Twenty Years of Challenge and Progress,* edited by Robert John Russell, Nancey Murphy, and William R. Stoeger, 179–99. Vatican City State: Vatican Observatory; Berkeley, Calif.: Center for Theology and the Natural Sciences, 2008.

Grene, Marjorie, and David Depew. *The Philosophy of Biology: An Episodic History.* Cambridge: Cambridge University Press, 2004.

Griffin, David Ray. "Interpreting Science from the Standpoint of Whiteheadian Process Philosophy." In *The Oxford Handbook of Religion and Science,* edited by Philip Clayton and Zachary Simpson, 453–71. Oxford: Oxford University Press, 2006.

Grygiel, Wojciech P. "Quantum Mechanics: A Dialectical Approach to Reality." *Thomist* 65 (2001): 223–38.

Guagliardo, Vincent. "Nature and Miracle." *CTNS Bulletin* 10, no. 2 (1990): 17–20.
Gunter, A. Y. "Six Scientific Alternatives to Darwinism." In *Back to Darwin: A Richer Account of Evolution,* edited by John B. Cobb, 128–44. Grand Rapids, Mich.: Eerdmans, 2008.
Gutiérrez, Gustavo. *On Job: God-Talk and the Suffering of the Innocent.* Translated by Matthew J. O'Connell. Maryknoll, N.Y.: Orbis Books, 1987.
Gwynne, Paul. *Special Divine Action: Key Issues in the Contemporary Debate (1965–1995).* Rome: Pontificia Universita Gregoriana, 1996.
Halligan, Patrick. "The Environmental Policy of Saint Thomas Aquinas." *Environmental Law* 19 (1989): 767–806.
Harris, Errol E. *The Foundations of Metaphysics in Science.* London: George Allen and Unwin, 1965.
Haslanger, Sally. "Parts, Compounds, and Substantial Unity." In *Unity, Identity, and Explanation in Aristotle's Metaphysics,* 129–70. Oxford: Clarendon Press, 1994.
Haught, John F. *Science and Religion: From Conflict to Conversation.* New York: Paulist Press, 1995.
Hawking, Stephen. *A Brief History of Time: From the Big Bang to Black Holes.* New York: Bantam Books, 1988.
Hebblethwaite, Brian L. "Providence and Divine Action." *Religious Studies* 14 (1978): 223–36.
———. "Some Reflections on Predestination, Providence, and Divine Foreknowledge." *Religious Studies* 15 (1979): 433–48.
———. *Evil, Suffering, and Religion.* Rev. ed. London: SPCK, 2000.
Hebblethwaite, Brian, and Edward Henderson. "Introduction." In *Divine Action: Studies Inspired by the Philosophical Theology of Austin Farrer,* 1–20. Edinburgh: T & T Clark, 1990.
Heisenberg, Werner. "Über den anschaulichen Inhalt der quantentheoretischen Kinematik und Mechanik." *Zeitschrift für Physik* 43 (1927): 172–98.
———. *Physics and Philosophy.* New York: Harper and Brothers, 1958.
Herbert, Nick. *Quantum Reality: Beyond the New Physics.* Garden City, N.Y.: Doubleday, 1987.
Hess, Peter M. J. "Creation, Design and Evolution: Can Science Discover or Eliminate God?" *University of St. Thomas Journal of Law and Public Policy* 4, no. 1 (2010): 102–16.
Hess, Peter M. J., and Paul L. Allen. *Catholicism and Science.* Westport, Conn.: Greenwood Press, 2008.
Hewlett, Martinez. "Molecular Biology and Religion." In *The Oxford Handbook of Religion and Science,* edited by Philip Clayton and Zachary Simpson, 172–86. Oxford: Oxford University Press, 2006.
Hill, William J. "Two Gods of Love: Aquinas and Whitehead." *Listening* 14 (1979): 249–65.

———. "Does Divine Love Entail Suffering in God?" In *God and Temporality*, edited by Bowman L. Clarke and Eugene T. Long, 55–71. New York: Paragon House Publishers, 1984.

———. "The Implicate World: God's Oneness with Mankind as a Mediated Immediacy." In *Beyond Mechanism: The Universe in Recent Physics and Catholic Thought*, edited by David L. Schindler, 78–98. Lanham, Md.: University Press of America, 1986.

Hodgson, Peter E. "Presuppositions and Limits of Science." In *The Structure and Development of Science*, edited by Gerard Radnitzky and Gunnar Andersson, 133–47. Boston: D. Reidl, 1979.

———. "God's Action in the World: The Relevance of Quantum Mechanics." *Zygon* 35 (2000): 505–16.

———. *Science and Belief in the Nuclear Age*. Naples, Fla.: Sapientia Press, 2005.

———. *Theology and Modern Physics*. Aldershot, U.K.: Ashgate, 2005.

Holder, Rodney D. *God, the Multiverse, and Everything: Modern Cosmology and the Argument from Design*. Aldershot, U.K.: Ashgate, 2004.

Houghton, John. "What Happens When We Pray." *Science and Christian Belief* 7 (1995): 3–20.

Hoyle, Fred. *The Intelligent Universe*. New York: Holt, Rinehart, and Winston, 1984.

Hübner, Johannes. *Aristoteles über Getrenntheit und Ursächlichkeit: Der Begriff des eidos choriston*. Hamburg: Meiner, 2000.

Hume, David. *An Enquiry Concerning Human Understanding*. Chicago: Open Court, 1930.

———. *A Treatise of Human Nature*. Edited by L. A. Selby-Bigge. Oxford: Clarendon Press, 1960.

Hutten, Ernest Hirschlaff. *The Language of Modern Physics: An Introduction to the Philosophy of Science*. New York: Macmillan, 1956.

International Theological Commission. *Communion and Stewardship: Human Persons Created in the Image of God*. Vatican City: 2004. Available at http://www.vatican.va/roman_curia/congregations/cfaith/cti_documents/rc_con_cfaith_doc_20040723_communion-stewardship_en.html.

Jaki, Stanley L. "Chance or Reality: Interaction in Nature versus Measurement in Physics." In *Chance or Reality and Other Essays*, 1–23. Lanham, Md.: University Press of America, 1986.

———. *Chesterton: A Seer of Science*. Urbana: University of Illinois Press, 1986.

———. *Miracles and Physics*. Front Royal, Va.: Christendom Press, 1989.

———. *Means to Message: A Treatise on Truth*. Grand Rapids, Mich.: Eerdmans, 1999.

———. "The Demarcation Line between Science and Religion." *Angelicum* 87 (2010): 81–89.

Jeffreys, Derek. "The Soul Is Alive and Well: Non-reductive Physicalism and Emergent Mental Properties." *Theology and Science* 2 (2004): 205–25.

Jenkins, David E. *Anglicanism, Accident, and Providence*. Wilton, Conn.: Morehouse-Barlow Co., 1987.

Jenkins, John. *Knowledge and Faith in Thomas Aquinas.* Cambridge: Cambridge University Press, 1997.

Jenkins, Willis. "Biodiversity and Salvation: Thomistic Roots for Environmental Ethics." *Journal of Religion* 83 (2003): 401–20.

John Paul II, Pope. *Fides et Ratio: On the Relationship between Faith and Reason.* Encyclical letter. Washington, D.C.: United States Catholic Conference, 1998.

Johnson, Mark. "Did St. Thomas Attribute a Doctrine of Creation to Aristotle?" *New Scholasticism* 63 (1989): 129–55.

Jonas, Hans. *The Phenomenon of Life: Toward a Philosophical Biology.* New York: Harper and Row, 1966.

Jorissen, Hans. "Schöpfung und Heil: Theologiegeschichtliche Perspektiven zum Vorsehungsglauben nach Thomas von Aquin." In *Vorsehung und Handeln Gottes*, edited by Theodor Schneider and Lothar Ullrich, 94–108. Leipzig: St. Benno Verlag, 1988.

Journet, Charles. *The Meaning of Evil.* Translated by Michael Barry. New York: P. J. Kennedy, 1963.

Judy, Albert. "Avicenna's Metaphysics in the *Summa Contra Gentiles*." *Angelicum* 52 (1975): 340–84, 541–86; 53 (1976): 185–226.

Kaufman, Gordon D. *God the Problem.* Cambridge, Mass.: Harvard University Press, 1972.

Keck, John W. "The Natural Motion of Matter in Newtonian and Post-Newtonian Physics." *Thomist* 71 (2007): 529–54.

Kocher, Richard. *Herausgeforderter Vorsehungsglaube. Die Lehre von der Vorsehung im Horizont der gegenwärtigen Theologie.* St. Ottilien: EOS Verlag, 1993.

Konyndyk, Kenneth J. "Aquinas on Faith and Science." *Faith and Philosophy* 12 (1995): 3–21.

Kosso, Peter. *Appearance and Reality: An Introduction to the Philosophy of Physics.* New York: Oxford University Press, 1998.

Krempel, A. *La doctrine de la relation chez saint Thomas.* Paris: Librairie Philosophique J. Vrin, 1952.

Kreyche, Gerald. "Some Causes of the Elimination of Causality in Contemporary Science." *Thomist* 29 (1965): 60–78.

Kuhn, Thomas S. *The Structure of Scientific Revolutions.* Chicago: University of Chicago Press, 1970.

Kumar, Manjit. *Quantum: Einstein, Bohr, and the Great Debate about the Nature of Reality.* New York: W. W. Norton, 2009.

Landen, Laura L. "Of Forests and Trees, Wholes and Parts." *Proceedings of the American Catholic Philosophical Association* 69 (1995): 81–89.

Lang, Helen S. *The Order of Nature in Aristotle's Physics: Place and the Elements.* Cambridge: Cambridge University Press, 1998.

Langford, Michael. *Providence.* London: SCM Press, 1981.

Laplace, Pierre Simon de. *Philosophical Essay on Probabilities*. Translated by Frederick Wilson Truscott and Frederick Lincoln Emory. New York: John Wiley and Sons, 1902.

Larson, Edward J. *Evolution: The Remarkable History of a Scientific Theory*. New York: Modern Library, 2006.

Larson, Thomas. "Natural Motion in Inanimate Bodies." *Thomist* 71 (2007): 555–76.

Lash, Nicholas. "Where Does *The God Delusion* Come from?" *New Blackfriars* 88 (2007): 507–21.

Lauer, Rosemary. "The Notion of Efficient Cause in the 'Secunda Via.'" *Thomist* 38 (1974): 754–67.

Lennox, James G. *Aristotle's Philosophy of Biology: Studies in the Origins of Life Science*. Cambridge: Cambridge University Press, 2001.

Leslie, John. "Observership in Cosmology: The Anthropic Principle." *Mind* 92 (1983): 573–79.

———. "The Anthropic Principle Today." In *Final Causality in Nature and Human Affairs*, edited by Richard Hassing, 163–87. Washington, D.C.: The Catholic University of America Press, 1997.

Lewin, Roger. *Complexity: Life at the Edge of Chaos*. Chicago: University of Chicago Press, 1999.

Lewis, C. S. *Letters to Malcolm: Chiefly on Prayer*. New York: Harcourt Brace Jovanovich, 1964.

Linzey, Andrew. *Why Animal Suffering Matters: Philosophy, Theology, and Practical Ethics*. New York: Oxford University Press, 2009.

Lonergan, Bernard. *Grace and Freedom: Operative Grace in the Thought of St. Thomas Aquinas*. New York: Herder and Herder, 1971.

Losch, Andreas. "On the Origins of Critical Realism." *Theology and Science* 7 (2009): 85–106.

Luisi, Pier Luigi. "Emergence in Chemistry: Chemistry as the Embodiment of Emergence." *Foundations of Chemistry* 4 (2002): 183–200.

Luyten, Norbert A. "Matter as Potency." In *The Concept of Matter*, edited by Ernan McMullin, 122–33. South Bend, Ind.: University of Notre Dame Press, 1965.

———. "Die Materie, Quelle des Geistes?" In *Ordo rerum: Schriften zur Naturphilosophie, philosophischen Anthropolgie und christlichen Weltanschauung*, 359–70. Fribourg, Switzerland: Editions Universitaires, 1969.

———. "Philosophical Implications of Evolution." In *Ordo rerum: Schriften zur Naturphilosophie, philosophischen Anthropolgie und christlichen Weltanschauung*, 135–50. Fribourg, Switzerland: Editions Universitaires, 1969.

Macquarrie, John. *Principles of Christian Theology*. New York: Charles Scribner's Sons, 1977.

Mahner, Martin, and Mario Bunge. *Foundations of Biophilosophy*. Berlin: Springer-Verlag, 1997.

Maldamé, Jean-Michel. *Le Christ et le cosmos: Incidence de la cosmologie moderne sur la théologie.* Paris: Desclée, 1993.

———. *Le Christ pour l'univers: Pour une collaboration entre science et foi.* Paris: Desclée, 1998.

———. "L'évolution et la question de Dieu." *Revue thomiste* 107 (2007): 531–60.

Maritain, Jacques. *Saint Thomas and the Problem of Evil.* Milwaukee: Marquette University Press, 1942.

———. "Toward a Thomist Idea of Evolution." In *Untrammeled Approaches*, 85–131. The Collected Works of Jacques Maritain, vol. 20. South Bend, Ind.: University of Notre Dame Press, 1977.

Mascall, E. L. *Christian Theology and Natural Science: Some Questions on Their Relations.* New York: Ronald Press, 1956.

Mason, David R. "Can We Speculate on How God Acts?" *Journal of Religion* 57 (1977): 16–32.

Massie, Pascal. "The Irony of Chance: On Aristotle's *Physics* B, 4–6." *International Philosophical Quarterly* 43 (2003): 15–28.

Maudlin, Tim. "Distilling Metaphysics from Quantum Physics." In *The Oxford Handbook of Metaphysics*, edited by Michael J. Loux and Dean W. Zimmerman, 461–87. Oxford: Oxford University Press, 2003.

Maurer, Armand. "Darwin, Thomists, and Secondary Causality." *Review of Metaphysics* 57 (2004): 491–514.

Mayr, Ernst. "Teleological and Teleonomic: A New Analysis." In *Evolution and the Diversity of Life: Selected Essays*, 383–404. Cambridge, Mass.: Harvard University Press, 1976.

———. *The Growth of Biological Thought: Diversity, Evolution, and Inheritance.* Cambridge, Mass.: Belknap Press of Harvard University Press, 1982.

———. *Toward a New Philosophy of Biology: Observations of an Evolutionist.* Cambridge, Mass.: Harvard University Press, 1988.

McCabe, Herbert. *God and Evil in the Theology of St. Thomas Aquinas.* Edited by Brian Davies. New York: Continuum, 2010.

———. "The Involvement of God." *New Blackfriars* 66 (1985): 464–76.

McGinn, Bernard. "The Development of the Thought of Thomas Aquinas on the Reconciliation of Divine Providence and Contingent Action." *Thomist* 39 (1975): 741–52.

McGrath, Alister. *Dawkins' God: Genes, Memes, and the Meaning of Life.* Oxford: Blackwell, 2005.

———. "Darwinism." In *The Oxford Handbook of Religion and Science*, edited by Philip Clayton and Zachary Simpson, 681–96. Oxford: Oxford University Press, 2006.

McInerny, Ralph. *Aquinas and Analogy.* Washington, D.C.: The Catholic University of America Press, 1996.

———. "Thomism." In *A Companion to Philosophy of Religion*, edited by Philip Quinn and Charles Taliarferro, 158–64. Cambridge, U.K.: Blackwell, 1997.

McMullin, Ernan. "How Should Cosmology Relate to Theology?" In *The Sciences and Theology in the Twentieth Century*, edited by Arthur R. Peacocke, 17–57. South Bend, Ind.: University of Notre Dame Press, 1981.

———. "A Case for Scientific Realism." In *Scientific Realism*, edited by Jarrett Leplin, 8–40. Berkeley and Los Angeles: University of California Press, 1984.

———. "Evolution and Special Creation." *Zygon* 28 (1993): 299–335.

———. "Anthropic Reasoning in Cosmology." In *Science and Theology: Ruminations on the Cosmos*, edited by Chris Impey and Catherine Petry, 79–109. Vatican City State: Vatican Observatory, 2003.

McNulty, T. Michael. "Evolution and Complexity." *American Catholic Philosophical Quarterly* 73 (1999): 435–48.

McShea, Daniel W. "Possible Largest-Scale Trends in Organismal Evolution: Eight 'Live Hypotheses.'" *Annual Review of Ecology and Systematics* 29 (1998): 293–318.

Meehan, Francis X. *Efficient Causality in Aristotle and St. Thomas*. Washington D.C.: The Catholic University of America Press, 1940.

Meurers, Joseph. "Thomas und die Naturwissenschaft Heute." In *Il cosmo e la scienza*, 41–59. Atti del congresso internazionale Tommaso d'Aquino nel suo settimo centenario, no. 9. Naples: Edizioni Domenicane Italiane, 1975.

Meyer, Stephen. "The Origin of Biological Information and the Higher Taxonomic Categories." *Proceedings of the Biological Society of Washington* 117 (2004): 213–39.

Micklethwait, John, and Adrian Wooldridge. *God Is Back: How the Global Revival of Faith Is Changing the World*. New York: Penguin Books, 2009.

Miller, Fred D. Jr. "Aristotelian Natural Form and Theology—Reconsidered." *Proceedings of the American Catholic Philosophical Association* 69 (1995): 69–79.

Miller, Kenneth R. *Finding Darwin's God: A Scientist's Search for Common Ground between God and Evolution*. New York: Cliff Street Books, 1999.

———. "Judgment Day: Intelligent Design on Trial." PBS *NOVA* program. Aired November 13, 2007. Transcript available at http://www.pbs.org/wgbh/nova/transcripts/3416_id_08.html.

Monod, Jacques. *Chance and Necessity: An Essay on the Natural Philosophy of Modern Biology*. New York: Alfred A. Knopf, 1972.

Mooney, Christopher F. "The Anthropic Principle in Cosmology and Theology." *Horizons* 21 (1994): 105–29.

———. *Theology and Scientific Knowledge: Changing Models of God's Presence in the World*. South Bend, Ind.: University of Notre Dame Press, 1995.

Moore, Andrew. "Not Explanation but Salvation: Scientific Theology, Christology, and Suffering." *Modern Theology* 22 (2006): 65–83.

Morchio, Renzo. "Reductionism in Biology." In *The Problem of Reductionism in Science*, 149–60. Dordrecht, The Netherlands: Kluwer Academic Publishers, 1991.

Moreno, Antonio. "Some Philosophical Considerations on Biological Evolution." *Thomist* 37 (1973): 417–54.

———. "The Law of Inertia and the Principle *'Quidquid movetur ab alio movetur.'*" *Thomist* 38 (1974): 306–31.

Moritz, Joshua M. "Rendering unto Science and God: Is NOMA Enough?" *Theology and Science* 7 (2009): 363–78.

Morris, Simon Conway. *Life's Solution: Inevitable Humans in a Lonely Universe.* Cambridge: Cambridge University Press, 2003.

———. "The Paradoxes of Evolution: Inevitable Humans in a Lonely Universe?" In *God and Design: The Teleological Argument and Modern Science,* edited by Neil A. Manson, 329–47. London: Routledge, 2003,

———. "What Is Written into Creation?" In *Creation and the God of Abraham,* edited by David Burrell, Carlo Coglioti, Janet Soskice, and William R. Stoeger, 176–91. New York: Cambridge University Press, 2010.

Murphy, Nancey. "Scientific Realism and Postmodern Philosophy." *British Journal for the Philosophy of Science* 41 (1990): 291–303.

———. "Divine Action in the Natural Order: Buridan's Ass and Schroedinger's Cat." In *Chaos and Complexity: Scientific Perspectives on Divine Action,* edited by Robert John Russell, Nancey Murphy, and Arthur R. Peacocke, 325–57. Vatican City State: Vatican Observatory; Berkeley, Calif.: Center for Theology and the Natural Sciences, 1995.

———. "On The Role of Philosophy in Theology-Science Dialogue." *Theology and Science* 1 (2003): 71–93.

———. "Scientific Cosmology: A New Challenge to Theology." In *Science and Theology: Ruminations on the Cosmos,* edited by Chris Impey and Catherine Petry, 109–28. Vatican City State: Vatican Observatory, 2003.

———. "Reductionism: How Did We Fall into It and Can We Emerge from It?" In *Evolution and Emergence: Systems, Organisms, Persons,* edited by Nancey Murphy and William R. Stoeger, 19–39. New York: Oxford University Press, 2007.

———. "Science and the Problem of Evil: Suffering as a By-product of a Finely Tuned Cosmos." In *Physics and Cosmology: Scientific Perspectives on the Problem of Natural Evil,* edited by Nancey Murphy, Robert John Russell, and William Stoeger, 131–51.Vatican City State: Vatican Observatory; Berkeley, Calif.: Center for Theology and the Natural Sciences, 2007.

Mutschler, Hans-Dieter. "Physik und Neothomismus: Das ontologische Grundproblem der modernen Physik." *Theologie und Philosophie* 68 (1993): 25–51.

Nahm, Milton C., ed. *Selections from Early Greek Philosophy.* New York: Appleton-Century-Crofts, 1964.

Nelson, Paul A. "Unfit for Survival: The Fatal Flaws of Natural Selection." *Touchstone: A Journal of Mere Christianity* 12, no. 4 (1999): 56–64.

Newman, John Henry Cardinal. *The Idea of a University.* New York: Longmans, Green and Co., 1947.

———. "On Certainty, Intuition and the Conceivable 1861–1863." In *The Theological*

Papers of John Henry Newman on Faith and Certainty, edited by J. Derek Holmes, 92–119. Oxford: Clarendon Press, 1976.

Newton, Isaac. *Mathematical Principles of Natural Philosophy.* In *Sir Isaac Newton's Mathematical Principles of Natural Philosophy and His System of the World,* translated by Andrew Motte, revised by Florian Cajori. Berkeley and Los Angeles: University of California Press, 1946.

Nichols, Terence. "Aquinas' Concept of Substantial Form and Modern Science." *International Philosophical Quarterly* 36 (1996): 303–18.

———. "Aristotle and the Metaphysics of Evolution." *Review of Metaphysics* 58 (2004): 3–59.

Oakes, E. T. "Final Causality." *Theological Studies* 53 (1992): 534–44.

Oderberg, David S. *Real Essentialism.* New York: Routledge, 2007.

Oldenburg, Henry. "Oldenburg to Boyle, no. 501 (24 March 1665/6)." In *The Correspondence of Henry Oldenburg,* edited and translated by A. Rupert Hall and Marie Boas Hall, 3.67–70. Madison: University of Wisconsin Press, 1966.

O'Leary, Don. *Roman Catholicism and Modern Science: A History.* New York: Continuum, 2006.

O'Rourke, Fran. *Pseudo-Dionysius and the Metaphysics of Aquinas.* Leiden: E. J. Brill, 1992.

Overman, Dean L. *A Case against Accident and Self-Organization.* New York: Rowman and Littlefield, 1997.

Page, Lyman A. "Teleology in Biology: Who Could Ask for Anything More?" *Zygon* 41 (2006): 427–33.

Pantin, C. F. A. "Life and the Conditions of Existence." In *Biology and Personality: Frontier Problems in Science, Philosophy, and Religion,* edited by Ian Thomas Ramsey, 83–105. Oxford: Blackwell, 1965.

Pasnau, Robert. "Form, Substance, and Mechanism." *Philosophical Review* 113 (2004): 31–87.

Peacocke, Arthur. *Science and the Christian Experiment.* London: Oxford University Press, 1971.

———. *Creation and the World of Science.* Oxford: Clarendon Press, 1979.

———. *Intimations of Reality: Critical Realism in Science and Religion.* South Bend, Ind.: University of Notre Dame Press, 1984.

———. "God's Action in the Real World." *Zygon* 26 (1991): 455–76.

———. *Theology for a Scientific Age: Being and Becoming—Natural, Divine and Human.* Minneapolis, Minn.: Fortress Press, 1993.

———. "Chance and Law in Irreversible Thermodynamics, Theoretical Biology, and Theology." In *Chaos and Complexity: Scientific Perspectives on Divine Action,* edited by Robert John Russell, Nancey Murphy, and Arthur R. Peacocke, 123–43. Vatican City State: Vatican Observatory; Berkeley, Calif.: Center for Theology and the Natural Sciences, 1995.

———. "God's Interaction with the World: The Implications of Deterministic 'Chaos' and of Interconnected and Interdependent Complexity." In *Chaos and Complexity: Scientific Perspectives on Divine Action,* edited by Robert John Russell, Nancey Murphy, and Arthur R. Peacocke, 282–87. Vatican City State: Vatican Observatory; Berkeley, Calif.: Center for Theology and the Natural Sciences, 1995.

———. "The Cost of New Life." In *The Work of Love: Creation as Kenosis,* edited by John Polkinghorne, 21–42. Grand Rapids, Mich.: Eerdmans, 2001.

———. "Articulating God's Presence in and to the World Unveiled by the Sciences." In *In Whom We Live and Move and Have Our Being: Panentheistic Reflections on God's Presence in a Scientific World,* edited by Philip Clayton and Arthur Peacocke, 137–55. Grand Rapids, Mich.: Eerdmans, 2004.

———. "Problems in Contemporary Christian Theology." *Theology and Science* 2 (2004): 2–3.

———. "Emergence, Mind, and Divine Action: The Hierarchy of the Sciences in Relation to the Human Mind-Brain-Body." In *The Re-emergence of Emergence: The Emergentist Hypothesis from Science to Religion,* edited by Philip Clayton and Paul Davies, 257–78. New York: Oxford University Press, 2006.

———. "Emergent Realities with Causal Efficacy: Some Philosophical and Theological Applications." In *God's Action in Nature's World: Essays in Honor of Robert John Russell,* edited by Ted Peters and Nathan Hallanger, 189–204. Aldershot, U.K.: Ashgate, 2006.

Pegis, Anton C. *St. Thomas and Philosophy.* Milwaukee, Wis.: Marquette University Press, 1964.

Pennock, Robert T. "The Pre-modern Sins of Intelligent Design." In *The Oxford Handbook of Religion and Science,* edited by Philip Clayton and Zachary Simpson, 732–48. Oxford: Oxford University Press, 2006.

Pesch, Otto Hermann. "Theologische Überlegungen zur 'Vorsehung Gottes' im Blick auf gegenwärtige natur- und humanwissenswchaftliche Erkenntnisse." In *Christlicher Glaube in Moderner Gesellschaft,* by Franz Böckle, et al., 74–104. Freiburg: Herder, 1982.

Peters, Ted, and Martinez Hewlett. *Evolution from Creation to New Creation: Conflict, Conversation and Convergence.* Nashville, Tenn.: Abingdon Press, 2004.

Peterson, Gregory R. "Species of Emergence." *Zygon* 41 (2006): 689–712.

Pius XII, Pope. "Modern Science and the Existence of God." *The Catholic Mind* 50 (1952): 182–92.

Placher, William C. *The Domestication of Transcendence: How Modern Thinking about God Went Wrong.* Louisville, Ky.: Westminster John Knox Press, 1996.

Plantinga, Alvin. "What Is 'Intervention'?" *Theology and Science* 6 (2008): 369–401.

Polkinghorne, John C. *The Quantum World.* Princeton, N.J.: Princeton University Press, 1985.

———. *One World: The Interaction of Science and Theology.* Princeton, N.J.: Princeton University Press, 1986.

———. "The Quantum World." In *Physics, Philosophy, and Theology: A Common Quest for Understanding*, edited by Robert J. Russell, William R. Stoeger, and George V. Coyne, 333–42. Vatican City State: Vatican Observatory; Berkeley, Calif.: Center for Theology and the Natural Sciences, 1988.

———. *Science and Creation: The Search for Understanding*. Boston: Shambhala, 1989.

———. *Science and Providence: God's Interaction with the World*. Boston: New Science Library, 1989.

———. *Reason and Reality: The Relation between Science and Theology*. Philadelphia: Trinity Press International, 1991.

———. "Chaos and Cosmos: A Theological Approach." In *Chaos: the New Science*. Nobel Conference 26, 105–17. Saint Peter, Minn.: Gustavus Adolphus College, 1993.

———. "The Laws of Nature and the Laws of Physics." In *Quantum Cosmology and the Laws of Nature: Scientific Perspectives on Divine Action*, edited by Robert John Russell, Nancey Murphy, and C. J. Isham, 437–48. Vatican City State: Vatican Observatory; Berkeley, Calif.: Center for Theology and the Natural Sciences, 1993.

———. *The Faith of a Physicist*. Princeton, N.J.: Princeton University Press, 1994.

———. "The Metaphysics of Divine Action." In *Chaos and Complexity: Scientific Perspectives on Divine Action*, edited by Robert John Russell, Nancey Murphy, and Arthur R. Peacocke, 147–56. Vatican City State: Vatican Observatory; Berkeley, Calif.: Center for Theology and the Natural Sciences, 1995.

———. "Chaos Theory and Divine Action." In *Religion and Science: History, Method and Dialogue*, edited by W. Mark Richardson and Wesley J. Wildman, 243–52. New York: Routledge, 1996.

———. *Belief in God in an Age of Science*. New Haven, Conn.: Yale University Press, 1998.

———. *Beyond Science: The Wider Human Context*. New York: Cambridge University Press, 1998.

———. "Kenotic Creation and Divine Action." In *The Work of Love: Creation as Kenosis*, edited by John Polkinghorne, 90–106. Grand Rapids, Mich.: Eerdmans, 2001.

———. *Quantum Theory: A Very Short Introduction*. New York: Oxford University Press, 2002.

———. "Space, Time, and Causality." *Zygon* 41 (2006): 975–83.

———. "Evolution and Providence: A Response to Thomas Tracy." *Theology and Science* 7 (2009): 317–22.

———. *Theology in the Context of Science*. New Haven, Conn.: Yale University Press, 2009.

Pollard, William G. *Chance and Providence: God's Action in a World Governed by Scientific Laws*. London: Faber and Faber, 1958.

Popper, Karl R. *The Logic of Scientific Discovery*. London: Hutchinson, 1959.

———. *Quantum Theory and the Schism in Physics*. Totowa, N.J.: Rowman and Littlefield, 1982.

Porter, Andrew P. *By the Waters of Naturalism: Theology Perplexed among the Sciences*. Eugene, Ore.: Wipf and Stock, 2001.

Powers, Jonathan. *Philosophy and the New Physics*. New York: Methuen, 1982.

Randall, John Herman Jr. *Aristotle*. New York: Columbia University Press, 1960.

Ratzinger, Joseph. *In the Beginning: A Catholic Understanding of the Story of Creation and the Fall*. Grand Rapids, Mich.: Eerdmans, 1986.

Ratzsch, Del. "There Is a Place for Intelligent Design in the Philosophy of Biology: Intelligent Design in (Philosophy of) Biology: Some Legitimate Roles." In *Contemporary Debates in Philosophy of Biology*, edited by Francisco J. Ayala and Robert Arp, 343–63. Chichester, U.K.: Wiley-Blackwell, 2010.

Rayski, Jerzy. "A Philosophy of Quantum Mechanics." *Philosophy in Science* 1 (1985): 139–48.

Rey, Georges. "Meta-atheism: Religious Avowal as Self-deception." In *Philosophers without Gods: Meditations on Atheism and the Secular Life*, edited by Louise M. Antony, 243–65. New York: Oxford University Press, 2007.

Rocca, Gregory. *Speaking the Incomprehensible God: Thomas Aquinas on the Interplay of Positive and Negative Theology*. Washington, D.C.: The Catholic University of America Press, 2004.

Rolston, Holmes. *Science and Religion: A Critical Survey*. New York: Random House, 1987.

Ruse, Michael. *Darwin and Design: Does Evolution Have a Purpose?* Cambridge, Mass.: Harvard University Press, 2003.

———. "Modern Biologists and the Argument from Design." In *God and Design: The Teleological Argument and Modern Science*, edited by Neil A. Manson, 308–28. London: Routledge, 2003.

———. "An Evolutionist Thinks about Religion." *Theology and Science* 6 (2008): 165–71.

Russell, Bertrand. "On the Notion of Cause." *Proceedings of the Aristotelian Society for the Systematic Study of Philosophy* 13 (1913): 1–26.

Russell, Robert John. "The Meaning of Causality in Contemporary Physics." In *Free Will and Determinism: Papers from an Interdisciplinary Research Conference, 1986*, edited by Viggo Mortensen and Robert Sorensen, 13–31. Aarhus: Aarhus University Press, 1987.

———. "Quantum Physics in Philosophical and Theological Perspective." In *Physics, Philosophy, and Theology: A Common Quest for Understanding*, edited by Robert J. Russell, William R. Stoeger, and George V. Coyne, 343–74. Vatican City State: Vatican Observatory; Berkeley, Calif.: Center for Theology and the Natural Sciences, 1988.

———. "Religion and the Theories of Science: A Response to Barbour." *Zygon* 31 (1996): 29–41.

———. "Does the 'God Who Acts' Really Act in Nature?" In *Science and Theology: The*

New Consonance, edited by Ted Peters, 77–102. Boulder, Colo.: Westview Press, 1998.

———. "Special Providence and Genetic Mutation: A New Defense of Theistic Evolution." In *Evolutionary and Molecular Biology: Scientific Perspectives on Divine Action*, edited by Robert John Russell, Willliam R. Stoeger, and Francisco J. Ayala, 191–223. Vatican City State: Vatican Observatory; Berkeley, Calif.: Center for Theology and the Natural Sciences, 1998.

———. "Divine Action and Quantum Mechanics: A Fresh Assessment." In *Quantum Mechanics: Scientific Perspectives on Divine Action*, edited by Robert John Russell, Philip Clayton, Kirk Wegter-McNelly, and John Polkinghorne, 293–328. Vatican City State: Vatican Observatory; Berkeley, Calif.: Center for Theology and the Natural Sciences, 2001.

———. "Bodily Resurrection, Eschatology, and Scientific Cosmology." In *Resurrection: Theological and Scientific Assessments*, edited by Ted Peters, Robert John Russell, and Michael Welker, 3–30. Grand Rapids, Mich.: Eerdmans, 2002.

———. "The Doctrine of Creation Out of Nothing in Relation to Big Bang and Quantum Cosmologies." In *The Human Search for Truth: Philosophy, Science, Theology: The Outlook for the Third Millennium, International Conference on Science and Faith, The Vatican, 23–25 May 2000*, 108–29. Philadelphia: Saint Joseph's University Press, 2002.

———. "Eschatology and Physical Cosmology: A Preliminary Reflection." In *The Far-Future Universe: Eschatology from a Cosmic Perspective*, edited by George F. R. Ellis, 266–315. London: Templeton Foundation Press, 2002.

———. "An Appreciative Response to Niels Henrik Gregersen's JKR Research Conference Lecture." *Theology and Science* 4 (2006): 129–35.

———. "Quantum Physics and the Theology of Non-Interventionist Objective Divine Action." In *The Oxford Handbook of Religion and Science*, edited by Philip Clayton and Zachary Simpson, 579–95. Oxford: Oxford University Press, 2006.

———. "Completing the Bridge: The New CTNS Logo." *Theology and Science* 6 (2008): 9–11.

———. *Cosmology from Alpha to Omega: The Creative Mutual Interaction of Theology and Science*. Minneapolis, Minn,: Fortress, 2008.

Russell, Robert John, Philip Clayton, Kirk Wegter-McNelly, and John Polkinghorne, eds. *Quantum Mechanics: Scientific Perspectives on Divine Action*. Vatican City State: Vatican Observatory; Berkeley, Calif.: Center for Theology and the Natural Sciences, 2001.

Russell, Robert John, Nancey Murphy, and C. J. Isham, eds. *Quantum Cosmology and the Laws of Nature: Scientific Perspectives on Divine Action*. Vatican City State: Vatican Observatory; Berkeley, Calif.: Center for Theology and the Natural Sciences, 1993.

Russell, Robert John, Nancey Murphy, Theo Meyering, and Michael Arbib. *Neuroscience and the Person: Scientific Perspectives on Divine Action*. Vatican City State: Vatican Observatory; Berkeley, Calif.: Center for Theology and the Natural Sciences, 1999.

Russell, Robert John, Nancey Murphy, and William R. Stoeger, eds. *Scientific Perspectives on Divine Action: Twenty Years of Challenge and Progress.* Vatican City State: Vatican Observatory; Berkeley, Calif.: Center for Theology and the Natural Sciences, 2008.

Russell, Robert John, Willliam R. Stoeger, and Francisco J. Ayala, eds. *Evolutionary and Molecular Biology: Scientific Perspectives on Divine Action.* Vatican City State: Vatican Observatory; Berkeley, Calif.: Center for Theology and the Natural Sciences, 1998.

Russell, Robert John, William R. Stoeger, and George Coyne, eds. *Physics, Philosophy, and Theology: A Common Quest for Understanding.* Vatican City State: Vatican Observatory; Berkeley, Calif.: Center for Theology and the Natural Sciences, 1988.

Sansbury, Timothy. "The False Promise of Quantum Mechanics." *Zygon* 42 (2007): 111–21.

Santmire, Paul. *The Travail of Nature: The Ambiguous Ecological Promise of Christian Theology.* Minneapolis, Minn.: Fortress, 1985.

Saunders, Nicholas. "Does God Cheat at Dice? Divine Action and Quantum Possibilities." *Zygon* 35 (2000): 517–44.

———. *Divine Action and Modern Science.* New York: Cambridge University Press, 2002.

Scaltsas, Theodore. "Substantial Holism." In *Unity, Identity, and Explanation in Aristotle's Metaphysics,* edited by Theodore Scaltsas, David Charles, and Mary Louise Gill, 107–28. Oxford: Clarendon Press, 1994.

Schillebeeckx, Edward. *Jesus: An Experiment in Christology.* New York: Seabury Press, 1979.

———. *Christ: The Experience of Jesus as Lord.* New York: Crossroad, 1983.

Schlick, Moritz. *Philosophy of Nature.* New York: Philosophical Library, 1949.

Schloss, Jeffrey. "Neo-Darwinism: Scientific Account and Theological Attributions." In *Back to Darwin: A Richer Account of Evolution,* edited by John B. Cobb, 99–118. Grand Rapids, Mich.: Eerdmans, 2008.

Schnall, Ira M. "Anthropic Observation Selection Effects and the Design Argument." *Faith and Philosophy* 26 (2009): 361–77.

Schulte, Raphael. "Wie ist Gottes Wirken in Welt und Geschichte theologisch zu verstehen?" In *Vorsehung und Handeln Gottes,* edited by Theodor Schneider and Lothar Ullrich, 116–67. Leipzig: St. Benno Verlag, 1988.

Scott, Alwyn. "Nonlinear Science and the Cognitive Hierarchy." In *Evolution and Emergence: Systems, Organisms, Persons,* edited by Nancey Murphy and William R. Stoeger, 173–97. New York: Oxford University Press, 2007.

Scott, Eugenie C. "'Science and Religion,' 'Christian Scholarship,' and 'Theistic Science': Some Comparisons." *Reports of the National Center for Science Education* 18, no. 2 (1988): 30–32.

Selvaggi, Filippo. *Causalità e indeterminismo: La problematica moderna alla luce della filosofia aristotelico-tomista.* Rome: Editrice Università Gregoriana, 1964.

Sentis, Laurent. *Saint Thomas d'Aquin et le mal. Foi chrétienne et théodicée.* Paris: Beauchesne, 1992.

Shanley, Brian J. "Divine Causation and Human Freedom in Aquinas." *American Catholic Philosophical Quarterly* 72 (1998): 99–122.

———. "Beyond Libertarianism and Compatibilism: Thomas Aquinas on Created Freedom." In *Freedom and the Human Person,* edited by Richard Velkley, 70–89. Washington, D.C.: The Catholic University of America Press, 2007.

Shapin, Steven. *Never Pure: Historical Studies of Science as if It Was Produced by People with Bodies, Situated in Time, Space, Culture, and Society, and Struggling for Credibility and Authority.* Baltimore: Johns Hopkins University Press, 2010.

Shields, G. W. "Davies, Eternity, and the Cosmological Argument." *International Journal for Philosophy of Religion* 21 (1987): 21–37.

Simpson, J. A., and E. S. C. Weiner, eds. *The Oxford English Dictionary.* 2nd. ed. 20 vols. Oxford: Clarendon Press, 1989.

Sloan, Phillip. "The Question of Natural Purpose." In *Evolution and Creation,* edited by Ernan McMullin, 121–50. South Bend, Ind.: University of Notre Dame Press, 1985.

Smedes, Taede A. *Chaos, Complexity, and God: Divine Action and Scientism.* Leuven: Peeters, 2004.

———. "Beyond Barbour or Back to Basics? The Future of Science-and-Religion and the Quest for Unity." *Zygon* 43 (2008): 235–58.

Smith, Huston. *Forgotten Truth: The Common Vision of the World's Religions.* San Francisco: HarperSanFrancisco, 1992.

Smith, Vincent Edward. *The General Science of Nature.* Milwaukee, Wis.: Bruce Publishing Company, 1958.

Smith, Wolfgang. *The Quantum Enigma: Finding the Hidden Key.* Peru, Ill.: Sherwood Sugden, 1995.

———. "From Schrödinger's Cat to Thomistic Ontology." *Thomist* 63 (1999): 49–63.

Sokolowski, Robert. "Formal and Material Causality in Science." *Proceedings of the American Catholic Philosophical Association* 69 (1995): 57–67.

———. *The God of Faith and Reason.* Washington, D.C.: The Catholic University of America Press, 1995.

Soontiëns, F. J. K. "Evolution: Teleology or Chance?" *Journal for General Philosophy of Science* 22 (1991): 133–41.

Spaemann, Robert, and Reinhard Löw. *Die Frage Wozu? Geschichte und Wiederentdeckung des teleologischen Denkens.* Munich: Piper, 1985.

Spitzer, Robert J, "Indications of Creation in Contemporary Big Bang Cosmology." *Philosophy in Science* 10 (2003): 35–106.

Steinhardt, Paul J., and Neil Turok. *Endless Universe: Beyond the Big Bang.* New York: Doubleday, 2007.

Stewart, Ian, and Jack Cohen. "Why Are There Simple Rules in a Complicated Universe?" *Futures* 26 (1994): 648–64.

Stoeger, William R. "The Evolving Interaction between Philosophy and the Sciences: Towards a Self-Critical Philosophy." *Philosophy in Science* 1 (1983): 21–43.

———. "The Origin of the Universe in Science and Religion." In *Cosmos, Bios, Theos: Scientists Reflect on Science, God and the Origins of the Universe, Life, and Homo Sapiens*, edited by Henry Margenau and Roy Abraham Varghese, 254–69. LaSalle, Ill.: Open Court, 1992.

———. "Contemporary Physics and the Ontological Status of the Laws of Nature." In *Quantum Cosmology and the Laws of Nature: Scientific Perspectives on Divine Action*, edited by Robert John Russell, Nancey Murphy, and C. J. Isham, 209–34. Vatican City State: Vatican Observatory; Berkeley, Calif.: Center for Theology and the Natural Sciences, 1993.

———. "Describing God's Action in the World in Light of Scientific Knowledge of Reality." In *Chaos and Complexity: Scientific Perspectives on Divine Action*, edited by Robert John Russell, Nancey Murphy, and Arthur R. Peacocke, 239–61. Vatican City State: Vatican Observatory; Berkeley, Calif.: Center for Theology and the Natural Sciences, 1995.

———. "Key Developments in Physics Challenging Philosophy and Theology." In *Religion and Science: History, Method and Dialogue*, edited by W. Mark Richardson and Wesley J. Wildman, 183–200. New York: Routledge, 1996.

———. "The Immanent Directionality of the Evolutionary Process, and Its Relation to Teleology." In *Evolutionary and Molecular Biology: Scientific Perspectives on Divine Action*, edited by Robert John Russell, William R. Stoeger, and Francisco Ayala, 163–90. Vatican City State: Vatican Observatory; Berkeley, Calif.: Center for Theology and the Natural Sciences, 1998.

———. "The Mind-Brain Problem, the Laws of Nature, and Constitutive Relationships." In *Neuroscience and the Person: Scientific Perspectives on Divine Action*, edited by Robert John Russell, Nancey Murphy, Theo Meyering, and Michael Arbib, 129–46. Vatican City State: Vatican Observatory; Berkeley, Calif.: Center for Theology and the Natural Sciences, 1999.

———. "Epistemological and Ontological Issues Arising from Quantum Theory." In *Quantum Mechanics: Scientific Perspectives on Divine Action*, edited by Robert John Russell, Philip Clayton, Kirk Wegter-McNelly, and John Polkinghorne, 81–98. Vatican City State: Vatican Observatory; Berkeley, Calif.: Center for Theology and the Natural Sciences, 2001.

———. "Are Anthropic Arguments, Involving Multiverses and Beyond, Legitimate?" In *Universe or Multiverse*, edited by Bernard Carr, 445–57. New York: Cambridge University Press, 2007.

———. "Reductionism and Emergence: Implications for the Interaction of Theology with the Natural Sciences." In *Evolution and Emergence: Systems, Organisms, Per-*

sons, edited by Nancey Murphy and William R. Stoeger, 229–47. New York: Oxford University Press, 2007.

———. "The Big Bang, Quantum Cosmology, and *creatio ex nihilo*." In *Creation and the God of Abraham*, edited by David Burrell, Carlo Coglioti, Janet Soskice, and William R. Stoeger, 152–75. New York: Cambridge University Press, 2010.

Stoeger, William R., G. F. R. Ellis, and U. Kirchner. "Multiverses and Cosmology: Philosophical Issues." 2008. Available at http://arxiv.org/PS_cache/astro-ph/pdf/0407/0407329v2.pdf.

Stump, Eleonore. "Non-Cartesian Substance Dualism and Materialism without Reductionism." *Faith and Philosophy* 12 (1995): 505–31.

———. *Aquinas*. New York: Routledge, 2003.

Stump, Eleonore, and Norman Kretzmann. "Being and Goodness." In *Divine and Human Action: Essays in the Metaphysics of Theism*, edited by Thomas V. Morris, 281–312. Ithaca, N.Y.: Cornell University Press, 1988.

Sturch, Richard. *The New Deism: Divine Intervention and the Human Condition*. New York: St. Martin's Press, 1990.

Susskind, Leonard. *The Cosmic Landscape: String Theory and the Illusion of Intelligent Design*. New York: Little, Brown, 2005.

Swinburne, Richard. *Providence and the Problem of Evil*. Oxford: Clarendon Press, 1998.

Tanner, Kathryn. *God and Creation in Christian Theology: Tyranny or Empowerment?* New York: Basil Blackwell, 1988.

———. *Jesus, Humanity, and the Trinity: A Brief Systematic Theology*. Minneapolis, Minn,: Fortress Press, 2001.

Te Velde, Rudi A. *Participation and Substantiality in Thomas Aquinas*. New York: Brill, 1995.

———. *Aquinas on God: The "Divine Science" of the Summa theologiae*. Aldershot, U.K.: Ashgate, 2006.

Thomas, Leo, with Jan Alkire. *Healing Ministry: A Practical Guide*. Kansas City, Mo.: Sheed and Ward, 1994.

Thomas, Owen C. "Introduction." In *God's Activity in the World: The Contemporary Problem*, edited by Owen C. Thomas, 1–14. Chico, Calif.: Scholars Press, 1983.

———. "Summary Analysis." In *God's Activity in the World: The Contemporary Problem*, edited by Owen C. Thomas, 231–40. Chico, Calif.: Scholars Press, 1983.

———. "Problems in Panentheism." In Philip Clayton and Zachary Simpson, eds., *The Oxford Handbook of Religion and Science*, 652–64. Oxford: Oxford University Press, 2006.

———. "Metaphysics and Natural Science." *Theology and Science* 7 (2009): 31–45.

Tracy, David. *Blessed Rage for Order: The New Pluralism in Theology*. New York: Seabury Press, 1975.

Tracy, Thomas F. *God, Action, and Embodiment*. Grand Rapids, Mich.: Eerdmans, 1984.

———. "Divine Action, Created Causes, and Human Freedom." In *The God Who Acts: Philosophical and Theological Explorations*, edited by Thomas F. Tracy, 77–102. University Park: Pennsylvania State University Press, 1994.

———. "Particular Providence and the God of the Gaps." *CTNS Bulletin* 15, no. 1 (1995): 1–18.

———. "Evolution, Divine Action, and the Problem of Evil." In *Evolutionary and Molecular Biology: Scientific Perspectives on Divine Action*, edited by Robert John Russell, Willliam R. Stoeger, and Francisco J. Ayala, 511–30. Vatican City State: Vatican Observatory; Berkeley, Calif.: Center for Theology and the Natural Sciences, 1998.

———. "Creation, Providence, and Quantum Chance." In *Quantum Mechanics: Scientific Perspectives on Divine Action*, edited by Robert John Russell, Philip Clayton, Kirk Wegter-McNelly, and John Polkinghorne, 235–58. Vatican City State: Vatican Observatory; Berkeley, Calif.: Center for Theology and the Natural Sciences, 2001.

———. "Theologies of Divine Action." In *The Oxford Handbook of Religion and Science*, edited by Philip Clayton and Zachary Simpson, 596–611. Oxford: Oxford University Press, 2006.

———. "The Lawfulness of Nature and the Problem of Evil." In *Physics and Cosmology: Scientific Perspectives on the Problem of Natural Evil*, edited by Nancey Murphy, Robert John Russell, and William Stoeger, 153–78. Vatican City State: Vatican Observatory; Berkeley, Calif.: Center for Theology and the Natural Sciences, 2007.

———. "Evolutionary Theologies and Divine Action." *Theology and Science* 6 (2008): 107–16.

———. "Special Divine Action and the Laws of Nature." In *Scientific Perspectives on Divine Action: Twenty Years of Challenge and Progress*, edited by Robert John Russell, Nancey Murphy, and William R. Stoeger, 249–83. Vatican City State: Vatican Observatory; Berkeley, Calif.: Center for Theology and the Natural Sciences, 2008.

———. "God and Creatures Acting: the Idea of Double Agency." In *Creation and the God of Abraham*, edited by David B. Burrell, Carlo Coglioti, Janet Soskice, and William R. Stoeger, 221–37. New York: Cambridge University Press, 2010.

Van Inwagen, Peter. "The Compatibility of Darwinism and Design." In *God and Design: The Teleological Argument and Modern Science*, edited by Neil A. Manson, 348–63. London: Routledge, 2003.

Vernier, Jean-Marie. *Théologie et métaphysique de la création chez saint Thomas d'Aquin*. Paris: Pierre Téqui, 1995.

Von Neumann, John. *Mathematical Foundations of Quantum Mechanics*. Translated by Robert T. Beyer. Princeton, N.J.: Princeton University Press, 1955.

Wallace, William A. *Causality and Scientific Explanation*. 2 vols. Ann Arbor: University of Michigan Press, 1972.

———. "Causality, Analogy and the Growth of Scientific Knowledge." In *Il cosmo e la scienza*, edited by D. Dubarle, W. Wallace, J. Meurers, et al., 26–40. Atti del congresso internazionale Tommaso d'Aquino nel suo settimo centenario, no. 9. Naples: Edizioni Domenicane Italiane, 1975.

———. *The Elements of Philosophy: A Compendium for Philosophers and Theologians.* New York: Alba House, 1977.

———. "Aquinas and Newton on the Causality of Nature and of God: The Medieval and Modern Problematic." In *Philosophy and the God of Abraham: Essays in Memory of James A. Weisheipl, O.P.*, edited by R. James Long, 255–79. Toronto: Pontifical Institute of Medieval Studies, 1991.

———. "A Place for Form in Science: The Modeling of Nature." *Proceedings of the American Catholic Philosophical Association* 69 (1995): 35–46.

———. *The Modeling of Nature: Philosophy of Science and Philosophy of Nature in Synthesis.* Washington, D.C.: The Catholic University of America Press, 1996.

———. "Is Finality Included in Aristotle's Definition of Nature?" In *Final Causality in Nature and Human Affairs*, edited by Richard F. Hassing, 52–82. Washington, D.C.: The Catholic University of America Press, 1997.

———. "Thomism and the Quantum Enigma." *Thomist* 61 (1997): 455–67.

Ward, Keith. *Divine Action.* London: Collins, 1990.

———. *God, Chance and Necessity.* Rockfort, Mass.: Oneworld, 1996.

———. *Religion and Creation.* Oxford: Clarendon Press, 1996.

———. *The Big Questions in Science and Religion.* West Conshohocken, Pa.: Templeton Foundation, 2008.

———. *God, Faith and the New Millennium: Christian Belief in an Age of Science.* Oxford: Oneworld Publications, 1998.

Waterlow, Sarah. *Nature, Change, and Agency in Aristotle's Physics: A Philosophical Study.* New York: Oxford University Press, 1988.

Wattles, Jeffrey. "Teleology Past and Present." *Zygon* 41 (2006): 445–64.

Wegter-McNelly, Kirk. "Atoms May Be Small, but They're Everywhere: Robert Russell's Theological Engagement with the Quantum Revolution." In *God's Action in the Nature's World: Essays in Honour of Robert John Russell*, edited by Ted Peters and Nathan Hallanger, 93–111. Aldershot, U.K.: Ashgate: 2006.

———. "Fundamental Physics and Religion." In *The Oxford Handbook of Religion and Science*, edited by Philip Clayton and Zachary Simpson, 156–71. Oxford: Oxford University Press, 2006,

Weinandy, Thomas G. *Does God Change? The Word's Becoming in the Incarnation.* Still River, Mass.: St. Bede's Publications, 1985.

———. *Does God Suffer?* South Bend, Ind.: University of Notre Dame Press, 2000.

Weinberg, Steven. *Dreams of a Final Theory.* New York: Vintage Books, 1994.

———. "A Designer Universe?" In *Facing Up: Science and Its Cultural Adversaries*, 243–46. Cambridge, Mass.: Harvard University Press, 2001.

Weisheipl, James A. "Space and Gravitation." *New Scholasticism* 29 (1955): 175–223.

———. "Thomas' Evaluation of Plato and Aristotle." *New Scholasticism* 48 (1974): 100–24.
———. "The Concept of Nature." In *Nature and Motion in the Middle Ages*, by James A. Weisheipl, 1–23. Edited by William E. Carroll. Washington, D.C.: The Catholic University of America Press, 1985.
———. "The Evolution of Scientific Method." In *Nature and Motion in the Middle Ages*, by James A. Weisheipl, 239–60. Edited by William E. Carroll. Washington, D.C.: The Catholic University of America Press, 1985.
White, Kevin. "Aquinas on Purpose." *Proceedings of the American Catholic Philosophical Association* 81 (2007): 133–47.
Whitehead, Alfred North. *Process and Reality*. Edited by David Ray Griffin and Donald W. Sherburne. New York: Free Press, 1978.
Whiting, Jennifer. "Aristotle on Form and Generation." In *Proceedings of the Boston Area Colloquium in Ancient Philosophy (Volume VI, 1990)*, edited by John J. Cleary and Daniel C. Sharatin, 35–63. Lanham, Md.: University Press of America, 1991.
Wildman, Wesley J. "Further Reflections on 'The Divine Action Project.'" *Theology and Science* 3 (2005): 71–83.
———. "Incongruous Goodness, Perilous Beauty, Disconcerting Truth: Ultimate Reality and Suffering in Nature." In *Physics and Cosmology: Scientific Perspectives on the Problem of Natural Evil*, edited by Nancey Murphy, Robert John Russell, and William Stoeger, 267–94. Vatican City State: Vatican Observatory; Berkeley, Calif.: Center for Theology and the Natural Sciences, 2007.
———. "The Divine Action Project, 1988–2003." In *Scientific Perspectives on Divine Action: Twenty Years of Challenge and Progress*, edited by Robert John Russell, Nancey Murphy, and William R. Stoeger, 133–76. Vatican City State: Vatican Observatory; Berkeley, Calif.: Center for Theology and the Natural Sciences, 2008.
Wildman, Wesley, and Robert John Russell. "Chaos: A Mathematical Introduction." In *Chaos and Complexity: Scientific Perspectives on Divine Action*, edited by Robert John Russell, Nancey Murphy, and Arthur R. Peacocke, 49–90. Vatican City State: Vatican Observatory; Berkeley, Calif.: Center for Theology and the Natural Sciences, 1995.
Wiles, Maurice. *The Remaking of Christian Doctrine*. London: SCM Press, 1974.
———. *God's Action in the World*. London: SCM Press, 1986.
———. "Divine Action: Some Moral Considerations." In *The God Who Acts: Philosophical and Theological Explorations*, edited by Thomas F. Tracy, 13–30. University Park: Pennsylvania State University Press, 1994.
Wippel, John F. *Metaphysical Themes in Thomas Aquinas*. Washington, D.C.: The Catholic University of America Press, 1984.
———. *Thomas Aquinas on the Divine Ideas*. Toronto: Pontifical Institute of Mediaeval Studies, 1993.
———. "The Latin Avicenna as a Source for Thomas Aquinas's Metaphysics." In

The Metaphysical Thought of Thomas Aquinas: From Finite Being to Uncreated Being, 31–64. Washington, D.C.: The Catholic University of America Press, 2000.

———. "Thomas Aquinas on Creatures as Causes of *Esse.*" *International Philosophical Quarterly* 40 (2000): 197–213.

———. "Thomas Aquinas on Our Knowledge of God and the Axiom that Every Agent Produces Something Like Itself." *Proceedings of the American Catholic Philosophical Association* 74 (2000): 81–101.

———. *Metaphysical Themes in Thomas Aquinas II.* Washington, D.C.: The Catholic University of America Press, 2007.

Witt, Charlotte. *Substance and Essence in Aristotle: An Interpretation of Metaphysics VII–IX.* Ithaca, N.Y.: Cornell University Press, 1989.

Worthing, Mark William. *God, Creation, and Contemporary Physics.* Minneapolis, Minn.: Fortress Press, 1995.

Wright, John H. "The Eternal Plan of Divine Providence." *Theological Studies* 27 (1966): 27–57.

———. *A Theology of Christian Prayer.* New York: Pueblo, 1979.

———. "Theology, Philosophy and Natural Science." *Theological Studies* 52 (1991): 651–68.

Yates, John C. *The Timelessness of God.* Lanham, Md.: University Press of America, 1990.

Zycinski, Jozef. *God and Evolution: Fundamental Questions of Christian Evolutionism.* Translated by Kenneth W. Kemp and Zuzanna Maslanka. Washington, D.C.: The Catholic University of America Press, 2006.

Index of Names

Albertson, James, 194n117, 269
Alexander, Samuel, 121, 269
Alkire, Jan, 263n13, 297
Allen, Paul, 4n13, 8n27, 269, 282
Alston, William, 251, 254, 269
Anaximander, 11
Anaximines, 11
Appleyard, Bryan, 45n1, 269
Aristotle, 1–2, 9–10, 12, 14n11, 15, 17–18, 21n26, 22n28, 23–27, 30–33, 35–41, 42n91, 42n92, 43–44, 46, 49, 53n34, 54n39, 62–64, 70–72, 81, 96–98, 100–101, 102n235, 103, 128, 143, 159–60, 172n46, 174, 177n65, 178–80, 182–84, 205, 229, 252, 259–60, 267–69
Artigas, Mariano, 46n6, 50n22, 62, 88, 95, 102, 177n62, 221n48, 269
Ashley, Benedict, 60n71, 203n147, 269
Augros, Robert, 48n13, 77n134, 84n159, 269
Auletta, Gennaro, 8n27, 51, 95, 184n82, 269
Austriaco, Nicanor, 152n125, 269
Avicenna, 23–24
Ayala, Francisco, 6, 51n26, 58n54, 79n141, 82n152, 83, 85–87, 88n180, 96n212, 97, 102n237, 104n246, 151n123, 233, 269

Bacon, Francis, 48, 54, 270
Barbour, Ian, 1, 2n2, 3, 7n24, 46n5, 60n71, 61n73, 64n85, 72n113, 101n233, 127, 131n52, 153, 217, 233, 234n15, 266n1, 270
Barrow, John, 75n125, 76n128, 76n130, 270
Bartholomew, David, 60n65, 60n66, 63n80, 73n116, 74–76, 77n134, 103n242, 104n243, 121–22, 126n31, 139, 140n87, 141n94, 142n96, 144, 148, 150n119, 158n148, 158n150, 213–15, 270
Behe, Michael, 91–92, 135, 150–51, 152n126, 152n127, 152n128, 271
Bielfeldt, Dennis, 116n53, 138–39, 145n105, 271
Bobik, Joseph, 12n4, 246n64, 271
Boeri, Marcelo, 36n75, 271
Bohm, David, 64, 65n88, 65n89, 66n93, 68n99, 69–70, 141n94, 147, 220n45, 271
Boland, Vivian, x, 13n7, 271
Booth, Edward, 6n22, 271
Boyd, Craig, 116, 210n10, 271
Brecha, Robert, 142n96, 271
Brierley, Michael, 166n27, 271
Brisson, Luc, 12n2, 271
Brooke, John, 95, 141n94, 272
Brümmer, Vincent, 112n33, 272
Bultmann, Rudolf, 109n19, 111, 133, 249n74, 250, 272
Bunge, Mario, 14n12, 48–49, 53n36, 64n85, 67, 79n143, 103, 104n243, 186n93, 272, 285
Burrell, David, 23n31, 29n53, 164n18, 164n19, 169, 174n55, 176n61, 206n1, 207n3, 226n58, 227n61, 227n62, 230n1, 239n44, 262n9, 272
Burtt, Edwin, 45, 46n5, 50n21, 50n23, 106, 272

Carr, Bernard, 71n109, 71n112, 72n113, 74n121, 272
Carroll, William, 3n6, 9n33, 46n5, 148n113, 198n130, 203n147, 209n6, 220n46, 272
Carter, Brandon, 75, 273
Charlton, William, 17n14, 18n17, 273
Chesterton, G. K., 9, 273

Clarke, William Norris, 15n13, 24n36, 101, 123, 149, 273
Clayton, Philip, 1n1, 2n3, 10n35, 25n39, 50n22, 56n46, 56n48, 57n52, 58, 61–62, 65, 82n153, 85, 87, 94n203, 96n212, 102n235, 102n236, 105n1, 108, 121, 123, 125n23, 126n30, 127, 129n43, 140n88, 141n93, 144, 147n108, 155, 158n149, 160n1, 166n29, 251n85, 251n86, 273
Cobb, Aaron, 116, 271
Cobb, John, 50n21, 53n36, 67n95, 106n4, 115, 180, 274
Code, Alan, 31n57, 274
Cohen, Jack, 59, 295
Cohen, Sheldon, 18n17, 274
Collins, James, 115n48, 274
Collins, John, 68, 274
Collins, Robin, 73n116, 274
Connell, Richard, 41n90, 57n52, 274
Cooper, John, 166n29, 274
Copleston, Frederick, 11n2, 41n90, 45n1, 51n24, 52n31, 53n35, 274
Coveney, Peter, 89, 274
Craig, William Lane, 135n65, 171, 274
Crain, Steven, 121, 124n21, 136n72, 137n73, 157, 250, 274

Dalferth, Ingolf, 166n29, 275
Darwin, Charles, 52n32, 55, 78–82, 83n154, 84–85, 87–88, 89n184, 92, 99–100, 150, 199, 201n142, 202n144, 233n14, 239, 275
Davies, Brian, 164n19, 166n29, 190n106, 230n1, 262n9, 275
Davies, Paul, 57, 145n105, 213, 249, 275
Dawkins, Richard, 56n45, 62, 188, 213, 275
Deacon, Terrence, 62, 96, 101, 103n239, 275, 280
Decaen, Christopher, 21n22, 276
de Duve, Christian, 4n15, 72, 83, 85n170, 89, 150n120, 276
Deely, John, 201n141, 276
De Koninck, Charles, 37n79, 39n84, 55, 188n98, 196n124, 202n145, 276
Dembski, William, 54n38, 91–93, 134–36, 148n111, 149, 150n119, 152, 158n148, 276

Denton, Michael, 73n116, 77n134, 103, 201n142, 276
Depew, David, 54n39, 81n148, 281
Descartes, René, 25, 49n19, 52, 54n39, 276
DeSchrijver, Georges, 110, 276
Desmond, Adrian, 85n166, 276
Dewan, Lawrence, 8n28, 14n10, 24n37, 101n232, 162n6, 186n91, 197n127, 176
Dickson, William, 65n89, 66n93, 277
Dilley, Frank, 108, 113, 277
Dirac, Paul, 47n8, 64n86, 277
Dodds, Michael, 101n232, 169n37, 178n66, 179n68, 183n81, 197n126, 236n23, 277
Donceel, Joseph, 202n144, 202n146, 277
Doolan, Gregory, 13n7, 22n28, 191n107, 192n114, 195n120, 196n124, 198n134, 277
Doran, Chris, 152, 153n129, 158n148, 277
Dowd, Sharon, 116n50, 278
Drees, Willem, 72n113, 72n114, 76n128, 76n129, 77n134, 138, 148n111, 148n112, 149n115, 278
Dubarle, Dominique, 52n33, 278
Dulles, Avery, 52n30, 278
Dupré, John, 58n54, 278

Ecklund, Elaine, 113n38, 278
Eddington, Arthur, 64n86, 94, 278
Edwards, Denis, 117, 164n18, 187n95, 278
Einstein, Albert, 2, 63, 64, 69, 71, 107, 141n94, 142n95, 179, 278
Elders, Leo, 12n4, 52n32, 64n86, 149n81, 98n223, 99, 199n137, 202n144, 278
El-Hani, Charbel, 56n46, 278
Ellis, George, 7n24, 57–58, 72n113, 74, 94n205, 96, 131n52, 135n65, 278
Ellis, Robert, 115, 145n105, 250n78, 279
Emery, Gilles, 174n53, 198, 279
Erbrich, Paul, 86, 279

Farrer, Austin, 107, 164n19, 177n63, 209–10, 279
Feynman, Richard, 47n9, 64n86, 279
Fiddes, Paul, 235–36, 279
Finance, Joseph de, 24n33, 191n110, 279
Fine, Arthur, 64n86, 126n29, 142n95, 279
Ford, Lewis, 115, 211n17, 234, 279

Index of Names · 305

Frank, Patrick, 149n115, 279
Freddoso, Alfred, 161n4, 190n106, 226n58, 279

Galileo Galilei, 8, 9n33, 46–47, 49n19, 81, 106, 179, 279
García-Rivera, Alejandro, 100n228, 201n142, 279
George, Marie, 77n133, 280
Gilby, Thomas, 207n2, 280
Gilkey, Langdon, 105, 113, 117, 175n57, 280
Gill, Mary, 18n17, 280
Gilson, Etienne, 3, 4n12, 29n53, 32n62, 48n13, 48n15, 50n22, 51n24, 52n33, 100n227, 101n232, 182n79, 190n105, 191n110, 208, 261, 262n10, 280
Gingerich, Owen, 90, 127, 280
Gleick, James, 59n63, 61, 280
Goodenough, Ursula, 103n239, 280
Goris, Harm, 39n84, 42n94, 163n15, 180n69, 190n106, 191n112, 280
Goyette, John, 20n21, 48n13, 151n124, 184, 280
Granger, E. Herbert, 62n77, 281
Graves, Mark, 63n81, 281
Green, Richard, 103n239, 104n243, 281
Greene, Brian, 74n121, 281
Greene, John, 56, 281
Gregersen, Niels, 59n57, 60n64, 60n65, 94n205, 121n4, 133, 141, 154, 161n3, 166n28, 168n31, 185, 213, 226n60, 281
Grene, Marjorie, 54n39, 81n148, 281
Griffin, David, 114, 281
Grygiel, Wojciech, 49n19, 69–70, 281
Guagliardo, Vincent, 253, 281
Gunter, A. Y., 201n142, 282
Gutiérrez, Gustavo, 231n1, 282
Gwynne, Paul, 2n2, 282

Harris, Errol, 90, 282
Haslanger, Sally, 25n40, 282
Haught, John, 7n24, 282
Hawking, Stephen, 73, 111, 282
Hebblethwaite, Brian, 113n34, 117, 177, 209n5, 211n16, 249, 250n79, 282
Heisenberg, Werner, 63–65, 67, 70n106, 96–98, 103, 126n30, 142n95, 179, 186, 282
Henderson, Edward, 177, 282

Heraclitus, 11
Herbert, Nick, 63n84, 282
Hess, Peter, 8n17, 135n68, 282
Hewlett, Martinez, 79n141, 282, 290
Highfield, Roger, 89, 274
Hill, William, 165, 166n28, 173n51, 183n81, 227n61, 261n3, 261n4, 282
Hodgson, Peter, 64n86, 66n93, 67–68, 69n102, 69n103, 70, 94n205, 140, 141n94, 142n95, 283
Holder, Rodney, 74, 76, 283
Houghton, John, 244, 283
Hoyle, Fred, 90, 283
Hübner, Johannes, 22n28, 27n46, 27n48, 283
Hume, David, 41n90, 53, 66, 186, 247–48, 283
Hutten, Ernest, 46n5, 283

International Theological Commission, 148n112, 203, 221, 283

Jaki, Stanley, 4, 45n2, 47n10, 50, 55, 98n221, 140, 201n142, 250, 283
Jeffreys, Derek, 100n226, 283
Jenkins, David, 107, 283
Jenkins, John, 8n28, 284
Jenkins, Willis, 241n51, 250n79, 284
John Paul II, Pope, 8n27, 284
Johnson, Mark, 182n79, 284
Jonas, Hans, 84n159, 284
Jorissen, Hans, 162n10, 191n110, 192n113, 284
Journet, Charles, 230, 284
Judy, Albert, 24n33, 284

Kaufman, Gordon, 107, 109n119, 111–12, 114n39, 158n149, 284
Keck, John, 48n13, 49n19, 284
Kirchner, U., 74, 296
Kocher, Richard, 246n64, 284
Konyndyk, Kenneth, 8n28, 284
Kosso, Peter, 4, 65n88, 220n45, 284
Krempel, A., 172n47, 173n50, 284
Kretzmann, Norman, 22n29, 297
Kreyche, Gerald, 49n19, 284
Kuhn, Thomas, 45, 284
Kumar, Manjit, 64n86, 284

Index of Names

Landen, Laura, 25n40, 102n236, 284
Lang, Helen, 31n58, 284
Langford, Michael, 142n96, 150n120, 284
Laplace, Pierre Simon de, 51n25, 285
Larson, Edward, 79n141, 285
Larson, Thomas, 18n18, 285
Lash, Nicholas, 51n27, 188n99, 285
Lauer, Rosemary, 196n125, 285
Lennox, James, 36n77, 285
Leslie, John, 73n116, 75n125, 76n127, 285
Lewin, Roger, 59n61, 59n63, 285
Lewis, C. S., 245, 285
Linzey, Andrew, 241n51, 285
Lonergan, Bernard, 206n1, 285
Losch, Andreas, 3, 285
Löw, Reinhard, 33n64, 81n147, 88n181, 295
Luisi, Pier, 57, 285
Luyten, Norbert, 17n16, 200–201, 202n145, 202n146, 222n49, 285

Macquarrie, John, 249, 285
Mahner, Martin, 104n243, 285
Maldamé, Jean-Michel, 77n133, 220n46, 241n49, 286
Maritain, Jacques, 99n225, 241n50, 280, 286
Mascall, E. L., 127, 191n107, 191n110, 286
Mason, David, 114n39, 286
Massie, Pascal, 36n76, 37n79, 38n82, 39n84, 286
Maudlin, Tim, 47n9, 66n93, 286
Maurer, Armand, 78n137, 85n166, 99n225, 199n137, 286
Mayr, Ernst, 46, 57–58, 82, 86–87, 88n181, 100–101, 102n236, 102n238, 286
McCabe, Herbert, 167n30, 231n7, 236n23, 286
McGinn, Bernard, 207n2, 286
McGrath, Alister, 188n99, 199, 286
McInerny, Ralph, 176n61, 180n69, 286
McMullin, Ernan, 4, 17n16, 75n125, 84n160, 148n113, 202n145, 287
McNulty, T. Michael, 150n119, 187
McShea, Daniel, 85n170, 287
Meehan, Francis, 12n4, 287
Meurers, Joseph, 97n215, 287
Meyer, Stephen, 90, 287
Micklethwait, John, 113n38, 287

Miller, Fred, 102n236, 287
Miller, Kenneth, 150, 213, 287
Monod, Jacques, 55n41, 83, 132, 212, 221n47, 287
Mooney, Christopher, 61n73, 76n125, 149, 287
Moore, Andrew, 230n4, 287
Moore, James, 85n166, 276
Morchio, Renzo, 82n151, 287
Moreno, Antonio, 71n111, 81n148, 82n152, 84n160, 204n149, 287
Moritz, Joshua, 6n20, 288
Morris, Simon, 56, 73, 89, 96n212, 149n115, 151, 288
Murphy, Nancey, 2n4, 3–4, 14n12, 58n23, 61n72, 100n227, 110, 116, 125, 128, 129n41, 131, 145–47, 154, 160n1, 233, 244n61, 251n84, 251n85, 255n101, 288
Mutschler, Hans-Dieter, 102n236, 288

Nahm, Milton, 11n1, 288
Nelson, Paul, 201n142, 288
Newman, John, 7, 176, 288
Newton, Isaac, 47n10, 48, 51, 54, 81, 95n209, 97, 128, 136, 179, 239, 255n101, 289
Nichols, Terence, 101, 289

Oakes, E. T., 6, 289
Oderberg, David, 97n219, 289
Oldenburg, Henry, 49, 289
O'Leary, Don, 8n27, 289
O'Rourke, Fran, 13n7, 32n61, 32n62, 48n13, 49n18, 53n34, 88n181, 97, 256n103, 289
Overman, Dean, 89, 289

Page, Lyman, 84n160, 289
Pantin, C. F. A., 90, 289
Pasnau, Robert, 49n17, 52n32, 53, 289
Peacocke, Arthur, 3, 5, 58n54, 63n80, 72n115, 104, 107, 116, 122–24, 137n75, 138, 139n83, 155–56, 158n149, 215, 244n59, 249, 289
Pegis, Anton, 161n3, 290
Pennock, Robert, 87, 290
Pereira, Antonio, 56n46, 278
Pesch, Otto, 143, 290
Peters, Ted, 79n141, 290
Peterson, Gregory, 58n57, 58n58, 62, 82n151, 102n235, 290

Index of Names • 307

Pius XII, Pope, 134, 148n111, 290
Placher, William, 211n15, 290
Plantinga, Alvin, 154, 290
Plato, 11–13, 23, 62, 100, 102n235, 136, 143, 152n126, 184, 196n125
Polkinghorne, John, 3, 4n15, 6, 11n1, 60n67, 60n68, 60n69, 60n71, 61n73, 63n82, 63n83, 63n84, 64n85, 65n89, 68, 77n132, 94–95, 104n246, 108n12, 112n29, 115–16, 124–26, 133n60, 135, 136n72, 137n73, 138–39, 144, 147n109, 154, 156–57, 166n27, 209, 232, 244n59, 290
Pollard, William, 127, 291
Popper, Karl, 57n49, 64n85, 142n95, 291
Porter, Andrew, 51n26, 291
Powers, Jonathan, 57, 291

Randall, John, 97, 292
Ratzinger, Joseph, 152n128, 292
Ratzsch, Del, 93n201, 292
Rayski, Jerzy, 64n86, 292
Rey, Georges, 108, 292
Rocca, Gregory, 176n61, 292
Rolston, Holmes, 14n12, 63n82, 64n85, 292
Ruse, Michael, 88, 136, 140, 292
Russell, Bertrand, 66, 292
Russell, Robert, 2n4, 7n24, 49n19, 64n85, 64n87, 67n97, 71n110, 104, 126n27, 129–34, 136, 139, 141, 142n97, 143n98, 144n103, 144n104, 145, 146n106, 148n113, 156–57, 218–19, 221, 266n1, 292–94

Sansbury, Timothy, 144n103, 244, 294
Santmire, Paul, 241n51, 294
Saunders, Nicholas, 66n93, 139, 144n103, 243n58, 294
Scaltsas, Theodore, 27n48, 294
Schillebeeckx, Edward, 4n15, 165n20, 174n55, 231n7, 239n44, 294
Schlick, Moritz, 11n1, 67n97, 294
Schloss, Jeffrey, 151n123, 201n142, 294
Schnall, Ira, 77n132, 294
Schulte, Raphael, 173n51, 192n113, 262n10, 294
Scott, Alwyn, 63n81, 294
Scott, Eugenie, 92–93, 294
Selvaggi, Filippo, 95n208, 96, 294

Sentis, Laurent, 230n1, 294
Shanley, Brian, 164, 194n117, 226n60, 294
Shapin, Steven, 113, 295
Shields, G.W., 69n103, 295
Simpson, J. A., 247n68, 295
Sloan, Phillip, 84n160, 295
Smedes, Taede, 45n1, 55, 106n4, 139n83, 154, 156, 158n147, 164n19, 295
Smith, Huston, 52, 295
Smith, Vincent, 39n84, 60n66, 69n101, 219n44, 295
Smith, Wolfgang, 52, 66n93, 70, 295
Sokolowski, Robert, 8n28, 48n14, 55, 295
Soontiëns, F. J. K., 86n172, 295
Spaemann, Robert, 33, 81n147, 88n181, 295
Spitzer, Robert, 135n66, 295
Steinhardt, Paul, 74n120, 295
Stewart, Ian, 59, 295
Stoeger, William, 2n4, 4n15, 5, 43n101, 58n56, 66n93, 74, 85n170, 120, 148, 149n115, 149n117, 187n95, 187n96, 188n97, 295
Stump, Eleonore, 22n29, 25n40, 42n93, 102, 297
Sturch, Richard, 110n23, 297
Susskind, Leonard, 74n121, 108, 297
Swinburne, Richard, 250, 297

Tanner, Kathryn, 165n20, 191n112, 297
Te Velde, Rudi, 162n10, 164n19, 180n71, 184n84, 185n88, 186n94, 190n106, 191, 192n114, 194n118, 226n58, 297
Thales, 11
Thomas Aquinas, 1–2, 5, 7–10, 12–13, 14n11, 18–20, 21n25, 22n29, 23–24, 26, 29–31, 33–34, 35n72, 37n78, 38, 39n84, 41, 42n93, 43, 63, 66, 68–70, 77, 96–98, 101–3, 143, 153n130, 159–61, 163–65, 167–70, 172–84, 188–91, 192n114, 194n117, 197, 198n130, 199–200, 202n143, 204n149, 205–7, 210–11, 214, 219n44, 220n46, 222–23, 224n55, 225, 226n60, 229, 231–32, 235–41, 243, 245–46, 248, 252–57, 259–60, 262, 267
Thomas, Leo, 263n13, 297
Thomas, Owen, 5, 111n28, 112n31, 113, 166n27, 297
Tipler, Frank, 75n125, 270

Tracy, David, 171, 297
Tracy, Thomas, 2n4, 109, 117, 119, 128–29, 131, 137n76, 139, 142n97, 143, 146n106, 162n9, 177n63, 187n95, 194n117, 213, 218–19, 226n60, 230n4, 232n11, 239n41, 297
Turok, Neil, 74n120, 295

van Inwagen, Peter, 221n48, 298
Vernier, Jean-Marie, 194n117, 298
Von Neumann, John, 65, 69n103, 298

Wallace, William, 4, 12n4, 21n25, 22n27, 23n30, 28n51, 32, 34, 35n72, 42n92, 44n102, 46n5, 49n19, 52n31, 54n39, 54n40, 63, 66n93, 77n133, 96n213, 98, 101, 150n152, 184n82, 186n93, 196n122, 298
Ward, Keith, 94n202, 95, 106, 120, 123, 157, 162n9, 234, 239n41, 244, 248, 255n99, 258n109, 299
Waterlow, Sarah, 26n42, 26n45, 299
Wattles, Jeffrey, 31n58, 299
Wegter-McNelly, Kirk, 50n22, 106, 109–10, 111n28, 132n56, 139, 154, 159n151, 160, 266n1, 299

Weinandy, Thomas, 171n44, 236n23, 299
Weinberg, Steven, 212, 299
Weiner, E. S. C., 247n68, 295
Weisheipl, James, 2, 13n7, 39n83, 43, 46n5, 52n33, 54n40, 255n101, 256n103, 299
White, Kevin, 36n77, 300
Whitehead, Alfred, 114, 115n48, 183n80, 211n17, 235–36, 300
Whiting, Jennifer, 21n26, 300
Wildman, Wesley, 138–39, 144n103, 158n150, 232n10, 300
Wiles, Maurice, 112, 113n34, 116, 158n149, 215, 247n67, 300
Wippel, John, 13n7, 23n31, 175n56, 195n120, 300
Witt, Charlotte, 31n58, 42n92, 301
Wooldridge, Adrian, 113n38, 287
Worthing, Mark, 141, 301
Wright, John, 165n23, 187n96, 222n50, 301

Yates, John, 226n59, 301

Zycinski, Jozef, 85n167, 301

Index of Subjects

analogy, 32n62, 55, 78, 92, 94, 121–23, 174–79, 185n87, 194n117, 204–5, 223n53, 255
anthropic principle, 71–77, 102, 134, 135n65, 148–49, 179–80, 260

Big Bang, 17n16, 71–74; and creation, 134–35, 148; and design, 134, 148; and final causality, 102; and material causality, 98

causality, 1–2, 9–10; in Aquinas, 11–44; dynamism of, 41–44; efficient, 12–13, 28–31, 265; and empirical science, 45–104, 160–204; exemplar (extrinsic formal cause), 11, 13, 23; final, 12–13, 28, 31–33, 265; formal, (intrinsic formal cause, substantial form), 13, 15–16, 18–27, 101–2, 265; Humean, 53, 66–67, 159n152, 186; material (primary matter), 1n1, 11–19, 24–27, 42n92, 49, 52, 72, 77, 130, 180n70, 259, 265; primary and secondary, 29–30, 266; principal and instrumental, 29, 265–66; top-down (emergence), 56–58, 60, 62, 99, 120–24, 125n26, 131n53, 147n108, 156, 218n41, 257, 260; univocal, 30n54, 52, 96–97, 266. *See also* emergence; God; science
causal joint, 107–9, 122–23, 130n49, 138, 161, 164n18, 168–69
chance, 10, 33–41, 60, 71, 73, 76. *See also* evolution; God; quantum mechanics; science
chaos theory, 59–61, 94, 104, 108, 259; and divine action, 124–26, 138–40, 154n134, 179, 244, 260
compatibilism, 226n60
contingency, 33–41, 206. *See also* chance; God

cosmology, 5, 27, 30, 33–34, 56, 71–77, 98, 104, 179, 253, 255–56, 260. *See also* Big Bang; multiverse; relativity
creation, 5, 77n132, 80–81, 108; act of, 110, 116–17, 134, 148, 154, 162–64, 169, 180n71, 190, 194, 198, 200, 203–4, 214, 232, 261
critical realism, 3–4

Darwinism, 29, 79n141, 201n142, 221n48. *See also* evolution
deism, 109–112, 148–49, 166
design, 103, 120, 260; and divine action, 134–36, 148–53; and evolution, 88–93, 233; intelligent design, 90–93, 134–36, 149–53, 158n148. *See also* anthropic principle; Big Bang
determinism, 51, 60, 66–67, 70–71, 95, 106, 109, 119, 223
divine action. *See* chance; chaos theory; contingency; design; emergence; freedom; God; quantum mechanics; science
double agency. *See* God
dualism, 24–27

emergence, 10n35, 56–63, 77, 82, 96, 99, 104; and divine action, 120–26, 138–40, 179, 251n85, 260; and substantial form, 101–2, 179, 183–86, 257. *See also* causality
evil, 115, 192, 229; and divine causality, 230–44, 250; and divine suffering, 235–36; and theodicy, 117, 230n1, 233, 241n51, 231–43, 249–50
evolution, 77–93; and chance, 77–79, 82–84, 88–92, 93n201, 135, 152n128, 201n142, 233n14; and divine action, 199–204;

309

evolution *(cont.)*
and purpose, 84–88; and secondary causality, 199–204; and species, 80–82. *See also* design

faith, 5–6, 115, 136, 143, 153, 166n29, 169, 177–78, 224n54, 235; and reason, 7–9
freedom, 10, 33–41. *See also* God

God: and causality of creatures, 205–10, 230; causality of, in modern science, 105–118; and chance, 116, 127, 131n52, 180, 205–8, 210–26, 237, 260; and contingency of creatures, 115, 205–25; and double agency, 108, 209–10; efficient causality of, 186–99; final causality of, 180–83; formal (exemplar) causality of, 180, 183–86, 198, 252, 257, 260, 261, 263, 265; freedom of, 117, 128, 158n150, 210; and human freedom, 10, 106, 115, 160, 205–12, 215–16, 225–28; immanence of, 164–68, 236–43; and material causality, 180n70, 180n71; as primary efficient cause, 127, 156, 188–93, 199–204, 206–10, 230, 245, 254, 260; as principal efficient cause, 193–99, 202–3; providence of, 41, 129, 131–33, 141, 156, 163, 169, 193, 198n130, 199n135, 204, 212–14, 216n35, 217n37, 217n38, 218, 222, 223n52, 223n53, 224n54, 225, 226n60, 227n62, 229–43; relationship to creatures, 169–74; transcendence of, 164–68, 236–43; Trinity, 173–74, 177–78, 261; as univocal and transcendent cause, 106–10, 115, 118, 137, 143, 147, 153–59, 163n17, 176, 179, 186, 191–93, 196n124, 197, 205, 209–28, 231–36, 243–47, 249, 251, 254–55, 260. *See also* causal joint; chaos theory; contingency; creation; design; emergence; evil; evolution; indeterminism; necessity; quantum mechanics; theology

immanence, divine. *See* God
indeterminism: and divine action, 126–34, 140–47. *See also* chaos theory; emergence; quantum mechanics

intelligent design (ID). *See* design
interventionism, 109–10

kenosis, 198, 210n10, 232n10. *See also* theology

materialism, 50, 92–93
miracle, 10, 93, 108, 111n26, 113, 129, 132–33, 135n67, 166n29, 192n114, 213n21, 229–30, 247–58
multiverse, 73n119, 74–75

nature, 2, 7, 17, 18n18, 23, 28, 30–33, 35–36, 38, 39n83, 39n84, 45n2, 46, 48n15, 49–51, 52n33, 53n36, 55, 62, 64, 66, 69n101, 71, 78–81, 84n159, 92–93, 96, 98, 100–102, 104, 110–11, 113–14, 119–21, 125–33, 135, 137, 139–40, 143, 146–47, 153–58, 179, 189–90, 197, 202, 206, 211, 216, 218–21, 238–39, 241, 244, 246–48, 250, 253–58, 260, 266; dynamism of, 41–44
necessity, 33–41, 54n40, 55n42, 77, 83n156, 93n201, 104, 170; and divine causality, 205–28, 233, 237, 246n65, 254, 258
NIODA (non-interventionist, objective divine action). *See* quantum mechanics

occasionalism, 128, 194n117, 210–11

panentheism, 123, 165–68
prayer, 10, 122, 229–30, 243–47, 250
primary matter. *See* causality
process theology. *See* theology
providence. *See* God

quantum mechanics, 5, 10n35, 56, 63–71, 95–96, 103–4, 108, 186, 259–60; and chance, 65n88, 65n89, 66n93, 69n101, 70–71, 131n52, 132, 141n94, 259; and divine action, 126–34, 140–47, 179, 217–21, 244; and NIODA, 129–34, 141–47, 219n44; and quantum indeterminacy, 69–70, 97–98, 127–29, 131, 133n60, 143–46, 233, 244

reductionism, 5, 50–51, 61, 77, 82, 95, 100–101, 106, 183
relativity, theory of, 5, 71, 108, 239

science: and chance, 82–84, 97, 103–4, 132, 150n119, 152n128, 179; contemporary, 53–104, 119–204; and final causality, 102–3; and formal causality, 99–102; limits of, 94, 203; and material causality, 97–99; methodology of, 46–51, 92, 94, 114, 187; modern (Newtonian), 46–53, 105–18. *See also* anthropic principle; Big Bang; causality; cosmology; emergence; evolution; God; quantum mechanics; relativity

scientism, 51–52, 55–56, 95, 106n4, 114, 249–50

sin. *See* evil

substantial form. *See* causality

theodicy. *See* evil

theology: and divine limitation (kenosis), 116–18, 232–34; liberal, 111–13; method of, 143, 178; process theology, 109, 114–16, 183, 211, 233–34

transcendence, divine. *See* God

Trinity. *See* God

univocal cause. *See* causality

Unlocking Divine Action: Contemporary Science and Thomas Aquinas
was designed and typeset in Filosofia by Kachergis Book Design of Pittsboro,
North Carolina. It was printed on 55-pound Natures Recycled and
bound by Sheridan Books of Ann Arbor, Michigan.

www.ingramcontent.com/pod-product-compliance
Lightning Source LLC
Chambersburg PA
CBHW031406290426
44110CB00011B/289